SSC GD

Constable Recruitment Exam

Latest Edition
Practice Kit

10 Tests

07 Mock Test

03 Previous Year Paper

Based On Real Exam Pattern

✓ Thoroughly Revised and Updated

✓ Detailed Analysis of all MCQs

Title	: SSC GD Constable Recruitment Exam
Author Name	: Mr. Rohit Manglik
Published By	: EduGorilla Community Pvt. Ltd.
Publishers Address	: 12/651, First Floor Opp. Arvindo Park, Near Jama Masjid, Indira Nagar, Lucknow, Uttar Pradesh-226016, India

Copyright EduGorilla

ISBN : 978-93-90257-82-9

First Edition

Disclaimer EduGorilla

Compiled and created by EduGorilla Community Pvt. Ltd

Printed By EduGorilla Community Pvt. Ltd.

ROHIT MANGLIK
CEO, EduGorilla

Dear Applicants,

People say *"Success comes to those who work hard."* But I've seen people working hard for their exams day in and day out for marginal success. While others succeed in their examinations by putting in just half the work. So are they God Gifted? No! I believe that it's because they work *smart* and not just *hard*. Similarly, for your exams, you should strategize your preparation so as to increase the likelihood of success. Well with EduGorilla get ready to increase your *chances of selection* in your exam by *16x*.

EduGorilla helps you in not only working *hard* but also working in a *smart and strategic* manner. With EduGorilla's preparation package, you get a chance to make your exam preparation easy, and a fun learning path towards selection. Finding the right path to your preparations can be difficult if you don't know in which direction to head. Don't worry, we have you covered! EduGorilla will be your guide to success in your journey. With our Preparation Package, you can prepare strategically and beat the exam in just one attempt.

EduGorilla's Preparation Package includes-

- **Test Series**
- **Books**

Our preparation package is handcrafted as per the latest changes, expert opinions, and students' discretion. Thus, enabling you to get through each stage of the selection process for your exam.

Our Books are designed by the teachers and experts of the respective exam with a combined 150+ years of experience; to provide you with easy, efficient, and effective learning. Our books are smart, in the sense that not only do they give you the answers to the questions but also provide similar questions for practice.

EduGorilla's competent Test Series gives you real-time experience and confidence through which you can clear your offline or online exam in just one attempt. We currently host 83,000+ mock tests for 1,440+ competitive and academic exams.

Thus, EduGorilla misses no chance to assist you in your preparation and covers all stages of the exam, so that you don't have to look anywhere else.

We provide complete preparation packages for defense, banking, teaching, and other National & State-Level exams. Hence, it doesn't matter which exam you aspire to because you will reach your success.

ALL THE BEST !

Let EduGorilla be your Guide to Success.

Rohit Manglik,
Founder and CEO, EduGorilla

INTRODUCTION

EduGorilla focuses on guiding students to succeed in their examinations. With that in mind, our book, titled "SSC GD : Constable Recruitment Exam", has been drafted through the collective efforts of our distinguished experts with 150+ years of combined experience. This book consists of questions that are created following the latest changes in the syllabus and exam pattern. We compiled the book on the basis of questions that are most likely to appear in the SSC GD Constable Recruitment Exam. Through EduGorilla's "SSC GD : Constable Recruitment Exam" your chances of success will increase 16x.

EduGorilla does this through our Complete Preparation Package. This package consists of well-conceptualized and structured content in the form of questions that are tailor-made according to your needs and will help you practice for exams in a smart way by pinpointing all the necessary information. It also provides hints and solutions, along with a smart answer sheet for your self-evaluation. You can assess your shortcomings and work accordingly on areas that may require more of your attention.

EduGorilla promises to help you succeed in your examination and accomplish your dream goals. We believe in our aspirants and see them at the top of the merit list. And the first step towards the top is to start preparing with us. EduGorilla's "SSC GD : Constable Recruitment Exam" includes the following attributes.

➤ Well-Researched Content

➤ Top-Notch Quality

➤ Detailed Answers and Analysis

➤ Smart Answer Sheet

➤ Exam Relevant Questions

Therefore, EduGorilla fortifies your preparation and makes it durable enough to help you stand tall and beat the examination.

SSC GD Constable Recruitment Exam
Scan QR code for Eligibility, Exam Pattern, Syllabus and more.

Book ID: 0244

TABLE OF CONTENTS

General Intelligence and Reasoning

Q.1 Five people are standing in a row. Aman is standing next to Karan who is not adjacent to Tanuj. Radhika is standing next to Priyanka who is standing on the extreme left and Tanuj is not standing next to Radhika. Who is Standing adjacent to Aman?

A. Radhika and Karan   **B.** Karan and Tanuj

C. Karan and Priyanka   **D.** Radhika and Tanuj

Q.2 Direction: In the following question a number of series is given with one term missing. Choose the correct alternative that will continue the same pattern.

225,336,447,558, __ 780

[Territorial Army Officer, 2019]

A. 690   **B.** 660   **C.** 689   **D.** 669

Q.3 Direction: A piece of paper is folded and cut as shown below in the question figure. From the given answer figures, indicate how it will appear when opened.

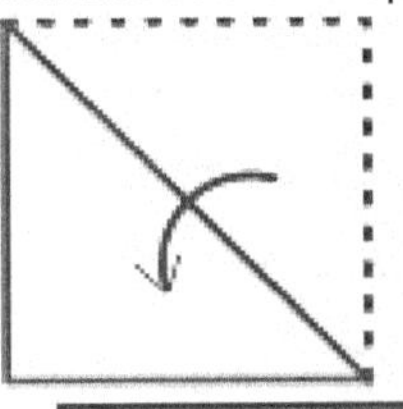  

A. 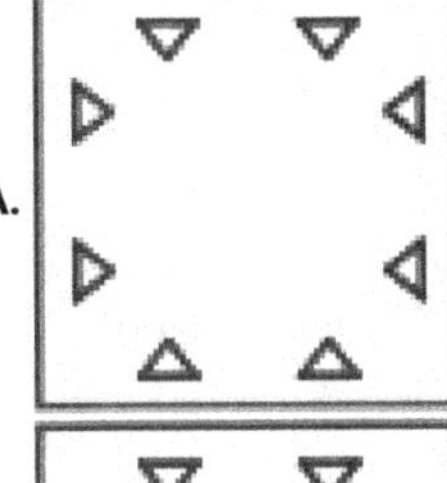   **B.** 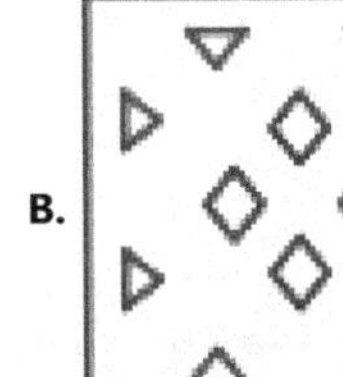

C. 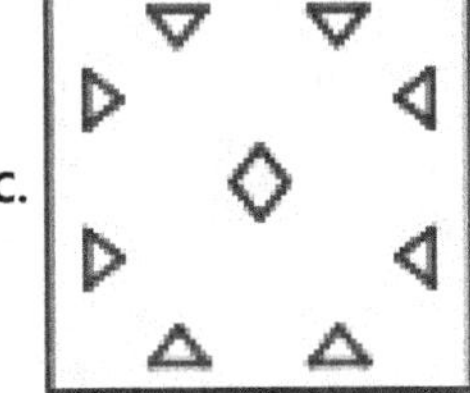   **D.** 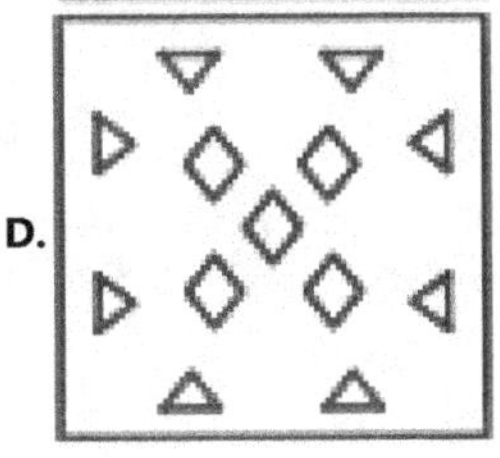

Q.4 Direction: Select out the odd word/letters/number /number pair from the given alternatives.

A. 85431   **B.** 23870   **C.** 99300   **D.** 11559

Q.5 Direction: Select the option in which the given figure is embedded. (Rotation of the figure is not allowed)

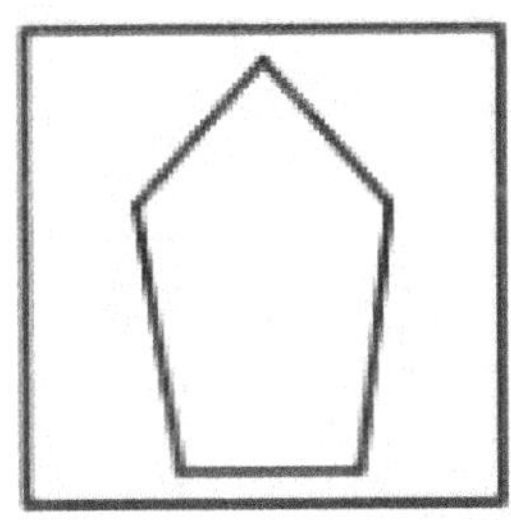

[SSC CHSL (Combined Higher Secondary Level), 2020]

A. 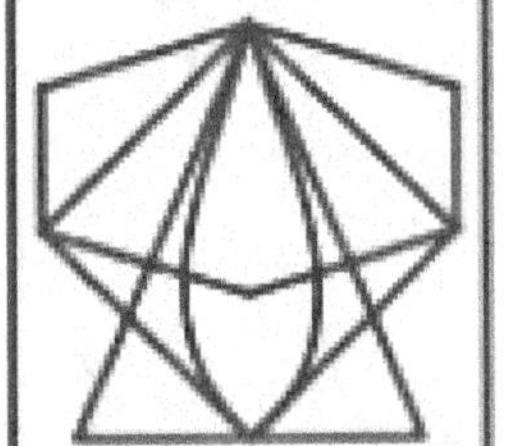

B. 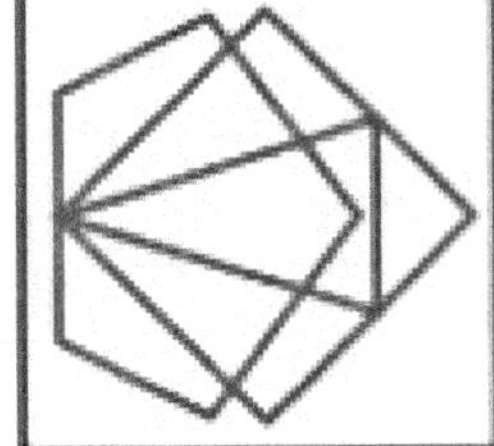

C. 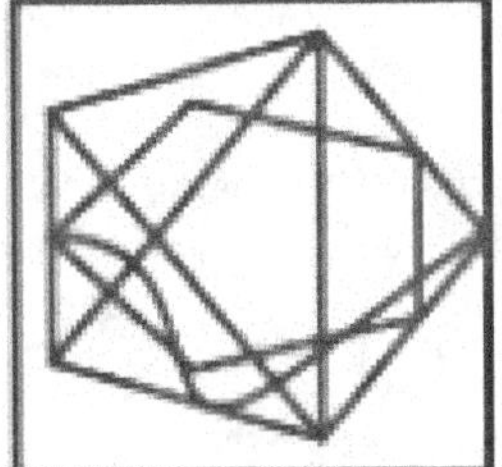

D.

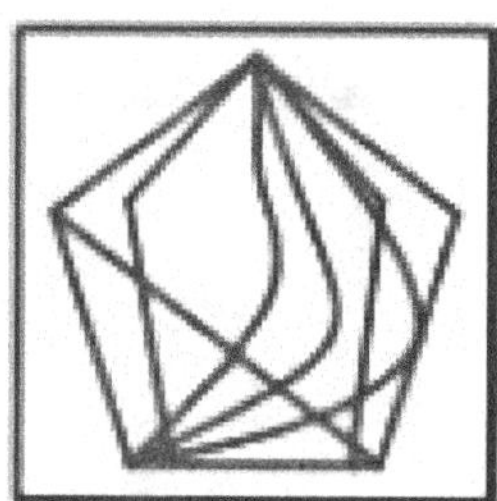

Q.6 Direction: In the given Venn diagram triangle represents doctors, the circle represents players and the rectangle represents artists.

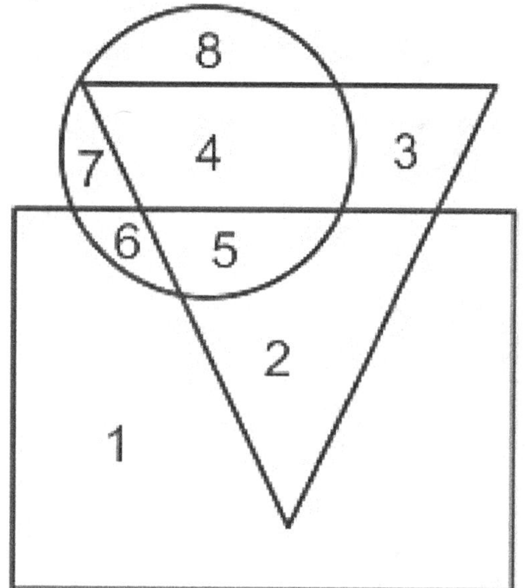

Which number represents artists who are also players only?

A. 4   B. 6   C. 7   D. 8

Q.7 If ' $+$ ' becomes ' $\div$ ' and ' $\times$ ' becomes ' $+$ ' then what will be the value of $\{(36 + 6) + 6\} \times 12$?

[RRB/RRC Group D, 2018]

A. 12   B. 6   C. 13   D. 21

Q.8 Direction: If a mirror is placed on the line AB, then which of the answer figures is the right image of the given figure?

A.

B.

C.

D.

Q.9 Direction: Find the one from option figures, which will replace the question mark from question figures.

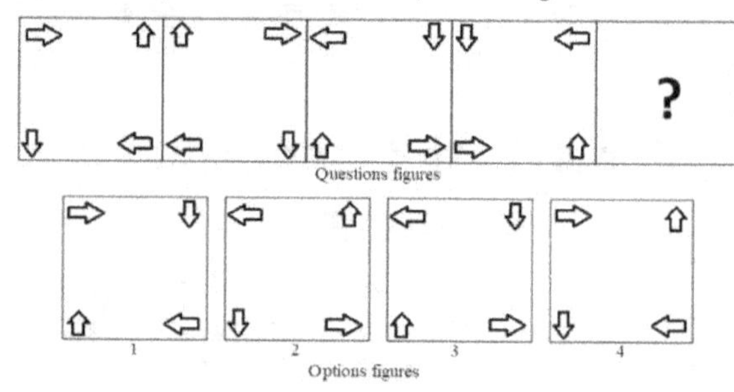

Questions figures

Options figures

A. 1   B. 2   C. 3   D. 4

Q.10 Direction: Select the number that will come into the place of the question mark (?).

24	20	36
15	11	18
55	40	?

A. 45   B. 65   C. 70   D. 80

Q.11 Direction: Arrange the given words in reverse order in which they occur in the dictionary.

1. Resign
2. Respect
3. Response
4. Resonance
5. Resolve

A. 1, 5, 4, 2, 3   B. 3, 2, 4, 5, 1
C. 5, 4, 3, 2, 1   D. 1, 2, 3, 4, 5

Q.12 The sum of twice a number and thrice its reciprocal is $\frac{25}{2}$. What is the number?

[Territorial Army Officer, 2021]

A. 7   B. 6   C. 5   D. 4

Q.13 Direction: Select the set in which the numbers are related in the same way as are the numbers of the following set.

$(3, 9, 27)$

A. $(5, 25, 125)$ B. $(6, 36, 215)$
C. $(8, 16, 512)$ D. $(11, 121, 110)$

Q.14 Direction: In the following figure, find out the best alternative of the boxes can be formed when the given figure is folded.

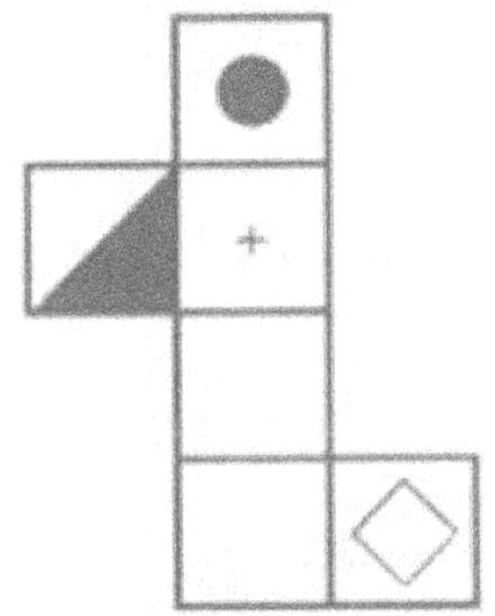

A.

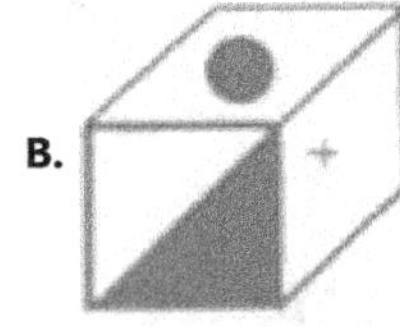

B.

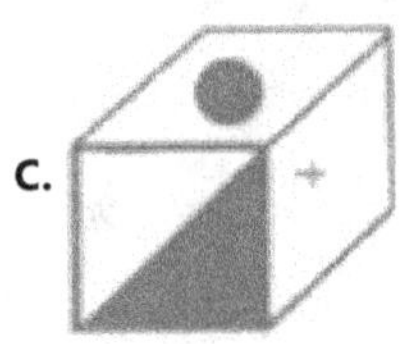

C.

D.

Q.15 Direction: Read the given statement(s) and conclusions carefully and select which of the conclusions logically follow(s) from the statement(s).

Statements:

I. All bottle is plastic

II. Some bags are plastic

Conclusions:

I. Some bags are not bottle

II. Some plastic are not bags

A. Only conclusion I follows

B. Only conclusion II follows

C. None follows

D. All Follows

Q.16 In a certain code language, BUTTER is coded as UVCSFU, then how will LETTER be coded in that language?

A. UFMSFU
B. UFMSTU
C. UFNSTV
D. None of these

Q.17 Direction: In the following question, select the related letters from the given alternatives.

HI : RS : : EF : ?

A. OQ
B. OO
C. UV
D. VU

Q.18 Direction: Read the following information carefully to answer the question given below.

I. 'A + B' means 'A is father of B'

II. 'A - B' means 'A is wife of B'

III. 'A × B' means 'A is brother of B'

IV. 'A ÷ B' means 'A is daughter of B'

If P ÷ R + S + Q, Which of the following is true?

A. P is the mother of Q

B. Q is the aunt of P
C. P is the daughter of Q
D. P is the aunt of Q

Q.19 Direction: Choose the option that will come into the place of the question mark (?).

729 : 324 : : 512 : ?

A. 144
B. 196
C. 64
D. 49

Q.20 Direction: Select the combination of letters that when sequentially placed in the blanks will create a repetitive pattern.

a_bc_a_bcda_ccd_bcd_

A. a, a, b, c, c, d
B. a, c, b, d, b, d
C. a, d, b, b, a, d
D. a, d, b, b, d, d

General Knowledge and General Awareness

Q.21 In which schedule 'Anti-Defection Law' is mentioned?

A. Tenth Schedule of the Constitution

B. Eleventh Schedule of the Constitution

C. Seventh Schedule of the Constitution

D. Twelfth Schedule of the Constitution

Q.22 According to which Article of Constitution of India, the Chief Minister is appointed by the Governor of a State?

[Uttarakhand Public Service Commission (UKPSC), 2016]

A. Article 163
B. Article 164
C. Article 165
D. Article 166

Q.23 In March 2022, who has launched TEJAS (Training for Emirates Jobs And Skills) programme?

A. Prem Kumar Dhumal

B. Jai Ram Thakur

C. Jyotiraditya Scindia

D. Anurag Thakur

Q.24 In January 2022, which of the following countries has become the 102nd country to join International Solar Alliance?

A. Saint Vincent and the Grenadines

B. Saint Kitts and Nevis

C. Antigua and Barbuda

D. Grenada

Q.25 Which company has signed a Memorandum of Understanding (MoU) with SIDBI to accelerate e-commerce for small industries in August 2022?

A. Flipkart
B. Zomato
C. Myntra
D. ONDC

Q.26 What is the contribution of India to the UN Women Core budget in 2022?

[Delhi Forest Guard, 2021], [HSSC Canal Patwari, 2021]

A. USD 10,000
B. USD 50,000
C. USD 100,000
D. USD 500,000

Q.27 Name the India's longest Rail cum Road Bridge.

[Territorial Army Officer, 2019]

A. Makum
B. Abhayapuri

C. Bogibeel   **D.** Nalbari

Q.28 The two volcanic islands in the Indian territory are:

[Territorial Army Officer, 2019]

A. Kavaratti and New Moor
B. Bitra and Kavaratti
C. Pamban and Barren
D. Narcondam and Barren

Q.29 Who among the followings has won the Australian Open Women's Singles title in January 2022?

A. Ashleigh Barty   **B.** Danielle Collins
C. Naomi Osaka   **D.** Serena Williams

Q.30 Defeat of which dynasty paved way for the establishment of Mauryan dynasty?

A. Aryanka Dynasty   **B.** Hoysala Dynasty
C. Nanda Dynasty   **D.** Chandela Dynasty

Q.31 Who was the court poet of Samudragupta?

A. Banabhatta   **B.** Harishena
C. Chand Bardai   **D.** Bhavabhuti

Q.32 The Treaty of Mangalore ended:
A. First Anglo Mysore war
B. Second Anglo Mysore war
C. Third Anglo Mysore war
D. Fourth Anglo Mysore war

Q.33 Who is the first woman of the world who climbed Mount Everest successfully from the Kangshung side?

[Rajasthan Teachers Eligibility Test - Level 1 Primary Level (RTET), 2021]

A. Bachendri Pal   **B.** Santosh Yadav
C. Premlata Agrawal   **D.** Arunima Sinha

Q.34 Which of the following is a non-Indian religion?

[Allahabad High Court ARO, 2020]

A. Buddhism   **B.** Jainism
C. Judaism   **D.** Hinduism

Q.35 Who among the following invented the medical thermometer?
A. Thomas Allbutt   **B.** Ralph Baer
C. James Chalmers   **D.** Hans Janssen

Q.36 Fiscal policy refers to:

[Territorial Army Officer, 2019]

A. Agricultural fertilizer policy
B. Rural credit policy
C. Interest policy
D. Related to revenue and expenditure policy of the government

Q.37 Which of the following has launched its Nifty 50 ETF Fund of Fund in July 2022?
A. Axis Mutual Fund
B. ICICI Prudential Mutual Fund
C. Quantum Mutual Fund
D. SBI Mutual Fund

Q.38 Who among the following invented the small pox vaccine?
A. Robert Koch   **B.** Edward Jenner
C. Robert Hooke   **D.** Louis Pasteur

Q.39 Which constitutional amendment act made constitutional provisions regarding "Urban Local Government"?

[UP Police Sub Inspector, 2021]

A. 74th Constitutional Amendment Act, 1992
B. 31st Constitutional Amendment Act, 1951
C. 44th Constitutional Amendment Act, 1976
D. 51st Constitutional Amendment Act, 1984

Q.40 In which city, Union Minister Nitin Gadkari has unveiled India's first Electric Double Decker bus on 18 August 2022?
A. Bengaluru   **B.** Bhopal
C. Mumbai   **D.** Nagpur

Elementary Mathematics

Q.41 The value of $3 \div 18$ of $3 \times 6 + 21 \times 6 \div 18 - 3 \div 2 + 3 - 3 \div 9$ of 3×9 is:

[SSC CGL, 2020]

A. $\frac{29}{6}$ **B.** $\frac{41}{9}$ **C.** $\frac{47}{6}$ **D.** $\frac{35}{9}$

Q.42 Direction: What will come in the place of the question mark $'?'$ in the following question?

$$240 \div 6 + \sqrt{529} \times 17 = ? + 150\% \text{ of } 80$$

A. 311   **B.** 310   **C.** 309   **D.** 312

Q.43 If 4A3164B is divisible by 88, then what is the value maximum possible value of 2A × B ?
A. 50   **B.** 70   **C.** 60   **D.** 80

Q.44 The difference between a number and $\frac{2}{7}$th of the number is 100. The number is:
A. 130   **B.** 140   **C.** 150   **D.** 160

Q.45 What is the correct ascending order for the given fractions?

A. $\frac{22}{7}, \frac{13}{17}, \frac{11}{19}, \frac{2}{3}$ **B.** $\frac{11}{19}, \frac{2}{3}, \frac{13}{17}, \frac{22}{7}$

C. $\frac{2}{3}, \frac{11}{19}, \frac{13}{17}, \frac{22}{7}$ **D.** $\frac{2}{3}, \frac{13}{17}, \frac{11}{19}, \frac{22}{7}$

Q.46 The total population of a town is 2800 where number of males is 720 more than that of females. If the number of males reduces by 40% and that of females increases by 20%, then find the new population of town.

[IBPS Clerk, 2021]

A. 2236   **B.** 2440   **C.** 2304   **D.** 2316

Q.47 In a compound, the ratio of carbon and oxygen is $1:4$. Find the percentage of carbon in the compound.
A. 20%   **B.** 10%   **C.** 5%   **D.** 80%

Q.48 If x is the mean proportional between 12.8 and 64.8 and y is the third proportional to 38.4 and 57.6, then $2x : y$ is equal to:

A. $3 : 4$ **B.** $1 : 2$ **C.** $2 : 3$ **D.** $4 : 5$

Q.49 The average of five consecutive odd numbers is 51. What is the difference between the highest and lowest number?

A. 3   **B.** 7   **C.** 8   **D.** 11

Q.50 What would be the compound interest obtained on an amount of Rs. $7,790$ at the rate of 10 percent per annum after two years?

A. Rs. 3,332.78   **B.** Rs. 3,335.35
C. Rs. 3,333.27   **D.** None of these

Q.51 A sum of Rs. $48,000$ was lent out at simple interest and at the end of 2 years and 3 months the total amount was Rs. $55,560$. Find the rate of interest per year.

[IBPS Clerk, 2021]

A. 7%   **B.** 8%   **C.** 9%   **D.** 10%

Q.52 If a man were to sell his chair for Rs. 720, he would lose 25 %. To gain 25% he should sell it for:

A. Rs. 1200   **B.** Rs. 1000   **C.** Rs. 960   **D.** Rs. 900

Q.53 A shopkeeper allows 10% discount on the marked price of an article and still makes a profit of 8%. If the marked price is Rs. 480, then what is the cost price (in Rs) of the article?

[SSC MTS, 2019]

A. 350   **B.** 400   **C.** 360   **D.** 420

Q.54 The successive discount of 15%, 20% and 25% on an article is equivalent to the single discount of:

A. 60%   **B.** 47%   **C.** 49%   **D.** 40%

Q.55 The length, breadth and height of a solid cuboid is 14 cm, 12 cm and 8 cm respectively. If cuboid is melted to form identical cubes of side 2 cm, then what will be the number of identical cubes?

A. 168   **B.** 144   **C.** 156   **D.** 128

Q.56 The sides of a triangle are 6.5 cm, 10 cm and x cm, where x is a positive number. What is the smallest possible value of x among the following?

[CTET Paper-II (Science & Mathematics), 2015]

A. 4.5   **B.** 2.8   **C.** 3.5   **D.** 4

Q.57 Three numbers are in ratio 1 : 2 : 3 and HCF is 12. The numbers are:

A. 12, 24, 36   **B.** 11, 22, 33
C. 12, 24, 32   **D.** 5, 10, 15

Q.58 A, B, C subscribe Rs. 50,000 for a business. A subscribes Rs. 4000 more than B and B Rs. 5000 more than C. Out of a total profit of Rs. 35,000, A receives:

A. Rs. 8400   **B.** Rs. 11,900

C. Rs. 13,600   **D.** Rs. 14,700

Q.59 A train travels a distance from P to Q with the speed of $70 km/h$ and returns to P from Q with the speed of $30 km/h$. Find the average speed of the train.

A. $50 km/h$ **B.** $42 km/h$
C. $100 km/h$ **D.** $40 km/h$

Q.60 Ganesh and Bhima can complete a work in 6 days. If Ganesh alone can finish it in 10 days, in how many days Bhima can complete the work?

A. 18   **B.** 14   **C.** 12   **D.** 15

English

Q.61 Direction: Select the correct antonym for the given word:

Frugal

A. Economical   **B.** Miserly
C. Extravagant   **D.** Greedy

Q.62 Direction: In this question, out of the four alternatives, choose the one which can be substituted for the given words/sentence:

The one who promotes the idea of the absence of government of any kind, when every man should be a law unto himself.

A. Agnostic   **B.** Belligerent
C. Iconoclast   **D.** Anarchist

Q.63 Direction: In this question, out of the four alternatives, choose the one which can be substituted for the given words/sentence.

Beams that support the roof

A. Portico   **B.** Porch   **C.** Rafter   **D.** Facade

Ques (64-67):Direction: Read the passage and answer the following questions.

The organization is working to end the inhumane culling of stray dogs, which many countries do in a **misguided** effort to eliminate rabies. The organization points out that vaccination programs are the only effective way to eliminate rabies and work with governments on vaccination programs. In 2012, a mass vaccination program was started in the Shaanxi, Guizhou, and Anhui provinces of China, working with the Chinese Animal Disease Control Centre; as of June 2014, 750 veterinarians have been trained and over 90,000 dogs have been vaccinated. A second focus is on stray dog population management itself, through proven humane methods such as education, improved legislation, registration and identification of dogs, sterilisation, and contraception, holding facilities, and rehoming centres. The charity has two disaster operations teams located in Asia and Latin America. In the **aftermath** of disasters, they travel to the worst affected areas to administer, distribute food and reunite animals with their owners where possible. The work is of particular benefit in developing world countries, where communities rely on animals for food, transport, and income.

Q.64 What is the major function of the organization?

A. To educate people on animal health

B. Disaster management in China

C. To take proper care of animals
D. To improve living conditions after disasters

Q.65 What does the organization suggest as a way to end rabies?
A. Emergency veterinary care
B. Stop culling of stray dogs
C. Vaccination programs
D. Establishment of rehoming centres

Q.66 Which of the following is MOST SIMILAR in meaning to the word 'aftermath'?
A. Casualty
B. After effects
C. Illness
D. Recovery

Q.67 Which of the following is MOST OPPOSITE in meaning to the word 'misguided'?
A. Effective
B. Fallacious
C. Obstruct
D. Well informed

Ques (68-70):Direction: Select the most appropriate option to substitute the underlined segment. If there is no need to substitute it, select No improvement.

Q.68 Bulbul is honest girl but she is also very rude.
A. Bulbul is an honest girl
B. Bulbul is very honest girl
C. Bulbul is a honest girl
D. No improvement

Q.69 I would be eternally indebted from you if you could help me.
A. indebted in you
B. indebted for you
C. No improvement
D. indebted to you

Q.70 I looked anywhere for my puppy but could not find it.
A. Everywhere
B. Somewhere
C. Nowhere
D. No improvement

Q.71 Direction: Choose the best expression amongst multiple choices for a given underlined idiom/proverb.
Get cold feet
A. To run for life
B. To get cold
C. To be afraid
D. To become discourteous

Q.72 Direction: Choose the appropriate preposition for the given sentence.
There is a heavy demand ______ these goods.
A. on
B. in
C. for
D. between

Q.73 Direction: Fill in the blanks with the correct form of a verb.
Don't _________ me you've lost your keys again.
A. say
B. tell
C. speak
D. inform

Q.74 Direction: Choose the correct form of tense for the given sentence.
This book ______ to her.
A. has belonged
B. belongs

C. is belonging
D. belong

Ques (75-76):Directions: In the following question, some part of the sentence may have errors. Find out which part of the sentence has an error and select the appropriate option. If a sentence is free from error, select 'No Error'.

Q.75 She has not/(A) completed her course,/(B) isn't it?/(C) No error/(D)
A. She has not
B. Completed her course
C. isn't it?
D. No error

Q.76 I need to get to the house in/(A) Landsdowne Road by/(B) ten o' clock./(C) No error/(D)
A. (A)
B. (B)
C. (C)
D. (D)

Q.77 Which of the following is most similar in meaning to the word 'Predicament' ?
A. Plight
B. Plunder
C. Stentorian
D. Occult

Q.78 Out of the given words, one word is misspelt find the misspelt word.
A. Malignancy
B. Frequency
C. Emergancy
D. Consistency

Q.79 Out of the given words, one word is misspelt find the misspelt word.
A. Phlegm
B. Mnemonic
C. Apropos
D. Rendezvos

Q.80 Direction: Choose the best expression amongst multiple choices for the given idiom/proverb.
Devil's advocate
A. An advocate
B. An advocate like a devil
C. Discussion of an advocate
D. To provoke debate or test the strength of opposing arguments

// Smart Answer Sheet //

Correct Percentage of students who answered correctly.   **Skipped** Percentage of students who skipped.

Q.	Ans.	Correct / Skipped	Q.	Ans.	Correct / Skipped	Q.	Ans.	Correct / Skipped	Q.	Ans.	Correct / Skipped	Q.	Ans.	Correct / Skipped
1	B	23.58 % / 21.4 %	17	C	43.45 % / 23.58 %	33	B	13.54 % / 27.07 %	49	C	23.36 % / 36.03 %	65	C	7.42 % / 78.82 %
2	D	58.3 % / 16.81 %	18	D	22.05 % / 23.8 %	34	C	55.68 % / 27.94 %	50	D	18.12 % / 37.99 %	66	B	7.42 % / 78.82 %
3	B	53.28 % / 12.22 %	19	C	20.52 % / 24.89 %	35	A	25.11 % / 28.17 %	51	A	16.38 % / 34.93 %	67	D	4.8 % / 78.39 %
4	B	39.52 % / 15.28 %	20	C	33.84 % / 23.15 %	36	D	34.06 % / 27.51 %	52	A	26.42 % / 32.75 %	68	A	8.73 % / 80.13 %
5	D	52.62 % / 13.76 %	21	A	24.89 % / 29.7 %	37	C	5.68 % / 28.6 %	53	B	22.05 % / 34.94 %	69	D	5.02 % / 80.13 %
6	B	47.82 % / 17.9 %	22	B	18.78 % / 27.94 %	38	B	31.44 % / 29.26 %	54	C	24.67 % / 29.92 %	70	A	11.57 % / 79.91 %
7	C	44.98 % / 16.81 %	23	D	16.81 % / 25.11 %	39	A	20.74 % / 32.54 %	55	A	11.79 % / 36.03 %	71	C	6.55 % / 79.69 %
8	A	54.59 % / 16.15 %	24	C	16.38 % / 25.76 %	40	C	20.09 % / 34.06 %	56	D	4.37 % / 30.13 %	72	C	9.83 % / 79.03 %
9	D	38.43 % / 14.41 %	25	D	10.7 % / 27.95 %	41	C	11.57 % / 34.28 %	57	A	43.45 % / 34.72 %	73	B	9.39 % / 80.35 %
10	B	27.95 % / 12.88 %	26	D	7.21 % / 25.54 %	42	A	20.09 % / 32.31 %	58	D	12.01 % / 36.24 %	74	B	11.57 % / 78.82 %
11	B	23.14 % / 13.1 %	27	C	22.05 % / 26.86 %	43	D	11.14 % / 34.27 %	59	B	20.74 % / 36.03 %	75	C	7.21 % / 79.47 %
12	B	17.03 % / 17.9 %	28	D	20.52 % / 26.42 %	44	B	33.62 % / 33.63 %	60	D	33.19 % / 31.0 %	76	A	8.52 % / 79.47 %
13	A	67.03 % / 15.5 %	29	A	13.97 % / 28.39 %	45	B	10.26 % / 37.56 %	61	C	3.06 % / 78.82 %	77	A	1.75 % / 79.91 %
14	B	32.97 % / 16.81 %	30	C	31.22 % / 24.24 %	46	C	16.16 % / 33.4 %	62	D	2.4 % / 78.39 %	78	C	9.39 % / 80.13 %
15	C	24.02 % / 20.96 %	31	B	24.02 % / 27.51 %	47	A	32.31 % / 34.5 %	63	C	4.59 % / 79.03 %	79	D	3.28 % / 80.34 %
16	A	36.46 % / 16.6 %	32	B	21.83 % / 25.55 %	48	C	12.88 % / 38.21 %	64	C	3.49 % / 78.61 %	80	D	6.33 % / 79.26 %

//Hints and Solutions//

1. Five people: Aman, Karan, Tanuj, Radhika, and Priyanka.

1) Radhika is standing next to Priyanka who is standing on the extreme left.

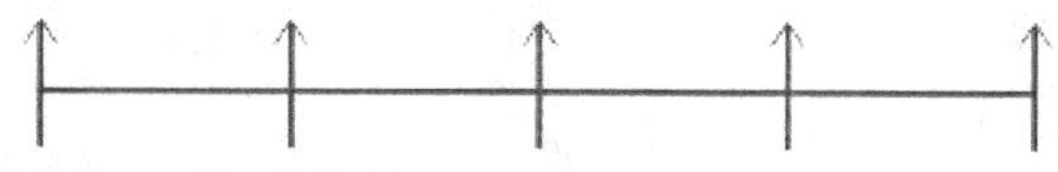

Priyanka   Radhika

2) Aman is standing next to Karan who is not adjacent to Tanuj.

3) Tanuj is not standing next to Radhika.

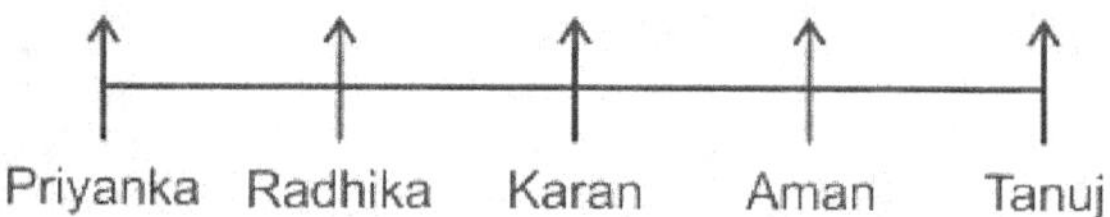

Priyanka   Radhika   Karan   Aman   Tanuj

So, Karan and Tanuj Standing adjacent to Aman.

Hence, the correct option is (B).

2. Given series,

225,336,447,558,___ 780

The pattern followed here is:

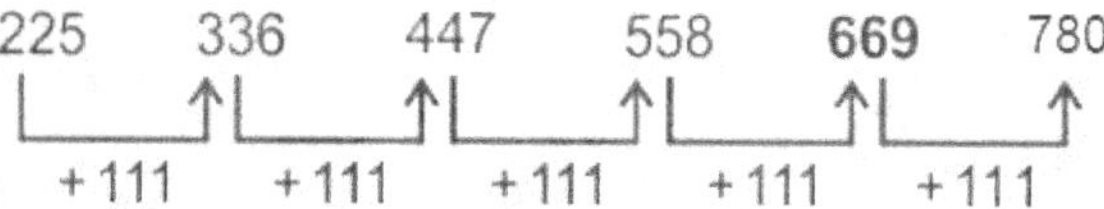

The next term is determined by adding 111 to the previous number.

So, 669 is the missing term.

Hence, the correct option is (D).

3. When the paper is unfolded it will appear like:

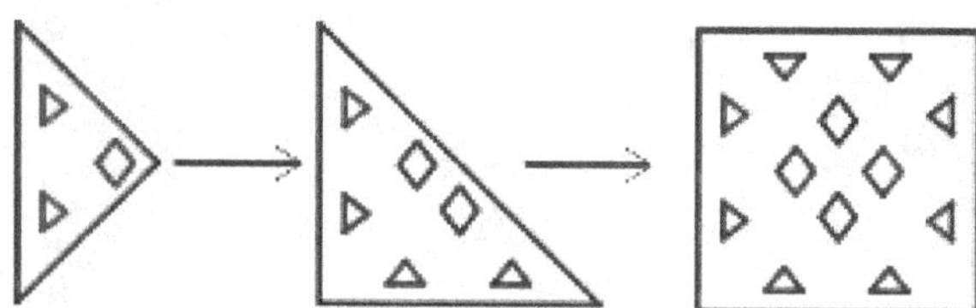

So, answer is the figure given below:

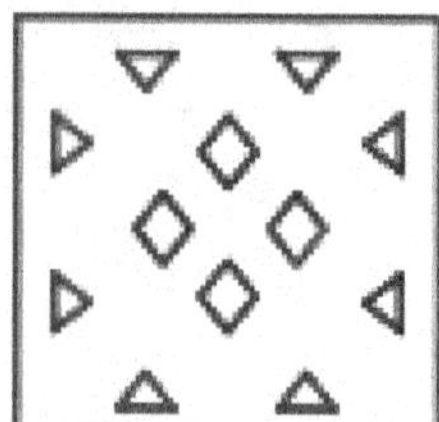

Hence, the correct option is (B).

4. In the given question, the sum of all the options except option (B) is 21.

8 + 5 + 4 + 3 + 1 = 21

2 + 3 + 8 + 7 + 0 = **20**

9 + 9 + 3 + 0 + 0 = 21

1 + 1 + 5 + 5 + 9 = 21

Hence, the correct option is (B).

5. The given figure is embedded in:

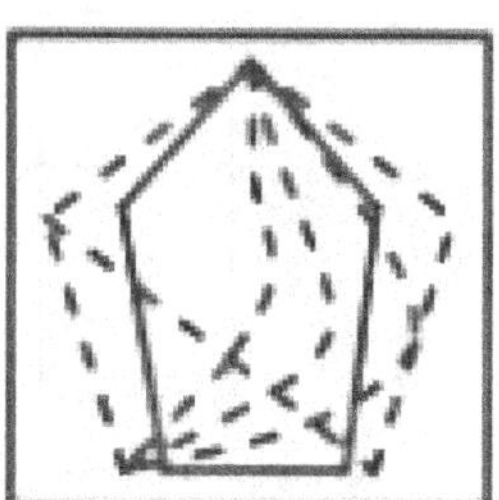

Hence, the correct option is (D).

6. Number which represents artists who are also players only are represented by shaded area as shown below:

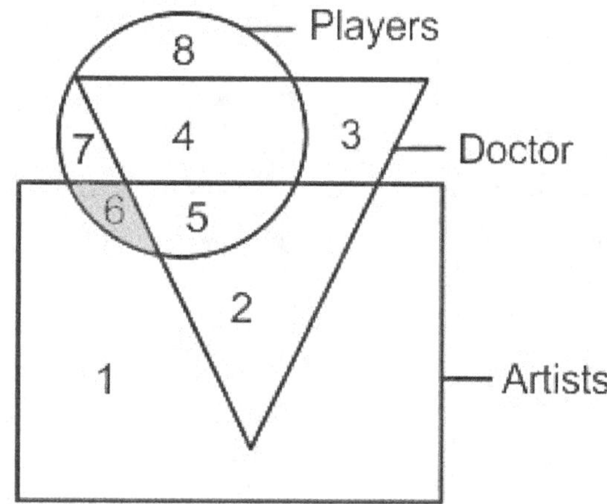

So, '6' is the correct answer.

Hence, the correct option is (B).

7.

Symbol	+	×
Meaning	÷	+

Given expression: $\{(36 + 6) + 6\} \times 12$

After changing the symbols:

$$\{(36 \div 6) \div 6\} + 12$$

$$= \{6 \div 6\} + 12$$

$$= 1 + 12$$

$$= 13$$

Therefore, "13" is the correct answer.

Hence, the correct option is (C).

8. The mirror image will be as follows:

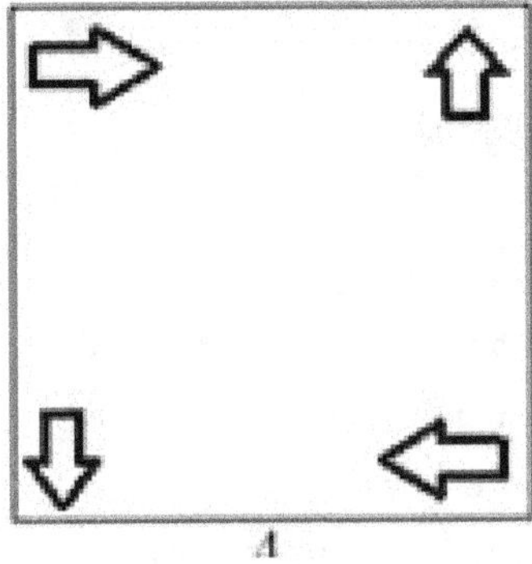

Hence, the correct option is (A).

9. By clockwise rotation of the arrow we get the correct figure as follows:

Hence, the correct option is (D).

10. The pattern that is being followed here is,

Sum of the first and third number of a row ÷ 3 = Second number of the same row

Therefore,

$$\Rightarrow \frac{(24+36)}{3} = \frac{60}{3} = 20$$

$$\Rightarrow \frac{(15+18)}{3} = \frac{33}{3} = 11$$

Similarly,

$$\frac{(55+?)}{3} = 40$$

$$\Rightarrow 55+? = 120$$

$$\Rightarrow ? = 120 - 55 = 65$$

Hence, the correct option is (B).

11. On arranging the words in reverse order as per the dictionary we get,

3) Response

2) Respect

4) Resonance

5) Resolve

1) Resign

So, the correct reverse order is "3, 2, 4, 5, 1" as per dictionary.

Hence, the correct option is (B).

12. Let number be x then its reciprocal be $\frac{1}{x}$.

According to the question,

$$2x + \frac{3}{x} = \frac{25}{2}$$

$$\Rightarrow 2x^2 + 3 = \frac{25x}{2}$$

$$\Rightarrow 4x^2 + 6 = 25x$$

$$\Rightarrow 4x^2 - 25x + 6 = 0$$

$$\Rightarrow (4x - 1)(x - 6) = 0$$

$$\Rightarrow x = 6, \frac{1}{4}$$

Value of number cannot be a fraction.

So, the number is 6.

Hence, the correct option is (B).

13. The pattern followed here is:

$$(3,9,27) \rightarrow (3, 3^2, 3^3)$$

Similarly,

$$(5,25,125) \rightarrow (5, 5^2, 5^3)$$

Hence, the correct option is (A).

14. We know that the half-shaded face will be opposite to the square face. So, option (A) and (D) are incorrect.

Now, as per the arrangement of folding of dice option (C) is also incorrect.

When the given figure is folded:

Hence, the correct option is (B).

15. The least possible Venn Diagram for the given statements will be as follows:

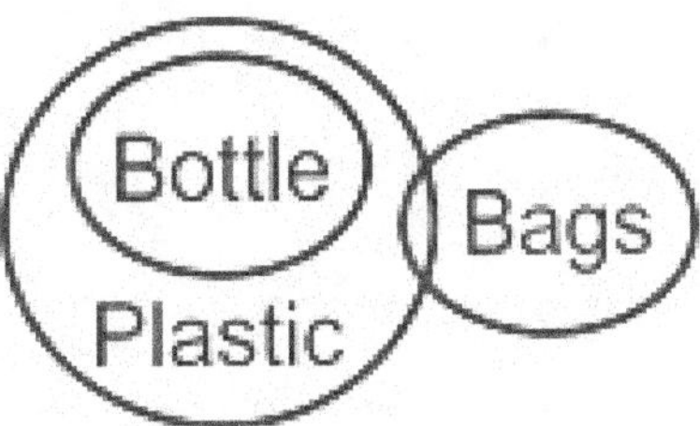

I. Some bags are not bottle → False (There is no direct relation given between bottle and bags so it can be possible but not definite, hence, false)

II. Some plastic are not bags → False (As "Some bags are plastic" given so some plastic can be bags it can be possible but some plastic are not bags it is not definite, hence, false)

So, None follows.

Hence, the correct option is (C).

16. The pattern for the code is as follows,

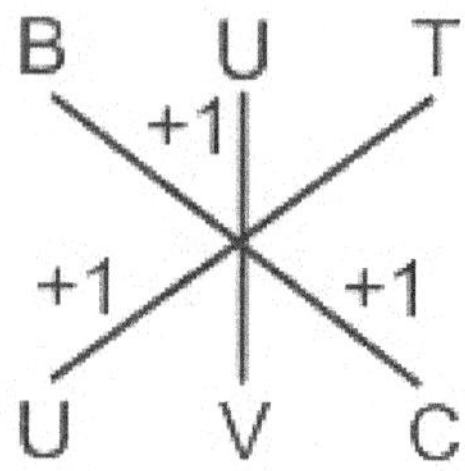
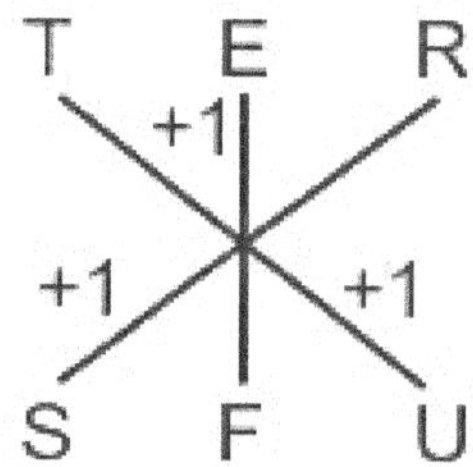

Similarly,

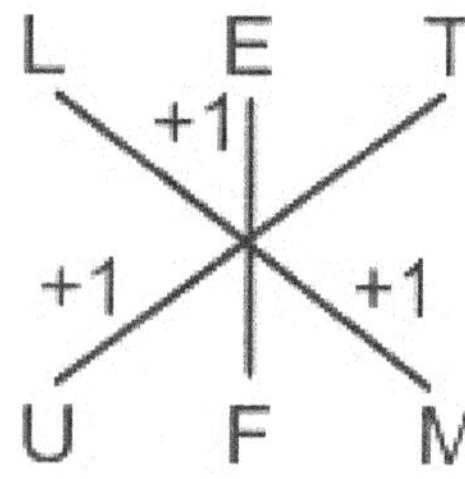
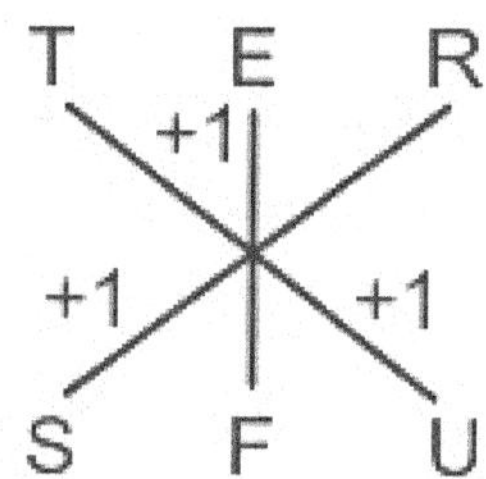

So, LETTER will be coded as UFMSFU.

Hence, the correct option is (A).

17. If we arrange alphabets with their opposite letters as shown below, we can see the pattern that is being followed here:

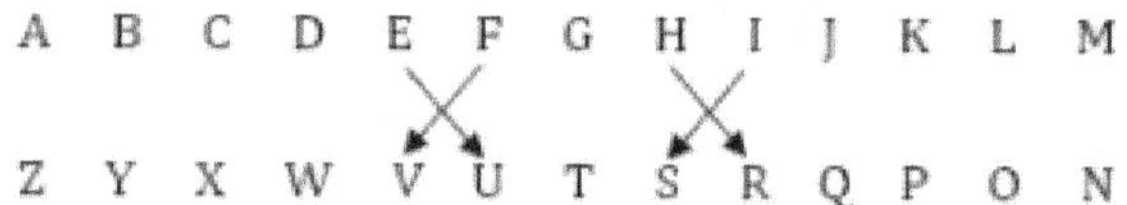

Thus, EF is related to UV.

Hence, the correct option is (C).

18. We can draw the following with the given information,

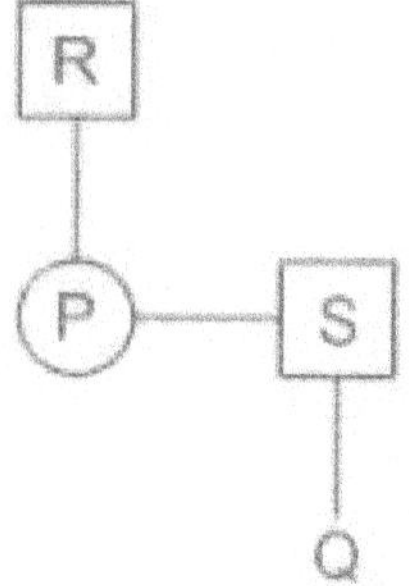

Checking the options:

(A) P is the mother of Q → False

(B) Q is the aunt of P → False

(C) P is the daughter of Q → False

(D) P is the aunt of Q → True

So, P is aunt of Q is the correct answer.

Hence, the correct option is (D).

19. The pattern that is being followed here is as follows,

$$729 \rightarrow 7 + 2 + 9 = 18^2 = 324$$

Similarly, 512 can be written as,

$$512 \rightarrow 5 + 1 + 2 = 8^2 = 64$$

Hence, the correct option is (C).

20. Given :-

a_bc_a_bcda_ccd_bcd_

By checking options and substituting accordingly.

(A). a, a, b, c, c, d → a a **b** c a - a **b** b c d - a **c** c c d - **c** b c d **d**

(B). a, c, b, d, b, d → a a **b** c **c** - a **b** b c d - a **d** c c d - **b** b c d **d**

(C). **a, d, b, b, a, d** → a a b c **d** - a **b** b c d - a **b** c c d - a **b** c d **d**

(D). a, d, b, b, d, d → a a **b** c d - a **b** b c d - a **b** c c d - **d** b c d **d**

Option (C) gives a cyclic pattern of **aa**bcd - a**bb**cd - abc**c**d - abc**dd**.

So, 'a, d, b, b, a, d' is the correct answer.

Hence, the correct option is (C).

21. The Tenth Schedule of the Indian Constitution, popularly known as the 'Anti-Defection Law', was brought in by the 52nd Constitutional Amendment in the year 1985.

- Defines the provisions relating to disqualification of defecting members.
- Its purpose is to disqualify the people's representatives who defected for the sake of political gain and office, so that the stability of Parliament is maintained.

Hence, the correct option is (A).

22. According to Article 164 of Constitution of India, the Chief Minister is appointed by the Governor of a State.

Article 164:

The Chief Minister shall be appointed by the Governor and the other Ministers shall be appointed by the Governor on the advice of the Chief Minister, and the Ministers shall hold office during the pleasure of the Governor.

Hence, the correct option is (B).

23. Union Minister Shri Anurag Thakur on 27 March 2022 has launched TEJAS (Training for Emirates Jobs And Skills) programme. It is a Skill India International Project to train overseas Indians.

The project is aimed at skilling, certification and overseas employment of Indians. Tejas is aimed at creating pathways to enable the Indian workforce to get equipped for skill and market requirements in UAE.

Hence, the correct option is (D).

24. Caribbean nation Antigua and Barbuda has become the 102nd country to join International Solar Alliance. The Prime Minister of Antigua and Barbuda Gaston Browne signed the International Solar Alliance Framework Agreement in the presence of Indian High Commissioner Dr. K J Srinivasa on 4 January 2022.

Hence, the correct option is (C).

25. ONDC has signed a Memorandum of Understanding (MoU) with SIDBI for the coordination of functions of institutions engaged in similar activities in August 2022.

- The partnership is aimed to change the landscape of MSMEs by bringing them into the ONDC network and accelerating their participation in eCommerce.
- The MoU was signed by Sivasubramanian Ramanan, Chairman & MD of SIDBI and T Koshy, MD & CEO of ONDC.

Hence, the correct option is (D).

26. India has contributed USD 500,000 to the UN Women, the United Nations agency for gender equality and women empowerment for their core budget.

India's Permanent Representative to the United Nations T.S.Tirumurti announced that India reaffirmed its partnership of women-led development and gender parity. UN Women Executive Director, Sima Bahous thanked India for its contribution.

Hence, the correct option is (D).

27. Bogibeel is the India's longest Rail cum Road Bridge.

- Bogibeel Bridge is a combined road and rail bridge in the Dibrugarh district of the northeastern Indian state of Assam.
- Upon its completion it will become the longest bridge of its kind in India and the longest bridge across the Brahmaputra river.
- It is Asia's second longest rail-cum-road bridge and was inaugurated by PM Narendra Modi on 25 December 2018.
- The bridge will reduce the distance by 100 km.
- The foundation stone of this project was laid down by the then Prime Minister H D Deve Gowda on January 22, 1997, and the work was then stalled. This work was again started by Atal Bihari Vajpayee on April 21, 2002.

Hence, the correct option is (C).

28. The two volcanic islands in the Indian territory are Narcondam and Barren.

- Narcondam: It is a small volcanic island located in the Andaman Sea. The island's peak rises to 710 m above mean sea level, and it is formed of andesite.
- Barren Island: It is an island located in the Andaman Sea, dominated by Barren Volcano, the only confirmed active volcano in South Asia, and the only active

volcano along a chain of volcanoes from Sumatra to Myanmar.

Hence, the correct option is (D).

29. Australian tennis player Ashleigh Barty defeated American Danielle Collins to win the Australian Open women's title on 29 January 2022. Barty is the first Australian player to win the Australian Open singles championship since 1978 . She won the French Open in 2019 and Wimbledon in 2021 and has been the number 1 ranked female player in the world for over 100 weeks.

Hence, the correct option is (A).

30. The Mauryan Dynasty was founded in 322 BCE by Chandragupta Maurya after overthrowing the Nanda Dynasty.

- He further expanded his powers to central and western parts of India too.
- The Maurya Empire is considered to be one of the largest empires in Indian history.

Hence, the correct option is (C).

31. Harishena was the court poet of the Gupta emperor Samudragupta.

- Samudragupta was the patron of many poets and scholars, one of whom was Harishena. Samudragupta was the son and successor of Chandragupta I and the greatest ruler of the Gupta dynasty. He was dubbed the Napoleon of India by VA Smith.
- Harishena was the court poet of the Gupta Emperor, Samudragupta. Allahabad Pillar inscription is also known as Prayag Prashasti consists of 33 lines composed by Harishena.

Hence, the correct option is (B).

32. The Treaty of Mangalore ended in Second Anglo Mysore war.

The Treaty of Mangalore was signed between Tipu Sultan and the British East India Company on 11 March 1784. It was signed in Mangalore.

Hence, the correct option is (B).

33. Santosh Yadav is the first woman of the world who climbed Mount Everest successfully from the Kangshung side.

Santosh Yadav:

- Santosh Yadav is a female mountaineer from India.
- She was born in Rewari district of Haryana in 1967.
- She is the first woman in the world to climb Mount Everest twice. She is awarded by the Padma Shri. The first woman to climb Mt. Everest from Kangshung Face (Eastern Facing side of Mt. Everest).
- She was the first Indian woman to climb Everest twice.
- She climbed the peak first in May 1992 and then again in May 1993 with an Indo-Nepalese Team.
- She has also been awarded the Tenzing Norgay National Adventure award in 1994.

Hence, the correct option is (B).

34. The correct answer is Judaism.

Judaism Religion

- Judaism is an Abrahamic, monotheistic, and ethnic religion comprising the collective religious, cultural, and legal tradition and civilization of the Jewish people, also sometimes called Israelites.
- Judaism is considered by religious Jews to be the expression of the covenant that God expression with the Children of Israel.
- It encompasses a wide body of texts, practices, theological positions, and forms of organization.
- Judaism is the tenth-largest religion in the world.

Hence, the correct option is (C).

35. Sir Thomas Clifford Allbutt was an English physician and he invented the medical thermometer in 1867.

A medical thermometer is used for measuring human or animal body temperature.

Thermometers are used to measure temperature gradients. Kelvin, Fahrenheit, and Celsius are common units for temperature. The invention of the first thermometer was credited to Galileo Galilei.

Hence, the correct option is (A).

36. Fiscal policy refers to related to revenue and expenditure policy of the government.

- Fiscal policy is the means by which a government adjusts its spending levels and tax rates to monitor and influence a nation's economy. It is the sister strategy to monetary policy through which a central bank influences a nation's money supply.
- Fiscal policy deals with the taxation and expenditure decisions of the government. Some of the major instruments of fiscal policy are as follows: Budget, Taxation, Public Expenditure, public revenue, Public Debt, and Fiscal Deficit in the economy.

Hence, the correct option is (D).

37. Quantum Mutual Fund (MF) has launched Quantum Nifty 50 ETF Fund of Fund in July 2022.

It is an open-ended fund of fund scheme investing in units of Quantum Nifty 50 ETF. It is India's first of its kind Nifty 50 ETF Fund of Fund (FoF). The New Fund Offer (NFO) will open on July 18, 2022 and close on August 1, 2022.

Hence, the correct option is (C).

38. Edward Jenner invented the smallpox vaccine.

The smallpox vaccine, introduced by Edward Jenner in 1796, was the first successful vaccine to be developed. He observed that milkmaids who previously had caught cowpox did not catch smallpox and showed that inoculated vaccinia protected against inoculated variola virus.

Hence, the correct option is (B).

39. 74th Constitutional Amendment Act, 1992 made constitutional provisions regarding "Urban Local Government".

The 74th Constitutional Amendment Act,1992 given to provision of Urban Local Self-government. The Municipal Corporation administers a region with a populace of more than 1 million. The individuals are straightforwardly chosen from wards known as councilors and the head is called Mayor.

Hence, the correct option is (A).

40. Highways and Road Transport Minister Nitin Gadkari on 18 August 2022 unveiled India's first Electric Double Decker bus in Mumbai.

Switch Mobility Ltd, a subsidiary of Ashok Leyland, has manufactured this unique electric double-decker bus called 'Switch EiV 22.'

The Switch electric double-decker can carry nearly twice the number of seated passengers compared to a single-decker bus.

Hence, the correct option is (C).

41. Given:

$$3 \div 18 \text{ of } 3 \times 6 + 21 \times 6 \div 18 - 3 \div 2 + 3 - 3 \div 9 \text{ of } 3 \times 9$$

Using the BODMAS rule to solve the above expression, we get

$$= 3 \div 54 \times 6 + 21 \times 6 \div 18 - 3 \div 2 + 3 - 3 \div 27 \times 9$$

$$= \frac{3}{54} \times 6 + 21 \times \frac{1}{3} - \frac{3}{2} + 3 - \frac{3}{27} \times 9$$

$$= \frac{1}{18} \times 6 + 21 \times \frac{1}{3} - \frac{3}{2} + 3 - \frac{1}{9} \times 9$$

$$= \frac{1}{3} + 7 - \frac{3}{2} + 3 - 1$$

$$= \left(\frac{1}{3} - \frac{3}{2}\right) + 9$$

$$= \frac{(54 + 2 - 9)}{6}$$

$$= \frac{47}{6}$$

Hence, the correct option is (C).

42. Given:

$$240 \div 6 + \sqrt{529} \times 17 = ? + 150\% \text{ of } 80$$

$$\Rightarrow 40 + 23 \times 17 = ? + 120$$

$$\Rightarrow 40 + 391 = ? + 120$$

$$\Rightarrow 431 - 120 = ?$$

$$\Rightarrow ? = 311$$

$\therefore$ The value of $?$ is 311.

Hence, the correct option is (A).

43. Given:

A number having unknown digits which is divisible by 88.

Divisibility rules of 11: If the difference between sum of digits at odd places and sum of digits at even places of a number is 0 or 11, then the number will be divisible by 11.

Divisibility rules of 8: If the last three digits of a number are divisible by 8, then the number will be divisible by 8.

Considering the given number 4A3164B.

By the rule of divisibility value of B = 0 and 8,

Maximum value is 8

648 is a multiple of 8.

Now the number will be 4A31648

Thus, (4 + 3 + 6 + 8) – (A + 1 + 4) = 11

$\Rightarrow$ 21 - 5 - A = 11

$\Rightarrow$ A = 5

Number will be 4531648

So, A = 5, B = 8

The value of 2A × B = 2 × 5 × 8 = 80

$\therefore$ The required answer is 80.

Hence, the correct option is (D).

44. Let the number be X.

$$\Rightarrow X - \frac{2X}{7} = 100$$

$$\Rightarrow \frac{7X - 2X}{7} = 100$$

$$\Rightarrow X = 140$$

Hence, the correct option is (B).

45. Option (B) is the correct ascending order for the given fractions.

Concept:

Divide the numerator by denominator.

$$\frac{11}{19} = 0.57$$

$$\frac{2}{3} = 0.66$$

$$\frac{13}{17} = 0.76$$

$$\frac{22}{7} = 3.14$$

$\Rightarrow$ 0.57 < 0.66 < 0.76 < 3.14

$$\therefore \quad \frac{11}{19} < \frac{2}{3} < \frac{13}{17} < \frac{22}{7}$$

Hence, the correct option is (B).

46. Given,

Total population of a town $= 2800$

Number of males $= 720 +$ Number of females

Let the number of females and males be x and $(x + 720)$ respectively.

According to the question,

$$x + x + 720 = 2800$$

$$\Rightarrow 2x + 720 = 2800$$

$$\Rightarrow 2x = 2080$$

$$\Rightarrow x = 1040$$

Number of males $= (1040 + 720) = 1760$

Now, New number of males after 40% reduction $=$ $1760 \times 60\% = 1056$

New number of females after 20% increment $=$ $1040 \times 120\% = 1248$

New population of town $= (1056 + 1248) = 2304$

$\therefore$ New population of town is 2304.

Hence, the correct option is (C).

47. Given:

The ratio of carbon and oxygen $= 1:4$

As we know,

$$\text{Percentage of carbon} = \left(\frac{\text{Value of carbon}}{\text{sum of ratio}}\right) \times 100$$

Sum of ratio $= 1 + 4 = 5$

$$\text{Percentage of carbon} = \left(\frac{1}{5}\right) \times 100$$

$$= 20\%$$

The percentage of carbon is 20%

Hence, the correct option is (A).

48. If x is the mean proportional between 12.8 and 64.8, then

$$12.8 : x :: x : 64.8$$

$$\Rightarrow \frac{12.8}{x} = \frac{x}{64.8}$$

$$\Rightarrow x^2 = 12.8 \times 64.8$$

$$\Rightarrow x = \sqrt{[16 \times 0.8 \times 0.8 \times 81]}$$

$$\Rightarrow x = 4 \times 0.8 \times 9$$

If y is the third proportional to 38.4 and 57.6, then

$$38.4 : 57.6 :: 57.6 : y$$

$\Rightarrow \dfrac{38.4}{57.6} = \dfrac{57.6}{y}$

$\Rightarrow y = \dfrac{(57.6 \times 57.6)}{38.4}$

$\Rightarrow y = 86.4$

Now,

$2x : y = 2 \times 4 \times 0.8 \times 9 : 86.4 = 2 : 3$

Hence, the correct option is (C).

49. Let the numbers be $x, x+2, x+4, x+6$ and $x+8$.

According to question,

$\dfrac{[x+(x+2)+(x+4)+(x+6)+(x+8)]}{5} = 51$

$\Rightarrow 5x + 20 = 255$

$\Rightarrow x = 47$

So, required difference $= (47+8) - 47 = 8$

Hence, the correct option is (C).

50. Given,

Principal, P = Rs. 7790

Rate, R = 10%

Time, T = 2 years

Compound Interest $= P\left[\left(1+\dfrac{R}{100}\right)^{T} - 1\right]$

$= 7790\left[\left(1+\dfrac{10}{100}\right)^{2} - 1\right]$

$= 7790\left(\dfrac{121}{100} - 1\right)$

$= \dfrac{7790 \times 21}{100}$

$= $ Rs. 1635.9

Hence, the correct option is (D).

51. Given,

Principal $= $ Rs. 48000

Amount $= $ Rs. 55560

Time $= 2$ year and 3 months

As we know,

S.I $= $ A $-$ P

S.I $= \dfrac{(P \times R \times T)}{100}$

S.I $= 55560 - 48000 = 7560$

Time $= 2\dfrac{1}{4} = \dfrac{9}{4}$ year

S.I $= \dfrac{\left(48000 \times R \times \frac{9}{4}\right)}{100}$

$\Rightarrow 7560 = \dfrac{\left(48000 \times R \times \frac{9}{4}\right)}{100}$

$\Rightarrow 756000 = 108000 \times R$

$\Rightarrow R = \dfrac{756}{108} = 7\%$

$\therefore$ The rate of interest per year is 7%.

Hence, the correct option is (A).

52. Let the cost price of the chair is x.

$SP = x - 25\%$ of x

$\Rightarrow 720 = 0.75x$

$\Rightarrow x = 960$

$\Rightarrow CP = $ Rs 960

So, To gain 25%, SP would be $= 960 + 25\%$ of $960 = $ Rs 1200

Hence, the correct option is (A).

53. Given:

Discount $= 10\%$

Profit $= 8\%$

MP of the article $= $ Rs. 480

SP of the article $= $ Marked price $\times \dfrac{\text{Marked price - Discount}}{100}$

SP of the article $= 480 \times \dfrac{90}{100}$

$= $ Rs. 432

CP of the article $= $ SP of the article $\times \dfrac{100}{100 \pm \text{Profit/Loss}}$

CP of the article $= 432 \times \dfrac{100}{108}$

$= $ Rs. 400

Hence, the correct option is (B).

54. Effective discount $\% = x + y - \dfrac{(xy)}{100}$

Where x and y are the successive rates of discount

Therefore,

Effective discount on 15% and $20\% = 15 + 20 - \dfrac{(15 \times 20)}{100} = 32\%$

Now apply it on 25% and 32%

Effective discount on 25% and $32\% = 25 + 32 - \frac{(25\times32)}{100} = 49\%$

Hence, the correct option is (C).

55. Given,

Sides of cuboid $= 14$ cm, 12 cm and 8 cm

Side of cube $= 2$ cm

We know that,

After melting and reformation volume remains same.

Volume of cuboid $= l \times b \times h$

Volume of cube $=$ side ^{3}

According to the question,

Volume of cuboid $= 14 \times 12 \times 8$

Volume of cube $= 2 \times 2 \times 2$

Number of cubes $= \frac{(14\times12\times8)}{(2\times2\times2)}$

$= 7 \times 6 \times 4$

$= 168$

Hence, the correct option is (A).

56. For a triangle the sum of any two sides should be greater than the third side.

Using this rule,

(1) 4.5

$\Rightarrow$ if third side is 4.5 cm, then 6.5 + 4.5 > 10   correct. But is 4.5 the smallest possible value.

Let's check more.

(2) 2.8

$\Rightarrow$ 2.8 + 6.5 = 9.3 < 10. Not a triangle

(3) 3.5

$\Rightarrow$ 6.5 + 3.5 = 10 = 10. Not possible

(4) 4

$\Rightarrow$ 4 + 6.5 = 10.5 >10. Correct and since 4 < 4.5 this is the smallest possible number among the options and hence it is the right answer.

Hence, the correct option is (D).

57. Since the numbers are given in the form of a ratio that means their common factors have been canceled.

Each one's common factor is HCF.

And here HCF = 12,

So, the numbers are 12, 24, and 36.
Hence, the correct option is (A).

58. Let C = x

Then, B = x + 5000 and A = x + 5000 + 4000 = x + 9000

So, x + x + 5000 + x + 9000 = 50000

$\Rightarrow$ 3x = 36000

$\Rightarrow$ x = 12000

A : B : C = 21000 : 17000 : 12000 = 21 : 17 : 12

So A's Share

$=$ Rs. $35000 \times \frac{21}{50}$

$=$ Rs. 14700
Hence, the correct option is (D).

59. Given:

Speed of train from P to $Q = 70 km/h$

Speed of train from Q to $P = 30 km/h$

Where,

$S_{avg} =$ Average speed of train

$S_1 =$ Speed of train from P to Q

$S_2 =$ Speed of train from Q to P

$(S)_{avg} = \frac{(2S_1 S_2)}{(S_1 + S_2)}$

$\Rightarrow (S)_{avg} = \frac{(2\times70\times30)}{(70+30)}$

$\Rightarrow (S)_{avg} = \frac{4200}{100}$

$\Rightarrow (S)_{avg} = 42 km/h$

$\therefore$ The average speed of train is $42 km/h$.

Hence, the correct option is (B).

60. As we know,

If a person completes a piece of work in 'n' days, then work of 1 day is $\frac{1}{n}$ part of work.

Time taken by Ganesh and Bhima complete a work $= 6$ days

The part of the work that is completed by Ganesh and Bhima in 1 day $= \frac{1}{6}$

Time taken by Ganesh to complete a work $= 10$ days

The part of work that is completed by Ganesh in 1 day $= \frac{1}{10}$

Now, we first find the part of work completed by Bhima in 1 day

$= \frac{1}{6} - \frac{1}{10}$

$= \frac{(10-6)}{60}$

$$= \frac{4}{60}$$

$$= \frac{1}{15}$$

∴ Bhima completes the whole work in 15 days.

Hence, the correct option is (D).

61. The meanings of the given words:

- Economical- Giving good value or return in relation to the money, time, or effort expended.
- Miserly - A person who hoards wealth and spends as little money as possible.
- Extravagant - Lacking restraint in spending money or using resources.
- Greedy - Having an excessive desire or appetite for food.

The given word 'Frugal' means sparing or economical with regard to money or food.

From the given options, the most appropriate antonym for the given word must be 'Extravagant'.

Hence, the correct option is (C).

62. One word substitute is Anarchist.

Anarchist: a person who believes in or tries to bring about anarchy

Belligerent: hostile and aggressive

Iconoclast: a person who attacks or criticizes cherished beliefs or institutions

Agnostic: a person who believes that nothing is known or can be known of the existence or nature of God

Hence, the correct option is (D).

63. Beams that support the roof are called rafters.

Sentence Usage: His voice got higher and slower as if he expected it to be rising into the church rafters.

Hence, the correct option is (C).

64. The passage clearly states that the organization wants to improve the living conditions of the animals and stop all sorts of cruel treatment against them. The author talks about the effective measures taken by the organization as well.

Hence, the correct option is (C).

65. It is mentioned in the passage 'The organization points out that vaccination programs are the only effective way to eliminate rabies, and work with governments on vaccination programs.'

Hence, the correct option is (C).

66. The word 'aftermath' means 'the consequences or after-effects of a significant unpleasant event'.

Hence, the correct option is (B).

67. The word 'misguided' means 'having or showing faulty judgment or reasoning.' Thus the word 'well informed' conveys the opposite meaning.

Hence, the correct option is (D).

68. 'an' and 'a' are definite articles whereas 'the' is an indefinite article.'an' is used when the word starts with a vowel sound - that is, 'a', 'e', 'i', 'o', 'u' and 'a' is used for words starting with a consonant sound. Here, 'honest', when pronounced, has a sound of 'o' which is a vowel. So, 'an' must be used before 'honest'.

So, the correct sentence is "Bulbul is an honest girl but she is also very rude".

Hence, the correct option is (A).

69. In the given sentence, there is an inappropriate use of prepositions.

Here, to will be used after indebted which is an appropriate preposition. To is used after adjectives and it also denotes destination.

Example: We are deeply indebted to you for your help.

We use from to refer to the place where someone or something starts or originates.

Example: The wind is coming from the north.

So, the correct sentence is "I would be eternally indebted to you if you could help me".

Hence, the correct option is (D).

70. The correct answer is 'everywhere'.

The adverb 'everywhere' means in or to all places.

The adverb 'anywhere' means in or to any place.

The adverb 'somewhere' means in or to someplace.

The adverb 'nowhere' means not in or to any place; not anywhere.

So the correct sentence is-

I looked everywhere for my puppy but could not find it.

Hence, the correct option is (A).

71. Get cold feet: suddenly become too frightened to do something one had planned to do

Example: The burglar has got cold feet when the dog started barking.

Hence, the correct option is (C).

72. There is a heavy demand **for** these goods.

The most appropriate preposition for the given sentence is 'for'.

We use for to talk about a purpose or a reason for something.

Example: I'm going for some breakfast.

Hence, the correct option is (C).

73. Don't **tell** me you've lost your keys again.

- The verb 'tell' means to communicate information to someone in spoken or written words.
- The verb 'say' means to utter words so as to convey information, an opinion, a feeling or intention, or an instruction.
- The verb 'speak' means to say something in order to convey information or to express a feeling.
- The verb 'inform' means to give (someone) facts or information.

Hence, the correct option is (B).

74. This book **belongs** to her.

In the given sentence 'book' is a singular auxiliary verb. So, it should be followed by a singular main verb.

And we know that the singular of 'belong' is 'belongs'.

The phrasal verb 'belongs to somebody' means 'to be someone's property'.

Hence, the correct option is (B).

75. The error should be corrected by 'has she' in place of 'isn't it'.

The auxiliary verb from the positive statement is repeated in the tag and changed to the negative and the negative verb in the original statement is changed to positive in the tag.

Example:

- We have finished, haven't we?
- You aren't English, are you?

The correct sentence is: 'She has not completed her course, has she?'

Hence, the correct option is (C).

76. The correct sentence is - 'I need to get to the house on Landsdowne Road by ten'o clock.'

The error is in part- I need to get to the house in.

In this part, the preposition 'in' should be replaced with 'on'. The preposition 'on' is used to designate names of streets, avenues etc.

Example- Ram house is on VIP road.

Hence, the correct option is (A).

77. The word 'predicament' means 'an unpleasant situation.'

The meanings of the words are:

- Plight - A dangerous, difficult, or otherwise unfortunate situation.
- Plunder- The violent and dishonest acquisition of property.
- Stentorian - Loud; harsh; raucous
- Occult - Mystical, supernatural, or magical powers, practices, or phenomena.

Hence, the correct option is (A).

78. Emergancy is the misspelt word.

Correct spelling is the emergency.

Emergency: a serious, unexpected, and often dangerous situation requiring immediate action.

Hence, the correct option is (C).

79. Rendezvos is the misspelt word.

Correct spelling is the Rendezvous.

Rendezvous: an agreement to be present at a specified time and place

Hence, the correct option is (D).

80. Devil's advocate: one who argues against something just for the sake of arguing, without actually being committed to the views

Example: He offered to play devil's advocate and argue against our case so that we could find out any flaws in it.

Hence, the correct option is (D).

General Intelligence and Reasoning

Q.1 Eight friends A, B, C, D, E, F, G and H are sitting around a circular table facing each other for a lunch. A is opposite F and third to the right of B. G is between F and D. H is to the left of D. E is between C and A. Who is sitting second to the left of C?

A. D   **B.** F   **C.** B   **D.** A

Q.2 Direction: What should come in place of question mark in the following Number Series?

12, 15, 75, ?, 738, 749

A. 259   **B.** 155   **C.** 90   **D.** 82

Q.3

Choose a figure which would most closely resemble the unfolded form of Figure (Z).

 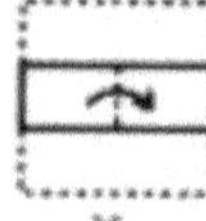  
X   Y   Z

 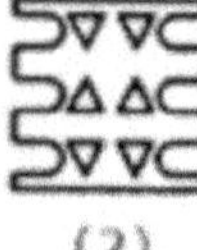  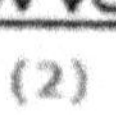 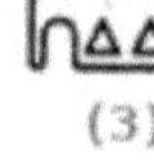  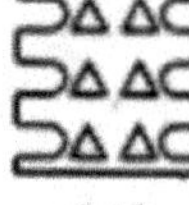
(1)   (2)   (3)   (4)

A. (1)   **B.** (2)   **C.** (3)   **D.** (4)

Q.4 In a group of people, S is brother of T, X is sister of S, B is brother of H and H is son of T. Who is B's uncle?

[UP Police Sub Inspector, 2017]

A. T   **B.** H   **C.** S   **D.** X

Q.5 Direction: Identify the option that is embedded in the following figure ? (rotation is NOT allowed).

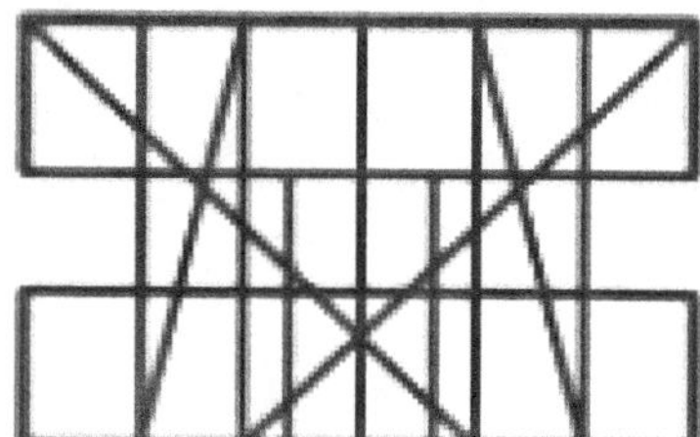

[SSC Sub Inspector (CPO), 2020]

A. 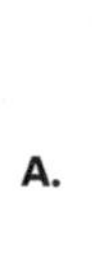 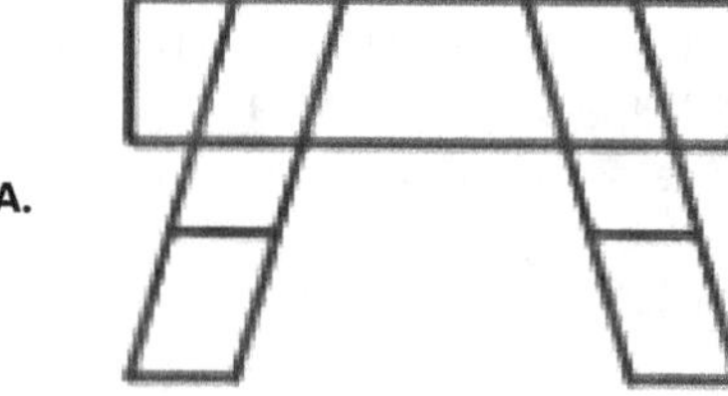

B. 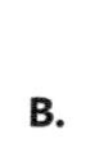 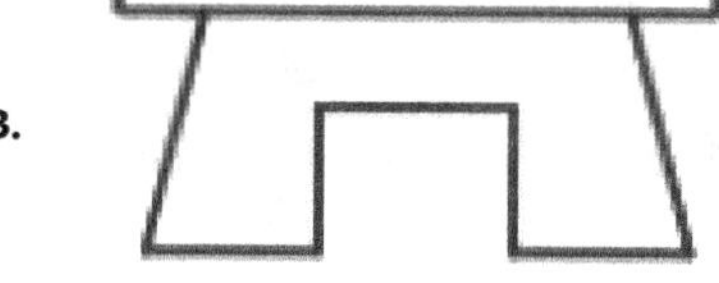

C. 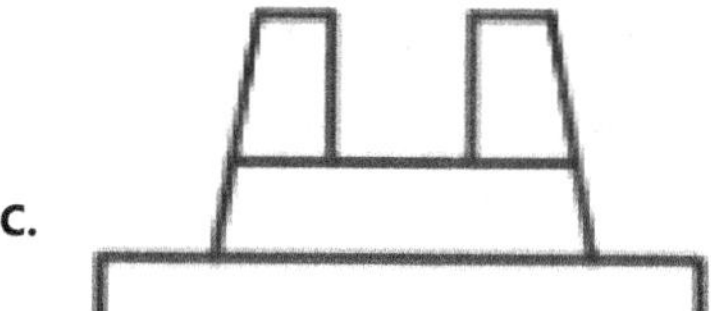

D. 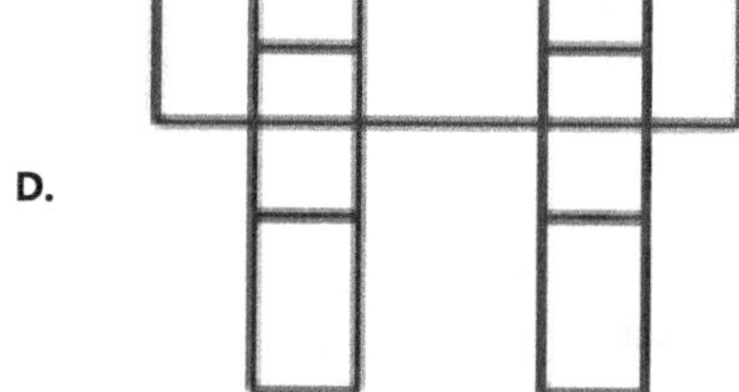

Q.6 Direction: Choose the Venn diagram that best represents the words.

India, Telangana, Hyderabad.

[RRB/RRC Group D, 2018]

A.  

B. 

C. 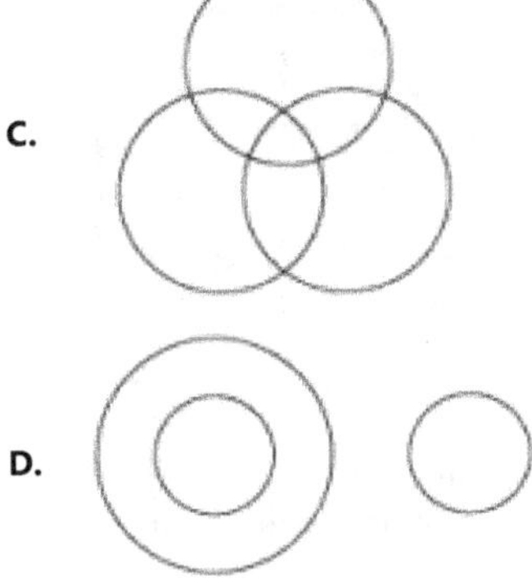

A. 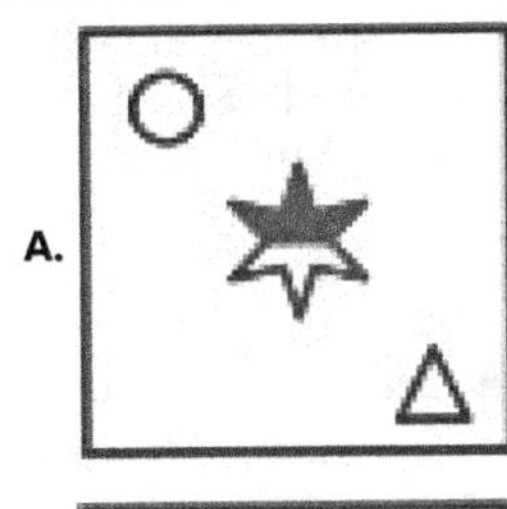

B. 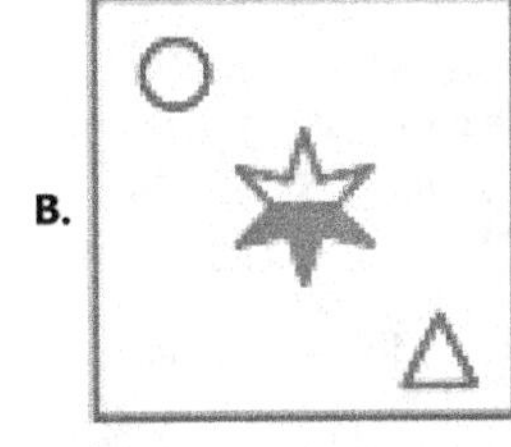

D.

C. 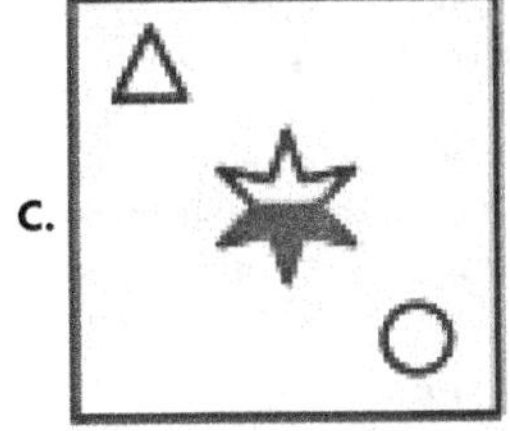

D. 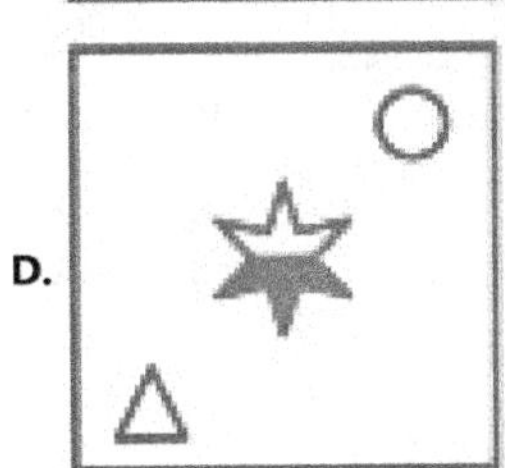

Q.7 If '÷' is coded as 'L', '+' is coded as 'M', '-' is coded as 'N', '×' is coded as 'P', then what is the value of 38 L 2 M 7 P 4 N 22?

A. 33   **B.** 25   **C.** 28   **D.** 21

Q.8 Direction: Study the image carefully and choose the correct mirror image.

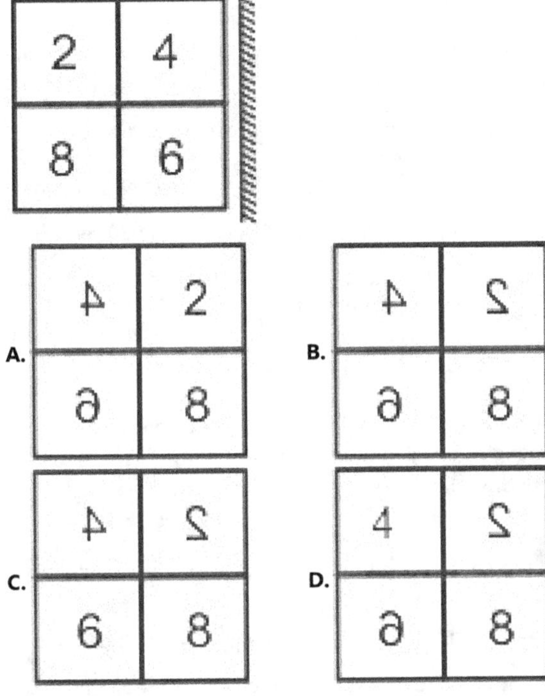

Q.9 Select the figure that will come next in place of the question mark [?] in the following figure series.

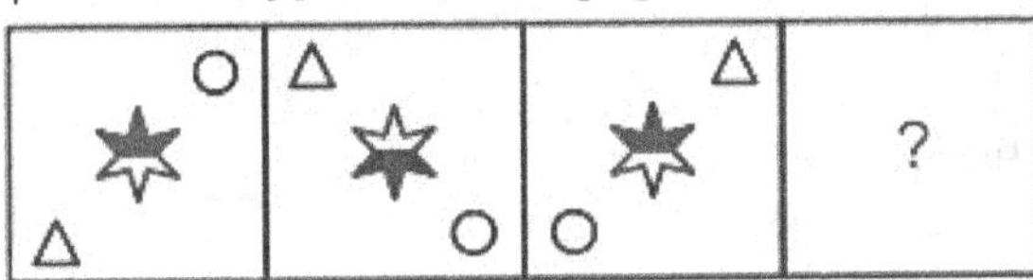

[SSC Selection Post Phase IX, 2020]

Q.10 Direction: In the following question, select the number which can be placed at the sign of question mark (?) from the given alternatives.

5	6	31
7	7	51
8	6	51
4	4	?

A. 22   **B.** 20   **C.** 27   **D.** 34

Q.11 Arrange the given words in the sequence in which they occur in the dictionary.

1. Decisive
2. Dethrone
3. Decision
4. Demand
5. Dearth

A. 5 1 4 3 2   **B.** 1 5 4 2 3   **C.** 5 3 1 4 2   **D.** 1 5 3 2 4

Q.12 Direction: Read the given statement(s) and conclusions carefully and select which of the conclusions logically follow(s) from the statement(s).

Statement:

All dark is night.

Some dark are black.

Conclusion:

I. All black is night.

II. Some black is not night.

A. Only I follows

B. Only II follows

C. Either I or II follows

D. Neither I nor II follows

Q.13 If TOUR is written as 1234, CLEAR is written as 56784 and SPARE is written as 90847, find the code for CARE.

[Intelligence Bureau Security Assistant, 2017]

A. 1247   **B.** 4847   **C.** 5247   **D.** 5847

Q.14 Select the option that is related to the third number in the same way as the second number is related to the first number and the sixth number is related to the fifth number.

72 : 108 :: 88 : ? :: 112 : 168

A. 138   **B.** 132   **C.** 142   **D.** 128

Q.15 In the following question, select the related letters from the given alternatives.

SLING : GNILS :: HINGE : ? : DRINK :: KNIRD

A. NGIHE   **B.** INEHG   **C.** HGEHI   **D.** EGNIH

Q.16 Out of the given number pairs, three are similar in a certain manner. However, one pair is NOT like the other three. Select the pair which is different from the rest:

A. 225 : 3375   **B.** 49 : 280

C. 64 : 512   **D.** 25 : 125

Q.17 Find out the odd number from the given alternatives.

A. 9613   **B.** 3823   **C.** 7855   **D.** 235

Q.18 Select the combination of letters that when sequentially placed in the blanks of the given series will complete the series.

d _ m c _ z _ h _ c s _ d _ m _ _ z

A. h s d z c h c s   **B.** h s d m z h c s

C. h s d m z h d s   **D.** h d s m z h c s

Q.19 Select the image that will be formed after the unfolded net of the cube is folded inwards to form the cube.

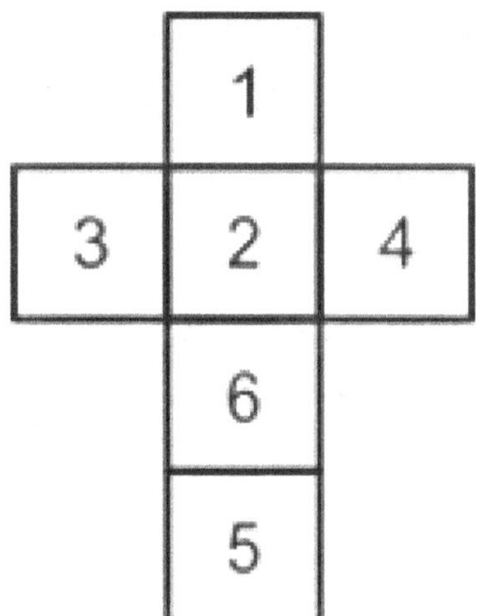

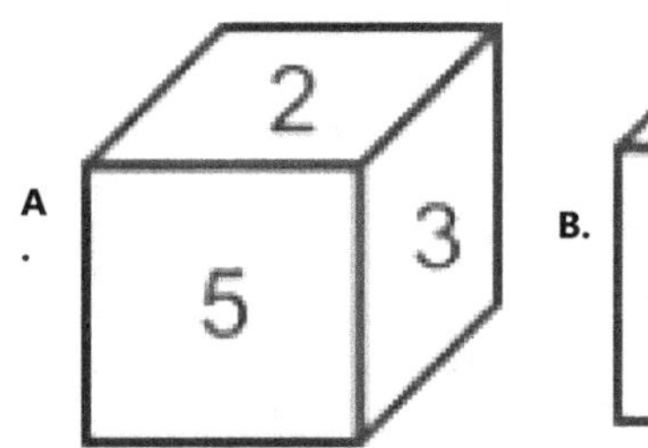

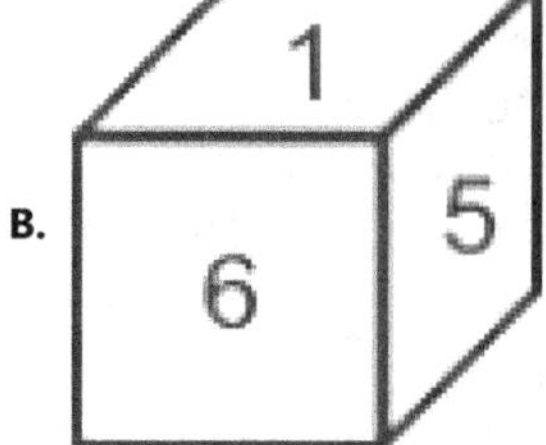

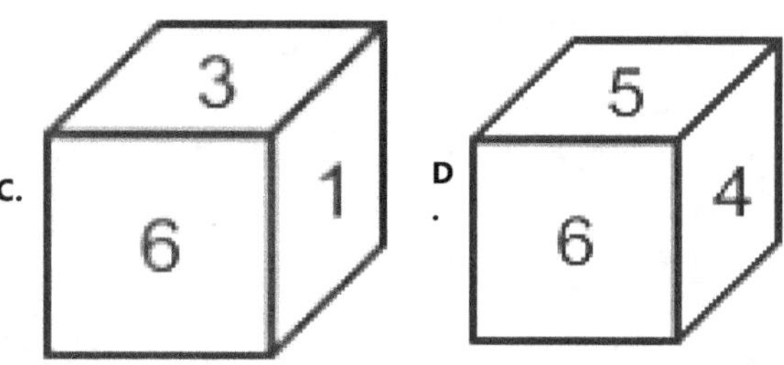

Q.20 In 2010, Shalu's age was six times the age of Stuti, whereas, in 2018, Shalu's age was two times the age of Stuti. What is Shalu's year of birth?

A. 1998   **B.** 2002   **C.** 1996   **D.** 2000

General Knowledge and General Awareness

Q.21 Reservation for women in India is available in:

[UPTET Paper - I, 2019]

A. Lok Sabha

B. Cabinet

C. Vidhan Sabha

D. Panchayati Raj Institutions

Q.22 In order to be appointed as the Governor of a state, one must have attained the age of:

[UPTET Paper - I, 2019]

A. 35 years   **B.** 50 years   **C.** 45 years   **D.** 30 years

Q.23 Which Constitutional amendment provided constitutional status to urban local government?

[Uttarakhand Public Service Commission (UKPSC), 2014]

A. 72nd   **B.** 73rd   **C.** 74th   **D.** 71st

Q.24 On 5 June, 2022 who has won the 14th French Open title by defeating Norwegian Casper Ruud?

A. Novak Djokovic   **B.** Rafael Nadal

C. Michael Chang   **D.** Max Decugis

Q.25 Which country was host the 44th FIDE Chess Olympiad 2022?

A. Russia   **B.** France   **C.** Italy   **D.** India

Q.26 Which of the following states recently launched Cheerag Scheme?

A. Uttar Pradesh   **B.** Haryana

C. Assam   **D.** Jharkhand

Q.27 The Hoysaleshwara Temple is an aspirant for the tag of World Heritage Site is located at which of the following state?

A. Himachal Pradesh   **B.** Karnataka

C. Odisha   **D.** Maharashtra

Q.28 Which Indian Institute of Technology (IIT) has collaborated with DRDO to develop defence technology in August 2022?

A. IIT Madras   **B.** IIT Dhanbad
C. IIT Roorkee   **D.** IIT Mumbai

Q.29 Charkula is famous folk dance of:
A. Bundelkhand   **B.** Brij bhumi
C. Avadh   **D.** None of the above

Q.30 What is the name of the potential COVID-19 vaccine, to be developed by Indian Council of Medical Research (ICMR)?
A. Covidin   **B.** Covaxin
C. Comedin   **D.** Coresearch

Q.31 The southernmost Himalayas are known as _________.
A. Shivaliks   **B.** Himadri
C. Himachal   **D.** Garhwal

Q.32 Which of the following mineral belts in India is famous for the production of iron ore and coal?
A. Himalayan belt
B. Chhotanagpur belt
C. Southern belt
D. North-Western Region

Q.33 What was the main occupation of the Paleolithic (Old Stone Age) people?
A. Hunting   **B.** Farming
C. Animal Husbandry   **D.** Fishing

Q.34 Who among the following was given the title of 'Khan-e-Khana' by Akbar?
A. Abul Fazl
B. Faizi
C. Tansen
D. Mirza Abdul Rahim Khan

Q.35 When was the Poona Pact signed?
A. August, 1932   **B.** October, 1932
C. September, 1932   **D.** November, 1932

Q.36 The Industrial licensing had been abolished for all projects EXCEPT for a short list of industries through the amendments in NIP (New Industrial Policy) in the year ______.
A. 1956   **B.** 1969   **C.** 1987   **D.** 1991

Q.37 Which of the following measuring instruments indicate an increase in economic development?
A. Increase in GDP
B. Increase in National Income
C. Increase in Poverty
D. Increase in Life Expectancy

Q.38 Which of the following gases used in manufacturing of vanaspati ghee from vegetable oil?
A. Hydrogen   **B.** Helium
C. Oxygen   **D.** Nitrogen

Q.39 Who has won the BBC Indian Sportswoman of the Year award for 2021 in March 2022?
A. Lovlina Borgohain   **B.** PV Sindhu
C. Mary Kom   **D.** Mirabai Chanu

Q.40 Who has been conferred with the 31st Vyas Samman on 25 August 2022?
A. Dr. Asghar Wajahat   **B.** Sudha Murty
C. Devdutt Pattanaik   **D.** R.K. Narayan

Elementary Mathematics

Q.41 The value of $\left[\frac{4}{7} \text{ of } 2\frac{4}{5} \times 1\frac{2}{3} - \left(3\frac{1}{2} - 2\frac{1}{6} \right) \right] \div \left(3\frac{1}{5} \div 4\frac{1}{2} \text{ of } 5\frac{1}{3} \right)$ is:

[SSC CGL, 2020]

A. 10   **B.** $7\frac{1}{2}$ **C.** $1\frac{1}{3}$ **D.** 15

Q.42 What will come in the place of the question mark '?' in the following question?
$$1456 \div 16 \times 14 + 22 = (?)^4$$
A. 6   **B.** 4   **C.** 16   **D.** 36

Q.43 In a two-digit number, the digit at the unit's place is 1 less than twice the digit at the ten's place. If the digits at unit's and ten's place are interchanged, the difference between the new and the original number is less than the original number by 20. The original number is:
A. 23   **B.** 35   **C.** 47   **D.** 59

Q.44 The numerator of a fraction is 4 less than its denominator. If the numerator is decreased by 2 and the denominator is increased by 1, then the denominator becomes eight times the numerator. Find the fraction.
A. $\frac{3}{7}$ **B.** $\frac{4}{8}$ **C.** $\frac{2}{7}$ **D.** $\frac{3}{8}$

Q.45 Convert $\frac{5}{8}$ to decimal.
A. 0.58   **B.** 0.625   **C.** 0.875   **D.** 0.058

Q.46 Marks of C is 25% less than A and marks of B are 30% more than C. Marks of B is how much percent less/more than the marks of A?
A. 2.5%   **B.** 3.5%   **C.** 4.5%   **D.** 5.5%

Q.47 A sum of money invested at simple interest becomes 6 times of itself at 5% per annum. Find the time period.
A. 50 years   **B.** 100 years
C. 125 years   **D.** 150 years

Q.48 The compound interest on $Rs.\,30000$ at 7% per annum for a certain time period is $Rs.\,4347$. Find the time period of investment.
A. 2 years   **B.** 3 years   **C.** 5 years   **D.** 7 years

Q.49 A seller offers 11% discount on a mini-refrigerator with a marked price of Rs. 8200. If he still earns a profit of Rs. 600, what is the cost price of the refrigerator?
A. Rs. 6698   **B.** Rs. 7600   **C.** Rs. 7350   **D.** Rs. 4960

Q.50 The average of $7.5, 3.2, 11.3, 20.5,$ and x is 10. Find the value of x.
A. 7.5   **B.** 4.5   **C.** 3.5   **D.** 6.5

Q.51 The marked price of an article is Rs 500 and three successive discounts of 10% each are given. What is the profit/loss,? (If cost price $= 350$)

A. Rs 14.5 **B.** Rs 12.5 **C.** Rs 13.5 **D.** Rs 11.5

Q.52 Radius ratio of three iron balls is $1:2:3$. They are melted and recast into a bigger iron ball of radius 6 cm. The diameter of the smallest ball is:

A. $\sqrt[3]{6}$ **B.** $\sqrt[3]{3}$ **C.** $2\sqrt[3]{6}$ **D.** $2\sqrt[3]{4}$

Q.53 A person crosses a road of length 1200 m in 10 minutes. What is the speed of the person?

A. 3 km/h **B.** 5 km/h **C.** 8.5 km/h **D.** 7.2 km/h

Q.54 A can do a piece of work in 10 days and B can do it in 15 days. Number of days to complete the work if they work together is:

A. 6 days **B.** 9 days **C.** 7 days **D.** 5 days

Q.55 3 men or 5 women can complete the work in 12 days then in how many days 3 men and 7 women will complete the same work?

A. 5 days **B.** 8 days **C.** 10 days **D.** 15 days

Q.56 Three friends A, B and C visited a cafe and at the end paid Rs 260. If the ratio of money paid by A to that of B is $1:2$ and that of B to C is $3:2$, then the amount paid by A was? (in Rs.)

A. 60 **B.** 65 **C.** 70 **D.** 75

Q.57 The average of 42 numbers is 102. In the calculation, If Rahul mistakenly added 40, 86 and 24 instead of 28, 30 and 50, then find the correct average.

A. 101 **B.** 102 **C.** 103 **D.** 104

Q.58 If the product of two numbers is 3360 and their LCM is 96, find their HCF.

[RRB (NTPC), 2017]

A. 35 **B.** 33 **C.** 34 **D.** 29

Q.59 Manish invests Rs.450 in a business for 4 monthes and Mahavir invests Rs.600 for 3 months. What is the share of Mahavir in the total profit of Rs.400?

A. 200 **B.** 100 **C.** 300 **D.** 150

Q.60 A pilgrim travelled a distance of $50km$ in 7.5 hours. He travelled partly on foot at $4km/hr$ and partly on a bullock cart at $12km/hr$. The distance travelled on foot is km.

A. 20 **B.** 30 **C.** 26 **D.** 24

English

Q.61 Direction: In the following question, some parts of the sentence may have errors. Find out which part of the sentence has an error and select the appropriate option. If a sentence is free from error, select 'No Error'.

Neither of (1)/ them (2)/ were looking for a mate. (3)/ No error (4)

A. 1 **B.** 2 **C.** 3 **D.** 4

Q.62 Direction: In the following question, some parts of the sentence may have errors. Find out which part of the sentence has an error and select the appropriate option. If a sentence is free from error, select 'No Error'.

This will reduce dependencies on (1)/ commercial journals and there (2)/ negative impact on research. (3)/ No error. (4)

A. 1 **B.** 2 **C.** 3 **D.** 4

Ques (63-65):Direction: In the following question, the sentence is given with blank to be filled in with an appropriate word. Select the correct alternative out of the four and indicate it by selecting the appropriate option.

Q.63 He knew that an apple _________ not be plucked while it is green.

A. Should **B.** Is **C.** Shall **D.** Can

Q.64 You haven't many teeth left, but ______ few you have are sharp enough to make me shudder.

A. A **B.** An **C.** Very **D.** The

Q.65 I can always tell when my friend is ______ because she bites her lip.

A. Lying **B.** Lain **C.** Lye **D.** Lay

Q.66 Direction: In the following question, out of the four alternatives, select the word opposite in meaning to the given word.

Gullible

A. Fickle **B.** Stylish
C. Easy **D.** Incredulous

Q.67 Direction: In the following question, out of the four alternatives, select the alternative which is the best substitute of the phrase.

A spot or a stain caused by a discolouring substance

A. Hue **B.** Blot **C.** Tint **D.** Dye

Q.68 Direction: Select single word or phrase which means most nearly the same as the given phrase.

An accomplished musician

A. Virtuoso **B.** Dilettante
C. Termagant **D.** Agnostic

Q.69 Direction: Select the correct synonym of the given word.

Opaque

A. Misty **B.** Uncovered
C. Clear **D.** Transparent

Ques (70-73):Direction: In the following passage there are blanks, which has been numbered. Choose the correct word from the given options which fits the blank appropriately.

Solar energy is considered one of the most important ___(1)___ energy sources, which is ___(2)___. Solar energy plays a huge role in the ___(3)___ to renewable energy, but there's a catch — recycling solar panels is ___(4)___ easy nor profitable.

Q.70 Select the most appropriate option to fill in the blank No. 1.

A. non-renewable **B.** recyclable
C. renewable **D.** industrial

Q.71 Select the most appropriate option to fill in the blank No. 2.

A. inexhaustible **B.** restless
C. inextinguishable **D.** indestructible

Q.72 Select the most appropriate option to fill in the blank No. 3.

A. tilt **B.** skip **C.** twist **D.** shift

Q.73 Select the most appropriate option to fill in the blank No. 4.

A. either **B.** neither
C. moreover **D.** whether

Q.74 Direction: Select the most appropriate meaning of the underlined idiom in the given sentence.

He makes himself a <u>laughing stock</u> by saying foolish things.

A. laughing at oneself
B. an object of ridicule
C. making people laugh
D. mocking others

Q.75 Direction: Select the option that means the same as the given idiom.

Go down like a lead balloon

A. Failure in exam leaving one dishearten
B. To lose all your belongings
C. Feeling lonely because of being ostracized
D. A speech, proposal, or joke that is poorly received

Q.76 Groups of four words are given, In each group, one word is correctly spelt. Find the correctly spelt word and mark your answer in the Answer Sheet.

A. Indeganeous **B.** Indigenous
C. Indegenous **D.** Indigeneous

Q.77 Direction: Identify the word that is spelt correctly.

A. Conscientiuous **B.** Consientious
C. Conscientious **D.** Consceintious

Q.78 Direction: Select the most appropriate option to substitute the underlined segment in the given sentence. If no substitution is required, select No improvement.

I usually <u>did not add</u> cheese to my toast

A. No Improvement **B.** did not adding
C. do not add **D.** do not added

Q.79 Direction: In the following questions a part of the sentence is underlined. Below are given alternatives to the underlined part at (A), (B) and (C) which may improve the sentence. Choose the correct alternative. In case no improvement is needed, your answer is 'D', Indicate your correct response.

I shall be honoured <u>if you would accept</u> my offer.

A. by your accepting **B.** if you shall' accept
C. if you accept **D.** No improvement

Q.80 Direction: For Underlined part of the sentence chooses part of the sentence from given choices, to correct or improve it.

Will you <u>lend me few rupees</u> in this hour of need?

A. lend me any rupees
B. borrow me a few rupees
C. lend me a few rupees
D. No improvement

// Smart Answer Sheet //

Correct Percentage of students who answered correctly. **Skipped** Percentage of students who skipped.

Q.	Ans.	Correct / Skipped	Q.	Ans.	Correct / Skipped	Q.	Ans.	Correct / Skipped	Q.	Ans.	Correct / Skipped	Q.	Ans.	Correct / Skipped
1	B	86.29 % / 12.82 %	17	A	47.93 % / 48.02 %	33	A	45.92 % / 39.9 %	49	A	83.95 % / 12.52 %	65	A	63.95 % / 31.44 %
2	D	83.0 % / 11.95 %	18	B	66.87 % / 30.1 %	34	D	81.77 % / 13.0 %	50	A	78.98 % / 11.23 %	66	D	44.81 % / 50.51 %
3	B	68.75 % / 30.58 %	19	D	53.57 % / 31.98 %	35	C	51.53 % / 43.5 %	51	A	86.57 % / 12.82 %	67	B	60.86 % / 33.33 %
4	C	82.04 % / 12.19 %	20	A	47.31 % / 49.82 %	36	D	67.93 % / 30.26 %	52	C	89.1 % / 10.54 %	68	A	42.03 % / 39.28 %
5	B	76.61 % / 15.98 %	21	D	81.3 % / 10.68 %	37	D	41.76 % / 54.24 %	53	D	89.22 % / 10.64 %	69	A	40.55 % / 45.8 %
6	A	81.05 % / 13.02 %	22	A	57.73 % / 37.04 %	38	A	87.6 % / 12.16 %	54	A	76.28 % / 18.77 %	70	C	68.64 % / 30.21 %
7	B	85.34 % / 13.1 %	23	C	54.53 % / 39.37 %	39	D	79.7 % / 19.0 %	55	A	84.45 % / 12.51 %	71	A	41.8 % / 32.59 %
8	B	79.63 % / 18.1 %	24	B	53.01 % / 31.47 %	40	A	65.5 % / 30.04 %	56	A	21.69 % / 71.09 %	72	D	56.51 % / 33.05 %
9	B	66.17 % / 33.43 %	25	D	43.68 % / 43.53 %	41	A	87.26 % / 10.27 %	57	A	50.88 % / 32.53 %	73	B	45.61 % / 34.25 %
10	B	77.4 % / 10.23 %	26	B	40.59 % / 45.08 %	42	A	89.31 % / 10.52 %	58	A	40.69 % / 59.08 %	74	B	63.74 % / 36.26 %
11	C	15.77 % / 77.15 %	27	B	57.29 % / 40.45 %	43	C	20.13 % / 71.63 %	59	A	65.49 % / 31.27 %	75	D	83.28 % / 13.38 %
12	C	86.41 % / 12.94 %	28	C	52.46 % / 46.92 %	44	A	46.97 % / 46.58 %	60	A	67.14 % / 32.43 %	76	B	43.79 % / 30.17 %
13	D	78.04 % / 21.86 %	29	B	80.31 % / 13.05 %	45	B	68.86 % / 30.62 %	61	C	77.55 % / 11.89 %	77	C	87.79 % / 11.2 %
14	B	61.55 % / 35.48 %	30	B	80.24 % / 16.19 %	46	A	59.45 % / 31.86 %	62	B	41.04 % / 32.11 %	78	C	66.53 % / 32.34 %
15	C	58.68 % / 39.61 %	31	A	62.58 % / 33.93 %	47	B	50.72 % / 37.18 %	63	A	56.11 % / 34.12 %	79	C	68.66 % / 30.13 %
16	B	58.88 % / 38.71 %	32	B	65.15 % / 33.56 %	48	A	68.62 % / 31.29 %	64	D	82.86 % / 13.78 %	80	C	32.65 % / 67.32 %

//Hints and Solutions//

1. 1. Eight friends A, B, C, D, E, F, G and H are sitting around circular table facing each other for a lunch. 2. A is opposite F and third to the right of B.

3. G is between F and D.

4. H is to the left of D.

5. E is between C and A.

The final arrangement will be as shown below:

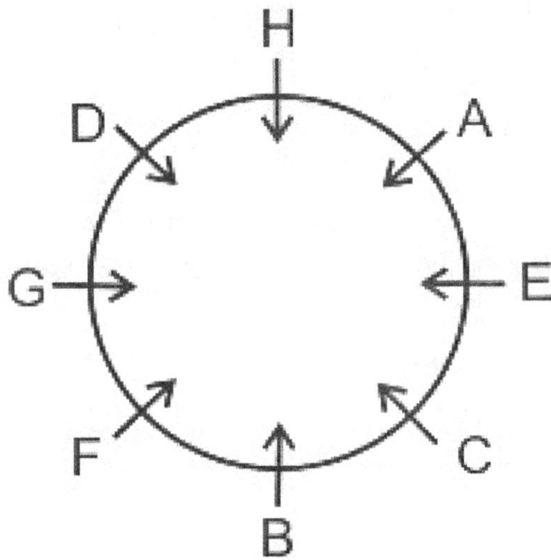

So, 'F' is sitting second to the left of C.

Hence, the correct option is (B).

2. The logic is:

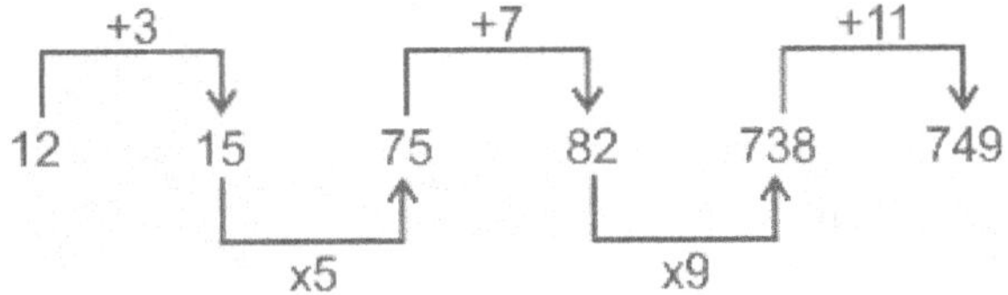

Therefore, '82' is the correct answer.

Hence, the correct option is (D).

3.

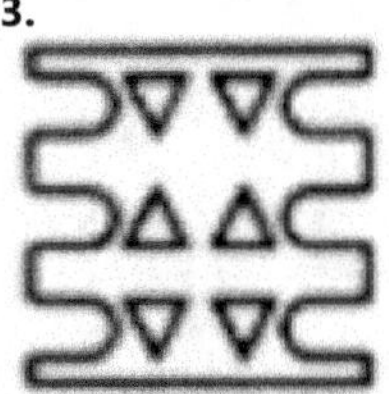

Figure (2), would most closely resemble the unfolded form of Figure (Z).

Hence, the correct option is (B).

4. S is the brother of T. So,

X is the sister of S. So,

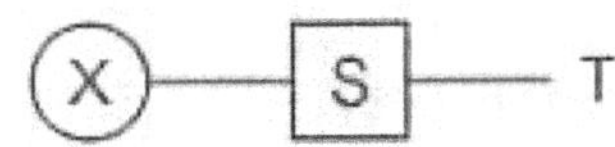

B is the brother of H and H is the son of T. So,

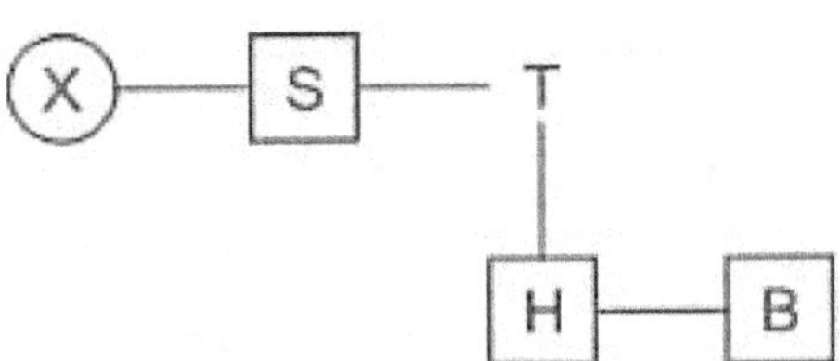

Therefore, 'S' is the uncle of 'B'

Hence, the correct option is (C).

5. The figure that is embedded in the given figure is:

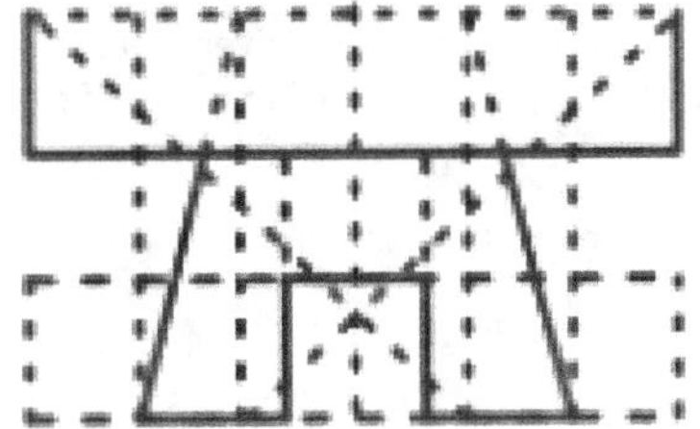

Hence, the correct option is (B).

6. India is a country.

Telangana is a state in India.

And,

Hyderabad is the capital of Telangana.

The correct Venn diagram representation is,

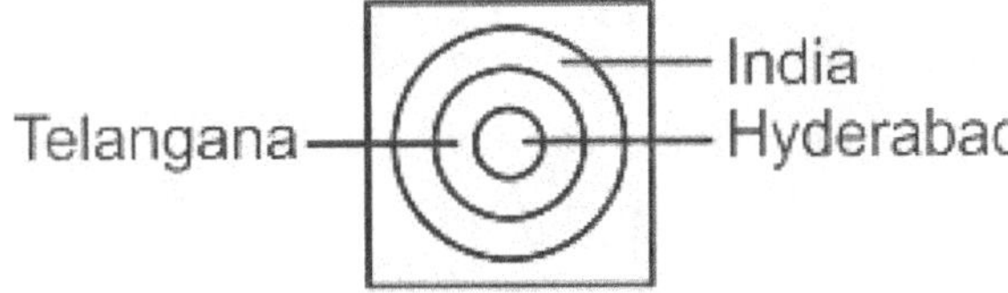

Hence, the correct option is (A).

7. Given:

38 L 2 M 7 P 4 N 22

Changing the signs according to the question,

38 ÷ 2 + 7 × 4 - 22

Solving by using BODMAS,

= 19 + 28 - 22

= 25

Hence, the correct option is (B).

8. The mirror image will be as follows:

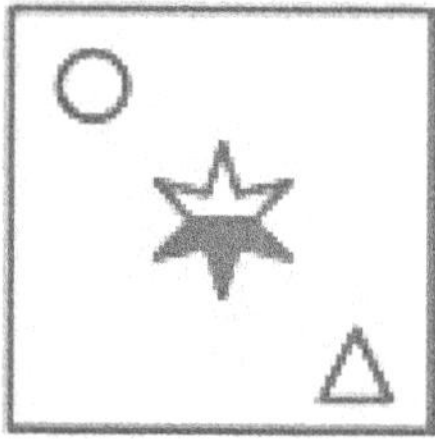

Hence, the correct option is (B).

9. Here, the pattern is:

(1) The position of the circle is changing clockwise from one corner to the other. → Therefore, the circle will be at the upper-left corner in the next figure of the series.

(2) The position of the triangle is changing clockwise from one corner to the other. → Therefore, the triangle will be at the lower-right corner in the next figure of the series.

(3) The shading pattern of the centre star in the given figures is- upper half, lower half, upper half. → Therefore, in the next figure of the series, the lower part of the star will be shaded.

So, based on this pattern the figure that can complete the given series is-

Thus, figure option (B) of the given options will complete the figure series.

Hence, the correct option is (B).

10. The pattern followed here is,

First box × Second box + the number of row = Third box

5 × 6 + 1 = 31

7 × 7 + 2 = 51

8 × 6 + 3 = 51

4 × 4 + 4 = 20

Hence, the correct option is (B).

11. According to the sequence in the dictionary:

5. Dearth

3. Decision

1. Decisive

4. Demand

2. Dethrone

So, "5 3 1 4 2" is the correct answer.

Hence, the correct option is (C).

12. The least possible Venn Diagram for the given statements will be as follows:

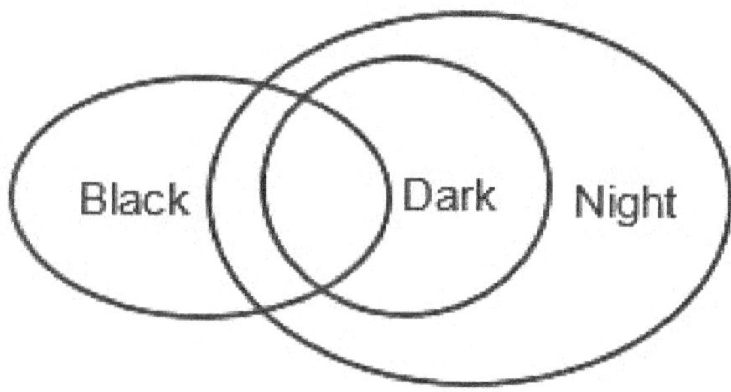

I. All black is night. → False (It is possible but not definite)

II. Some black is not night. → False (It is possible but not definite)

So, Either I or II follows.

Hence, the correct option is (C).

13. The code for TOUR is:

T	O	U	R
1	2	3	4

The code for CLEAR is:

C	L	E	A	R
5	6	7	8	4

The code for SPARE is:

S	P	A	R	E
9	0	8	4	7

Similarly,

The code for CARE is:

C	A	R	E
5	8	4	7

So, '5847' is the correct answer.

Hence, the correct option is (D).

14. The pattern followed here is:

1st number × 1.5 = 2nd number

Now follow the steps:

72 : 108

= 72 × 1.5

= 108 = 2nd number

And,

112 : 168

= 112 × 1.5

= 168 = 2nd number

Similarly,

88 : ?

= 88 × 1.5

= 132 = 2nd number

Thus, "132" is correct answer.

Hence, the correct option is (B).

15. The pattern here is as follows,

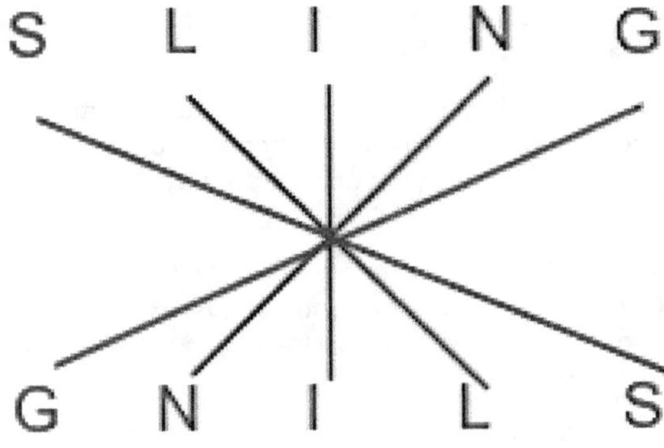

and,

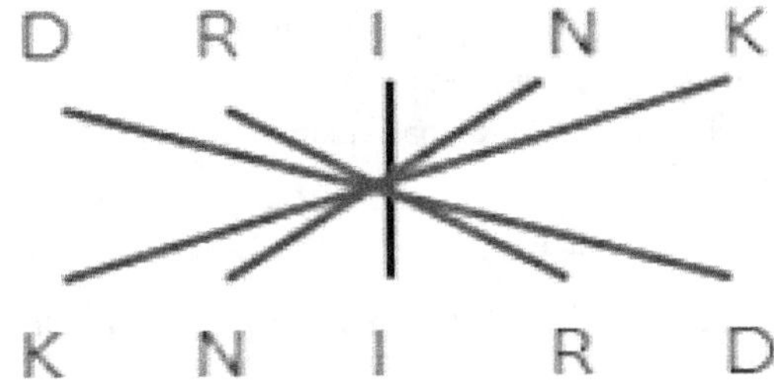

Similarly,

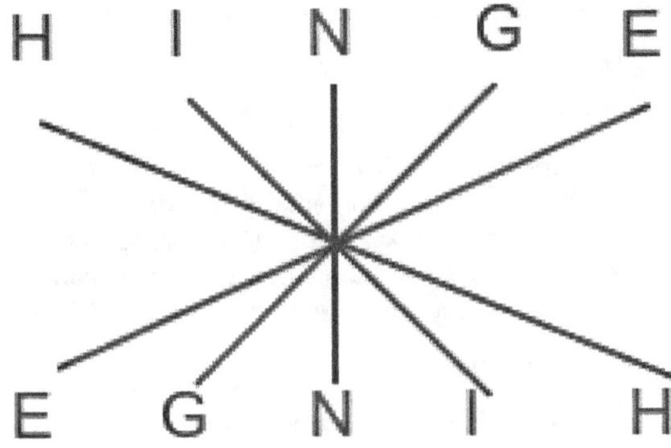

Therefore, EGNIH is the correct answer.

Hence, the correct option is (C).

16. The logic is:

the pattern being followed here is:

$$(\,\text{Number}\,)^2 : (\,\text{Number}\,)^3$$

1. $225 : 3375 \rightarrow 15^2 : 15^3$

2. $49 : 280 \rightarrow 7^2 : 7^3 = 343 \neq 280$

3. $64 : 512 \rightarrow 8^2 : 8^3$

4. $25 : 125 \rightarrow 5^2 : 5^3$

Thus, '49 : $280'$ is the odd one out.

Hence, the correct option is (B).

17. $9613 \Rightarrow (9 \times 6) - 1 \neq 13$

$3823 \Rightarrow (3 \times 8) - 1 = 23$

$7855 \Rightarrow (7 \times 8) - 1 = 55$

$235 \Rightarrow (2 \times 3) - 1 = 5$

Thus, "9613" is the odd one from the given alternatives.

Thus, the correct option is (A).

18. Given: d _ m c _ z _ h _ c s _ d _ m _ _ z

1. h s d z c h c s → d h m c s z - d h z c s c - d h m c s z

2. h s d m z h c s → d h m c s z - d h m c s z - d h m c s z

3. h s d m z h d s → d h m c s z - d h m c s z - d h m d s z

4. h d s m z h c s → d h m c d z - s h m c s z - d h m c s z

Option (B) follow the cycle of **dhmcsz/dhmcsz/dhmcsz**.

Thus, the correct answer is "h s d m z h c s".

Hence, the correct option is (B).

19. In the given figure the opposite faces are:

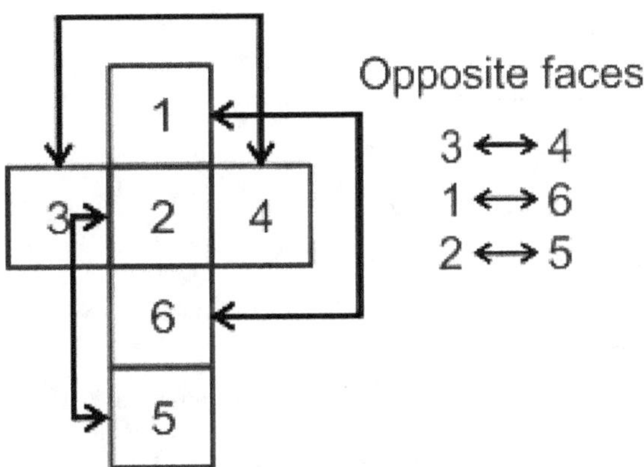

Here, the opposite faces are 3 ⟺ 4, 1 ⟺ 6, and 2 ⟺ 5.

Opposite faces are not on the adjacent side of the dice.

The opposite pair 2 ⟺ 5 in option(A) and 1 ⟺ 6 is in options (B) and (C).

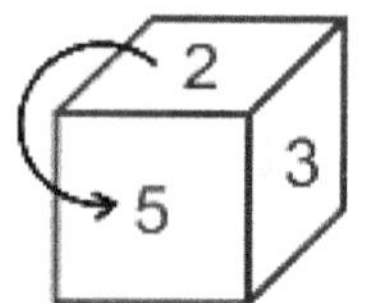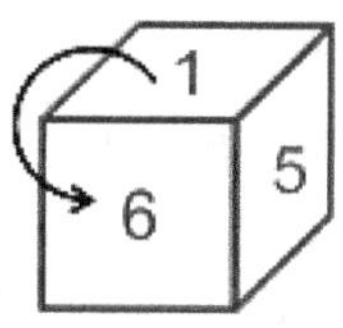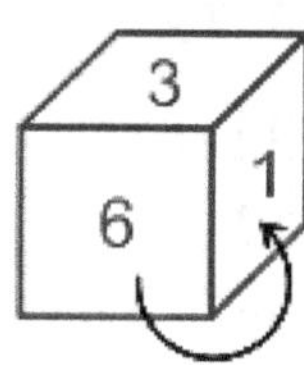

Hence, the correct option is (D).

20. Given,

In 2010, Shalu's age was six times the age of Stuti

Shalu's age = 6 Stuti's age

Let Shalu = 6x years

then Stuti = x years

In 2018

Shalu's age = 6x + 8

Stuti's age= x + 8

According to given question, in 2018 Shalu's age was two times of the age of Stuti,

Shalu's age = 2 times Stuti's age

6x + 8 = 2 (x + 8)

6x + 8 = 2 (x + 8)

6x + 8 = 2x + 16

6x - 2x = 16 - 8

4x = 8

$x = \dfrac{8}{4}$

x = 2

In 2010, Age of Shalu = 6x = 6 × 2 = 12 years

Year of birth of Shalu = 2010 - 12

Year of birth of Shalu = 1998

Hence, the correct option is (A).

21. Reservation for women in India is available in Panchayati Raj Institutions.

Panchayati Raj is a system of rural local self-government. 73rd and 74th Amendment Acts added two new parts to the Constitution of India. Part IX was titled "The Panchayats" (added by 73rd Amendment) and Part IX-A was titled "The Municipalities" (added by 74th Amendment). The Act provides for the reservation of not less than one-third of the total number of seats for women (including the number of seats reserved for the SCs and STs).

Hence, the correct option is (D).

22. In order to be appointed as the Governor of a state, one must have attained the age of 35 years.

The Governor of an Indian state generally holds office for a period of 5 years. The Governor of the state is similar (not the same) to the President of the Union. Article 157 and Article 158 of the Constitution of India specify eligibility requirements for the post of governor. A governor must:

- Be a citizen of India.
- Be at least 35 years of age.
- Not be a member of either house of the parliament or the house of the state legislature.
- Not hold any office of profit.

Hence, the correct option is (A).

23. The 74th Constitutional amendment provided constitutional status to urban local government.

The 74th constitutional amendment act mandated the setting up and devolution of powers to Urban local bodies or city governments as the lowest unit of governance in cities and towns.

The constitution 74th Amendment Act 1992, relating to Municipalities (Urban local Government) was passed by the parliament in 1992. It received the assent of the president of India on 20th April 1993.

Hence, the correct option is (C).

24. On 5 June, 2022 Rafael Nadal has won the 14th French Open title by defeating Norwegian Casper Ruud.

Spain's Rafael Nadal lifts the trophy after winning the final match against Norway's Casper Ruud in three sets, $6 - 3, 6 - 3, 6 - 0$, at the French Open tennis tournament in Roland Garros stadium in Paris, France.

Hence, the correct option is (B).

25. India was host the 44th FIDE Chess Olympiad 2022. It was originally scheduled to be hosted in Russia. FIDE has recently announced that it pulled out from Russia following the Ukraine invasion. After the announcement, Tamil Nadu government and All-India Chess Federation made a joint bid to host the tournament It is the first time that India is hosting FIDE Chess Olympiad since its inception in 1927.

Hence, the correct option is (D).

26. Haryana Government recently launched the Haryana Cheerag Scheme. Under the scheme, government will provide free education to Economically Weaker section (EWS) students of Government schools in private school. Cheerag Scheme stands for, "Chief Minister Equal Education Relief, Assistance and Grant".

Hence, the correct option is (B).

27. The Hoysaleshwara Temple is an aspirant for the tag of World Heritage Site is located at Karnataka state.

- Tiong Kian Boom, an expert from International Commission on Monuments and Sites (ICOMOS), visited the Hoysaleshwara temple in Halebeedu, Karnataka on September 14, 2022.
- The Hoysala structure is an aspirant for the tag of World Heritage Site, which is given by UNESCO.

- It is a 12th-century Hindu temple dedicated to Lord Shiva.

Hence, the correct option is (B).

28. With the aim to develop defence technology and produce indigenous defence equipment, DRDO has collaborated with IIT Roorkee in August 2022.

IIT Roorkee in collaboration with the Defence Electronics Application Laboratory (DEAL) of DRDO has developed indigenous radio frequency power amplifiers to meet the futuristic requirements of programmable radios.

Hence, the correct option is (C).

29. Charkula is a dance performed in the Braj region of Uttar Pradesh. In this dance, veiled women balancing large multi-tiered circular wooden pyramids on their heads dance to songs about Krishna.

Hence, the correct option is (B).

30. Indian Council of Medical Research (ICMR) has partnered with Bharat Biotech for development of potential COVID-19 vaccine called Covaxin.

The Drugs Controller General of India has granted permission to conduct phase-1 and 2 human clinical trials. ICMR has announced that it is acting in accordance with the globally accepted standards to develop the vaccine.

Hence, the correct option is (B).

31. The southernmost Himalayas are known as Shivaliks.

Shivalik:

- Also known as the Outer Himalayas, they are known by different names in different places. For example, they are called Jammu hills in Jammu, Dudhwa hills in Uttarakhand, Darjeeling hills in West Bengal, etc.
- The Shivaliks are the southernmost range of the Himalayas.
- The Teesta River cuts the Shivalik ranges in Sikkim.
- Beyond Sikkim, the Shivalik ranges merge with the Lesser Himalayas, also known as the Outer Himalayas.
- The Shivalik range lies between the Great Plains and the Lesser Himalayas.
- The altitude varies from 600 to 1500 m.
- It runs for a distance of 2,400 km from the Potwar plateau to the Brahmaputra valley.

Hence, the correct option is (A).

32. The Chhotanagpur belt in India is famous for the production of iron ore and coal.

Chhotanagpur belt:

- This belt comprising of Chota Nagpur plateau and Orissa Plateau in the states of Jharkhand, West Bengal and Orissa is the richest mineral belt of India.

- It contains large quantities of coal, iron ore, manganese, mica, bauxite, copper, kyanite, chromite, beryl, apatite and many more minerals.
- In fact, you ask for any major mineral of India and you will find it in this belt.
- Thus it is a mineral region par excellence.
- The Chota Nagpur plateau is known as the mineral heartland of India.
- According to Wadia, this region possesses India's 100 per cent Kyanite, 93 per cent iron ore, 84 per cent coal, 70 per cent chromite, 70 per cent mica, 50 per cent fire clay, 45 per cent asbestos, 45 per cent china clay, 20 per cent limestone and 10 per cent manganese.
- However, many changes have taken place in the recent years.

Hence, the correct option is (B).

33. The main occupation of the Paleolithic (Old Stone Age) people was hunting.

- The Paleolithic people were grouped into small societies survived by hunting and gathering.
- They practised fishing, hunting, or scavenging wild animals and gathering resources from plants.
- The Paleolithic age was characterized by the use of stone tools along with wooden or bone tools.
- They were used as simple stone tools for chipping and chopping during hunting.
- They were not aware of agriculture as well as home construction.

Hence, the correct option is (A).

34. Akbar gave the title of 'Khan-e-Khana' to Mirza Abdul Rahim Khan.

- Khanzada Mirza Khan Abdul Rahim was the real name of Rahim.
- He was one of the nine important ministers in his court, also known as the Navaratnas.
- The Navaratnas of Akbar were as follows: Raja Birbal, Tansen, Abul Fazl, Faizi, Raja Man Singh, Raja Todar Mal, Mullah Do Piaza, Fakir Aziao-Din, Abdul Rahim Khan-e-Khana.

Hence, the correct option is (D).

35. In the Yerwada Central Jail in Pune, Mahatma Gandhi and Dr. B R Ambedkar signed the Poona Pact on September 24, 1932.

- The agreement was formed at Poona (now Pune, Maharashtra) in response to the British government's Racial Award of August 4, 1932, which proposed that seats in India's several legislatures be allocated to various ethnicities to calm communal tensions.
- The plan was backed by Dalit leaders, particularly Bhimrao Ramji Ambedkar, who believed it would empower Dalits to further their interests.

- On the other hand, Mahatma Gandhi objected to the creation of a distinct Dalit electorate from the Hindu electorate, believing that it would harm India's drive for independence.

Hence, the correct option is (C).

36. On 24th July, 1991, in Lok-Sabha the Minister of States for industries, Mr. P. J. Kurian declared the Industrial Policy, 1991.

- The new policy contained policy directions for reforms and thus for LPG (Liberalisation, Privatisation and Globalisation).
- With the exception of three industrial sectors, it expanded the scope of private sector involvement.
- The strategy has simultaneously welcomed foreign technology and investment.
- This has ended the era of license raj or red tapism in the country.

Hence, the correct option is (D).

37. An increase in Life Expectancy indicates an increase in economic devlopment.

- Life Expectancy means the number of years a person can expect to live.
- Life expectancy in India is almost 70 years (as of 2014-18 data).

Economic Growth: It refers to an increase in the real output of goods and services in the country. It relates to a gradual increase in one of the components of GDP, consumption, government spending, investment, and net exports.

Economic Development: It implies progressive changes (institutional and technological changes) in the socio-economic structure of the country along with income, savings, and investment. It deals with the growth of human capital, reduction of inequality figures and structural changes that improve the quality of life of the population, which increases in life expectancy.

Hence, the correct option is (D).

38. Hydrogen gas is used in the manufacture of Vanaspati Ghee from vegetable oil.

- Hydrogenation - to treat with hydrogen - is a chemical reaction between molecular hydrogen (H_2) and another compound or element, usually in the presence of a catalyst.
- The process is commonly employed to reduce or saturate organic compounds.
- The largest scale application of hydrogenation is for the processing of vegetable oils (fats to give margarine and related spreads and shortenings).
- Typical vegetable oils are derived from polyunsaturated fatty acids (containing more than one carbon-carbon double bonds).
- Their partial hydrogenation reduces most but not all, of these carbon-carbon double bonds.

- Hydrogenation converts liquid vegetable oils into solid or semi-solid fats, such as those present in margarine.

Hence, the correct option is (A).

39. Weightlifter Mirabai Chanu has won the BBC Indian Sportswoman of the Year award for 2021 on 29 March 2022.

- Chanu became the first Indian weightlifter to win a silver medal at an Olympic Games when she finished second in the 49kg category in Tokyo.
- Chanu won the gold medal in the 48kg division at the 2017 World Championships in Anaheim and followed up with Commonwealth Games gold in 2018.
- The BBC Emerging Player award was presented to 18-year-old cricketer Shafali Verma, who has recently been playing at the Women's World Cup in New Zealand.

Hence, the correct option is (D).

40. Dr Asghar Wajahat, a well-known Hindi writer, was conferred with the 31st Vyas Samman on 25 August 2022.

- He has been chosen for the prestigious award for his play 'Mahabali', which focuses on Mughal emperor Akbar & poet Tulsidas.
- The Vyas Samman is a Hindi literary award in India, first awarded in 1991.
- It is awarded annually by the K.K. Birla Foundation & carries an award of 4 lakh rupees.

Hence, the correct option is (A).

41. Given:

$$\left[\frac{4}{7} \text{ of } 2\frac{4}{5} \times 1\frac{2}{3} - \left(3\frac{1}{2} - 2\frac{1}{6}\right)\right] \div \left(3\frac{1}{5} \div 4\frac{1}{2} \text{ of } 5\frac{1}{3}\right)$$

Using the BODMAS rule to solve the above expression, we get

$$= \left[\frac{4}{7} \times \frac{14}{5} \times \frac{5}{3} - \frac{4}{3}\right] \div \left(\frac{16}{5} \div \left(\frac{9}{2} \times \frac{16}{3}\right)\right)$$

$$= \left[\left(\frac{4}{7} \times \frac{14}{5} \times \frac{5}{3}\right) - \frac{4}{3}\right] \div \left(\frac{16}{5} \times \frac{1}{24}\right)$$

$$= \left(\frac{8}{3} - \frac{4}{3}\right) \div \left(\frac{2}{15}\right)$$

$$= \frac{4}{3} \div \frac{2}{15}$$

$$= \frac{4}{3} \times \frac{15}{2}$$

$$= 10$$

Hence, the correct option is (A).

42. We know that:

Follow the BODMAS rule according to the table given below:

B	Brackets in order ( ), { } , [ ]	ब्रैकेट ( ), { } , [ ] क्रम में
O	of	का
D	Division (÷)	विभाजन (÷)
M	Multiplication (x)	गुणा (x)
A	Addition (+)	जोड़ (+)

S	Subtraction (-)	घटाव (−)

Given:

$$1456 \div 16 \times 14 + 22 = (?)^4$$
$$\Rightarrow 91 \times 14 + 22 = (?)^4$$
$$\Rightarrow 1274 + 22 = (?)^4$$
$$\Rightarrow (?)^4 = 1296$$
$$\Rightarrow ? = 6$$

∴ The value of $?$ is 6.

Hence, the correct option is (A).

43. Let unit's digit be x and ten's digit by y

∴ Number formed = 10y + x ...(i)

According to the question,

2y − 1 = x ...(ii)

Also, (New number) − (Original number)

= Original number − 20

(10x + y) − (10y + x) = (10y + x) − 20

10x + y − 10y − x = 10y + x − 20

9x − 9y = 10y + x − 20 ...(iii)

On substituting the value of x = 2y − 1 from equation (i), we get

9 (2y − 1) − 9y = 10y + 2y − 1 − 20

= 18y − 9 − 9y = 10y + 2y − 1 − 20

= 3y = 12

∴ y = 4

On putting the value of y in equation (ii), we get

x = 2 × 4 − 1

= 8 − 1 = 7

∴ Required number

= 10y + x

= 10 × 4 + 7

= 47

Hence, the correct option is (C).

44. Let denominator of fraction = x

Then, numerator = x − 4

∴ Fraction = $\dfrac{(x-4)}{x}$

Now, according to the question,

$$\dfrac{(x-4)-2}{(x+1)} = \dfrac{1}{8}$$

$$\Rightarrow x-6 = \dfrac{(x+1)}{8}$$

$$\Rightarrow 8x - 48 = x + 1$$

$$\Rightarrow 8x - x = 48 + 1$$

7x = 49

∴ x = 7

∴ Fraction = $\dfrac{(7-4)}{7} = \dfrac{3}{7}$

Hence, the correct option is (A).

45. As we know,

By dividing, we can get the desired decimal.

$$\dfrac{1}{8} = 0.125$$

$$\dfrac{5}{8} = \dfrac{1}{8} \times 5 = 0.125 \times 5 = 0.625$$

∴ Required value = 0.625

Hence, the correct option is (B).

46. Given:

Marks of C is 25% less than A.

And, marks of B are 30% more than C

Let the marks of A is 100x

∴ Marks of C = 75% of 100x = 75x

∴ Marks of B = 130% of 75x = 97.5x

∴ Required percentage = $\dfrac{100-97.5}{100} \times 100 = 2.5\%$

So, the marks of B is 2.5% less than the marks of A.

Hence, the correct option is (A).

47. Given-

A sum of money invested at simple interest becomes 6 times of itself at 5% per annum.

Let the sum $P = Rs.\, X$

Amount $A = Rs.\, 6X$

Simple Interest $SI = A - P$

$$\Rightarrow SI = Rs.\,(6X - X)$$

$$\Rightarrow SI = Rs.\,5X$$

Rate $R = 5\%$ per annum

According to the formula-

$$T = \dfrac{100 \times SI}{P \times R} \quad \text{[where } T \text{ is time period]}$$

$$\Rightarrow T = \dfrac{100 \times 5X}{X \times 5}$$

$$\Rightarrow T = 100 \text{ years}$$

Hence, the correct option is (B).

48. Given-

The compound interest on $Rs.\,30000$ at 7% per annum for a certain time period is $Rs.\,4347$.

Principal $P = Rs.\,30000$

Rate $R = 7\%$ per annum

Compound Interest $CI = Rs.\,4347$

Amount $A = P + CI$

$\Rightarrow A = Rs.\,(30000 + 4347)$

$\Rightarrow A = Rs.\,34347$

According to the formula-

$A = P\left(1 + \dfrac{R}{100}\right)^{T}$ [where T is time period of investment]

$\Rightarrow 34347 = 30000\left(1 + \dfrac{7}{100}\right)^{T}$

$\Rightarrow \dfrac{34347}{30000} = \left(1 + \dfrac{7}{100}\right)^{T}$

$\Rightarrow \dfrac{11449}{10000} = \left(1 + \dfrac{7}{100}\right)^{T}$

$\Rightarrow \left(\dfrac{107}{100}\right)^{2} = \left(\dfrac{107}{100}\right)^{T}$

On equating the powers,

$\Rightarrow T = 2$ years

Hence, the correct option is (A).

49. Let cost price of the mini-refrigerator = x

$\Rightarrow$ Marked price × (100 - discount%) = Selling price

$\Rightarrow 8200 \times \left(\dfrac{100 - 11}{100}\right) =$ Selling price

$\Rightarrow$ Selling price = Rs. 7298

Cost price = Selling price - profit

$\Rightarrow$ x = 7298 - 600 = Rs. 6698

Hence, the correct option is (A).

50. Given,

The average of $7.5, 3.2, 11.3, 20.5$, and $x = 10$

As we know,

Average of n numbers $= \dfrac{\text{sum of total numbers}}{n}$

According to the question,

$10 = \dfrac{(7.5 + 3.2 + 11.3 + 20.5 + x)}{5}$

$\Rightarrow 50 = 42.5 + x$

$\therefore x = 7.5$

Hence, the correct option is (A).

51. Given:

Marked price $=$ Rs 500

Three successive discounts of 10% each.

We know that,

$$Selling\ price = Marked\ price \times \dfrac{(100 - Discount\%)}{100}$$

So, Selling price(S.P.) $= 500 \times \left(\dfrac{90}{100}\right)\left(\dfrac{90}{100}\right)\left(\dfrac{90}{100}\right)$

S.P. $= 364.5$

We know that,

Profit $=$ Selling price $-$ Cost price

Profit $= 364.5 - 350$

$= 14.5$

Hence, the correct option is (A).

52. Ratio of three iron balls $= x : 2x : 3x$

We know that,

Volume of sphere $= \dfrac{4}{3} \times \pi r^{3}$

According to the question,

$\dfrac{4}{3} \times \pi \times [x^{3} + (2x)^{3} + (3x)^{3}] = \dfrac{4}{3} \times \pi \times 6^{3}$

$\Rightarrow x^{3} + 8x^{3} + 27x^{3} = 216$

$\Rightarrow 36x^{3} = 216$

$\Rightarrow x^{3} = 6$

$\Rightarrow x = \sqrt[3]{6}$

$\therefore$ Diameter of the smallest ball is $= 2\sqrt[3]{6}$

Hence, the correct option is (C).

53. Given:

Length of road = 1200 m

Time taken to cross a road = 10 min

Formula Used:

Speed $= \dfrac{Distance}{Time}$

Speed $= \dfrac{1200 \times 60}{10 \times 1000} = 7.2$ km/hr

$\therefore$ The speed of the person is 7.2 km/hr.

Hence, the correct option is (D).

54. Given,

A can do work in 10 days.

A's 1 day's work $= \dfrac{1}{10}$

B can do work in 15 days.

B's 1 day's work $= \dfrac{1}{15}$

(A + B)'s 1 day's work $= \dfrac{1}{10} + \dfrac{1}{15}$

$= \dfrac{(3+2)}{30}$

$= \dfrac{1}{6}$

∴ Together they can complete work in 6 days.

Hence, the correct option is (A).

55. Given,

3 men or 5 women can complete the work in 12 days.

Work done by 3 men = Work done by 5 women

1 men $= \dfrac{5}{3} \times$ women

Now, 3 men $+7$ women $= 3 \times \left(\dfrac{5}{3}\right) + 7$ women $= 12$ women

As we know,

$$W_1 \times D_1 = W_2 \times D_2$$

$$\therefore 5 \times 12 = 12 \times D_2$$

$$\Rightarrow D_2 = 5 \text{ days}$$

Hence, the correct option is (A).

56. Given that,

Amount paid by A : Amount paid by $B = 1:2$

Amount paid by B: Amount paid by $C = 3:2$

$\Rightarrow$ Ratio of amount paid by A, B and C is $3:6:4$

$\Rightarrow$ Amount paid by $A = 3k$

$\Rightarrow$ Amount paid by $B = 6k$

$\Rightarrow$ Amount paid by $C = 4k$

$\Rightarrow 3k + 6k + 4k = 260$

$\Rightarrow 13k = 260$

$\Rightarrow k = 20$

∴ Amount paid by A is $3k = 3(20) =$ Rs. 60

Hence, the correct option is (A).

57. Given:

The average of 42 numbers = 102

Mistakenly added numbers = 40, 86 and 24

Required numbers = 28, 30 and 50

Sum of n numbers = average of n number × n

The average of 42 numbers = 102

The sum of all 42 numbers = 102 × 42 = 4284

Now,

Sum of all mistakenly added numbers = 40 + 86 + 24 = 150

Sum of all required numbers = 28 + 30 + 50 = 108

Now,

The sum of all correct 42 numbers = 4284 - 150 + 108 = 4242

The average of all 42 numbers = $\dfrac{4242}{42} = 101$

Therefore, '101' is the required answer.

Hence, the correct option is (A).

58. Given:

Product of two numbers $= 3360$

LCM $= 96$

Product of two numbers $= LCM$ of those numbers $\times HCF$ of those numbers

Let the HCF be x

According to the condition-

$3360 = x \times 96$

$\Rightarrow x = \dfrac{3360}{96}$

$\Rightarrow x = 35$

∴ Required value of HCF is 35.

Hence, the correct option is (A).

59. Given:

Investment of Manish = Rs. 450

Time period of Investment of Manish = 4 months

Investment of Mahavir = Rs. 600

Time period of Investment of Mahavir = 3 months

Distribution of share through investment ratio

Ratio of investment of Manish and Mahavir = 450 × 4 : 600 × 3

$\Rightarrow$ 1800 : 1800

$\Rightarrow$ 1 : 1

Share of Mahavir = 400 × $\dfrac{1}{2}$

$\Rightarrow$ Rs. 200

∴ The share of Mahavir is Rs. 200

Hence, the correct option is (A).

60. Given,

A pilgrim travelled a distance of $50 km$ in 7.5 hours

He travelled partly on foot at $4 km/hr$ and partly on a bullock cart at $12 km/hr$.

$$\text{Speed} = \frac{Distance}{Time}$$

Let time taken to cover distance by foot be t hrs, then

$\Rightarrow$ Time taken to cover distance by bullock cart $= (7.5 - t)\ hr$

According to the question,

$$4t + 12(7.5 - t) = 50$$

$$\Rightarrow 4t + 90 - 12t = 50$$

$$\Rightarrow 12t - 4t = 90 - 50$$

$$\Rightarrow 8t = 40$$

$$\Rightarrow t = \frac{40}{8}$$

$$\Rightarrow t = 5\ hr$$

$\therefore$ Distance covered on foot in 5 hr with the speed of 4 $km/hr = 4 \times 5 = 20 km$

Hence, the correct option is (A).

61. The correct sentence is Neither of them was looking for a mate.

The error lies in the third part of the sentence. The subject here is "neither of them" which is singular; thus, the singular verb "was" should be used with it.

Hence, the correct option is (C).

62. The correct sentence would be: This will reduce dependencies on commercial journals and their negative impact on research.

The error lies in the incorrect usage of a pronoun. "Their" is a related term for "they're", while one refers to a place (there). "Their" is the possessive plural pronoun belonging to, from, of, or relating to them. It is the correct word. The segment requires "their" as it reflects a relationship between men and children.

Hence, the correct option is (B).

63. He knew that an apple should not be plucked while it is green.

The V_2 verb in the first part of the sentence indicates that there should be a past form of the verb in the second part of the sentence too. Should is the only verb that is in the past form. So 'should' is the correct choice.

Hence, the correct option is (A).

64. You haven't many teeth left, but the few you have are sharp enough to make me shudder.

A few means some. It has a positive meaning. The few means not many, but all of those. Here we are talking about all the teeth that are left, so 'the' is the correct choice here.

Hence, the correct option is (D).

65. I can always tell when my friend is lying because she bites her lip.

Lying: to make an untrue statement with intent to deceive

Hence, the correct option is (A).

66. Gullible: someone who easily believe others, credulous

Incredulous: one who is unable or not willing to believe others

The opposite meaning of the gullible is incredulous

Hence, the correct option is (D).

67. A spot or a stain caused by a discolouring substance is blot.

Blot means a dark mark or stain made by ink, paint, dirt, etc.

Hence, the correct option is (B).

68. An accomplished musician is virtuoso.

'Virtuoso' is 'a person highly skilled in music or another artistic pursuit'.

Hence, the correct option is (A).

69. The word 'Opaque' means that you cannot see through, difficult to understand; not clear.

Misty: used to describe glass or a similar surface that is covered with a mist that makes it difficult to see through.

From the meanings of the given words, the word similar in meaning to the given word 'Opaque' is "Misty."

Hence, the correct option is (A).

70. Renewable is the most appropriate option to fill in the blank.

- Renewable: it is a form of energy that can be produced as quickly as they are used
- Non-renewable: forms of energy can be produced as quickly as they are used
- Recyclable: able to be recycled
- Industrial: in or related to the industry

The context of the sentence is that the energy we get from the sun is unlimited and it is constantly getting replenished.

According to the above-mentioned points, the most appropriate word to fill the blank is **"renewable."**

Hence, the correct option is (C).

71. Inexhaustible is the most appropriate option to fill in the blank.

- Inexhaustible: existing in very great amounts that will never be finished
- Restless: having a lot of movement as a characteristic
- Inextinguishable: unable to be stopped from burning or existing

- Indestructible: impossible to destroy or break

The context of the sentence is that solar energy can not be consumed completely by human activities as it exists in unlimited amounts.

According to the above-mentioned points, the most appropriate word to fill the blank is **"inexhaustible."**

Hence, the correct option is (A).

72. Shift is the most appropriate option to fill in the blank.

- Shift: to cause something or someone to move or change from one position or direction to another, especially slightly

- Tilt: to cause to move into a sloping position

- Skip: to move lightly and quickly, making a small jump after each step

- Twist: to turn something, especially repeatedly, or to turn or wrap one thing around another

The context of the sentence is as the world is advancing in science and technology we need to move from nonrenewable sources of energy to renewable energy which is good for the environment.

According to the above-mentioned points, the most appropriate word to fill the blank is **"shift."**

Hence, the correct option is (D).

73. Neither is the most appropriate option to fill in the blank.

- Neither: used when referring to none of the choices between two possibilities

- Either: used when referring to a choice between two possibilities

- Moreover: used to add information also and more importantly

- Whether: used to refer to one or more possibilities or to express uncertainty

The context of the sentence is none of the choices between easy or profitable is applicable for recycling solar panels. 'Neither...nor' is a pair of correlative conjunctions.

According to the above-mentioned points, the most appropriate word to fill the blank is **"neither."**

Hence, the correct option is (B).

74. The most appropriate meaning of the underlined idiom 'laughing stock' is 'an object of ridicule'.

Laughing stock: someone or something that seems stupid or silly, especially by trying to be serious or important and not succeeding

Example: Another performance like that and this team will be the laughing stock of the league.

Hence, the correct option is (B).

75. The correct answer is A speech, proposal, or joke that is poorly received.

If something that you say or show to people goes down like a lead balloon, they do not like it at all i.e. it is poorly received by all.

Examples:

- My joke about the alcoholic went down like a lead balloon.

- The tax proposals went down like a lead balloon at the party conference.

Hence, the correct option is (D).

76. The correct spelt word is Indigenous.

Indigenous is used to refer to, or relating to, the people who originally lived in a place, rather than people who moved there from somewhere else.

- Eg: The indigenous population has long suffered exclusion and profound injustice.

- Eg: Are there any species of frog indigenous to the area?

All the other spellings (given in the options) are not acceptable in English.

Hence, the correct option is (B).

77. Conscientious is the word that is spelt correctly.

- Conscientious(adjective): Putting a lot of effort into your work.

- Example: She was a conscientious worker, and I'll miss her.

Hence, the correct option is (C).

78. The correct sentence is: 'I usually do not add cheese to my toast.'

- The error lies in the incorrect usage of tense.

- The given sentence is in the simple past tense.

- Let's take a look at the word 'usually' which suggests that it is a habitual action.

- Simple present tense: It is used for habitual actions, planned routines, newspaper headlines and commentaries.

Structure:

Subject+ do/does+ not+ the first form of verb.

- Example: I do not want to go to school.

Thus, 'did' needs to be replaced with 'do'.

Hence, the correct option is (C).

79. The correct sentence is: I shall be honoured if you accept my offer.

The sentence is in the First Conditional. The First Conditional is used to talk about the result of an imagined future situation, when we believe the imagined situation is quite likely.

Structure: If + present simple + modal verb with future meaning (will, shall, might etc.)

- Ex: If he gets a job in Liverpool, he will have to get up early. It's a long drive.

The question sentence has 'would' in 'if-clause', which should be improved.

Option (C): i.e., 'if you accept' has 'if-clause' in present simple, therefore, it is the correct improvement

Hence, the correct option is (C).

80. The correct sentence is: Will you lend me a few rupees in this hour of need?

- 'Few' means not many (people or things).
- It is used to say that there are not a lot of people or things.
- 'A few' means some (people or things).
- It is used to say that there are a small number of people or things.
- Example: I have a few friends. (I have some/a small number of friends)

Therefore, in the underlined part of the given sentence, the usage of 'few' is incorrect and it should be replaced with 'a few'.

Hence, the correct option is (C).

General Intelligence and Reasoning

Q.1 Select the option that is related to the third number in the same way as the second number is related to the first number.

30 : 56 :: 20 : ?

A. 24   **B.** 51   **C.** 33   **D.** 42

Q.2 Five teachers, H, K, P, R and T, are sitting around a circular table facing towards the centre (not necessarily in the same order). T is between H and R. P is second to the right of R. H is to the immediate left of T. Who is sitting to the immediate left of K?

A. T   **B.** H   **C.** P   **D.** R

Q.3 A piece of paper is folded and punched as shown below in the question figures. From the given answer figures, indicate how it will appear when opened?

Question figure

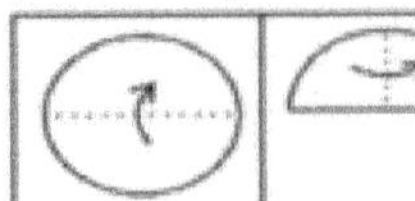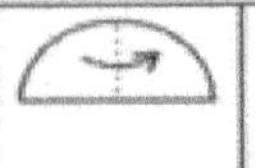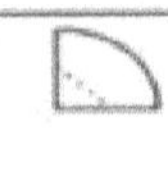

Answer figure

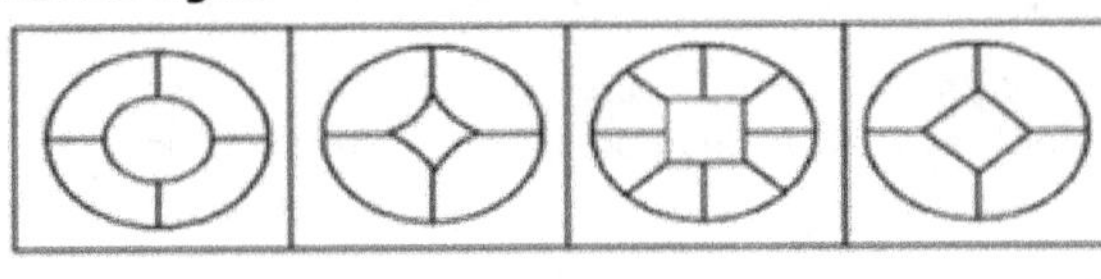

    (A)   (B)   (C)   (D)

A. A   **B.** B   **C.** C   **D.** D

Q.4 Select the odd word/letters/number /number pair from the given alternatives.

A. 256   **B.** 289   **C.** 343   **D.** 144

Q.5 There are six members in a family, consisting of 2 couples. A is grandfather of X. C is only sister in law of T who is a female. X is only child of R. Q if a female.

How is Q related to R?

A. Mother   **B.** Aunt

C. Father   **D.** Daughter

Q.6 Select the option figure which is NOT embedded in the figure (X) given below (rotation is NOT allowed).

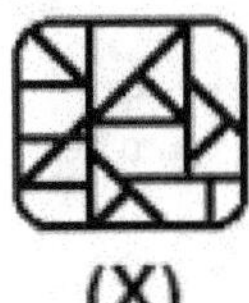

(X)

A.    **B.** 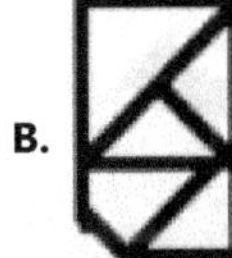

C. 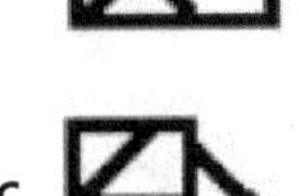   **D.** 

Q.7 If '\$' means '÷', '@' means '×', '#' means '-', then find the value of 10 # 5 @ 1 \$ 5.

A. 11   **B.** 9   **C.** 13   **D.** 7

Q.8 Identify the mirror image of the figure.

A. 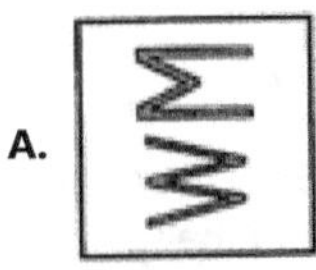   **B.** 

C. 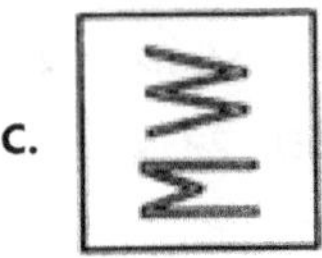   **D.** 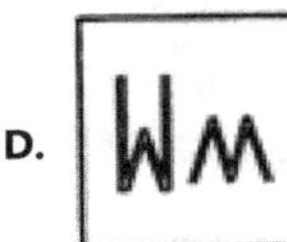

Q.9 Select the figure that will come next in place of the question mark (?).

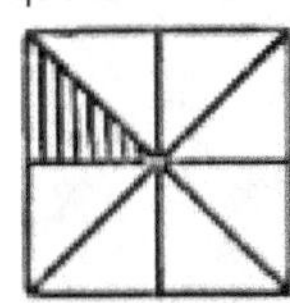 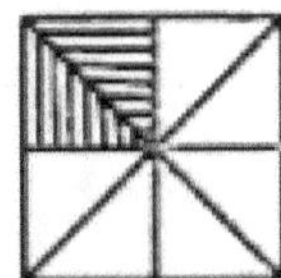 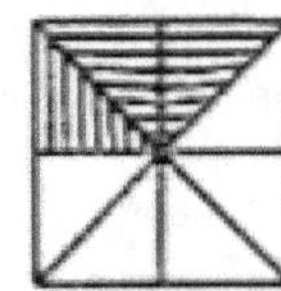

    (1)   (2)   (3)   (4)

A. 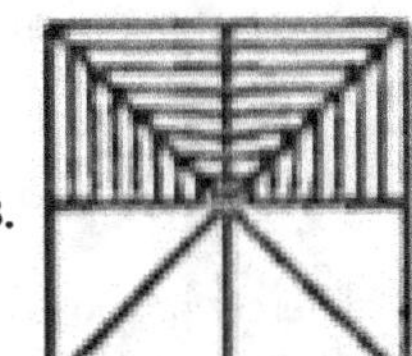   **B.** 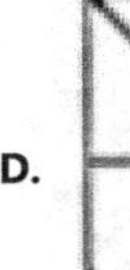

C. 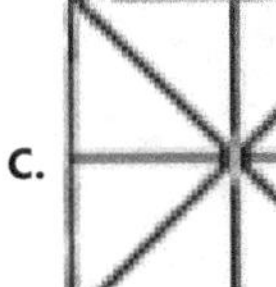   **D.** 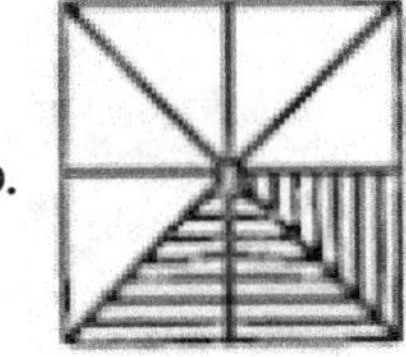

Q.10 Find the missing number in the following figure.

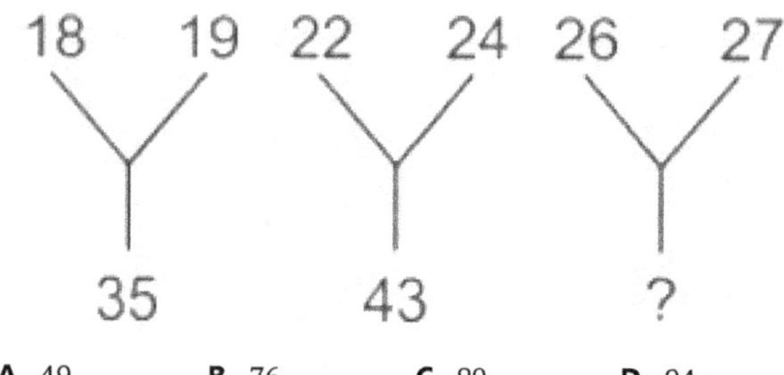

A. 49   **B.** 76   **C.** 89   **D.** 94

Q.11 Read the given statement(s) and conclusions carefully and select which of the conclusions logically follow(s) from the statement(s).

Statement:

I. Some bells are golden

II. Some bells are red.

Conclusion:

I. Some red are golden

II. No golden is red

A. Only conclusion I follows

B. Both conclusions I and II follow

C. Only conclusion II follows

D. Either conclusion I or II follow

Q.12 In a code language, if BOX is written as 725 and GLAND is written as 16493, then how will BOND be written in the same language?

[SSC Selection Post Phase IX, 2020]

A. 7276   **B.** 7553   **C.** 9293   **D.** 7293

Q.13 In the following question, select the related letters from the given alternatives.

LMOI : OHRD : : EUTX : ?

A. HPVS   **B.** IQWS   **C.** IPVS   **D.** HPWS

Q.14 Which number will replace the question mark (?) in the following series.

0, 6, 24, 60, ?

A. 100   **B.** 200   **C.** 120   **D.** 360

Q.15 Select the combination of letters that when sequentially placed in the gaps of the given letter series will complete the series.

T _ C _ _ H _ Q T _ C Q

A. HQCTH   **B.** HQTHC   **C.** HQTCH   **D.** HTQHC

Q.16 Three different positions of the same dice are shown, the six faces of which are numbered 1 to 6. Which number is on the face opposite the face showing '6'?

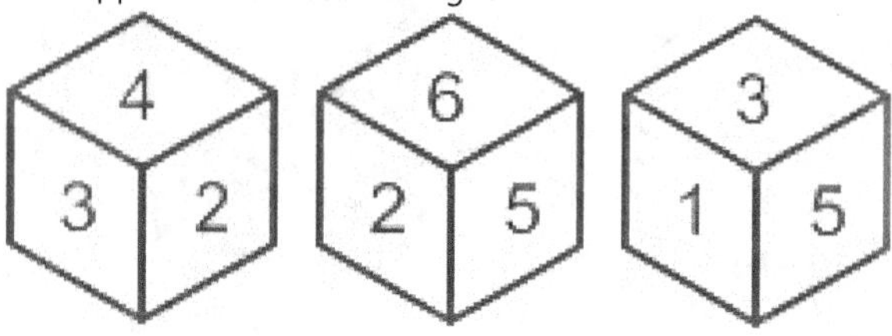

A. 4   **B.** 3   **C.** 2   **D.** 5

Q.17 In the given venn diagram, 'A' denotes 'likes teaching', 'B' denotes 'likes cooking', and 'C' denotes 'likes playing'. How many persons like only teaching and playing but NOT cooking?

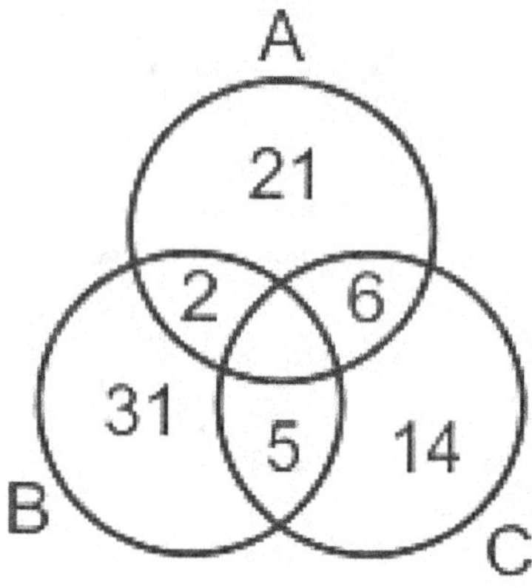

A. 41   **B.** 23   **C.** 48   **D.** 29

Q.18 Ten years ago, the ages of father and son were in the ratio 3 : 1. Ten years hence this ratio will be 2 : 1. What is the age of the father now?

A. 65   **B.** 55   **C.** 70   **D.** 75

Q.19 Four number-pairs have been given, out of which three are alike in some manner and one is different. Select the number-pair that is different from the rest.

A. (23, 4, 45)   **B.** (94, 5, 99)

C. (47, 3, 78)   **D.** (29, 7, 99)

Q.20 Select the option that represents the correct order of the given words as they would appear in an English dictionary.

1. Profess

2. Product

3. Prosecute

4. Precaution

5. Proctor

A. 2, 5, 4, 1, 3   **B.** 3, 5, 2, 1, 4

C. 4, 5, 2, 3, 1   **D.** 4, 5, 2, 1, 3

General Knowledge and General Awareness

Q.21 Who has been appointed as the World Bank's Country Director for India in August 2022?

A. Penny Goldberg

B. Aart Kraay

C. Carmen Reinhart

D. Auguste Tano Kouamé

Q.22 Which is the venue of the 11th World Urban Forum held in 2022?

A. Spain   **B.** Poland   **C.** Australia   **D.** France

Q.23 Which state government launched 'e-Adhigam' scheme to provide tablets to five lakh students?

A. New Delhi   **B.** Haryana

C. West Bengal   **D.** Odisha

Q.24 In April 2022, the Mazagon Dock Shipbuilders launched _______, the last of the six submarines under Project 75.

A. INS Vela   **B.** INS Vagsheer
C. INS Kalvari   **D.** INS Vagir

Q.25 Which of the following has been named as an official sponsor of the FIFA World Cup Qatar 2022 in March 2022?

A. BYJU'S   **B.** Vedantu
C. Unacademy   **D.** Udemy

Q.26 Which are the rivers included as "Western rivers" under Indus Waters Treaty?

[UP Police ASI, 2018]

A. Indus, Ravi and Sutlej
B. Indus, Beas and Sutlej
C. Indus, Chenab and Jhelum
D. Indus, Chenab and Sutlej

Q.27 Who was the first recipient of the Dronacharya Award in 1985?

[Madhya Pradesh Public Service Commission (MPPSC), 2018]

A. O. M. Nambiar
B. Om Prakash Bhardwaj
C. Bhalchandra Bhaskar Bhagwat
D. All of them

Q.28 Which among the following steps is most likely to be taken at the time of an economic recession?

[UPSC Prelims, 2021]

A. Cut in tax rates accompanied by increase in interest rate
B. Increase in expenditure on public projects
C. Increase in tax rates accompanied by reduction of interest rate
D. Reduction of expenditure on public projects

Q.29 Who developed the indigenous Overhauser Magnetometer, one of the most accurate magnetometer in the world?

A. Indian Institute of Geomagnetism
B. Indian Institute of Technology, Delhi
C. Indian Space Research Organization
D. None of the above

Q.30 Which is the only part of the constitution that has been completely removed?

[UP Police Sub Inspector, 2017]

A. Part 22   **B.** Part 11   **C.** Part 7   **D.** Part 5

Q.31 In which year was the first amendment to the Constitution of India made?

A. 1951   **B.** 1952   **C.** 1950   **D.** 1953

Q.32 The Bhakra Nangal dam is situated on the ______ river.

[SSC Selection Post Phase IX, 2019]

A. Sutlej   **B.** Chenab   **C.** Ravi   **D.** Beas

Q.33 Who was called as the 'Napoleon of India'?

A. Samudragupta   **B.** Skandagupta
C. Chandragupta II   **D.** Chandragupta I

Q.34 Who presided over the first session of the All India Trade Union Congress in 1920?

A. Purshottam Das Tandon
B. Lala Lajpat Rai
C. Kasturbhai Lalbhai
D. Govind Vallabh Pant

Q.35 What was the capital of the southern part of Avanti Mahajanapada?

A. Mahishmati   **B.** Mathura
C. Ujjain   **D.** Taxila

Q.36 Which God is worshipped in the Tusu festival of Jharkhand?

A. Sun   **B.** Durga   **C.** Mansa   **D.** Saran

Q.37 Which of the following gas is also known as laughing gas?

A. Nitrous oxide   **B.** Nitrogen dioxide
C. Nitrogen hydroxide   **D.** Nitrogen peroxide

Q.38 When people are engaged in production of goods and services they are said to be engaged in:

A. Labour   **B.** Economic activity
C. Work   **D.** Manufacturing

Q.39 Which famous personality founded the Marathi newspaper 'Kesari'?

A. Lokmanya Tilak   **B.** Vallabhbhai Patel
C. Lala Lajpat Rai   **D.** Mahatma Gandhi

Q.40 Who is the constitutional head of state?

A. Chief Minister
B. Chief Justice of High court
C. Governor
D. Vidhan Sabha Speaker

Elementary Mathematics

Q.41 If 123457Y is completely divisible by 8, then what will be the digit in place of Y?

[SSC MTS, 2017]

A. 4   **B.** 5   **C.** 8   **D.** 6

Q.42 Which smallest number to be subtracted from 300, so that the resulting number is completely divisible by 9?

[SSC MTS, 2017]

A. 5   **B.** 6   **C.** 3   **D.** 1

Q.43 In an examination 15% of the students failed. If 1500 students appeared in the examination, how many passed?

A. 1250   **B.** 1375   **C.** 1275   **D.** 1150

Q.44 If 658 bags are divided into three parts, proportional to $\left(\frac{3}{2}\right) : \left(\frac{5}{3}\right) : \left(\frac{3}{4}\right)$, what is the third part?

A. 126   **B.** 123   **C.** 156   **D.** 186

Q.45 The ratio of three numbers is 7 : 8 : 9. The sum of their squares is 776. What is the sum of the given three numbers?

A. 68   **B.** 78   **C.** 64   **D.** 48

Q.46 Average of 60 observations is 42. If a number of the value of 50 is replaced by 20. Find the new average of 60 observations.

A. 46   **B.** 44   **C.** 45.5   **D.** 41.5

Q.47 Find the compound interest on Rs. 1000 at the rate of 20% per annum for 18 month when interest is compounded half yearly.

A. Rs. 331   **B.** Rs. 1331   **C.** Rs. 320   **D.** Rs. 325

Q.48 Alan sold his two iPods for Rs 8400 each without any profit or loss. If he sold one of the mobiles at a 30% loss then at what profit percent should he sell the other mobile?

A. 55%   **B.** 80%   **C.** 60%   **D.** 75%

Q.49 Rohan bought a mobile for Rs 15000 and sold it at a 30% loss. If he had sold it for Rs 2000 more then what will be the loss percent?

A. 16.66%   **B.** 50.3%   **C.** 57.2%   **D.** 63.2%

Q.50 A shopkeeper marks his goods 30% above his cost price but allows a discount of 10% at the time of sale. His gain is:

A. 21%   **B.** 20%   **C.** 18%   **D.** 17%

Q.51 The perimeter of an equilateral triangle whose area is $4\sqrt{3}\ cm^2$ is equal to:

[Joint Entrance Examination (Polytechnic), 2019]

A. 10 cm   **B.** 12 cm   **C.** 20 cm   **D.** 15 cm

Q.52 A solid metallic ball of radius 9 cm is melted to form cylinders of radius 6 mm and height 1 cm. Find the number of such solid cylinders that can be formed.

A. 2200   **B.** 3000   **C.** 2500   **D.** 2700

Q.53 If the ratio of two numbers is in the ratio 4 : 9 and their LCM is 720, then find the sum of both the numbers?

A. 260   **B.** 240   **C.** 180   **D.** 390

Q.54 In a business, A, B and C invested Rs 380, Rs 400, and Rs 420 respectively. Divide a net profit of Rs 180 among the partners.

A. $A = 45, B = 56, C = 76$
B. $A = 57, B = 60, C = 63$
C. $A = 12, B = 23, C = 34$
D. $A = 18, B = 34, C = 56$

Q.55 What will come in place of question mark '?' in the following question?

$$\left(\frac{3}{4} \times \frac{2}{9}\right) + \left(\frac{8}{5} \div \frac{12}{5}\right) - \left(\frac{2}{3} \times \frac{1}{4}\right) = ?$$

A. $\frac{1}{4}$ **B.** $\frac{2}{3}$ **C.** $\frac{3}{4}$ **D.** $\frac{5}{8}$

Q.56 Direction: Simplify the given expression.

$$19 \div \left[1 - \frac{1}{2} + 2\frac{2}{3}\right] = ?$$

A. $\frac{1}{6}$ **B.** 6   **C.** $\frac{1}{2}$ **D.** $\frac{1}{19}$

Q.57 If 2 is added to the numerator of a fraction, it reduces to $\left(\frac{1}{2}\right)$ and if 1 is subtracted from the denominator, it reduces to $\left(\frac{1}{3}\right)$. Find the fraction.

A. $\frac{5}{7}$ **B.** $\frac{1}{10}$ **C.** $\frac{2}{5}$ **D.** $\frac{3}{10}$

Q.58 Travelling at $\frac{3}{4}$ of the normal speed, a person reaches his workplace 15 minutes late. How many minutes does he take usually to reach the workplace?

A. 60 minutes   **B.** 30 minutes
C. 42 minutes   **D.** 45 minutes

Q.59 A person invests Rs. 30000 as a fixed deposit at a bank of 10% p.a. S.I. But due to some problem, he has to withdraw the entire money after 3 yrs for which the bank allowed him a lower rate of interest. If he gets Rs. 7800 less than what he would have got at the end of 5 yrs; Find R.O.I allowed by the bank?

A. 2%   **B.** 5%   **C.** 4%   **D.** 8%

Q.60 A, B, and C can do a work in 24, 16 and 12 days respectively. How many days will it take them to complete the work, if the three of them decide to work together?

A. $5\frac{1}{3}$ days   **B.** $5\frac{2}{3}$ days   **C.** $5\frac{1}{2}$ days   **D.** $5\frac{3}{4}$ days

English

Q.61 In the question, some part of the sentence may have errors. Find out which part of the sentence has an error and select the appropriate option. If the sentence is free from error, select 'No error'.

Aradhaya learnt (A)/ the alphabets (B)/ at her play school. (C)/ No error (D)

A. A   **B.** B   **C.** C   **D.** D

Q.62 In the question, some part of the sentence may have errors. Find out which part of the sentence has an error and select the appropriate option. If the sentence is free from error, select 'No error'.

Me and my husband (A)/ were at party (B)/ last night. (C)/ No error (D)

A. A   **B.** B   **C.** C   **D.** D

Q.63 Complete the sentence with the most appropriate word.
Making pies and cakes ____ Mrs Kumar's speciality.

A. have   **B.** is
C. has   **D.** are being

Q.64 Complete the sentence with the most appropriate word.
Laxmi's sons are the most ________ thing in her life.

A. Importancy   **B.** Importance
C. Importantly   **D.** Important

Q.65 Complete the sentence with the most appropriate word.
Students are not expected to leave without ________.

A. tolerance   **B.** indulgence
C. permission   **D.** freedom

Q.66 Select the word similar in meaning to the given word.
OBSTREPEROUS
A. Boisterous   **B.** Bashful
C. Reticent   **D.** Taciturn

Q.67 Select the word opposite in meaning to the given word.
Eternity
A. Perpetuity   **B.** Yonder
C. Aeon   **D.** Ephemeral

Q.68 In the question, out of the four alternatives, select the alternative which is the best substitute of the phrase.
Sums of money expressed in a specified monetary unit.
A. To denominate   **B.** To monetise
C. To nominate   **D.** Demarche

Q.69 In the question, you need to replace the bold part of the sentence by the most suitable idiom/expression given as an option.
Maths is the only subject that seems **extremely difficult for me to understand.**
A. a piece of cake   **B.** all greek to me
C. ducks and drakes   **D.** ace in the hole

Q.70 Out of the four alternatives, choose the one which can be substituted for the given words/sentences.
One who eats everything.
A. Omnivorous   **B.** Omniscient
C. Irresistible   **D.** Insolvent

Q.71 Out of the four alternatives, choose the one which can be substituted for the given words.
Preventing the light from travelling through.
A. Oblique   **B.** Optical   **C.** Opaque   **D.** Opulent

Q.72 In the question, a word has been written in four different ways out of which only one is correctly spelled. Select the correctly spelled word.
A. Comittee   **B.** Commitee
C. Commmitte   **D.** Committee

Q.73 In the question, a word has been written in four different ways out of which only one is correctly spelled. Select the correctly spelled word.
A. Gibberish   **B.** Giberish
C. Ggiberrish   **D.** Gibberrish

Ques (74-77):Directions: Read the passage closely and pick up the answer for each question.

There is no general agreement about how the planets were formed. The most widely accepted theory is that about 5000 million years ago swirling clouds of matter began to condense.

Through the action of centrifugal force, the heavier molecules were concentrated near the center of the eddies, and the lighter, gaseous material was thrown out towards the

periphery. Such is the theory. What is known is that nine satellites began orbiting around the sun.

These are the planets. The planet on which man lives is the third closest to the sun, with the third shortest orbit. It also has been something none of the others has - an atmosphere that can support life in all the manifold forms that exist on our planet. There may be satellites circling other stars in other parts of the universe that have the right ingredients for some sort of life to evolve, but the earth is the only one in the solar system.

Q.74 The theory of the formation of the planets:
A. Is generally agreed upon by everyone
B. Covers a very wide area
C. Is widely known
D. None of the above

Q.75 According to the passage, the planets are:
A. Nothing but condensed clouds
B. A collection of gaseous material
C. A collection of condensed swirling material
D. A collection of centrifugal forces

Q.76 One essential difference between the earth and the-
A. The atmosphere of the earth makes possible the presence of life on it
B. The earth draws the heavier molecules into its centre through the action of centrifugal force
C. Only the earth is on the periphery of the solar system
D. The earth has the capacity to come into closer contact with the sun

Q.77 A planet is a 'heavenly body' that moves round:
A. The sun
B. A star
C. A satellite of the solar system
D. The universe

Q.78 In the question, a part of the sentence is made bold. Below are given alternatives to the bold part at (A), (B), and (C) which may improve the sentence. Choose the correct alternative. In case no replacement is needed, mark (D) as your answer.
There are very few **people in the world that doesn't** like ice cream.
A. people in the world whom don't
B. people in the world who don't
C. people in the world which don't
D. No replacement required

Q.79 In the question, a part of the sentence is made bold. Below are given alternatives to the bold part at (A), (B), and (C) which may improve the sentence. Choose the correct alternative. In case no replacement is needed, mark (D) as your answer.
No sooner **do the bell ring** than the students ran out of their classes.
A. Did the bell ring
B. Did the bells ring
C. Do the bell rang

D. No replacement required

Q.80 In the question, a part of the sentence is made bold. Below are given alternatives to the bold part at (A), (B), and (C) which may improve the sentence. Choose the correct alternative. In case no replacement is needed, mark (D) as your answer.

For **decade company which** make soap, lotions and perfumes have relied on a chemical called Bourgeonal.

A. decades company that

B. decade companies which

C. decades companies that

D. No replacement required

// Smart Answer Sheet //

Correct Percentage of students who answered correctly. **Skipped** Percentage of students who skipped.

Q.	Ans.	Correct / Skipped
1	D	30.54 % / 67.27 %
2	D	84.09 % / 12.7 %
3	D	57.42 % / 34.72 %
4	C	89.68 % / 10.09 %
5	A	44.72 % / 34.78 %
6	B	82.45 % / 17.27 %
7	B	83.7 % / 15.46 %
8	B	79.12 % / 13.42 %
9	B	59.79 % / 37.87 %
10	A	84.37 % / 11.29 %
11	D	87.65 % / 11.89 %
12	D	86.44 % / 13.42 %
13	D	44.88 % / 50.56 %
14	C	51.2 % / 45.75 %
15	C	89.11 % / 10.62 %
16	B	50.12 % / 34.72 %

Q.	Ans.	Correct / Skipped
17	A	60.51 % / 31.22 %
18	C	54.48 % / 38.36 %
19	C	49.74 % / 34.66 %
20	D	68.96 % / 31.03 %
21	D	62.88 % / 33.08 %
22	B	55.37 % / 34.46 %
23	B	61.2 % / 34.35 %
24	B	45.7 % / 48.59 %
25	A	51.5 % / 46.77 %
26	C	59.89 % / 37.33 %
27	D	10.96 % / 81.12 %
28	B	65.1 % / 32.42 %
29	A	45.87 % / 44.24 %
30	C	53.26 % / 40.86 %
31	A	82.22 % / 10.83 %
32	A	66.46 % / 30.61 %

Q.	Ans.	Correct / Skipped
33	A	51.37 % / 43.6 %
34	B	61.41 % / 37.55 %
35	A	13.1 % / 79.68 %
36	A	57.45 % / 30.83 %
37	A	64.02 % / 33.6 %
38	B	81.61 % / 11.26 %
39	A	65.94 % / 33.99 %
40	C	63.58 % / 35.44 %
41	D	55.78 % / 40.05 %
42	C	59.31 % / 34.35 %
43	C	53.99 % / 31.16 %
44	A	78.54 % / 15.38 %
45	D	86.95 % / 10.32 %
46	D	83.46 % / 11.96 %
47	A	85.89 % / 11.85 %
48	D	48.15 % / 47.74 %

Q.	Ans.	Correct / Skipped
49	A	47.55 % / 50.57 %
50	D	81.29 % / 15.31 %
51	B	84.37 % / 12.83 %
52	D	82.23 % / 10.74 %
53	A	84.44 % / 10.83 %
54	B	42.66 % / 31.36 %
55	B	48.35 % / 50.45 %
56	B	65.43 % / 30.37 %
57	D	44.0 % / 38.87 %
58	D	40.28 % / 58.7 %
59	D	46.16 % / 35.72 %
60	A	56.48 % / 35.78 %
61	B	84.43 % / 13.28 %
62	A	69.0 % / 30.87 %
63	B	84.37 % / 10.38 %
64	D	88.04 % / 11.08 %

Q.	Ans.	Correct / Skipped
65	C	86.66 % / 12.67 %
66	A	58.86 % / 32.92 %
67	D	84.19 % / 11.46 %
68	A	44.74 % / 31.58 %
69	B	43.75 % / 35.97 %
70	A	41.04 % / 41.98 %
71	C	43.3 % / 52.97 %
72	D	47.29 % / 44.36 %
73	A	51.27 % / 36.6 %
74	C	58.27 % / 31.49 %
75	B	67.86 % / 31.54 %
76	A	47.28 % / 36.87 %
77	A	42.32 % / 35.3 %
78	B	61.83 % / 35.96 %
79	B	47.61 % / 36.5 %
80	C	69.41 % / 30.02 %

//Hints and Solutions//

1. The logic follows here is;

In 30 : 56;

$30 = 5 \times 6$

$(5 + 2) \times (6 + 2)$

$= 7 \times 8$

$= 56$

Similarly;

$20 = 4 \times 5$

$(4 + 2) \times (5 + 2)$

$= 6 \times 7$

$= 42$

Hence, the correct option is (D).

2. Teachers: H, K, P, R and T

All are facing towards the centre.

1) T is between H and R.

2) P is second to the right of R.

3) H is to the immediate left of T.

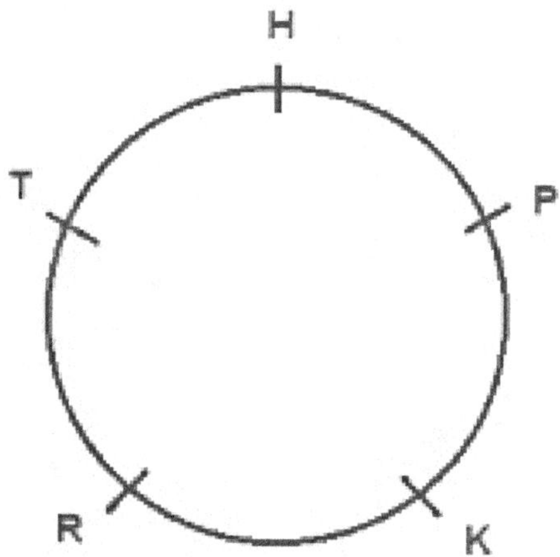

R sits immediate left of K.

So, R is the correct answer.

Hence, the correct option is (D).

3. After opening the paper folding and cut we get:

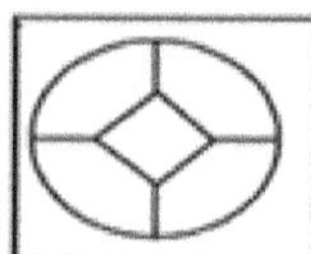

Hence, the correct option is (D).

4. All are square of some number except '343', which is a cube of '7'.

$256 = 16^2$

$289 = 17^2$

$144 = 12^2$

$343 = 7^3$

Hence, the correct option is (C).

5. From the given information

Symbol in Diagram	Meaning
◯	Female
☐	Male
═	Married Couple
—	Siblings
│	Difference of A Generation

A is the grandfather of X.

C is the only sister-in-law of T.

X is the only child of R.

Q is a female so must be the wife of A.

So, the complete figure would be like this:-

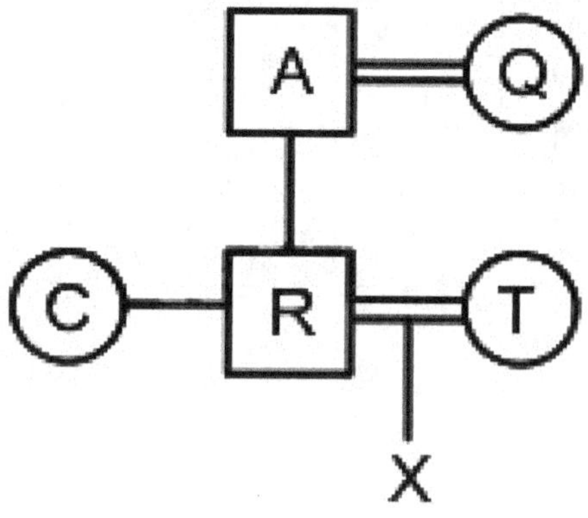

Therefore, Q is the mother of R.

Hence, the correct option is (A).

6. Except figure (B), all figures have been embedded in the question figure.

The embedded figures have been shown below.

Option (A):

option (C):

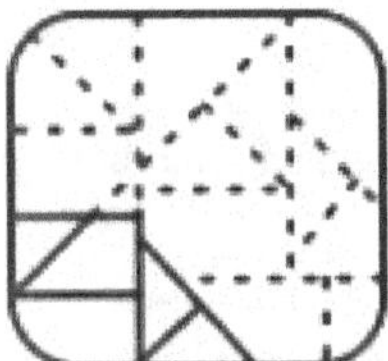

Option (D):

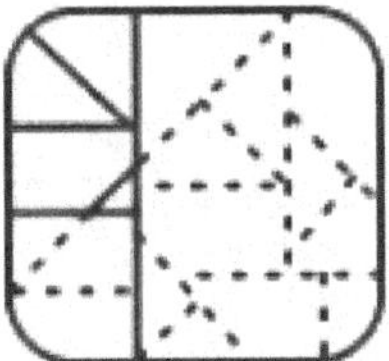

Hence, the correct option is (B).

7. Given:

10#5@1$5

Changing the signs according to the question,

10 - 5 × 1 ÷ 5

Solving by using BODMAS,

= 10 -1

= 9

Hence, the correct option is (B).

8.

So, (B) is the correct figure.

Hence, the correct option is (B).

9. In each figure, one portion is shaded in the clockwise direction. In the first figure one portion is shaded, then two and so on. Therefore, the next figure:

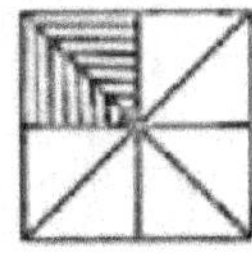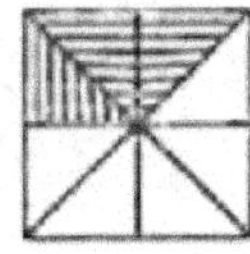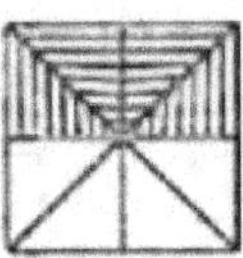

Hence, the correct option is (B).

10. Logic:

Figure $(1) \rightarrow 18 + 19 - 2 = 35$

Figure $(2) \rightarrow 22 + 24 - 3 = 43$

Similarly,

Figure $(3) \rightarrow 26 + 27 - 4 = 49$

Hence, the correct option is (A).

11. The least possible Venn Diagram for the given statements will be as follows:

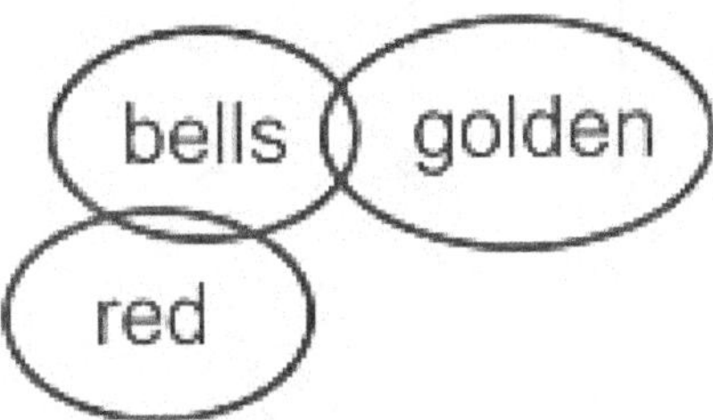

I. Some red are golden. (False, it can be true but not definite.)

II. No golden is red. (False, it can be true but not definite.)

So, Either conclusion I or II follow.

Hence, the correct option is (D).

12. In a code language, if BOX is written as 725

B	O	X
7	2	5

and GLAND is written as 16493,

G	L	A	N	D
1	6	4	9	3

Then BOND be written as

B	O	N	D
7	2	9	3

BOND is written as 7293.

Hence, the correct option is (D).

13. As

L M O I
+3 -5 +3 -5
↓   ↓   ↓   ↓
O H R D

Similarly,

E U T X
+3 -5 +3 -5
↓   ↓   ↓   ↓
H P W S

Thus, EUTX is related to HPWS.

Hence, the correct option is (D).

14. The pattern followed here is:

$(1)^3 - 1 = 1 - 1 = 0$

$(2)^3 - 2 = 8 - 2 = 6$

$(3)^3 - 3 = 27 - 3 = 24$

$(4)^3 - 4 = 64 - 4 = 60$

Similarly,

$(5)^3 - 5 = 125 - 5 = 120$

Hence, the correct option is (C).

15. The pattern followed here is,

T H C Q | T H C Q | T HC Q

Hence, the correct option is (C).

16. Here, 3, 4, 6 and 5 cannot be opposite to 2.

So, 1 must be opposite 2.

Also, 1, 2, 3 and 6 are not opposite to 5. So, 4 must be opposite 5.

If 1 is opposite 2, 4 is opposite 5 then 3 must be opposite 6.

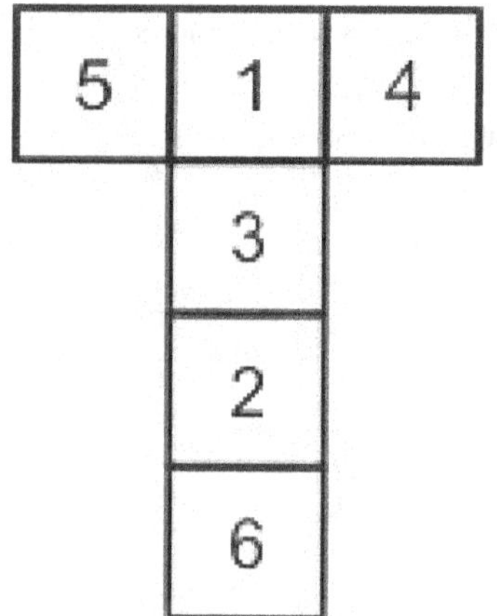

Hence, the correct option is (B).

17. Number of persons who like only teaching and playing but NOT cooking = 21 + 6 + 14 = 41

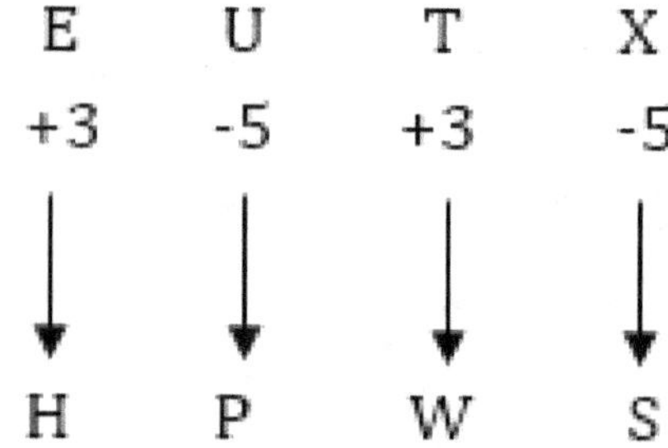

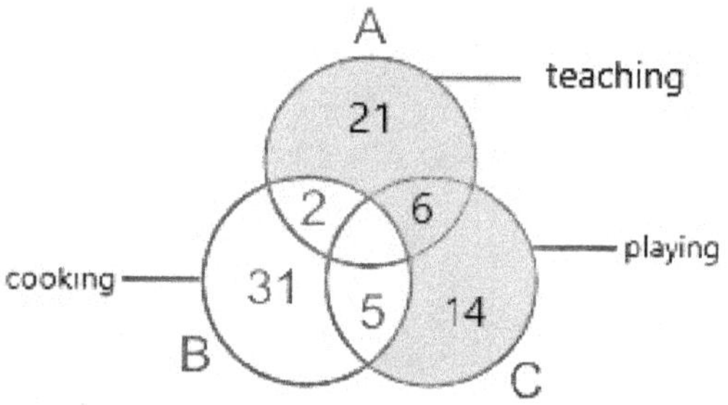

Hence, the correct option is (A).

18. Let the present age of father be F and that of son be S.

Ten years ago, the ages of father and son were in the ratio $3:1$

$\therefore \dfrac{F-10}{S-10} = \dfrac{3}{1}$

$\Rightarrow F - 10 = 3S - 30$

$\Rightarrow 3S = F - 10 + 30$

$\Rightarrow 3S = F + 20$

$\Rightarrow S = \dfrac{(F+20)}{3}$ ....(i)

Ten years hence this ratio will be $2:1$

$\therefore \dfrac{F+10}{S+10} = \dfrac{2}{1}$

$\Rightarrow F + 10 = 2S + 20$..........(ii)

Substituting the value of equation (i) in (ii), we get:

$\Rightarrow F + 10 = 2\left(\dfrac{F+20}{3}\right) + 20$

$\Rightarrow 3(F + 10) = 2F + 40 + 60$

$\Rightarrow 3F + 30 = 2F + 100$

$\Rightarrow 3F - 2F = 100 - 30$

$$\Rightarrow F = 70$$

Hence, the correct option is (C).

19. The logic here is:

Sum of digits of third number - sum of digits of first number = Second number

(23, 4, 45) → (4 + 5) - (2 + 3) = 9 - 5 = 4

(94, 5, 99) → (9 + 9) - (9 + 4) = 18 - 13 = 5

(47, 3, 78) → (7 + 8) - (4 + 7) = 15 - 11 = 4 ≠ 3

(29, 7, 99) → (9 + 9) - (2 + 9) = 18 - 11 = 7

Hence, (47, 3, 78) is the odd one out.

Hence, the correct option is (C).

20. The arrangement of the given words in the order in which they appear in an English dictionary is as shown below :

4. **Prec**aution

5. **Proc**tor

2. **Prod**uct

1. **Prof**ess

3. **Pros**ecute

Hence, the correct option is (D).

21. The World Bank has appointed Auguste Tano Kouamé as the Country Director for India. He replaced Junaid Kamal Ahmad who recently completed a five-year term.

Auguste, a national of Côte d'Ivoire, most recently served as the World Bank's Country Director for the Republic of Turkey.

Hence, the correct option is (D).

22. The 11th World Urban Forum was held in Poland. The National Institute of Urban Affairs' (NIUA) Climate Centre for Cities (NIUA C-Cube), World Resources Institute India (WRI India) and their partners launched India's first national coalition platform for urban nature-based solutions (NbS).

'India Forum for Nature-Based Solutions' aims to create a collective of NbS entrepreneurs, government entities and like-minded organisations, to aid in scaling urban nature-based solutions.

Hence, the correct option is (B).

23. Haryana government launched 'e-Adhigam' scheme to provide tablets to five lakh students. Under the Haryana Government, around five lakh school students of classes 10th and 12th will receive tablets.

These devices come with pre-loaded content along with personalised and adaptive learning software, and 2GB of free data. Haryana government has also announced to form two task forces for the education sector, to work on the infrastructure and sanitation of schools.

Hence, the correct option is (B).

24. The Mazagon Dock Shipbuilders on 20 April 2022, launched INS Vagsheer, the last of the six submarines under Project 75. The submarine was launched by Defence Secretary Ajay Kumar.

Named after sandfish, a deadly deep water sea predator of the Indian Ocean, the first submarine 'Vagsheer' was commissioned in Indian navy December 1974. It was decommissioned in Indian navy April 1997.

Hence, the correct option is (B).

25. Ed-tech company BYJU'S has been named as an official sponsor of the FIFA World Cup Qatar 2022 on 24 March 2022. The 2022 FIFA World Cup is scheduled to take place in Qatar from 21 November to 18 December, 2022. FIFA is dedicated to harnessing the power of football towards the goal of enacting positive societal change.

Hence, the correct option is (A).

26. Indus, Chenab, and Jhelum are the rivers included as "Western rivers" under Indus Waters Treaty.

- India was allocated about 20% of the total water carried by the Indus system while Pakistan was allocated the remaining.

- The treaty allows India to use the western river waters for limited irrigation use and unlimited non-consumptive use for such applications as power generation, navigation, floating of property, fish culture, etc.

Hence, the correct option is (C).

27. The first recipients of the award were Bhalchandra Bhaskar Bhagwat (Wrestling), Om Prakash Bhardwaj (Boxing), and O. M. Nambiar (Athletics), who were honored in 1985.

Dronacharya Award: It was instituted in 1985 to honor eminent Coaches for producing medal winners at prestigious International sports events.

Hence, the correct option is (D).

28. An increase in expenditure on public projects steps is most likely to be taken at the time of an economic recession.

An economic recession is typically defined as a decline in the gross domestic product (GDP) for two or more consecutive quarters. High-interest rates are a cause of recession because they limit liquidity, or the amount of money available to invest. So, statements 1 and 3 are not correct.

Inflation refers to a general rise in the prices of goods and services over a period of time. As inflation increases, the percentage of goods and services that can be purchased with the same amount of money decreases.

An increase in public expenditure rises GDP by the same amount, other things equal. Moreover, since income is an important determinant of consumption, that increase in income will be followed by a rise in consumption. Public expenditure plays four main roles:

1. It contributes to current effective demand;

2. It expresses a coordinated impulse on the economy, which can be used for stabilization, business cycle inversion, and growth purposes;

3. It increases the public endowment of goods for everybody;

4. It gives rise to positive externalities to the economy and society as a whole (or in specific sectors and geographical areas), the more so through its capital component. So, statement 2 is correct.

Hence, the correct option is (B).

29. The Indian Institute of Geomagnetism (IIG), an autonomous research institute, developed an indigenous Overhauser magnetometer, which is one of the most accurate magnetometers widely used in all magnetic observatories across the world.

A team from IIG's Instrumentation Division used a variety of spectroscopic tools and theoretical simulations to understand the work. They also conducted various control experiments which included changing the sensor structure and checking the performance of the sensor.

Hence, the correct option is (A).

30. Part 7 of the constitution was repealed by the 7th Amendment Act. It consisted of states in the B part of the First schedule.

Part B states were Hyderabad, Jammu and Kashmir, Madhya Bharat, Mysore, Patiala, and East Punjab States Union (PEPSU), Rajasthan, Saurashtra, and Travancore-Cochin.

- Part 22 deals with Short Text, Commencement, Authoritative Text in Hindi, and Repeal.
- Part 11 deals with Relations Between The Union And The States.
- Part 5 deals with the Union.

Hence, the correct option is (C).

31. The first amendment to the Constitution of India was made in 1951. The amendment was made for the welfare of scheduled castes, tribes and backward classes. It provided a 10 per cent quota for economically weaker sections in educational or academic institutions. It amended Articles 15, 19, 85, 87, 174, 176, 341, 342, 372 and 376. It also inserted Ninth Schedule to the Indian Constitution. Articles 31A and 31B were also inserted.

Hence, the correct option is (A).

32. The Bhakra Nangal dam is situated on the Sutlej river.

Bhakra dam is constructed on Satluj river and located in Himachal Pradesh and Punjab border near Nangal city. It is intended for irrigation as well as hydro-electric purposes.

Hence, the correct option is (A).

33. Samudragupta was called the 'Napoleon of India'.

Samudragupta:

- He ruled from 335 AD to 380 AD.

- Samudragupta was the greatest king of the Gupta dynasty.

- The most detailed and authentic record of Samudragupta's reign is preserved in the Prayaga Prasasti/Allahabad pillar inscription, composed by his court poet Harisena.

- Samudragupta's military campaigns justify the description of him as the Napoleon of India by V.A. Smith.

- He assumed titles such as Kaviraja, Param Bhagavat, Ashvamedha- parikrama, Vikram Sarva-raj-ochchhetta, only the Gupta ruler had the title of Sarva-raj-ochchhetta.

Hence, the correct option is (A).

34. On October 31, 1920, the first session of the All India Trade Union Congress was held at Bombay under Lala Lajpat Rai, thus marking the beginning of the AITUC (All India Trade Union Congress).

Hence, the correct option is (B).

35. The capital of the southern part of Avanti Mahajanapada was located at Mahishmati. It was located in the present-day malwa region on the banks of river Narmada. Avanti mahajanapada was significant in the rise of Buddhism.

Hence, the correct option is (A).

36. In the Tusu festival of Jharkhand, the Sun God is worshipped.

- The festival is celebrated by the Mahato community of the tribal people of the Singhbhum district on the day of Makar Sankranti.
- It is a folk festival.
- It is celebrated on the day of Makar Sankranti, which is the last day of the Bengali month of Poush.
- In the local language, it is also called Makar Parav.
- The festival is celebrated to unify the local common faith and to enjoy the joy of harvest.
- In the festival, rural fairs are also organized.

Hence, the correct option is (A).

37. Nitrous oxide, commonly known as laughing gas is a colourless non-flammable gas, with a slight metallic scent and taste. It is also used in surgery and dentistry, for its anesthetic and pain reducing effects.

Hence, the correct option is (A).

38. The production, distribution, and consumption of commodities is termed as economic activity. When people are engaged in the production of goods and services they are said to be engaged in economic activities.

Hence, the correct option is (B).

39. Lokmanya Tilak founded the Marathi newspaper 'Kesari'. The Kesari newspaper is a Marathi-language Indian newspaper.

- The newspaper was initially founded in 1881 by a prominent personality of the Indian Independence Movement, Lokmanya Bal Gangadhar Tilak.
- The Kesari newspaper was originally started as a co-operative effort by Agarkar (the paper's first editor), Chiplunkar, and Tilak, and was published along with Tilak's English newspaper, the Mahratta, to encourage people to rise against the oppressive regime of the time, instead of being submissive.
- the Kesari is still published from the original offices in Pune. Reporting local, national, and international news, the paper today is still one of the leading dailies of Maharashtra.

Hence, the correct option is (A).

40. Governor is the constitutional head of the state.

- Governor has all the executive and legislative powers of the state.
- Governor is the first person in the state.
- Article 153 of the Constitution states that should be a governor in each state.

Hence, the correct option is (C).

41. Given,

123457Y

If a number is completely divisible by 8, then the last three digits of the number must also be divisible by 8.

$\Rightarrow$ 57Y must be divisible by 8 and the only three-digit number starting with '57' which is divisible by 8 is = 576

$\Rightarrow$ Y=6

Hence, the correct option is (D).

42. On dividing 300 by 9, we get : 300 = 9 × 33 + 3

Thus, the smallest number which should be subtracted from 300 = 3

Also, 300 - 3 = 297 is completely divisible by 9.

Hence, the correct option is (C).

43. Given,

In an examination 15% students failed

Total students appeared in examination = 1500

Students passed in examination = 85%

Number of students passed in the examination =

$\left(\frac{85}{100}\right) \times 1500 = 1275$

$\therefore$ Number of students passed in the examination is 1275.

Hence, the correct option is (C).

44. Given:

If 658 bags are divided into three parts, proportional to

$\left(\frac{3}{2}\right) : \left(\frac{5}{3}\right) : \left(\frac{3}{4}\right)$

Third part $= \dfrac{(\text{Third ratio} \times \text{Total})}{\text{Sum of the ratio}}$

Ratio $= \dfrac{3}{2} : \dfrac{5}{3} : \dfrac{3}{4}$

$= 18 : 20 : 9$

Sum of the ratio $= 47$

Third part $= \dfrac{(9 \times 658)}{47} = 126$

Hence, the correct option is (A).

45. Given,

The ratio of the three numbers is 7 : 8 : 9.

The sum of their squares is 776.

Let the three numbers are 7X, 8X and 9X.

Square of first number + square of second number + square of third number = 776

$\Rightarrow$ (7X)^2 + (8X)^2 + (9X)^2 = 776

$\Rightarrow$ 49X^2 + 64X^2 + 81X^2 = 776

$\Rightarrow$ 194X^2 = 776

$\Rightarrow$ X$^2 = \dfrac{776}{194}$

$\Rightarrow$ X^2 = 4

$\Rightarrow$ X = 2

First number = 7X = 14

Second number = 8X = 16

Third number = 9X = 18

Sum = 14 + 16 + 18 = 48

$\therefore$ Required sum is 48.

Hence, the correct option is (D).

46. Given,

Average of 60 observations $= 42$

As we know,

Average $= \dfrac{\text{Sum of all observations}}{\text{Total number of all observations}}$

Sum of all 60 observations $= 60 \times 42 = 2520$

New sum of all 60 observations if 50 is replaced by 20

$= 2520 - 50 + 20 = 2490$

$\therefore$ New average of 60 observations $= \dfrac{2490}{60} = 41.5$

Hence, the correct option is (D).

47. Given,

Principal, $P =$ Rs. 1000

Compoind rate, $R = 20\%$ per annum

$= \frac{20}{2} = 10\%$ half - yearly

Time $= 18$ month $= 3$ half - years

Amount,

$$A = \left\{ P \times \left[1 + \left(\frac{R}{100} \right) \right]^n \right\}$$

$$= \left\{ 1000 \times \left[1 + \left(\frac{10}{100} \right) \right]^3 \right\}$$

$$= \frac{1000 \times 11 \times 11 \times 11}{10 \times 10 \times 10}$$

$A =$ Rs. 1331

So, compound interest $=$ Rs. 331

Hence, the correct option is (A).

48. Alan sold his two iPods for Rs 8400 each without any profit or loss.

The total SP $= 8400 + 8400 = 16800$

The cost price of 1st mobile $= 8400 \left(\frac{100}{70} \right)$

$= 12000$

The selling price of 2nd mobile $= 8400$

The cost price of 2nd mobile $= 16800 - 12000$

$= 4800$

Profit percent $= \left(\frac{8400 - 4800}{4800} \right) \times 100$

$= 75\%$

Hence, the correct option is (D).

49. Cost price $= 15000$

Selling price $= \left(\frac{70}{100} \right) \times 15000$

$= 10500$

New selling price $= 10500 + 2000$

$= 12500$

Loss percent $= \left(\frac{15000 - 12500}{15000} \right) \times 100$

$= \frac{50}{3}$

$= 16.66\ \%$

Hence, the correct option is (A).

50. Let the cost price be Rs. 100

then the mark up price which is 30% above the cost price,

Mark price $= (100 + 30\%$ of $100\ ) =$ Rs. 130

Shopkeeper gives a discount of 10% on mark up price, then the

Selling Price $= (130 - 10\%$ of $130\ ) =$ Rs. 117

Gain $= 117 - 100 =$ Rs. 17

$\%$ gain $= \frac{17 \times 100}{100}$

$= 17\%$

Hence, the correct option is (D).

51. Given:

Area of an equilateral triangle $= 4\sqrt{3}\ cm^2$

$\Rightarrow \frac{\sqrt{3}}{4} a^2 = 4\sqrt{3}\ cm^2$

$\Rightarrow a^2 = 16$

$\Rightarrow a = 4\ cm$

Perimeter of an equilateral triangle $= 3a$

$= 4 \times 3$

$= 12\ cm$

Hence, the correct option is (B).

52. Let, 'n' be the number of cylinders that can be formed;

$\therefore$ Volume of spherical ball $= n \times$ Volume of one cylinder

$\Rightarrow \frac{4}{3} \pi r^3 = n \times \pi r^2 h$

$\Rightarrow \frac{4}{3} \times \frac{22}{7} \times 9 \times 9 \times 9 = n \times \frac{22}{7} \times 0.6 \times 0.6 \times 1$

$\Rightarrow n = 2700$

Hence, the correct option is (D).

53. Given:

Ratio of numbers = 4 : 9

LCM of the numbers = 720

Let the numbers be $4a$ and $9a$.

$\therefore$ Prime factors of $4a = a \times 2 \times 2$

Prime factors of $9a = a \times 3 \times 3$

$\therefore$ LCM of $4a$ and $9a = a \times 2 \times 2 \times 3 \times 3$

$= 36 \times a$

LCM of 4 and $9a = 720$ ..... (Given)

$\therefore 36 \times a = 720$

$\Rightarrow a = \frac{720}{36}$

$\Rightarrow a = 20$

$\therefore$ Numbers are $4a = 4 \times 20 = 80$

$9a = 9 \times 20 = 180$

$\therefore$ Sum of numbers $= 180 + 80$

$= 260$

Hence, the correct option is (A).

54. The ratio of investments corresponds to the ratio of profits:

A's profit: B's profit: C's profit

$= A : B : C$

$= 380 : 400 : 420$

$= 19 : 20 : 21$

Profit share of $A = \dfrac{19}{60} \times 180 =$ Rs. 57

Profit share of $B = \dfrac{20}{60} \times 180 =$ Rs. 60

Profit share of $C = \dfrac{21}{60} \times 180 =$ Rs. 63

Hence, the correct option is (B).

55. $\left(\dfrac{3}{4} \times \dfrac{2}{9}\right) + \left(\dfrac{8}{5} \div \dfrac{12}{5}\right) - \left(\dfrac{2}{3} \times \dfrac{1}{4}\right) = ?$

$\Rightarrow \left(\dfrac{3}{4} \times \dfrac{2}{9}\right) + \left(\dfrac{8}{5} \times \dfrac{5}{12}\right) - \left(\dfrac{2}{3} \times \dfrac{1}{4}\right) = ?$

$\Rightarrow \dfrac{1}{6} + \dfrac{2}{3} - \dfrac{1}{6} = ?$

$\therefore ? = \dfrac{2}{3}$

Hence, the correct option is (B).

56. Given,

$19 \div \left[1 - \dfrac{1}{2} + 2\dfrac{2}{3}\right] = ?$

$\Rightarrow ? = 19 \div \left[1 - \dfrac{1}{2} + \dfrac{8}{3}\right]$

$\Rightarrow ? = 19 \div \left[\dfrac{6 - 3 + 16}{6}\right]$

$\Rightarrow ? = 19 \div \left[\dfrac{3 + 16}{6}\right]$

$\Rightarrow ? = 19 \div \left[\dfrac{19}{6}\right]$

$\Rightarrow ? = 19 \times \dfrac{6}{19}$

$\Rightarrow ? = 6$

Hence, the correct option is (B).

57. Let the required fraction be $\dfrac{x}{y}$.

Then, we have:

2 is added to the numerator of a fraction, it reduces to $\left(\dfrac{1}{2}\right)$

$\dfrac{x+2}{y} = \dfrac{1}{2}$

$\Rightarrow 2(x + 2) = y$

$\Rightarrow 2x + 4 = y$

$\Rightarrow 2x - y = -4 \ldots \text{(i)}$

1 is subtracted from the denominator, it reduces to $\left(\dfrac{1}{3}\right)$

$\dfrac{x}{y-1} = \dfrac{1}{3}$

$\Rightarrow 3x = 1(y - 1)$

$\Rightarrow 3x - y = -1 \quad \ldots \text{(ii)}$

On subtracting (i) from (ii), we get:

$x = (-1 + 4) = 3$

On substituting $x = 3$ in (i), we get:

$2 \times 3 - y = -4$

$\Rightarrow 6 - y = -4$

$\Rightarrow y = (6 + 4) = 10$

$\therefore x = 3$ and $y = 10$

Thus, the required fraction is $\dfrac{3}{10}$.

Hence, the correct option is (D).

58. Let the normal speed be 4 km/hr

Travelling speed $= 4 \times \left(\dfrac{3}{4}\right) = 3 \; km/hr$

Ratio of normal speed to travelling speed = 4x : 3x

As we know,

Time is inversely proportional to time.

Ratio of normal time to travelling time = 3x : 4x

4x – 3x = 15

$\Rightarrow$ x = 15

$\therefore$ Normal time = 3x = 3 × 15 = 45 min

Hence, the correct option is (D).

59. Given:

Principal $=$ Rs. 30000

Rate $= 10\%$

Time $= 5$ years

Let the R. O. I allowed by bank be r%

According to question

$$7800 = \left(\frac{30000 \times 10 \times 5}{100}\right) - \left(\frac{30000 \times r \times 3}{100}\right)$$

$$7800 = 15000 - 900r$$

$$r = 8\%$$

$\therefore$ R.O.I allowed by bank is 8%.

Hence, the correct option is (D).

60. Given,

A can do the work in 24 days.

B can do the work in 16 days.

C can do the work in 12 days.

$$\text{Efficiency} = \frac{\text{Total work}}{\text{Time taken}}$$

LCM of 24,16 and $12 = 48 =$ Total work

Efficiency of $A = \dfrac{48}{24} = 2$ units/day

Efficiency of $B = \dfrac{48}{16} = 3$ units/day

Efficiency of $C = \dfrac{48}{12} = 4$ units/day

Total efficiency of A, B and C together $= (2 + 3 + 4) = 9$ units/day

Time taken by A, B and $C = \dfrac{48}{9} = \dfrac{16}{3} = 5\dfrac{1}{3}$ days

$\therefore$ Time taken if all of them work together is $5\dfrac{1}{3}$ days.

Hence, the correct option is (A).

61. The error is in part (B) of the sentence. The noun 'alphabet' is not used in plural form. It is because it is a collective noun which is used for the letters referring to a to z in English language. So, replace 'alphabets' with 'alphabet'.

Hence, the correct option is (B).

62. The error is in part (A) of the sentence. Replace objective case 'me' with nominative case 'I'. Also, the order of pronoun should be 231 (i.e. Second Person, Third Person, First Person). Hence, replace 'me and my husband' with 'My husband and I'.

Hence, the correct option is (A).

63. Making pies and cakes is Mrs Kumar's speciality.

The given sentence needs a verb, the subject is singular as 'pies and cakes' are slotted together with the conjunction 'and'.

Hence it is counted as one unit.

The sentence is in the present tense so the perfect 'has/have' would be incorrect.

The only auxiliary correct for the sentence: 'is'.

'Making' is a gerund and it becomes the subject of the sentence.

For example: Making [pies and cakes] [food] is Mrs Kumar's speciality.

Hence, the correct option is (B).

64. Laxmi's sons are the most _______ thing in her life.

The given sentence is about the sons being a significant part of her life, so the right word is 'Important'.

Importancy- is an incorrect word.

Importance- being of great significance or value.

Importantly-used to emphasize a significant point.

Important-of great significance or value.

Hence, the correct option is (D).

65. Students are not expected to leave without permission.

The sentence is about students leaving a class so the right word is 'Permission'.

Tolerance=capacity to endure pain or hardship.

Indulgence= treating someone with special kindness.

Permission= allowing someone to do a particular thing.

Freedom= allowed to do, say, think whatever you want to.

Hence, the correct option is (C).

66. The correct answer is 'Boisterous'.

'Obstreperous': noisy and difficult to control.

Boisterous: (used about a person or behaviour) noisy and full of energy.

Hence, the correct option is (A).

67. Eternity means forever; infinite or unending time.

Perpetuity means continuance; the state or quality of lasting forever.

Yonder means farther; at some distance in the direction indicated.

Aeon means lifetime; an indefinite and very long period of time.

Ephemeral means short-lived; lasting for a very short time.

So, 'Ephemeral' is the opposite word for 'Eternity'.

Hence, the correct option is (D).

68. Denominate- be expressed in a specified monetary unit.

Monetise- convert into or express in the form of currency.

Nominate- propose or formally enter as a candidate for election or for an honour or award.

Demarche- a political step or initiative.

Hence, the correct option is (A).

69. All greek to me (idiom): Something difficult to understand.

A piece of cake (idiom): Something very easy.

Ducks and Drakes (Idiom): Behave recklessly.

Ace in the hole (Idiom): A hidden strength.

Hence, the correct option is (B).

70. Omnivorous is the right word which means feeding on a variety of food of both plant and animal origin.

Omniscient: knowing everything.

Irresistible: too powerful or convincing to be resisted.

Insolvent: unable to pay debts owed.

Hence, the correct option is (A).

71. Oblique- Neither perpendicular nor parallel to a given line or surface; slanting.

Optical- A pair of glasses.

Opaque- Not transmitting radiation, sound, heat, etc.

Opulent- Expensive or luxurious.

Thus, the correct answer is Opaque which means "Preventing the light from traveling through"

Hence, the correct option is (C).

72. Committee: a group of people appointed for a specific function by a larger group and typically consisting of members of that group.

The correct spelling is 'committee'.

Hence, the correct option is (D).

73. Gibberish, also called jibber-jabber or gobbledygook, is speech that is (or appears to be) nonsense. It may include speech sounds that are not actual words, or language games, and specialized jargon that seems nonsensical to outsiders.

The correct spelling is 'gibberish'.

Hence, the correct option is (A).

74. The theory of the formation of the planets is widely known.

It can be concluded from the given lines of the passage: "There is no general agreement about how the planets were formed. The most widely accepted theory is that about 5000 million years ago swirling clouds of matter began to condense."

Hence, the correct option is (D).

75. From the lines in the passage, 'There is no general agreement about how the planets were formed. The most widely accepted theory is that about 5000 million years ago swirling clouds of matter began to condense.'

So, the planets are a collection of gaseous material.

Hence, the correct option is (B).

76. From the lines in the passage "It also has been something, none of the others has - an atmosphere that can support life in all the manifold forms that exist on our planet."

One essential difference between the earth and the atmosphere of the earth makes possible the presence of life on it.

Hence, the correct option is (A).

77. From the lines in the passage "What is known is that nine satellites began orbiting around the sun."

A planet is a 'heavenly body' that moves around the sun.

Hence, the correct option is (A).

78. "Who" is always used to refer to people. "That" is always used when you are talking about an object.

So, people in the world that doesn't are replaced with people in the world who don't to make the sentence grammatically correct.

Among the given choices, only option (B) replaces the given bold part most appropriately.

The sentence after replacement becomes:

There are very few people in the world who don't like ice cream.

Hence, the correct option is (B).

79. The given sentence is an example of subject-verb inversion with negative adverb fronting.

In other words, when a negative adverb (e.g. no sooner . . . than) heads a sentence, an auxiliary verb (e.g. did) changes places with the subject (e.g. the bell).

We need an auxiliary verb for the inversion to work here, so we should replace "do" with "did" and we also change the verb according to the tense to make the sentence grammatically correct.

Among the given choices, only option (B) replaces the given bold part most appropriately.

The sentence after replacement becomes:

No sooner did the bells ring than the students ran out of their classes.

Hence, the correct option is (B).

80. The original sentence is incorrect.

Reason:

1st. The phrase 'For decades' and not 'for decade' is used to denote a very long time. Therefore, 'decade' must be replaced by 'decades' here.

2nd. As the verb 'make' is used in its plural form, it's clear that the subject has to be plural too. Therefore, the noun 'company' must be replaced by 'companies' here.

3rd. As we need a restrictive relative pronoun in the given case, 'that' should be used in place of 'which' here.

Therefore, among the given choices option C replaces the bold part most appropriately.

The sentence after replacement becomes:

For decades companies that make soap, lotions and perfumes have relied on a chemical called Bourgeonal.

Hence, the correct option is (C).

General Intelligence and Reasoning

Q.1 Direction: In the following question choose the set of numbers from the four alternative sets that is similar to the given set.

Given set: (246, 257, 358)

A. (233, 343, 345) **B.** (273, 365, 367)
C. (143, 226, 237) **D.** (145, 235, 324)

Q.2 Eight friends A, B, C, D, E, F, G, and H are sitting around a circular table facing each other for a lunch. A is opposite F and third to the right of B. G is between F and D. H is to the left of D. E is between C and A. Who is sitting opposite C?

A. D **B.** F **C.** B **D.** A

Q.3 Direction: What should come in place of question mark in the following Number Series?

34, 42, 50, 56, 62, 66, ?

A. 68 **B.** 72 **C.** 67 **D.** 70

Q.4 Direction: From the given options, select the one in which the given question figure is embedded. (Rotation is allowed)

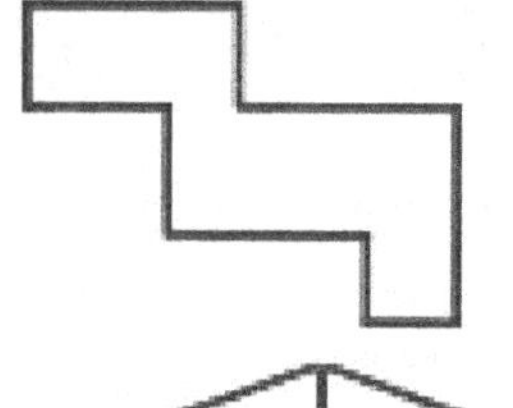

A.
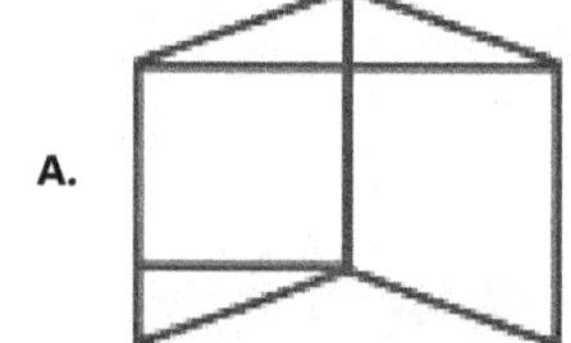

B.
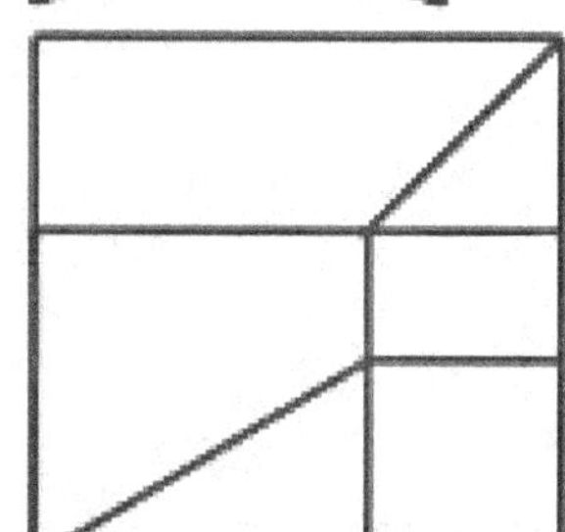

C.
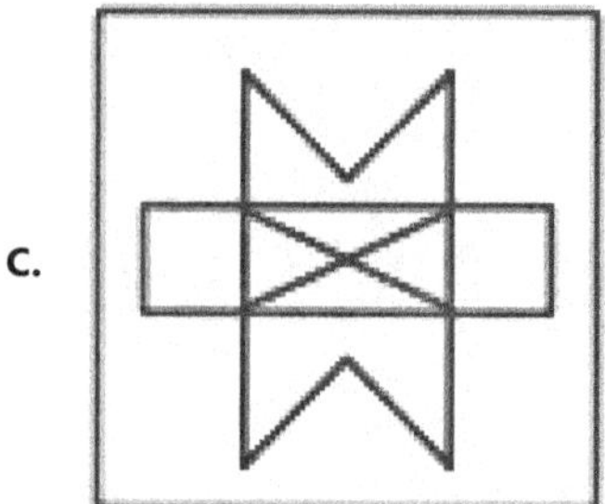

D.
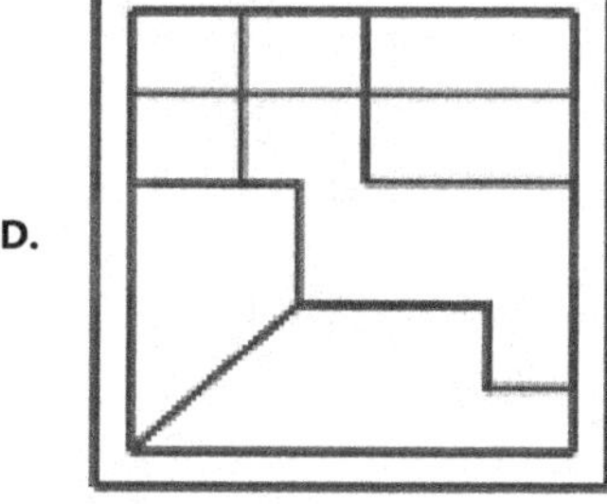

Q.5 If a mirror is placed on the line MN, then which will be the correct mirror image of the given figure?

[Rajasthan Police Constable, 2020]

A.

B.
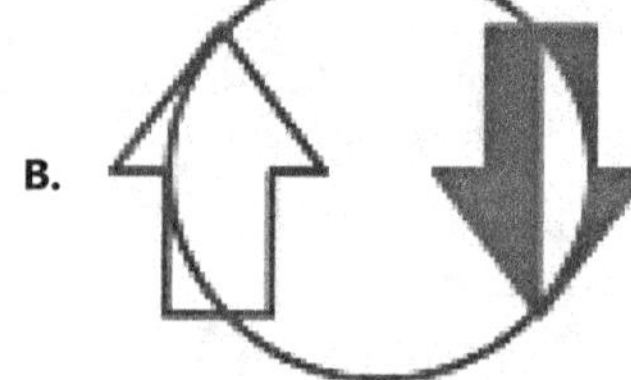

C.

D.

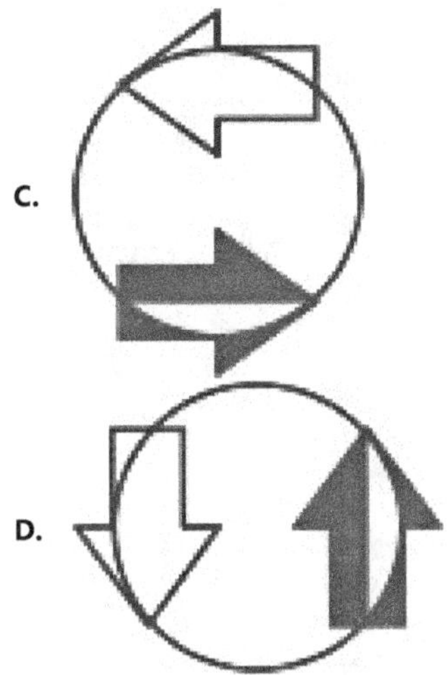

Q.6 Direction: The following question consists of four figures. Select the answer figure which will complete the series established by the question.

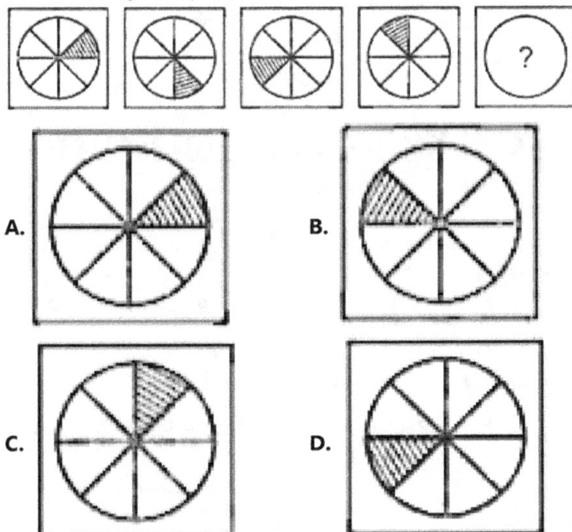

A.

B.

C.

D.

Q.7 Direction: In the following question, select the number which can be placed at the sign of question mark (?) from the given alternatives.

4	8	20
9	3	15
6	6	?

A. 22   **B.** 18   **C.** 16   **D.** 26

Q.8 Arrange the following words as per the order of dictionary-

1. Live
2. Litter
3. Little
4. Literacy
5. Living

A. 34215   **B.** 32451   **C.** 43521   **D.** 42315

Q.9

The total of ages of Amar, Akbar and Anthony is 80 years. What was the total of their ages three years ago?

A. 71 years   **B.** 72 years   **C.** 74 years   **D.** 77 years

Q.10 Four positions of the same dice are shown below, find the side opposite to the side with face 1?

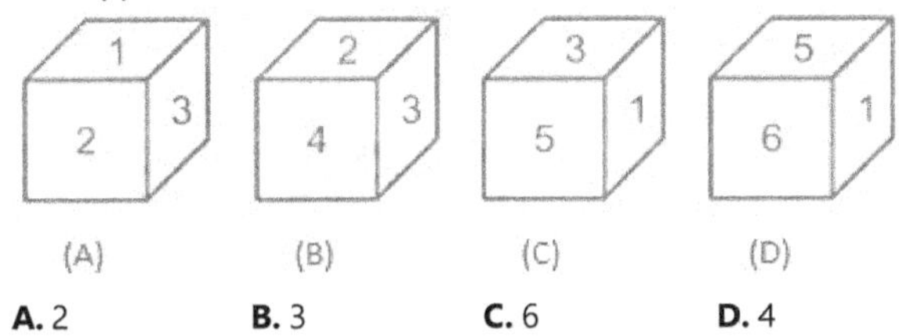

(A)   (B)   (C)   (D)

A. 2   **B.** 3   **C.** 6   **D.** 4

Q.11 Direction: Read the given statement(s) and conclusions carefully and select which of the conclusions logically follow(s) from the statement(s).

Statements:

All Sky are Clouds.

All Clouds are Rain.

Conclusions:

I. All Sky are Rain.

II. Some Rain are Sky.

A. Only I follows

B. Only II follows

C. Both I and II follows

D. Neither I nor II follows

Q.12 In a code language, INDICATOR is written as JOEJBCVQT. How will EMOTIONAL be written in that language?

[SSC Selection Post Phase IX, 2020]

A. FNAUJQPCN   **B.** FNPUHQPCN

C. GNPUHTRCM   **D.** FNPDKQPCN

Q.13 Select the correct option which is related to the third term in the same way as second term is related to the first:

KCA : HBE : : EBH : ?

[KVS Trained Graduate Teacher, 2018]

A. CBM   **B.** CGE   **C.** BCM   **D.** CBE

Q.14 Direction: A piece of paper is folded and cut as shown below in the question figures From the given answer figures, indicate how it will appear when opened:

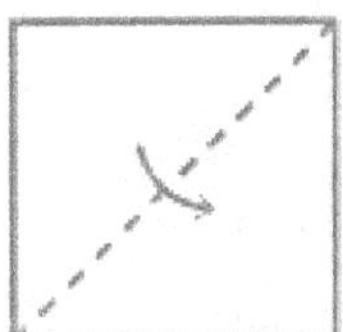 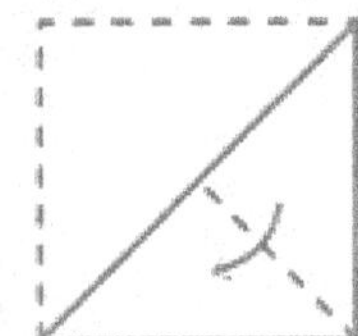 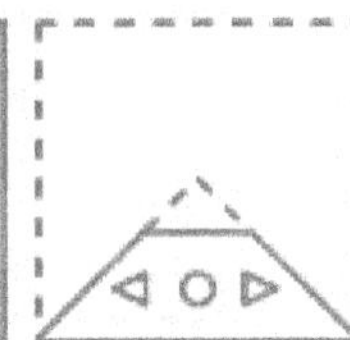

A.

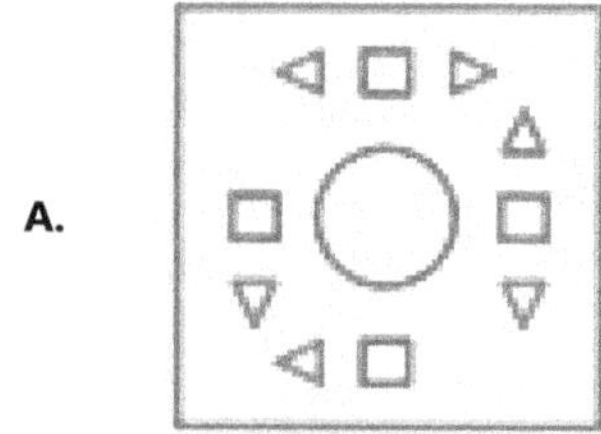

B.

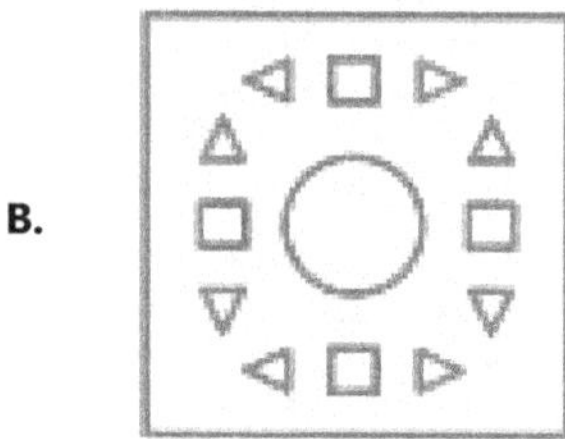

C.

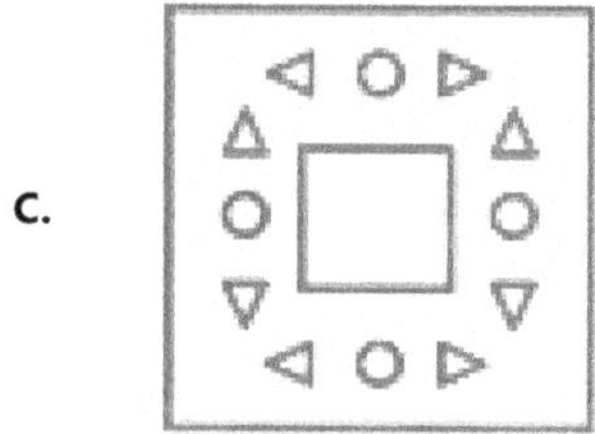

D.

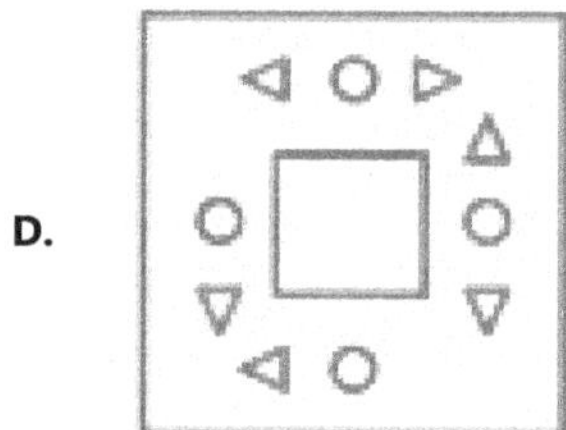

Q.15 What will come in place of the question mark '?' in the following question?

$$3140 - 55 \times 1422 \div 79 = ? \times 22 + 1428 \div 8.4$$

A. 90   **B.** 85   **C.** 80   **D.** 95

Q.16 Direction: Choose the odd one out of the given alternatives.

A. 22   **B.** 33   **C.** 44   **D.** 51

Q.17 Direction: Select the combination of letters that when sequentially placed in the gaps of the given letter series will complete the series.

AA _ AB _ ABC _ A _C_E

A. BCDBD   **B.** AABCD   **C.** BCCBD   **D.** BABCD

Q.18 A + B means A is the mother of B.

A > B means A is the sister of B.

A = B means A is the brother of B.

If C = K = M > T + Q, then how is C related to Q?

A. Maternal uncle   **B.** Paternal uncle

C. Son   **D.** Father

Q.19 Direction: In the following diagram, the square represents the male, the triangle represents the manager, and the circle represents the engineer. Which numbered section represents men who are managers but not engineers?

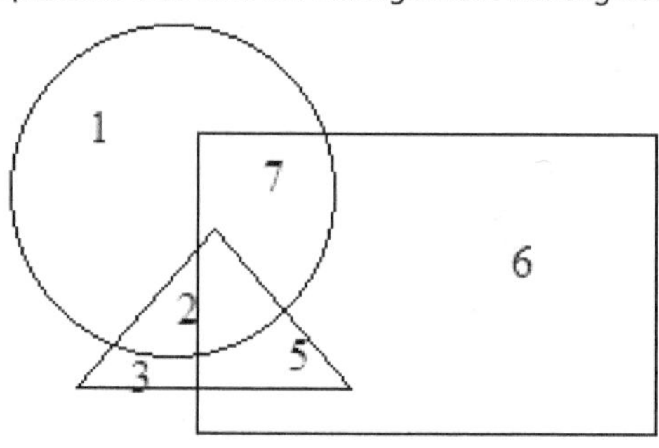

A. 5   **B.** 6   **C.** 2   **D.** 1

Q.20 Direction: In the following question, select the related Number/Numbers from the given alternatives.

4578 : 8 :: 289 : ?

A. 7   **B.** 8   **C.** 9   **D.** 10

General Knowledge and General Awareness

Q.21 Which of the following system is established on the basis of the direct election ?

[HSSC Canal Patwari, 2021]

A. Gram Panchayat   **B.** Block Committee

C. Zila Parishad   **D.** Both (B) and (C)

Q.22 In Panchayati Raj System, what does the word 'Raj' means ?

[HSSC Canal Patwari, 2021]

A. Rule   **B.** Review

C. Role   **D.** None of these

Q.23 Which organisation has partnered with NITI Aayog to use AI, IoT, Blockchain and Drones to support small and marginal farmers?

A. World Bank   **B.** WEF

C. IMF   **D.** ADB

Q.24 Which ship building company has been conferred with the Green Channel Certification by Ministry of Defence?

A. Goa Shipyard

B. Cochin Shipyard

C. Garden Reach Shipbuilders and Engineers

D. Mazagon Dock Shipbuilders

Q.25 Who was sworn in for a second term as president of Angola on 15 September 2022?

A. Jeremias Chitunda

B. Arlete Chimbinda

C. Abdelmadjid Tebboune

D. Joao Lourenco

Q.26 Name the operation launched by india to evacuate indian students from Ukraine?

A. Operation Maitri **B.** Operation Ganga
C. Operation Abhaya **D.** Operation Sahay

Q.27 Which among the following is a west flowing River?

A. Godavari **B.** Mahanadi
C. Cauvery **D.** Tapti

Q.28 Syed Mushtaq Ali Trophy is associated with which sport?

A. Hockey **B.** Cricket
C. Foot Ball **D.** Golf

Q.29 Kathak is the principal classical dance of:

A. South India **B.** Eastern India
C. Northern India **D.** Western India

Q.30 Researchers at which Institution has developed 'Fifth-generation (5G) microwave absorbers'?

A. IISc Bengaluru **B.** IIT Madras
C. Kerala University **D.** IIT Bombay

Q.31 What is the number of Schedules in Constitution of India?

A. 8 **B.** 10 **C.** 11 **D.** 12

Q.32 In which of the following Himalayan ranges is the Banihal Pass situated?

A. The great Himalayas
B. Pir Panjal
C. Ladakh
D. Zaskar

Q.33 Which of the following has started the revolt of 1857?

A. Zamindars **B.** Sepoys
C. Peasants **D.** Peasants

Q.34 Which of the following is not an Indus Valley Civilization site?

A. Kalibangan **B.** Ropar
C. Patliputra **D.** Lothal

Q.35 Which of the following is one of the holy books of Buddhism?

A. Tora **B.** The avesta
C. Kalpa Sutra **D.** Tripitaka

Q.36 A passenger in a moving bus is thrown forward when the bus suddenly stops. This is explained:

A. by Newton's first law
B. by Newton's second law
C. by Newton's third law
D. by the principle of conservation of momentum

Q.37 Per Capita Income of a country is obtained by dividing National Income by which of the following?

A. Total working population
B. Total population of the country
C. Area of the country
D. Volume of the capital used

Q.38 The most appropriate measure of a country's economic growth is.

A. GDP
B. NDP
C. Per capita real income
D. GNP

Q.39 Who presented the 5th National Award for Innovations and Good Practices in Educational Administration virtually in February 2022?

A. Jagannath Sarkar **B.** Nisith Pramanik
C. John Barla **D.** Dr Subhas Sarkar

Q.40 In which city of Haryana has the country's first 'Green Energy' plant been set up in 2022?

A. Rewari **B.** Karnal **C.** Kaithal **D.** Hisar

Elementary Mathematics

Q.41 The value of $\left(2.\overline{4} \times 0.\overline{6} \times 30 \times 0.1\overline{6}\right) \times [0.2\overline{7} \times \left(0.8\overline{3} \div 0.1\overline{6}\right)]$ is:

[SSC CGL, 2020]

A. $0.1\overline{1}$ **B.** $1.\overline{36}$ **C.** 11.3 **D.** $1.8\overline{14}$

Q.42 What is the value of $2^{2^{3}}$?

A. 256 **B.** 1024 **C.** 128 **D.** 64

Q.43 Which of the following fractions is greater than $\dfrac{3}{4}$ and less than $\dfrac{5}{6}$?

[HSSC Canal Patwari, 2021]

A. $\dfrac{1}{4}$ **B.** $\dfrac{2}{4}$ **C.** $\dfrac{4}{5}$ **D.** $\dfrac{8}{10}$

Q.44 When the price of sugar decreases by 10%, a man is able to buy 1 kg more for $Rs.270$. The original price of sugar per kg is-

A. $Rs.30$ **B.** $Rs.27$ **C.** $Rs.32$ **D.** $Rs.25$

Q.45 In what time will ₹ 1000 amount to ₹ 1331 at 20% per annum, compounded half-yearly?

A. $\dfrac{3}{2}$ years **B.** 2 years
C. 1 year **D.** $2\dfrac{1}{2}$ years

Q.46 The greatest number of four digit which is divisible by 15, 25, 40 and 75 is:

[Haryana Primary Teacher (PRT), 2021]

A. 9000 **B.** 9400 **C.** 9600 **D.** 9800

Q.47 A, B and C invested Rs. 5000, Rs. 7000 and Rs. 6000 respectively in a business. If at the end of two years, they got a profit of Rs. 10800. The share of B in this total profit is:

A. Rs. 4500 **B.** Rs. 4200 **C.** Rs. 1800 **D.** Rs. 1500

Q.48 The average of four consecutive even numbers is 29. Find the largest of these numbers.

A. 42   **B.** 28   **C.** 32   **D.** 36

Q.49 The length of sides of a triangle are in the ratio $3:4:5$ and its perimeter is 144 cm. The area of a triangle is:

[Joint Entrance Examination (Polytechnic), 2019]

A. 764 cm²   **B.** 684 cm²   **C.** 864 cm²   **D.** 664 cm²

Q.50 A train is moving at a speed of 72 km/h. If the length of the train is 220 meters, then how long will it take to cross the 330 metre long platform?

[UP Police Sub Inspector, 2017]

A. 48.5 seconds   **B.** 11 seconds
C. 16.5 seconds   **D.** 27.5 seconds

Q.51 6 women and 8 men can complete a task in 10 days where a woman is twice efficient as a man. Find the time taken by 40 men to complete the same task.

A. 15 days   **B.** 20 days   **C.** 5 days   **D.** 10 days

Q.52 12 men work 8 hours per day and require 10 days to build a wall. If 8 men are available, how many hours per day must they work to finish the work in 8 days?

[Indian Military Academy (IMA), 2018]

A. 10 hours   **B.** 12 hours
C. 15 hours   **D.** 18 hours

Q.53 The MRP of the I-phone is Rs $80,000$, but it is available at Rs $60,000$. Find the rate of discount.

A. 10%   **B.** 15%   **C.** 20%   **D.** 25%

Q.54 The average of 45 numbers is 150. Later it is found that a number 46 is wrongly written as 91, then find the correct average.

A. 151   **B.** 147   **C.** 149   **D.** 153

Q.55 If a certain sum of money becomes 9 times itself in 2 years. Find the rate of compound interest.

A. 50%   **B.** 100%   **C.** 200%   **D.** 80%

Q.56 The highest four-digit number which is divisible by each of the numbers 16, 36, 45, 48 is:

[Indian Military Academy (IMA), 2018]

A. 9180   **B.** 9360   **C.** 9630   **D.** 9840

Q.57 The curved surface area of a right circular cone of radius 28 cm is 4664 cm2. What is the slant height of the cone?(Use $\pi = \dfrac{22}{7}$)

A. 53 cm   **B.** 56 cm   **C.** 64 cm   **D.** 48 cm

Q.58 The average speed of a car which covers half the distance with a speed of 20 km/hr and the other half with a speed of 30 km/hr, will be:

A. 50 km/hr   **B.** 25 km/hr   **C.** 26 km/hr   **D.** 24 km/hr

Q.59 Direction: What will come in the place of the question mark '?' in the following question?

22% of 4350 + 47.25 × 4 + 17 × 51 − 1013 = ?

A. 1005   **B.** 900   **C.** 1200   **D.** 1000

Q.60 If the number 22144 is divided in the ratio $\dfrac{1}{3}:\dfrac{3}{5}:\dfrac{5}{7}$, the difference between the largest and smallest part is:

A. 3150   **B.** 4530   **C.** 6210   **D.** 5120

English

Ques (61-62):Direction: In the following question, some parts of the sentence may have errors. Find out which part of the sentence has an error and select the appropriate option. If a sentence is free from error, select 'No Error'.

Q.61 The important point is that (1)/ humans does not observe (2)/ scenes passively or neutrally. (3)/ No error (4)

A. 1   **B.** 2   **C.** 3   **D.** 4

Q.62 It emerge from within constraint like a breath, (1)/ it is about breath, (2)/ it is about breathing. (3)/ No error (4)

A. 1   **B.** 2   **C.** 3   **D.** 4

Q.63 Direction: In the following question, the sentence is given with a blank to be filled in with an appropriate word. Select the correct alternative out of the four and indicate it by selecting the appropriate option.

I am awful ______ picking vegetables.

A. for   **B.** at   **C.** of   **D.** as

Q.64 Direction: Complete the given sentence using the appropriate pronoun from the following options:

This is the boy ______ scored the highest marks.

[Allahabad High Court Review Officer (RO), 2019]

A. it   **B.** whose   **C.** which   **D.** who

Q.65 Direction: Fill in the blank with the most appropriate option as given:

Giving money to the poor is a/an ______ act of service to the poor.

[Allahabad High Court Review Officer (RO), 2019]

A. benevolent   **B.** bemused
C. atrocious   **D.** bad

Ques (66-67):Direction: In the following question, out of the four alternatives, select the word similar in meaning to the given word.

Q.66 Jeer
A. Compliment   **B.** Hoot
C. Flatter   **D.** Praise

Q.67 Bombastic
A. Eloquent   **B.** Ornate
C. Glorious   **D.** Grandiloquent

Q.68 Direction: In the following question, four alternatives are given for the meaning of the given sentence. Choose the Idiom/Phrase which best expresses the meaning of the given sentence.

Math is the only subject that seems **extremely difficult for me to understand**.

A. A piece of cake   **B.** All greek to me

C. Ducks and drakes **D.** Ace in the hole

Q.69 Direction: In the following question, four alternatives are given for the meaning of the given Idiom/Phrase. Choose the alternative which best expresses the meaning of the Idiom/Phrase.

In the offing

A. In danger **B.** Appear soon
C. Side by side **D.** Worrisome

Ques (70-71):Direction: Select the word which means the same as a group of words given.

Q.70 A place where government records are kept.

A. Asylum **B.** Apiary
C. Archives **D.** Aquarium

Q.71 The supervising person during an examination.

A. Invigilator **B.** Calligrapher
C. Introvert **D.** Radio Jockey

Ques (72-73):Direction: In the following question, a word has been written in four different ways out of which only one is correctly spelled.

Q.72 Select the correctly spelled word.

A. Apalling **B.** Appalling
C. Appaling **D.** Aapaling

Q.73 Select the correctly spelled word.

A. Ocasion **B.** Ocassion
C. Occassion **D.** Occasion

Ques (74-75):Direction: In the given question, a part of the sentence is made bold. Below are given alternatives to the bold part at (A), (B), and (C) which may improve the sentence. Choose the correct alternative. In case no replacement is needed, mark (D) as your answer.

Q.74 These hand woven shawls **are much in demand** in many European countries.

A. Were much demand
B. Are lots of demand
C. Demanded much
D. No replacement required

Q.75 The dacoits and the police **was firing at each other** when one bullet hit the young man.

A. Were firing at each other
B. Were firing against each other
C. Was firing against each other
D. No replacement required

Q.76 Direction: In the given question, a part of the sentence is made bold. Below are given alternatives to the bold part at (A), (B), and (C) which may improve the sentence. Choose the correct alternative. In case no replacement is needed, mark (D) as your answer.

Shivani **was annoyed at the** childish behaviour of her friends who were behaving like lunatics in the mall.

A. Was annoyed with the
B. Was annoyed in the

C. Was annoyed with respect to the
D. No replacement required

Ques (77-80):Direction: In the following passage, some words have been deleted. Fill in the blanks with the help of the alternatives given. Select the most appropriate option for each blank.

Ram Singh whistled cheerfully as he pushed his bicycle up the hill towards old Mrs. Gupta's house. His work for the (1)_____was almost finished (2)_____his bag, which was usually (3)_____ when he started from the post office (4)_____now become empty except for the letter that he had to deliver Mrs.Gupta.

Q.77 Select the most appropriate option to fill in blank no. (1).
[SSC Sub Inspector (CPO), 2019]

A. month **B.** day **C.** year **D.** week

Q.78 Select the most appropriate option to fill in blank no. (2).
[SSC Sub Inspector (CPO), 2019]

A. although **B.** but **C.** and **D.** unless

Q.79 Select the most appropriate option to fill in blank no. (3).
[SSC Sub Inspector (CPO), 2019]

A. large **B.** dirty **C.** torn **D.** heavy

Q.80 Select the most appropriate option to fill in blank no. (4).
[SSC Sub Inspector (CPO), 2019]

A. had **B.** have **C.** were **D.** has

// Smart Answer Sheet //

Correct — Percentage of students who answered correctly.　　**Skipped** — Percentage of students who skipped.

Q.	Ans.	Correct / Skipped	Q.	Ans.	Correct / Skipped	Q.	Ans.	Correct / Skipped	Q.	Ans.	Correct / Skipped	Q.	Ans.	Correct / Skipped
1	B	28.78 % / 69.71 %	17	A	65.71 % / 33.39 %	33	B	52.96 % / 37.58 %	49	C	80.55 % / 16.91 %	65	A	56.92 % / 38.75 %
2	A	82.62 % / 11.17 %	18	A	58.25 % / 38.04 %	34	C	50.74 % / 40.4 %	50	D	80.1 % / 16.89 %	66	B	61.67 % / 33.17 %
3	D	83.28 % / 16.2 %	19	A	49.89 % / 34.68 %	35	D	79.05 % / 15.31 %	51	C	88.04 % / 10.34 %	67	D	42.73 % / 40.26 %
4	D	80.54 % / 13.11 %	20	C	68.46 % / 31.23 %	36	A	77.87 % / 20.29 %	52	C	86.89 % / 11.36 %	68	B	62.11 % / 33.05 %
5	A	79.48 % / 13.45 %	21	A	49.72 % / 44.84 %	37	B	48.09 % / 40.05 %	53	D	52.86 % / 34.38 %	69	B	12.23 % / 75.05 %
6	A	41.75 % / 49.64 %	22	A	53.43 % / 42.61 %	38	C	44.6 % / 43.67 %	54	C	57.7 % / 34.24 %	70	C	64.87 % / 32.49 %
7	B	85.05 % / 14.69 %	23	B	47.39 % / 46.81 %	39	D	42.97 % / 56.51 %	55	C	63.48 % / 32.89 %	71	A	54.22 % / 41.54 %
8	D	43.43 % / 38.58 %	24	C	41.25 % / 42.82 %	40	A	56.69 % / 34.7 %	56	B	51.38 % / 48.37 %	72	B	85.17 % / 13.13 %
9	A	43.44 % / 54.07 %	25	D	55.3 % / 39.27 %	41	C	80.73 % / 14.15 %	57	A	58.76 % / 30.58 %	73	D	83.21 % / 12.05 %
10	D	81.82 % / 16.81 %	26	B	51.41 % / 47.24 %	42	A	76.3 % / 20.45 %	58	D	43.57 % / 39.97 %	74	D	53.83 % / 40.31 %
11	C	76.92 % / 15.99 %	27	D	84.61 % / 11.39 %	43	C	43.46 % / 41.08 %	59	D	62.25 % / 34.69 %	75	A	46.91 % / 35.76 %
12	B	81.32 % / 15.81 %	28	B	22.99 % / 74.0 %	44	A	20.96 % / 75.21 %	60	D	45.19 % / 52.82 %	76	D	68.26 % / 30.76 %
13	B	76.66 % / 11.07 %	29	C	61.52 % / 32.61 %	45	A	81.36 % / 17.87 %	61	B	44.87 % / 53.21 %	77	B	40.4 % / 54.53 %
14	C	64.74 % / 34.32 %	30	C	69.47 % / 30.51 %	46	C	87.8 % / 10.46 %	62	A	50.99 % / 46.01 %	78	C	69.1 % / 30.05 %
15	A	49.52 % / 37.96 %	31	D	49.55 % / 42.47 %	47	B	57.51 % / 31.13 %	63	B	45.8 % / 40.73 %	79	D	50.12 % / 35.65 %
16	D	69.33 % / 30.06 %	32	B	47.61 % / 33.77 %	48	C	89.05 % / 10.82 %	64	D	77.99 % / 18.17 %	80	A	45.18 % / 36.61 %

//Hints and Solutions//

1. The pattern followed in (246, 257, 358)

As in 246 → 2 + 4 + 6 = 12

257 → 2 + 5 + 7 = 14

358 → 3 + 5 + 8 = 16

Now we will check for given sets,

(233, 343, 345)

233 → 2 + 3 + 3 = 8

343 → 3 + 4 + 3 = 10

345 → 3 + 4 + 5 = 12

(273, 365, 367)

273 → 2 + 7 + 3 = 12

365 → 3 + 6 + 5 = 14

367 → 3 + 6 + 7 = 16

(143, 226, 237)

143 → 1 + 4 + 3 = 8

226 → 2 + 2 + 6 = 10

237 → 2 + 3 + 7 = 12

(145, 235, 325)

145 → 1 + 4 + 5 = 10

235 → 2 + 3 + 5 =10

325 → 3 + 2 + 4 = 9

Thus (273, 365, 367) is the answer.

Hence, the correct option is (B).

2. 1. Eight friends A, B, C, D, E, F, G and H are sitting around circular table facing each other for a lunch.

2. A is opposite F and third to the right of B.

3. G is between F and D.

4. H is to the left of D.

5. E is between C and A.

The final arrangement will be as shown below:

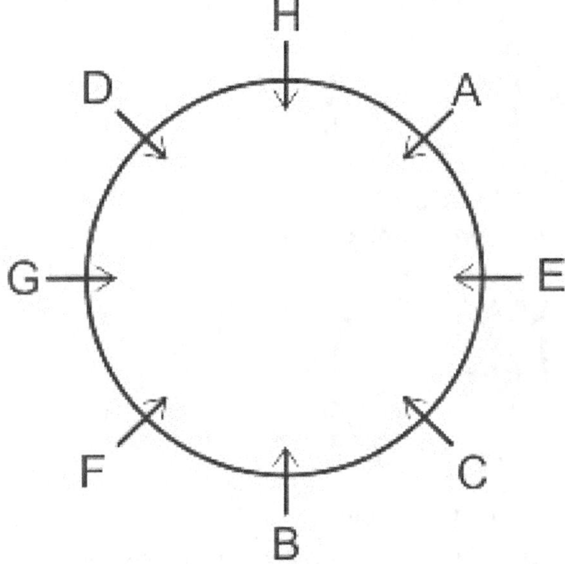

So, 'D' is sitting opposite C.

Hence, the correct option is (A).

3. Given series is: $34, 42, 50, 56, 62, 66, ?$

The pattern followed here is:

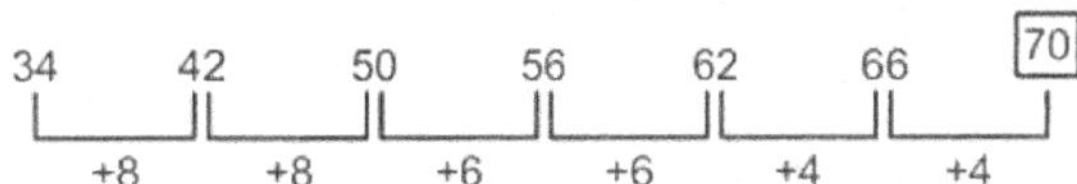

Hence, the correct option is (D).

4. On close observation, we find that the question figure is embedded in option (D) as shown below:

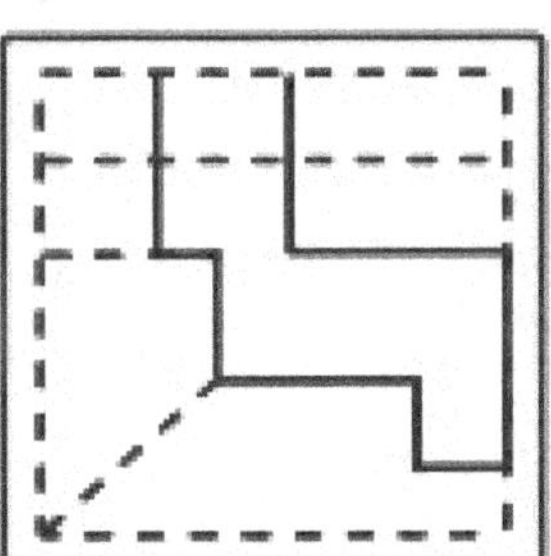

Hence, the correct option is (D).

5. The mirror image will be as follows:

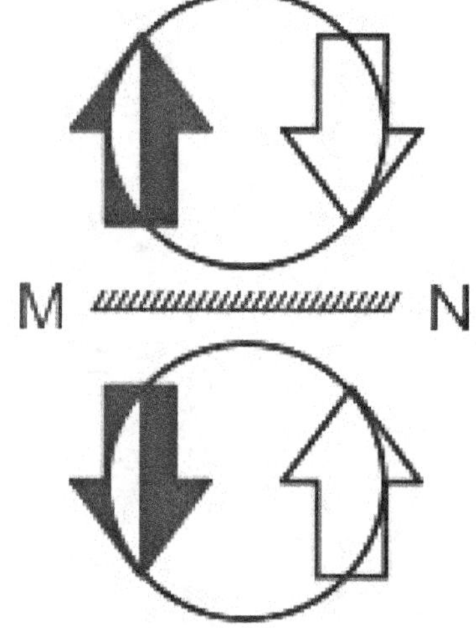

Hence, the correct option is (A).

6. In each figure, the shaded part is moving two parts in a clockwise direction.

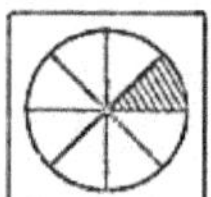 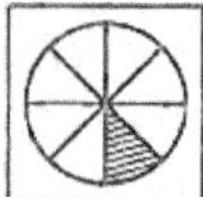 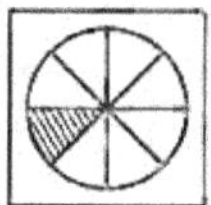 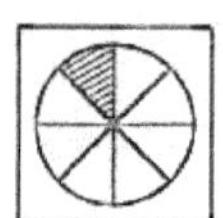 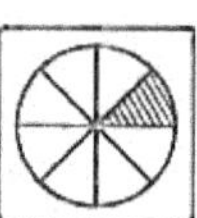

Hence, the correct option is (A).

7. The pattern is:

$$\Rightarrow 20 = 8 \times 2 + 4$$

$$\Rightarrow 15 = 3 \times 2 + 9$$

The number on the blank space,

$$\Rightarrow 6 \times 2 + 6 = 18$$

Hence, the correct option is (B).

8. The correct dictionary order of the words is-

4. Literacy

2. Litter

3. Little

1. Live

5. Living

Hence, the correct option is (D).

9. Given:

The total of ages of Amar, Akbar and Anthony is 80 years.

Required sum = (80 - 3 ✕ 3) years

= (80 - 9) years

= 71 years

Hence, the correct option is (A).

10. Considering the Dice 'A' and 'D', clockwise pair of numbers are

1 3 2

1 6 5

Number 4 is missing, therefore 4 will be the opposite number of 1.

Hence, the correct option is (D).

11. The least possible Venn Diagram for the given statements will be as follows:

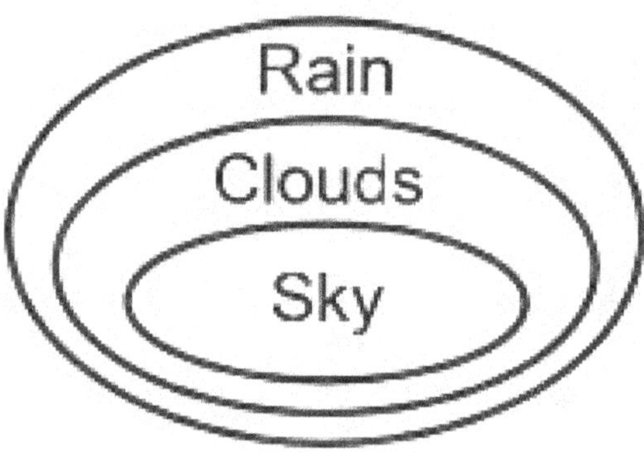

I. All Sky are Rain → True (As all sky are clouds and all clouds are rain. Thus, All sky are rain)

II. Some Rain are Sky → True.

So, Both I and II follows.

Hence, the correct option is (C).

12. In a code language, INDICATOR is written as JOEJBCVQT.

First four letter of the word take next letter of the word, middle letter of the word take previous letter of the word and last four word letter of the word take add 2 in each letter of the word.

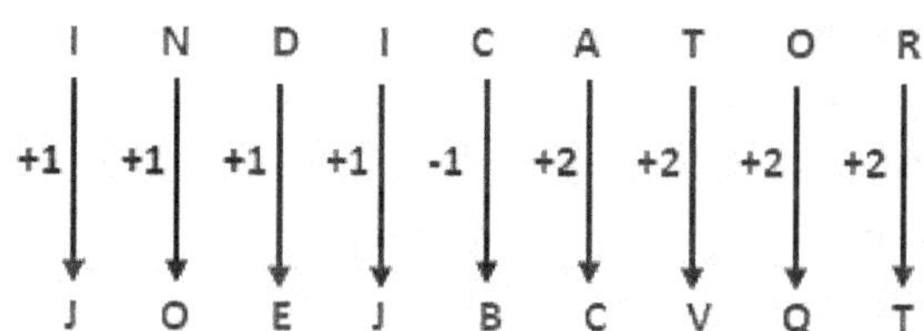

Similarly, EMOTIONAL be written as:

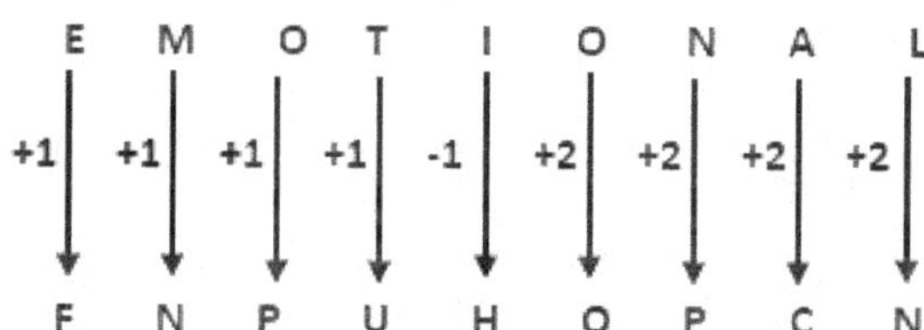

EMOTIONAL is written as FNPUHQPCN.

Hence, the correct option is (B).

13. KCA ⇒ 11 + 3 + 1 = 15

HBE ⇒ 8 + 2 + 5 = 15

Similarly,

EBH ⇒ 5 + 2 + 8 = 15

CGE ⇒ 3 + 7 + 5 = 15

Hence, the correct option is (B).

14.

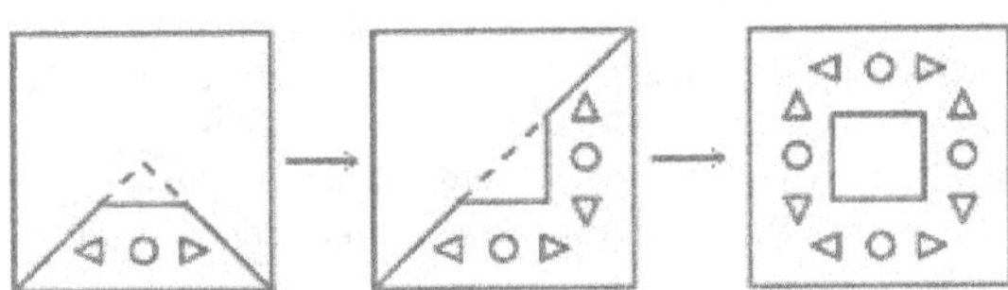

Hence, the correct option is (C).

15. The given expression is, $3140 - 55 \times 1422 \div 79 = ? \times 22 + 1428 \div 8.4 = ?$

Applying the BODMAS Rule;

$$\Rightarrow 3140 - 55 \times 18 = 22 \times ? + 170$$

$$\Rightarrow 3140 - 990 = 22 \times ? + 170$$

$$\Rightarrow 22 \times ? = 1980$$

$$\Rightarrow ? = 90$$

Hence, the correct option is (A).

16. 22, 33, 44 all are multiples of 11 whereas 51 is not.

Therefore, '51' is the odd one out.

Hence, the correct option is (D).

17. Given: AA _ AB _ ABC _ A _C_E

By checking options and substituting accordingly.

Option (A) BCDBD → A - AB - ABC - ABCD - ABCDE

Option (B) AABCD → A - AA - ABA - ABCB - ACCDE

Option (C) BCCBD → A - AB - ABC - ABCC - ABCDE

Option (D) BABCD → A - AB - ABA - ABCB - ACCDE

So, 'BCDBD' is the correct answer.

Hence, the correct option is (A).

18. A + B means A is the mother of B.

A > B means A is the sister of B.

A = B means A is the brother of B.

If C = K = M > T + Q, then:

Symbol in Diagram	Meaning
○	Female
□	Male
=	Married Couple
—	Siblings
|	Difference of A Generation

C is the maternal uncle of Q.

Hence, the correct option is (A).

19. The common area for the square and triangle represents male managers who are not engineers. The required field number is 5.

Hence, the correct option is (A).

20. The logic is:

4578 = 4 + 5 + 7 + 8 = 24 = 2 × 4 = 8

Then we get,

289 = 2 + 8 + 9 = 19 = 1 × 9 = 9

Therefore, the correct answer is 9.

Hence, the correct option is (C).

21. The Gram Panchayat is established on the basis of direct election.

Gram Panchayat is a basic village governing institute in Indian villages.

The panchayat is chaired by the president of the village, known as a Sarpanch.

Hence, the correct option is (A).

22. In Panchayati Raj System, the word raj means "rule" and panchayat means "assembly" (ayat) of five (panch).

Panchayati Raj system is a system of rural local self-government.

73rd Constitutional Amendment Act, 1992 is related to the Panchayati Raj system.

Hence, the correct option is (A).

23. The World Economic Forum (WEF) has partnered with Government's think-tank Niti Aayog to use emerging technologies such as artificial intelligence (AI), Internet of Things (IoT), blockchain and drones, to support small and marginal farmers.

WEF had established a 'Centre for the Fourth Industrial Revolution' (C4IR) in India, to implement various innovative projects across the country.

Hence, the correct option is (B).

24. Garden Reach Shipbuilders and Engineers Ltd (GRSE), has been conferred with the coveted Green Channel Certification by Ministry of Defence.

It is one of the leading Public Sector Undertaking and Mini-Ratna Category 1 Shipyard. The certification was conferred for supply of Portable Steel Bridges (Bailey Type) of various configurations to Indian Army.

Hence, the correct option is (C).

25. Joao Lourenco was sworn in for a second term as president of Angola on 15 Sept 2022.

Lourenco, 68, was sworn in alongside Esperanca da Costa, Angola's first female vice president in the capital, Luanda. The ruling MPLA party garnered 51% of the votes and 124 seats in the 220-member parliament in the Aug 24 election. Angola is a country located on the west coast of Southern Africa.

Hence, the correct option is (D).

26. Operation Ganga was an evacuation operation by the Government of India to evacuate the Indian citizens amidst the 2022 Russian invasion of Ukraine, who had crossed over to neighboring countries.

Hence, the correct option is (B).

27. The Tapi is a river of central India. It is one of the major rivers of peninsular India with a length of around 724 km; it runs from east to west. Tapi river rises near Multai in the Betul district of Madhya Pradesh at an elevation of about 752 m and flows for about 724 km before outfalling into the Arabian Sea through the Gulf of Cambay.

Hence, the correct option is (D).

28. The Syed Mushtaq Ali trophy is an Indian domestic cricket championship organized by the Board of Control for Cricket in India (BCCI). The championship is named after Syed Mushtaq Ali, the famous Indian cricketer.

Hence, the correct option is (B).

29. Kathak is the major classical dance form of northern India. The word kathak means "to tell a story". It is derived from the dance dramas of ancient India. When the patronage shifted from the temples to the royal court, there was a change in the overall emphasis.

Hence, the correct option is (C).

30. A Professor and Research Scholar Department of Physics at Kerala University, have developed fifth-generation (5G) microwave absorbers, which can be used as an effective shield against electromagnetic radiation

Electromagnetic interference (EMI) is known to be dangerous to the health of living organisms. It also affects the high-end electronic devices. They used new shielding material, 'mayenite electride' for microwave absorption in high frequency region.

Hence, the correct option is (C).

31. The number of Schedules in Constitution of India is 12. One of the first mentions of Schedules was made in the Government of India Act, 1935 where it included 10 Schedules. Later, when the Indian Constitution was adopted in 1949, it consisted of 8 Schedules.

Hence, the correct option is (D).

32. The Banihal Pass is situated in Pir Panjal Himalayan Range.

The Pir Panjal Range is a range of Inner Himalayan mountains stretching from east-southeast (ESE) to west-northwest (WNW) through Himachal Pradesh, the Indian state, and Jammu and Kashmir, Indian Union Territory. Pir Panjal is the greatest range of the Lesser Himalayas.

Hence, the correct option is (B).

33. The revolt of 1857 was the conscious beginning of the Independence struggle against the colonial tyranny of the British. The revolt began on May 10, 1857, at Meerut as a sepoy mutiny. It was initiated by sepoys in the Bengal Presidency against the British officers.

Hence, the correct option is (B).

34. Patliputra is not an Indus Valley Civilization site.

The Indus Valley Civilization covered parts of Sind, Baluchistan, Afganistan, West Punjab, Gujarat, Uttar Pradesh, Haryana, Rajasthan, Jammu and Kashmir, Punjab. The sites of Indus civilization are Harappa, Mohenjo - Daro, Kalibangan, Lothal, Rangpur, Surkotada, Malavan, Chanhudaro, Balakot, Ropar, Banawali, and Dholavira.

Hence, the correct option is (C).

35. Tripitaka is one of the holy books of Buddhism.

There are three types of Tripitakas:

- Vinaya Pitaka rules of monastic discipline for monks.
- The Sutta Pitaka is a collection of Buddha's teachings.
- The Abhidhamma Pitaka is a vision of the Buddha's teachings.

Hence, the correct option is (D).

36. Newton's laws of motion-

- Newton's first law states that, if a body is at rest or moving at a constant speed in a straight line, it will remain at rest or keep moving in a straight line at constant speed unless it is acted upon by force.

  - This postulate is known as the law of inertia. The law of inertia was first formulated by Galileo Galilei for horizontal motion on Earth and was later generalized by René Descartes.

  - Before Galileo, it had been thought that all horizontal motion required a direct cause. Still, Galileo deduced from his experiments that a body in motion would remain in motion unless a force (such as friction) caused it to come to rest.

Hence, the correct option is (A).

37. Per capita income or average income measures the average income earned per person in a given area in a specified year. It is calculated by dividing the area's total income by its total population.

Hence, the correct option is (B).

38. The most appropriate measure of a country's economic growth is its per capita real income. Per capita income is average income, a measure of the wealth of the population of a nation. It is used to measure a country's standard of living thus a better indicator of economic growth.

Hence, the correct option is (C).

39. Minister for State for Education Dr Subhas Sarkar presented the 5th National Award for Innovations and Good Practices in Educational Administration virtually on 10 February 2022.

More than hundred officers received Award or Certificate of Appreciation for 2022. The National Institute of Educational Planning and Administration has instituted the National Award.

Hence, the correct option is (D).

40. The country's first green power plant to generate electricity from stubble has been set up in Khursaidnagar village of Rewari district.

- The green energy plant has generated 48,000 units of power from 600 quintal stubble in 24 hours without pollution.

- The plant has been set up by the Haryana Renewable Energy Development Agency (HREDA) along with a private sector company.

- The plant is working on a biomass gas method instead of a boiler, thus, there is no possibility of polluting the environment.

Hence, the correct option is (A).

41. Given:

$$\left(2.\overline{4} \times 0.\overline{6} \times 30 \times 0.1\overline{6}\right) \times [0.2\overline{7} \times \left(0.8\overline{3} \div 0.1\overline{6}\right)]$$

Using the BODMAS rule to solve the above expression, we get

$$= \left(\frac{22}{9} \times \frac{2}{3} \times 30 \times \frac{1}{6}\right) \times \left[\frac{5}{18} \times \left(\frac{5}{6} \div \frac{1}{6}\right)\right]$$

$$= \left(\frac{22}{9} \times \frac{2}{3} \times 30 \times \frac{1}{6}\right) \times \left[\frac{5}{18} \times \left(\frac{5}{6} \times 6\right)\right]$$

$$= \left(\frac{22}{9} \times \frac{2}{3} \times 30 \times \frac{1}{6}\right) \times \left[\frac{25}{18}\right]$$

$$= \left(\frac{22}{9} \times 10 \times \frac{1}{3}\right) \times \frac{25}{18}$$

$$= \frac{22}{9} \times 5 \times \frac{1}{3} \times \frac{25}{9}$$

$$= \left(\frac{2750}{243}\right)$$

$$= 11.31$$

$\therefore$ the value of $\left(2.\overline{4} \times 0.\overline{6} \times 30 \times 0.1\overline{6}\right) \times [0.2\overline{7} \times \left(0.8\overline{3} \div 0.1\overline{6}\right)]$ is 11.31.

Hence, the correct option is (C).

42. $\Rightarrow 2^{2^3}$

$\Rightarrow 2^8$

$\Rightarrow 256$

Hence, the correct option is (A).

43. $\frac{3}{4} = 0.75$

$\frac{5}{6} = 0.833$

$\frac{1}{2} = 0.5$

$\frac{2}{3} = 0.66$

$\frac{4}{5} = 0.8$

$\frac{9}{10} = 0.9$

Clearly, 0.8 lies between 0.75 and 0.833.

$\therefore \frac{4}{5}$ lies between $\frac{3}{4}$ and $\frac{5}{6}$.

Hence, the correct option is (C).

44. Let the original price of sugar per kg be $Rs.\,A$.

Quantity of sugar purchased in $Rs.\,270 = \frac{270}{A}$ kg

According to the question,

The price of sugar decreases by 10%,

New price of sugar $= A - (10\% \times A)$

$$= A - \frac{A}{10}$$

$$= Rs.\frac{9A}{10}$$

New quantity of sugar purchased in $Rs.\,270 = \dfrac{270}{\frac{9A}{10}} = \dfrac{300}{A}$ kg

A man is able to buy 1 kg more for $Rs.\,270$.

$$\Rightarrow \frac{300}{A} - \frac{270}{A} = 1$$

$$\Rightarrow \frac{30}{A} = 1$$

$$\Rightarrow A = Rs.\,30$$

Original price of sugar per kg $= Rs.\,30$

Hence, the correct option is (A).

45. Let the required time $= t$ years

Interest is compounded half-yearly

$t = 2t$ half years and rate $= \dfrac{20}{2} = 10\%$

We know that:

$$\because A = P\left(1 + \frac{r}{100}\right)^{t}$$

$$\therefore 1000\left(1 + \frac{10}{100}\right)^{2t} = 1331$$

$$\Rightarrow \left(\frac{11}{10}\right)^{2t} = \frac{1331}{1000}$$

$$\Rightarrow \left(\frac{11}{10}\right)^{2t} = \left(\frac{11}{10}\right)^{3}$$

$$\Rightarrow 2t = 3$$

$$\therefore t = \frac{3}{2}\text{ years}$$

Hence, the correct option is (A).

46. The greatest number of four-digit is 9999.

L.C.M. of 15, 25, 40 and 75 is 600.

On dividing 9999 by 600, we get the remainder of 399.

∴ Required number = (9999 - 399) = 9600

Hence, the correct option is (C).

47. Given:

A invested = Rs. 5000

B invested = Rs. 7000

C invested = Rs. 6000

We know that,

Profit = Amount invested × Time

Ratio of shares of A, B and C = Ratio of their investments for 2 years

= [(5000×2) : (7000×2) : (6000×2)]

= [10000 : 14000 : 12000] = 5 : 7 : 6

Net profit earned = Rs. 10800

∴ B's share = $\dfrac{7}{18}$ × 10800 = Rs. 4200

Hence, the correct option is (B).

48. Let the four consecutive even numbers is $x, x+2, x+4$ and $x+6$.

Average of even numbers $= 29$

We know that:

$$\text{Average of even numbers} = \frac{\text{Sum of Even Numbers}}{\text{Total Number}}$$

$$29 = \frac{x+x+2+x+4+x+6}{4}$$

$$29 = \frac{4x+12}{4}$$

$$29 = x + 3$$

$$x = 26$$

Therefore, the largest number is $= x + 6 = 26 + 6 = 32$.

Hence, the correct option is (C).

49. Let Sides $= 3x, 4x$ and 5x

Then, $3x + 4x + 5x = 144$ cm

$$12x = 144$$

$$\Rightarrow x = 12$$

Area of triangle

$$= \frac{1}{2} \times 4x \times 3x$$

$$= \frac{1}{2} \times 12x^{2}$$

$$= \frac{1}{2} \times 12 \times 12 \times 12$$

$$= 144 \times 6$$

$$= 864 \text{ cm}^{2}$$

Hence, the correct option is (C).

50. Given:

Speed of train = 72 km/h

Length of train = 220 metre

Length of platform = 330 metre

Formula used: Speed $= \dfrac{Distance}{Time}$

Speed (in m/s) = Speed (in km/h) × $\left(\dfrac{5}{18}\right)$

Speed = 72 × $\left(\dfrac{5}{18}\right)$ = 4 × 5 = 20 m/s

Total distance to travel = 220 + 330 = 550 m

Time taken to cover the distance = $\dfrac{Distance}{Speed}$

$\Rightarrow \dfrac{550}{20}$ = 27.5 seconds

∴ The train takes 27.5 seconds to cross the 330 m long platform.

Hence, the correct option is (D).

51. Given:

6 women and 8 men can complete a task in 10 days

A woman is twice efficient as a man: $\dfrac{W}{M} = \dfrac{2}{1}$

Formula used:

M_1 × Eff_1 × D_1 = M_2 × Eff_2 × D_2, where M = number of workers, D = number of days and Eff. = efficiency of the worker

Let 'D' be the time taken by 40 men to complete the same task.

(6 × 2 + 8 × 1) × 10 = (40 × 1) × D

$\Rightarrow$ D = $\dfrac{200}{40}$ = 5 days

∴ Time taken by 40 men to complete the same task is 5 days.

Hence, the correct option is (C).

52. 12 men build a wall in 10 days working for 8 hours per day

Total no. of hours 12 men took = 10 × 8 = 80 hours

No. of hours 1 man will take = 12 × 80 = 960 hours

No. of hours 8 men will take = $\dfrac{960}{8}$ = 120 hours

But, 8 men have only 8 days to finish the work,

∴ No. of hours per day 8 men must work = $\dfrac{120}{8}$ = 15 hours

Hence, the correct option is (C).

53. Discount = Marked price − Selling price

$= 80,000 - 60,000$

$= 20,000$

Therefore, Rate of discount will be,

Discount $\% = \dfrac{Discount}{Marked\ Price} \times 100$

$= \dfrac{20000}{80000} \times 100$

$= 25\%$

Hence, the correct option is (D).

54. Given,

The average of 45 data is 150.

46 is wrongly written as 91

As we know,

Average $= \dfrac{\text{Sum of total observations}}{\text{Total number of observations}}$

The total sum of all 45 number $= 150 \times 45 = 6750$

Now, 46 is wrongly written as 91,

The correct sum of data $= 6750 - (91 - 46) = 6705$

Then, correct average of the data $= \dfrac{6705}{45} = 149$

∴ The correct average is 149.

Hence, the correct option is (C).

55. Given:

The sum becomes 9 times in 2 years.

Let P be the principal.

∴ $A = 9P$

As we know,

$$A = P\left(1 + \dfrac{r}{100}\right)^t$$

$$\therefore 9P = P\left(1 + \dfrac{r}{100}\right)^2$$

$$\Rightarrow 9 = \left(1 + \dfrac{r}{100}\right)^2$$

$$\Rightarrow \sqrt{9} = 1 + \dfrac{r}{100}$$

$$\Rightarrow 3 = 1 + \dfrac{r}{100}$$

$$\Rightarrow 3 - 1 = \dfrac{r}{100}$$

$$\Rightarrow 2 = \dfrac{r}{100}$$

$$\Rightarrow r = 200\%$$

∴ The rate of interest is 200%.

Hence, the correct option is (C).

56. We can write,

$\Rightarrow$ 16 = 2⁴

$\Rightarrow$ 36 = 2² × 3²

$\Rightarrow$ 45 = 3² × 5

$\Rightarrow$ 48 = 2⁴ × 3

LCM of the numbers = Product of highest powers of prime factors = 2⁴ × 3² × 5 = 720

Now, Highest 4-digit number = 9999

On dividing 9999 by 720, remainder = 639

∴ Required number = 9999 - 639 = 9360

Hence, the correct option is (B).

57. Given:

Curved surface area of a cone $= 4664$ cm2

Radius $= 28$ cm

Formula:

Curved surface area of cone $= \pi r l$ where $l =$ slant height

Curved surface area $= \pi r l = 4664$

$\Rightarrow \dfrac{22}{7} \times 28 \times l = 4664$

$\Rightarrow l = 53$ cm

∴ Slant height i.e. l is 53 cm.

Hence, the correct option is (A).

58. Formula:

Average speed $=$ Total distance covered $\div$ Total time

Let the total distance be 240 km

Time for which speed is 20 km/hr $= \dfrac{120}{20} = 6$ hrs

Time for which speed is 30 km/hr $= \dfrac{120}{30} = 4$ hrs

Total time $= 6 + 4 = 10$ hrs

Average speed $= \dfrac{240}{10} = 24$ km/h

The average speed is 24 km/h.

Hence, the correct option is (D).

59. Given:

22% of 4350 + 47.25 × 4 + 17 × 51 − 1013 = ?

$\Rightarrow$ 957 + 47.25 × 4 + 17 × 51 − 1013 = ?

$\Rightarrow$ 957 + 189 + 867 − 1013 = ?

$\Rightarrow$ 2013 − 1013 = ?

$\Rightarrow$? = 1000

∴ The value of ? is 1000.

Hence, the correct option is (D).

60. Given:

The number 22144 is divided in the ratio of $\dfrac{1}{3} : \dfrac{3}{5} : \dfrac{5}{7}$

Taking the L.C.M of the denominators $(3,5,7) = 105$

Now, the new ratio thus formed is $= 35 : 63 : 75$

The smallest number is $= \dfrac{35}{35+63+75} \times 22144$

$\dfrac{35}{173} \times 22144 = 4480$

The largest number is $= \dfrac{75}{173} \times 22144 = 9600$

Difference of the two $= 9600 - 4480 = 5120$

∴ The answer is 5120.

Hence, the correct option is (D).

61. The error lies in the incorrect usage of the verb. "Does" is the third person singular present tense of the verb "do". While the verb "do" is used when referring to more than one person or thing, the word "does" is used in sentences that refer to a single person or thing. For example: "It does look nice on you. They do look nice together."

The correct sentence would be:

The important point is that humans do not observe scenes passively or neutrally.

Hence, the correct option is (B).

62. The error lies in the incorrect usage of a verb. The sentence is in the simple present tense. In a simple present sentence where he, she, it, or a name is the subject, verbs can end in "-s or –es" depending on the way the verb ends.

The correct sentence would be:

It emerges from within constraint like a breath, it is about breath, it is about breathing.

Hence, the correct option is (A).

63. I am awful at picking vegetables.

The correct preposition here is 'at' as someone is awful 'at' an action.' Being awful means 'too bad at doing that thing.'

Hence, the correct option is (B).

64. This is the boy who scored the highest marks.

The most suitable pronoun for the given blank is 'who'. A pronoun is a word that replaces a noun to avoid its repetition.

A relative pronoun is one which is used to refer to nouns mentioned previously, whether they are people, places, things, animals, or ideas" (i.e. Who, whom, that, which, etc.). Who should be used to refer to the subject of a sentence.

For example: Jack is the one who wants to go.

Hence, the correct option is (D).

65. Correct sentence: Giving money to the poor is a/an **benevolent** act of service to the poor.

Benevolent: kind and helpful, giving money or help to people or organizations that need it.

According to the given sentence, giving money to the poor is an act of charity. Therefore, we need a word whose meaning is close to kind/helpful.

So, according to the context of the sentence, 'benevolent' fits appropriately in the given blank.

Hence, the correct option is (A).

66. Jeer = a rude and mocking remark.

Compliment = a polite expression of praise or admiration.

Hoot = a shout expressing scorn or disapproval.

Flatter = lavish praise and compliments on (someone), often insincerely and with the aim of furthering one's own interests.

Praise = express warm approval or admiration.

So, the word 'Hoot' has a similar meaning as 'Jeer'.

Hence, the correct option is (B).

67. Bombastic = sounding important but in actual meaningless; pompous, grandiloquent

Eloquent = fluent or persuasive in speaking or writing

Grandiloquent = pompous or extravagant in language, style, or manner, especially in a way that is intended to impress; bombastic

Ornate = highly decorated

Glorious = having great beauty and splendor

So, the word 'Grandiloquent' has a similar meaning as 'Bombastic'.

Hence, the correct option is (D).

68. A piece of cake (Idiom): Something very easy.

All greek to me (Idiom): Something difficult to understand.

Ducks and Drakes (Idiom): Behave recklessly.

Ace in the hole (Idiom): A hidden strength.

Clearly option (B) is the most suitable idiom.

Hence, the correct option is (B).

69. In the offing: Likely to happen or appear soon. E.g: "There are several initiatives in the offing."

Hence, the correct option is (B).

70. Archives(noun)- "a collection of historical records relating to a place, organization, or family".

A place where government records are kept : Archives

- E.g: These old photographs should go in the family archives.

Let's have a look at the meaning of the other given options:

- Asylum(noun)- "the protection granted by a state to someone who has left their home country as a political refugee".

- Apiary(noun)- "a place where people keep bees".

- Aquarium(noun)- "a transparent tank of water in which live fish and other water creatures and plants are kept".

Hence, the correct option is (C).

71. The word is 'Invigilator' is a noun, and its meaning is a person whose job is to watch people taking an exam in order to check that they do not cheat.

- Example: If you need more paper, please ask the invigilator.

Hence, the correct option is (A).

72. The correct spelling is 'Appalling'.

Appalling means causing shock or dismay; horrific.

For example, Because he lied to everyone, his actions were considered appalling in his circle of friends.

Hence, the correct option is (B).

73. The correct spelling is 'Occasion'.

Occasion means a particular event or the time at which it takes place.

For example, The wedding of my friend was a very grand occasion.

Hence, the correct option is (D).

74. The original sentence is absolutely correct and hence the bold part needs no replacement.

Hence, the correct option is (D).

75. The original sentence is erroneous.

"The dacoits and the police" is a plural subject.

So, the verb 'was' is inappropriate. The correct verb should have been 'were'.

The rest of the sentence is correct.

Among the given choices, only option (A) replaces the given bold part most appropriately.

The sentence after replacement becomes:

The dacoits and the police were firing at each other when one bullet hit the young man.

Hence, the correct option is (A).

76. The original sentence is absolutely correct and hence the bold part needs no replacement.

Hence, the correct option is (D).

77. Day is the most appropriate option to fill in blank no. (1).

It is clear from the passage that the author is talking about a particular day.

The sentence will be:

Ram Singh was whistling cheerfully as the work allotted to him for that day was finished.

Hence, the correct option is (B).

78. "and" is the most appropriate option to fill in blank no. (2).

And is used to join similar words or sentences.

Although means in spite of the fact.

But is used to introduce a contradicting statement.

Unless means except if; if not.

In this sentence, the author is talking about his work and his bag and is combining two sentences. So, 'and' should be used.

Hence, the correct option is (C).

79. "heavy" is the most appropriate option to fill in blank no. (3).

In the next sentence, the author has said that the bag became empty which means that when he started from the post office the bag must have been heavy.

There is no mention of the size or cleanliness of the bag.

The word 'heavy' means weighing a lot; difficult to lift or move.

Large : greater in size, amount, etc. than usual; big.

Dirty : not clean.

Torn : pull (something) apart or to pieces with force.

Hence, the correct option is (D).

80. "had" is the most appropriate option to fill in blank no. (4).

The sentence uses the past participle form of the verb i.e., started. So, the sentence is in past tense.

Have is used in the present tense.

Example- "I have only six nails," he said, "and it will take a little time to hammer out ten more."

Were is used with plural nouns and bag is singular.

Example- My parents were deeply grieved and perplexed.

Has is used in present tense with pronouns like he/she/it.

Example- If Len has time, maybe he could help me.

Hence, the correct option is (A).

General Intelligence and Reasoning

Q.1 Select the related letters/number from the given alternatives.

$DE : 10 :: HI : ?$

A. 17   **B.** 20   **C.** 36   **D.** 46

Q.2 Direction: In the following question, select the related word/letters/number from the given alternatives.

6 : 72 : : 8 : ?

A. 94   **B.** 96   **C.** 74   **D.** 92

Q.3 Five students P, Q, R, S and T are sitting in a row facing north. P is adjacent to T. T is in the middle of the row. T is to the immediate right of P. P is not adjacent to Q or R. Then S is adjacent to whom?

A. S   **B.** P
C. Q   **D.** Can't be determine

Q.4 Complete the series choosing the missing number:

5, 15, 45, 135, _____

A. 455   **B.** 395   **C.** 305   **D.** 405

Q.5 A piece of paper is folded and punched as shown below in the question figures. From the given answer figures, indicate how it will appear when opened.

 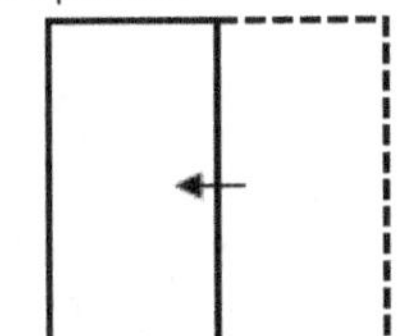 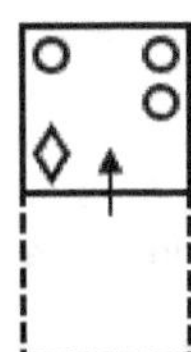

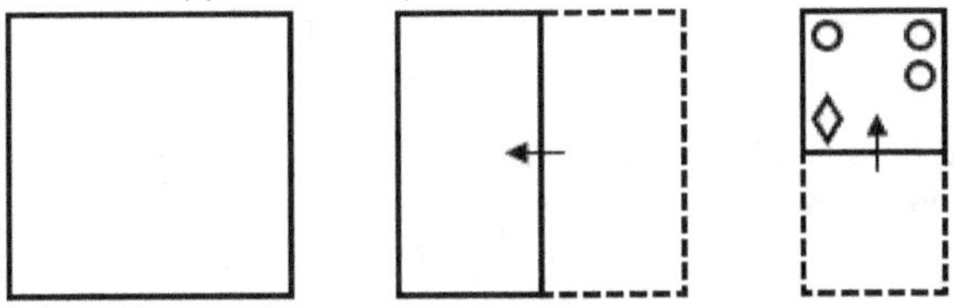

[SSC MTS, 2019], [UP Police Constable, 2019]

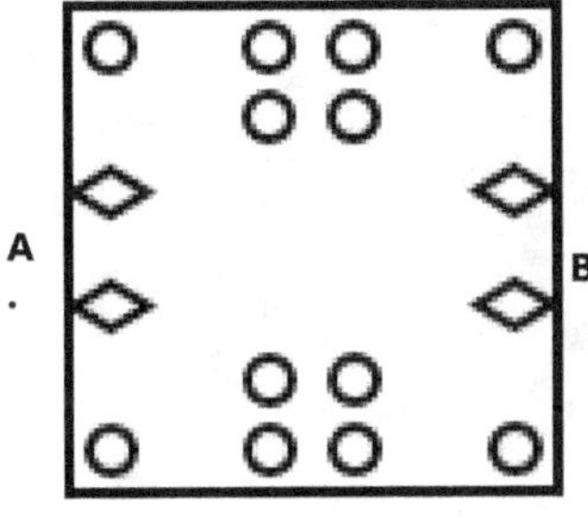 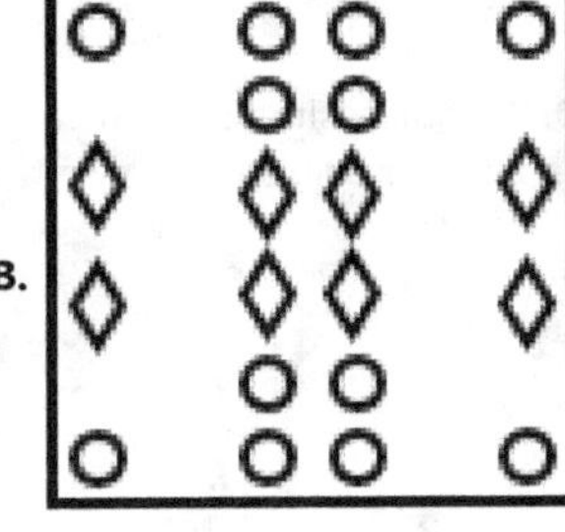

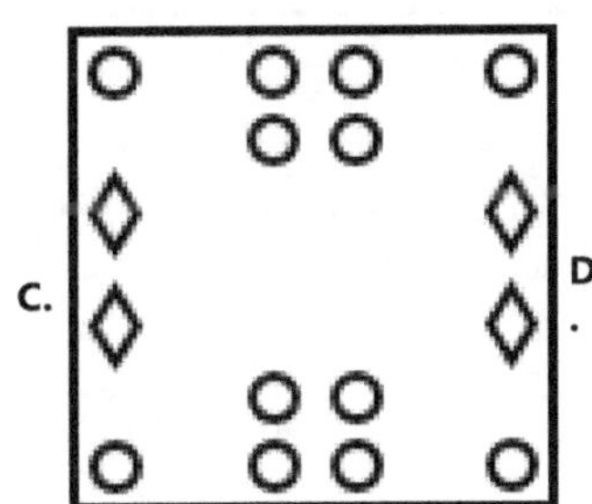 

Q.6 Which one set of letters when sequentially placed at the gaps in the given letter series shall complete it ?

_ bc _ ca _ aba _ c _ ca

A. abcbb   **B.** abcbb   **C.** baaba   **D.** bbcc

Q.7 Four pairs of numbers have been given, out of which three are alike in some manner, while one is different. Choose out the odd one.

A. 17 : 306   **B.** 21 : 420   **C.** 13 : 182   **D.** 19 : 380

Q.8 A = B means 'A is the sister of B'

A @ B means 'A is the husband of B'

A # B means 'A is the daughter of B'

If C # U = K # V @ M, then how is V related to U?

A. Son-in-law   **B.** Father
C. Paternal uncle   **D.** Brother

Q.9 Direction: Select the option figure that is embedded in the given figure (rotation is NOT allowed).

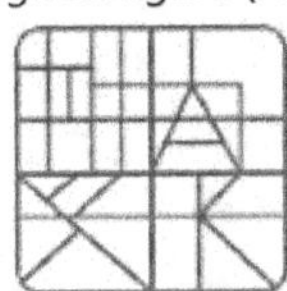

[SSC CGL, 2021]

A. 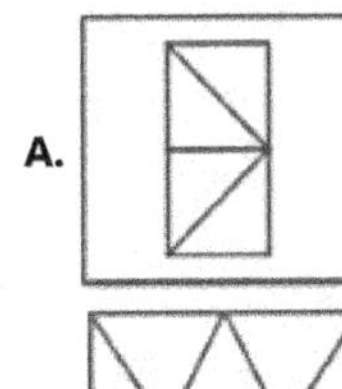   **B.** 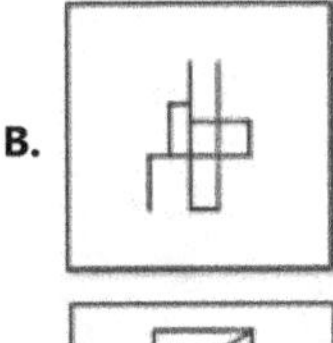

C. 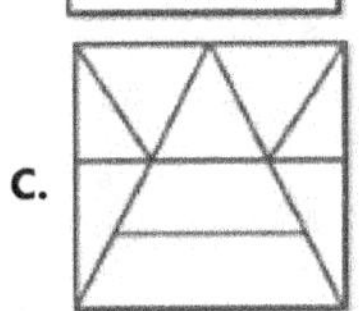   **D.** 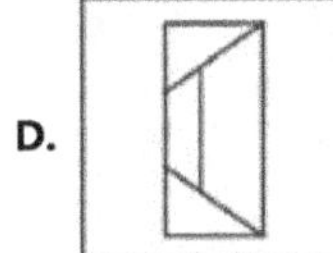

Q.10 Identify the diagram that best represents the relationship among the classes given below :

Sparrow, Bird, Cat

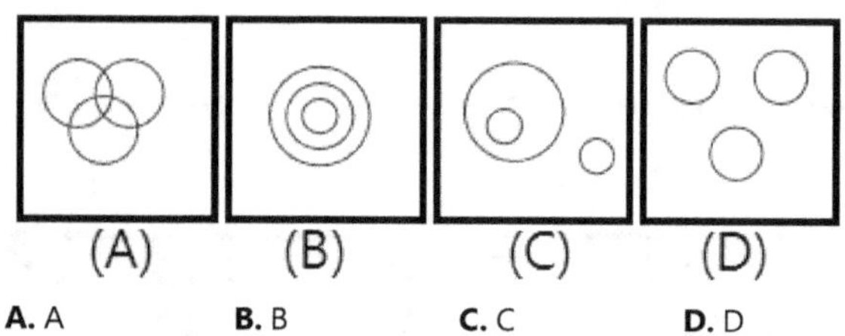

(A)   (B)   (C)   (D)

A. A   **B.** B   **C.** C   **D.** D

Q.11 Direction: Select the correct combination of mathematical signs to replace * signs and to balance the following equation:

8 * 8 * 1 * 7 = 8

A. × ÷ +   **B.** + × ÷   **C.** ÷ × +   **D.** - × ÷

Q.12 If a mirror is placed on line AB, then which will be the correct mirror image of the given figure?

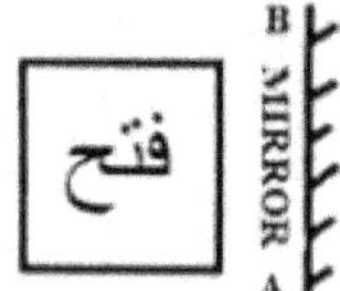

[Rajasthan Police Constable, 2020]

A. 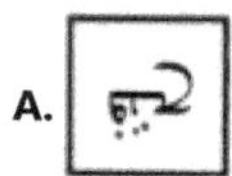   **B.**    **C.** 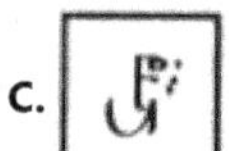   **D.** 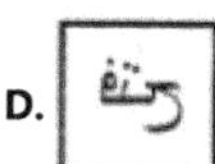

Q.13 Direction: A series of figures are given with one figure missing. Select the correct alternative from the given ones that will complete the series.

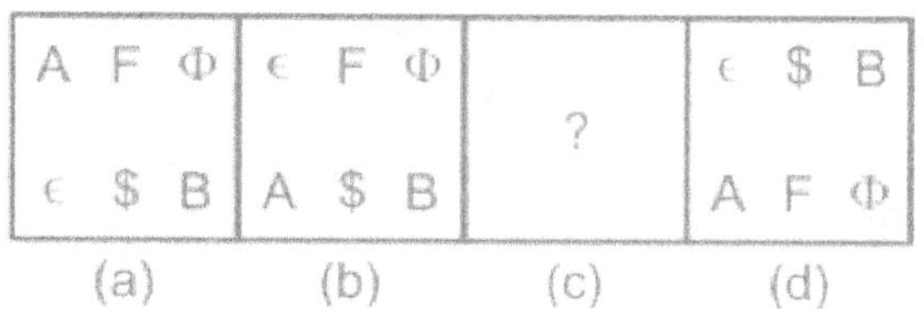

(a)   (b)   (c)   (d)

A.

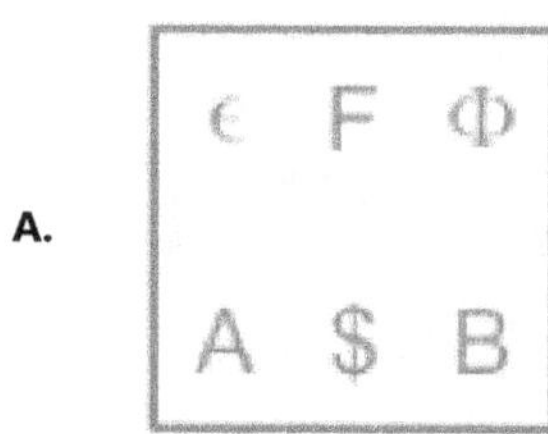

B.

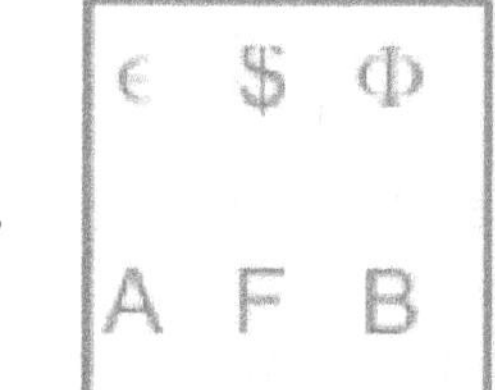

C.

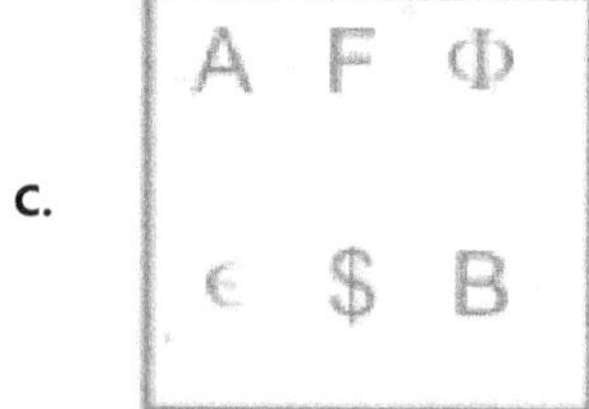

D.

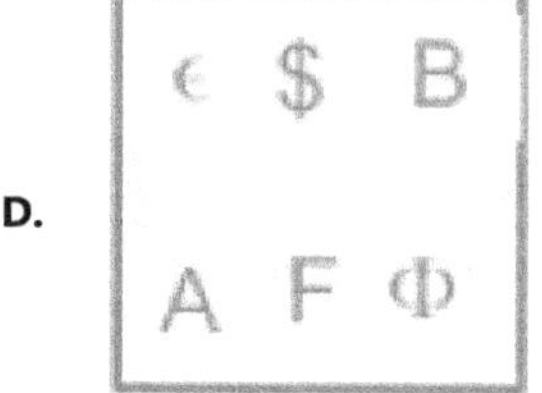

Q.14 Direction: What number should replace the question mark shown below?

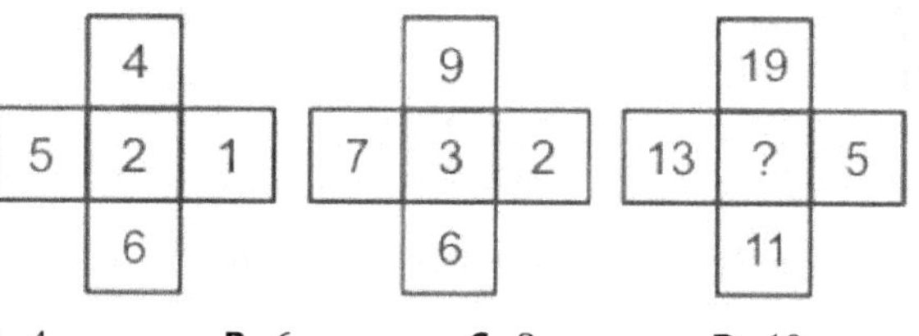

A. 4   **B.** 6   **C.** 8   **D.** 10

Q.15 Direction: Arrange the given words in the reverse dictionary order and choose the one that comes second.

Severe, Sentiment, Shower, Surpass

A. Severe   **B.** Sentiment
C. Shower   **D.** Surpass

Q.16 The sum of a number and its four times is 60. Find the 100 times the number.

A. 1200   **B.** 800   **C.** 900   **D.** 1000

Q.17 In the following question, select the odd letters from the given alternatives.

A. ACEG   **B.** MOQS   **C.** FHIK   **D.** PRTV

Q.18 Four positions of a dice are given below. Look at them carefully and find which number is opposite to 5?

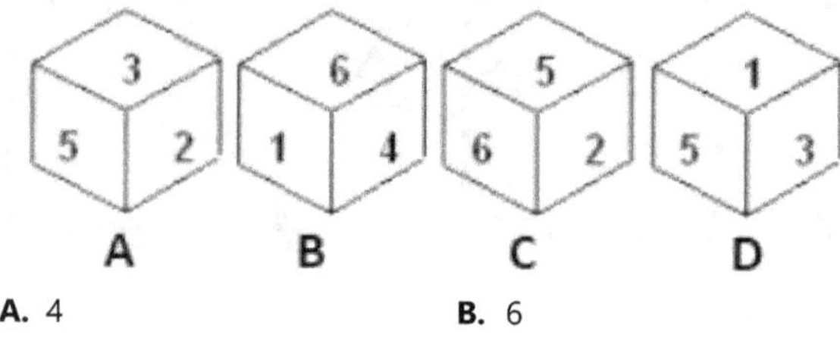

A   B   C   D

A. 4   **B.** 6
C. 1   **D.** 3

Q.19 Direction: Read the given statement(s) and conclusions carefully and select which of the conclusions logically follow(s) from the statement(s).

Statements:

All Paint are Wall.

No Wall is Tall.

Conclusions:

I. No Paint are Tall.

II. Some Paint are Tall.

A. Only I follows

B. Only II follows

C. Both I and II follows

D. Neither I nor II follows

Q.20 If B = 25, SUN = 27, then CAR = ?

A. 54   **B.** 59   **C.** 56   **D.** 49

General Knowledge and General Awareness

Q.21 Which of the following commission was appointed by the Central Government on Union-State relations in 1983?

A. Sarkariya commission

B. Dutt commission

C. Setalvad commission

D. Rajamannar commission

Q.22 The First Election Commissioner of India was?

A. S.P. Sen Verma   **B.** Dr Nagendra Singh

C. K.V.K. Sundram   **D.** Sukumar Sen

Q.23 According to which Article of the Constitution, the State of Jammu and Kashmir had a Special Status?

[Uttarakhand Public Service Commission (UKPSC), 2016]

A. Article 1   **B.** Article 360

C. Article 270   **D.** Article 370

Q.24 Which of the following is among the 'pull factors of migration'?

A. Security of life

B. Unemployment

C. Poor living condition

D. Unpleasant

Q.25 Who has been appointed as the Managing Director and Chief Executive Officer of SBI General Insurance Company Limited in July 2022?

A. T Raja Kumar

B. Paritosh Tripathi

C. Vijay Shekhar Sharma

D. Gyanesh Bharti

Q.26 Who has become the first Indian to win gold in the World Cadet Judo Championship 2022?

A. Avtar Singh

B. Linthoi Chanambam

C. Poonam Chopra

D. Kalpana Devi

Q.27 A special meeting of the UN Security Council's (UNSC) Counter-Terrorism Committee hosted on 28th and 29th of October, 2022, was held in which place?

A. Mumbai   **B.** Delhi

C. Jaipur   **D.** Both (A) and (B)

Q.28 The Centre and____________ government have signed a tripartite peace accord with 8 tribal outfits of the state on 15 September 2022.

A. Tripura   **B.** Assam

C. Manipur   **D.** Nagaland

Q.29 Which one of the following statements is not correct regarding the Himalayas?

A. The Himalayas have napped and recumbent folds.

B. The Himalayas rose up from the Tethys sea.

C. The Himalayas contain three mountain ranges- Shiwaliks, the Great Himalayas, and Kunlun Ranges.

D. The orogeny took place in the Tertiary Era.

Q.30 The shaded area in the map given below is the major producer of which one of the following?

A. Cotton   **B.** Groundnut

C. Wheat   **D.** Mustard

Q.31 Which Indian player has become the first Indian to win the Diamond League in 2022?

A. Neeraj Chopra   **B.** Vikas Goda

C. Mandeep Singh   **D.** Vikas Yadav

Q.32 Who of the following was/were economic critic/ critics of colonialism in India?

1. Dadabhai Naoroji

2. G. Subramania Iyer

3. R. C. Dutt

A. 1 only   **B.** 1 and 2 only

C. 2 and 3 only   **D.** 1, 2 and 3

Q.33 The Kalinga war was fought in which year of Ashoka reign?

A. 6   **B.** 7   **C.** 8   **D.** 9

Q.34 Who defeated Humayun in the battle of Chausa in 1539?

[Territorial Army Officer, 2019]

A. Sher Shah   **B.** Bahadur Shah

C. Rana Sanga   **D.** None of these

Q.35 Who has become the 1st beneficiary in the 2nd phase of nationwide vaccination against the coronavirus?

A. Ram Nath Kovind   **B.** Narendra Modi

C. Uddhav Thackeray   **D.** Amit Shah

Q.36 With which form of performing art is Teejan Bai associated?

A. Burra Katha B. Pandavani
C. Lavani D. Nautanki

Q.37 Graphite is commonly known as _______.

A. Fool's Gold B. Black Gold
C. Black Lead D. Soft Diamond

Q.38 What does invisible export mean?

A. Export of services
B. Export of prohibited goods
C. Export of restricted goods
D. Export of goods as per OGL list

Q.39 Which one of the following is the advantage of capitalist economy?

A. There is more efficiency in the capitalist economy as the products are produced according to the demand of the consumers.
B. There is less intervention from the government or bureaucratic interference.
C. Both (A) and (B)
D. None of above

Q.40 Who invented the air conditioner?

A. John Gorrie
B. Geraud Darnis
C. David Gitlin
D. Willis Haviland Carrier

Elementary Mathematics

Q.41 Find the value of $(999)^2 - 2^2$.

A. 998007 B. 995997 C. 996997 D. 997997

Q.42 Find the value of $\dfrac{4-\sqrt{0.04}}{4+\sqrt{0.4}}$.

A. 0.8 B. 1.0 C. 0.4 D. 1.4

Q.43 The square root of which of the following numbers is a rational number?

A. 53824 B. 81025 C. 62472 D. 23568

Q.44 There are some cocks and tigers. If the total number of their heads is 48 and total number of their legs is 140 then find the number of cocks.

A. 21 B. 28 C. 23 D. 26

Q.45 Arrangement of following fractions in ascending order.
$$\frac{1}{3}, \frac{3}{4}, \frac{2}{5}, \frac{6}{7}$$

A. $\frac{1}{3}, \frac{3}{4}, \frac{2}{5}, \frac{6}{7}$ B. $\frac{6}{7}, \frac{2}{5}, \frac{3}{4}, \frac{1}{3}$
C. $\frac{1}{3}, \frac{2}{5}, \frac{3}{4}, \frac{6}{7}$ D. $\frac{6}{7}, \frac{3}{4}, \frac{2}{5}, \frac{1}{3}$

Q.46 Preeti spends 30% of his income on grocery and 40% of remaining on travels. After this, she spends 25% on education. If his annual income is ₹ 2,00,000. Find her annual savings.

A. ₹ 63,000 B. ₹ 36,000 C. ₹ 63,500 D. ₹ 60,000

Q.47 The ratio of the number of boys to the number of girls at a party is 5: 9. If there are 99 girls at the party, the total number of persons at the party are:

A. 99 B. 55 C. 132 D. 154

Q.48 If $A:B = 7:3$, find the value of $\dfrac{AB+B^2}{A^2-B^2}$.

A. $\frac{3}{4}$ B. $\frac{4}{3}$ C. $\frac{7}{3}$ D. $\frac{3}{7}$

Q.49 The average of 25 results is 18 . The average of first 12 of those is 14 and the average of last 12 is 17 . What is the 13th result?

A. 74 B. 75 C. 69 D. 78

Q.50 If a certain amount doubles itself in 5 years at simple interest then find the rate of interest per annum at which the sum was invested.

A. 12.50% B. 15% C. 16.66% D. 20%

Q.51 What is the compound interest earned on 3rd year if Rs. 10000 is invested at the rate of 40% per annum?

A. Rs. 8840 B. Rs. 8120 C. Rs. 7430 D. Rs. 7840

Q.52 A tradesman allows a discount of 15% on the marked price. Find the ratio of the cost price to the Marked price in the particular case that the tradesman gets a profit of 19% on the cost price.

A. $7:5$ B. $3:4$ C. $5:7$ D. $15:19$

Q.53 By selling 30 articles, a man gains the selling price of 5 articles. What is the profit percentage?

A. 25% B. 30% C. 15% D. 20%

Q.54 Applied to a bill for Rs.1,00,000 the difference between a discount of 40% and two successive discounts of 36% and 4% is:

A. Rs. 3,440 B. Rs. 1,440
C. Rs. 2,500 D. Rs. 4,000

Q.55 The ratio of length and breadth of a rectangle is 5 : 4. The perimeter of the rectangle is 54 cm. Find the area of the rectangle.

A. 180 cm² B. 160 cm² C. 210 cm² D. 280 cm²

Q.56 The length of the base of a triangle is $\dfrac{5}{7}$ of the base of a parallelogram. The area of the triangle and the parallelogram is the same. Find the ratio of the respective heights of the triangle and the parallelogram.

A. 5 : 3 B. 7 : 5 C. 14 : 5 D. 21 : 10

Q.57 If two numbers are greater than 13 and the H.C.F of two numbers be 13, L.C.M 273, then the sum of the numbers is:

A. 286 B. 130 C. 288 D. 290

Q.58 Jalal, Amit and Firoz share partnerships. Jalal has invested 4 times more than Amit and the amount invested by Firoz is $\left(\dfrac{3}{4}\right)^{th}$ of the amount invested by Amit. At the end of the financial year, the total profit earned is Rs. 19,000. Find out the part of the Jalal?

A. Rs. 15000   B. Rs. 12000
C. Rs. 13000   D. Rs. 10000

Q.59 A train moving at the rate of 72 kmph crosses a pole in 20 seconds. How much time will the train require to cross car moving at speed of 18 kmph in opposite direction?

A. 20 s   B. 16 s   C. 10 s   D. 12 s

Q.60 If A and B together can finish a piece of work in 20 days, B and C in 10 days and C and A in 12 days, then A, B, C jointly can finish the same work in:

A. $\frac{7}{60}$ days   B. $8\frac{4}{7}$ days   C. $4\frac{2}{7}$ days   D. 30 days

English

Ques (61-62):Direction: In the following question, some part of the sentence may have errors. Find out which part of the sentence has an error and select the appropriate option. If the sentence is free from error, select 'No error'.

Q.61 This boy is (A)/ the most strongest (B)/ of the group. (C)/ No error (D)

A. A   B. B   C. C   D. D

Q.62 No sooner had she (A)/ seen one show (B)/ when she saw another. (C)/ No error (D)

A. A   B. B   C. C   D. D

Q.63 Direction: Select the most appropriate option to fill in the blank.
The nationalists followed a policy of non-violence to make their _____ successful.

A. encounter   B. struggle
C. politics   D. speeches

Q.64 Select the most appropriate option to fill in the blank.
Generally people use _____ oils for their cooking.

A. cleared   B. refined
C. improved   D. washed

Q.65 Direction: Select the most appropriate option to fill in the blank.
The committee's suggestion was not acceptable to everyone as it was _____.

A. considerate   B. controversial
C. concrete   D. convenient

Q.66 Direction: Choose the word which best expresses nearly the same meaning of the given word:
SARDONIC

A. Carelessly dressed   B. Threatening
C. Mocking   D. Flirty

Q.67 Pick out the synonym of 'ERUDITE' from the following:

A. Execute   B. Expanse
C. Academic   D. Settle

Ques (68-69):Direction: In the following question, four alternatives are given for the idiom/phrase. Choose the alternative which best expresses the meaning of the idiom/phrase.

Q.68 To get cold feet

A. Drenched   B. Fear
C. Felicitate   D. Fever

Q.69 To pay heed

A. To submit   B. To listen
C. To care for   D. To understand

Ques (70-71):Direction: Select the most appropriate word for the given group of words.

Q.70 To try to achieve something is difficult circumstances despite setbacks

A. Persuade   B. Persevere
C. Picturesque   D. Perspective

Q.71 A person who forsakes religion

[Territorial Army Officer, 2017]

A. Renegade   B. Apostle
C. Charlatan   D. Apotheosis

Q.72 Direction: In the following question, a word has been spelt in four different ways out of which only one is correctly spelt. Select the correctly spelt word.

A. Curiociti   B. Curiocity
C. Curiosity   D. Curiositi

Q.73 Direction: In the following question, a word has been spelt in four different ways out of which only one is correctly spelt. Select the correctly spelt word.

A. Superflos   B. Superflus
C. Superflous   D. Superfluous

Ques (74-76):Direction: Improve the bracketed part of the sentence.

Q.74 To become a professional banjo player, you (need spend) thousands of hours practicing.

A. Need spends   B. Need to spend
C. Dare to spend   D. No improvement

Q.75 Either the bears or the lion (has escaped) from the zoo.

A. Have escaped   B. Were escaped
C. Are escaped   D. No improvement

Q.76 If he is (on the influence) of alcohol he will not be allowed to sail.

A. Under the influence
B. Out on the influence
C. In the influence
D. No improvement

Ques (77-80):Direction: Read the passage carefully and select the best answer to each question out of the given four alternatives.

Female foeticide in India is the abortion of a female foetus outside of legal methods. The frequency of female foeticide in India is increasing day by day. The natural ratio is assumed to be between 103 and 107, and any number above it is considered as suggestive of female foeticide. According to the decennial Indian census, the sex ratio in the 0 to 6 age group in India has risen from 102.4 males per 100 females in 1961 to 104.2 in 1980, to 107.5 in 2001, to 108.9 in 2011.

The child sex ratio is within the normal natural range in all eastern and southern states of India, but significantly higher in certain western and particularly northwestern states such as Maharashtra, Haryana, Jammu & Kashmir (118, 120, and 116, as of 2011, respectively). The western states of Maharashtra and Rajasthan 2011 census found a child sex ratio of 113, Gujarat at 112, and Uttar Pradesh at 111.

The Indian census data suggests there is a positive correlation between abnormal sex ratio and better socio-economic status and literacy. This may be connected to the dowry system in India where dowry deaths occur when a girl is seen as a financial burden. Urban India has a higher child sex ratio than rural India according to 1991, 2001, and 2011 Census data, implying a higher prevalence of female foeticide in urban India. Similarly, child sex ratio greater than 115 boys per 100 girls is found in regions where the predominant majority is Hindu, Muslim, Sikh, or Christian; furthermore "normal" child sex ratio of 104 to 106 boys per 100 girls are also found in regions where the predominant majority is Hindu, Muslim, Sikh or Christian. These data contradict any hypotheses that may suggest that sex selection is an archaic practice that takes place among uneducated, poor sections or particular religions of the Indian society.

There is an ongoing debate as to whether these high sex ratios are only caused by female foeticide or some of the higher ratios is explained by natural causes. The Indian government has passed the Preconception and Prenatal Diagnostic Techniques Act (PCPNDT) in 1994 to ban and punish prenatal sex screening and female foeticide. It is currently illegal in India to determine or disclose the sex of the foetus to anyone. However, there are concerns that PCPNDT Act has been poorly enforced by authorities.

Q.77 What trend do the decennial census of India show amongst the age group of 0-6 years?

A. Increasing number of boys compared to girls

B. Increasing number of girls compared to boys

C. Male infanticide started gaining popularity

D. The male population has been subjected to exponential growth

Q.78 As per Indian census data, what is the effect on sex ratio of boys compared to girls, as the socio-economic and literacy rate increases?

A. Sex ratio is inversely proportional to the socio-economic status

B. Sex ratio increases as socio-economic and literacy rates increase

C. There is no relation between sex ratio and living conditions of the population

D. The relation varies with time and most of the hypotheses get contradicted by the data

Q.79 Which of following is where sex selection is most prevalent in the country?

A. Urban area with Hindu - Muslim majority

B. Rural areas with Hindu - Muslim majority

C. Semi-urban areas with Sikh - Christian majority

D. None of the above

Q.80 Even though the PCPNDT bans determination of sex of the fetus, why is female foeticide prevalent in the country?

A. The ban is still being worked upon in the parliament

B. The prevalence of the Dowry system

C. The fine against breaking the rule is marginal

D. The ban is yet to be implemented properly

// Smart Answer Sheet //

Correct Percentage of students who answered correctly. **Skipped** Percentage of students who skipped.

Q.	Ans.	Correct / Skipped	Q.	Ans.	Correct / Skipped	Q.	Ans.	Correct / Skipped	Q.	Ans.	Correct / Skipped	Q.	Ans.	Correct / Skipped
1	C	87.21 % / 10.77 %	17	C	53.56 % / 38.98 %	33	C	30.06 % / 69.37 %	49	D	81.95 % / 13.67 %	65	B	77.15 % / 20.53 %
2	B	85.69 % / 12.29 %	18	A	65.41 % / 31.98 %	34	A	68.42 % / 30.96 %	50	D	50.13 % / 35.66 %	66	C	44.32 % / 32.12 %
3	B	80.09 % / 17.57 %	19	A	88.51 % / 11.36 %	35	B	29.98 % / 68.41 %	51	D	42.55 % / 30.5 %	67	C	84.3 % / 11.55 %
4	D	86.22 % / 11.11 %	20	B	77.16 % / 12.08 %	36	B	77.91 % / 12.04 %	52	C	59.92 % / 35.29 %	68	B	51.88 % / 35.09 %
5	C	53.44 % / 31.57 %	21	A	58.22 % / 35.82 %	37	C	47.24 % / 35.85 %	53	D	40.8 % / 49.05 %	69	B	87.76 % / 10.35 %
6	A	57.67 % / 38.82 %	22	D	68.6 % / 30.63 %	38	A	67.6 % / 31.89 %	54	B	86.58 % / 10.28 %	70	B	58.69 % / 34.28 %
7	B	81.46 % / 13.63 %	23	D	63.15 % / 32.1 %	39	C	45.37 % / 36.82 %	55	A	82.9 % / 13.91 %	71	A	51.23 % / 33.41 %
8	B	54.8 % / 40.5 %	24	A	54.16 % / 33.81 %	40	D	14.9 % / 83.51 %	56	C	81.31 % / 18.46 %	72	C	88.39 % / 11.16 %
9	B	85.47 % / 14.42 %	25	B	42.77 % / 43.5 %	41	D	79.62 % / 16.95 %	57	B	76.81 % / 10.01 %	73	D	63.98 % / 30.2 %
10	C	77.14 % / 22.78 %	26	B	40.19 % / 33.05 %	42	A	76.59 % / 16.45 %	58	B	58.35 % / 34.28 %	74	B	81.55 % / 10.22 %
11	C	79.06 % / 19.1 %	27	D	63.37 % / 32.13 %	43	A	17.69 % / 72.36 %	59	B	80.34 % / 13.23 %	75	D	82.7 % / 16.98 %
12	D	89.61 % / 10.16 %	28	B	20.53 % / 75.43 %	44	D	54.58 % / 36.71 %	60	B	89.37 % / 10.29 %	76	A	81.53 % / 17.35 %
13	B	31.13 % / 67.9 %	29	C	45.87 % / 44.62 %	45	C	84.9 % / 11.83 %	61	B	87.28 % / 11.03 %	77	A	22.84 % / 69.45 %
14	B	85.46 % / 11.9 %	30	A	87.36 % / 10.31 %	46	A	25.67 % / 69.67 %	62	C	66.41 % / 30.6 %	78	B	20.04 % / 72.84 %
15	C	40.12 % / 49.52 %	31	A	63.9 % / 31.87 %	47	D	89.73 % / 10.07 %	63	B	19.8 % / 78.75 %	79	D	21.98 % / 76.42 %
16	A	82.74 % / 14.23 %	32	D	81.94 % / 12.47 %	48	A	84.58 % / 14.94 %	64	B	80.39 % / 19.26 %	80	D	25.83 % / 71.61 %

//Hints and Solutions//

1. As given, $DE = \dfrac{4 \times 5}{2} = 10$ (according to series)

we have, $HI = \dfrac{8 \times 9}{2} = 36$

Hence, the correct option is (C).

2. Given,

As 6: 72

72 = 6×12

Similarly

8:?

? = 8×12 =96

? =96

8: 96

Hence, the correct option is (B).

3.

Clearly, S is adjacent to P.

Hence, the correct option is (B).

4. The series 5, 15, 45, 135, _____ followed the pattern

$\Rightarrow$ 5 × 3 = 15

$\Rightarrow$ 15 × 3 = 45

$\Rightarrow$ 45 × 3 = 135

Similarly

$\Rightarrow$ 135 × 3 = 405

∴ The missing number is 405.

Hence, the correct option is (D).

5. According to the question, after unfolding the paper, it will look like:

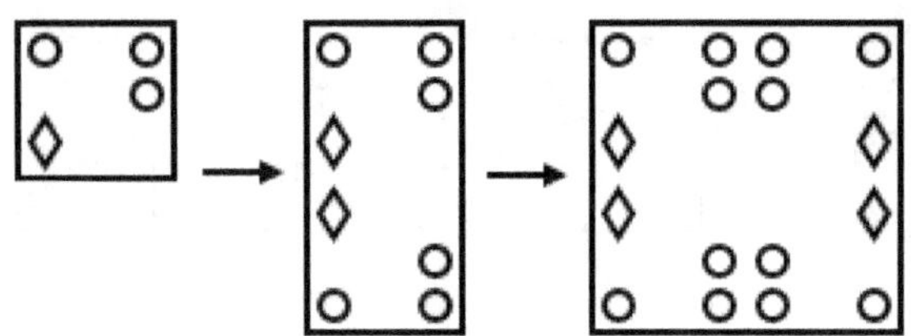

Hence, the correct option is (C).

6. The letters are changing their place in a cycling order.

The series is,

abcbcacababcbca

Hence, the correct option is (A).

7. The pattern followed is,

Option (A) → 17 : 306 → 17 : 17^2 + 17

Option (B) → 21 : 420 → 21 : 21^2 - 21

Option (C) → 13 : 182 → 13 : 13^2 + 13

Option (D) → 19 : 380 → 19 : 19^2 + 19

All follow the same pattern, except 21 : 420.

Hence, the correct option is (B).

8. By using the symbols in the table given below, we can draw the following family tree:

Symbol in Diagram	Meaning
◯	Female
▢	Male
══	Married Couple
──	Siblings
|	Difference of A Generation

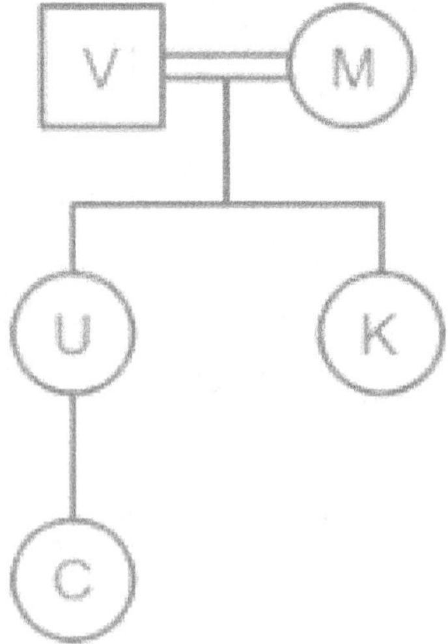

Clearly, V is the father of U.

Thus, 'Father' is the correct answer.

Hence, the correct option is (B).

9. On close observation, we find that the question figure is embedded in option (B) as shown below:

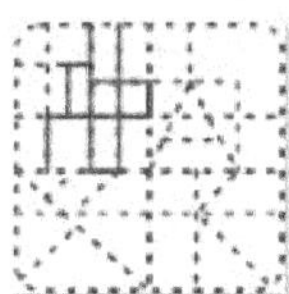

Hence, the correct option is (B).

10. All Sparrow is Birds. But Cat is entirely different.

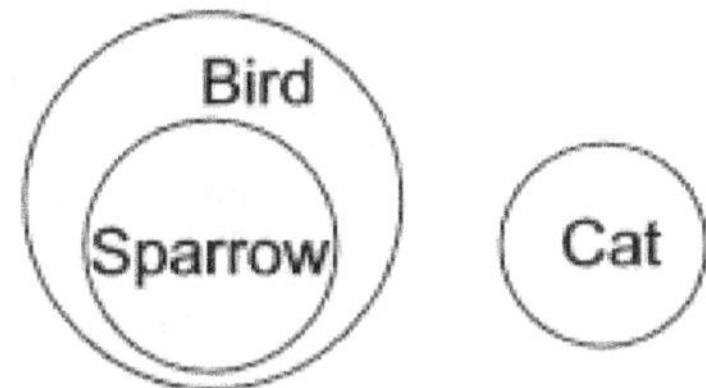

Hence, the correct option is (C).

11. Given:

8 * 8 * 1 * 7 = 8

From the option (C) we get:

$\Rightarrow 8 \div 8 \times 1 + 7 = 8$

$\Rightarrow 1 \times 1 + 7 = 8$

Hence, the correct option is (C).

12. The mirror image will be as follows:

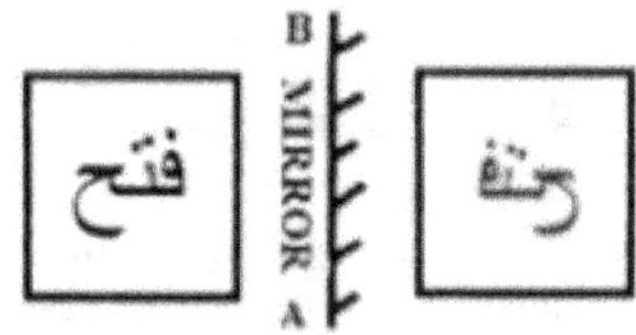

Hence, the correct option is (D).

13. In figure (b), elements of the 1st column are interchanged. In figure (c), elements of the 2nd column are interchanged. In figure (d), elements of the 3rd column are interchanged.

So,

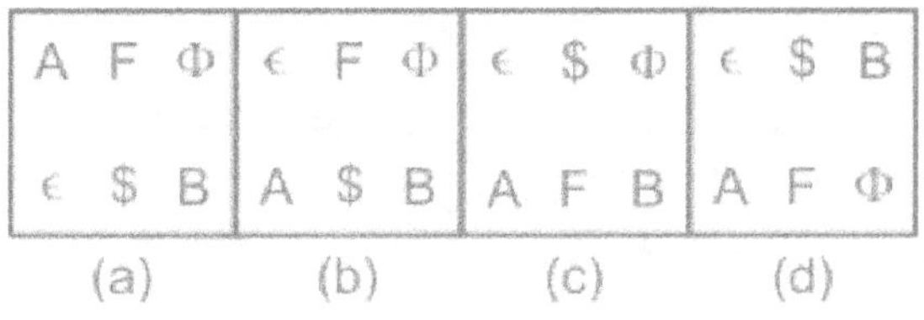

Hence, the correct option is (B).

14. The logic is:

$$5 + 4 + 1 + 6 = 16 \text{ and } 2 \times 8 = 16$$

$$7 + 9 + 2 + 6 = 24 \text{ and } 3 \times 8 = 24$$

Similarly,

$$13 + 19 + 5 + 11 = 48 \text{ and } 6 \times 8 = 48$$

Therefore, $? = 6$

Hence, the correct option is (B).

15. Reverse dictionary order:

S is the common letters in all four words.

'u' comes after 'h' in dictionary order so Surpass comes first and Shower second in reverse dictionary order.

Se is common letters in Severe and Sentiment

'v' comes after 'n' in dictionary order so Severe comes third and Sentiment fourth in reverse dictionary order.

Thus, the reverse dictionary order is:

Surpass, Shower, Severe, Sentiment

So, Shower is second word.

Hence, the correct option is (C).

16. Let the number be x.

$$x + 4x = 60$$

$$5x = 60$$

$$x = 12$$

Then, the 100 times the number = 100×12 = 1200

Hence, the correct option is (A).

17. F (+2 letters) = H (+1 letter) = I (+2 letters) = K

A (+2 letters) = C (+2 letters) = E (+2 letters) = G

M (+2 letters) = O (+2 letters) = Q (+2 letters) = S

P (+2 letters) = R (+2 letters) = T (+2 letters) = V

Hence, the correct option is (C).

18. Given-

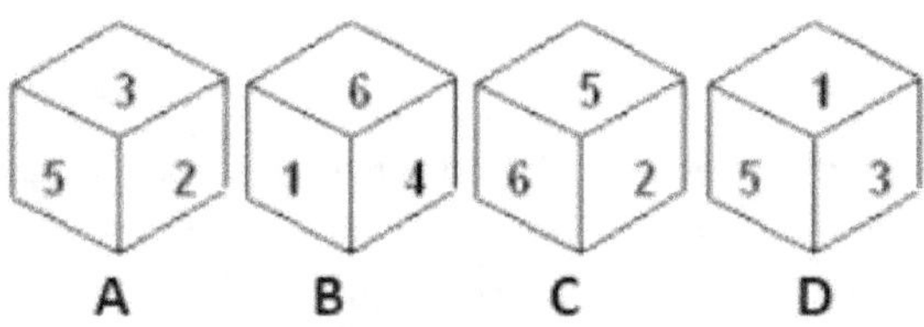

In position (A) and position (D), 5 and 3 are common which means 2 and 1 are opposite to each other.

In position (A) and position (C), 5 and 2 are common which means 3 and 6 are opposite to each other.

4 and 5 are opposite to each other.

Hence, the correct option is (A).

19. The least possible Venn Diagram for the given statements will be as follows:

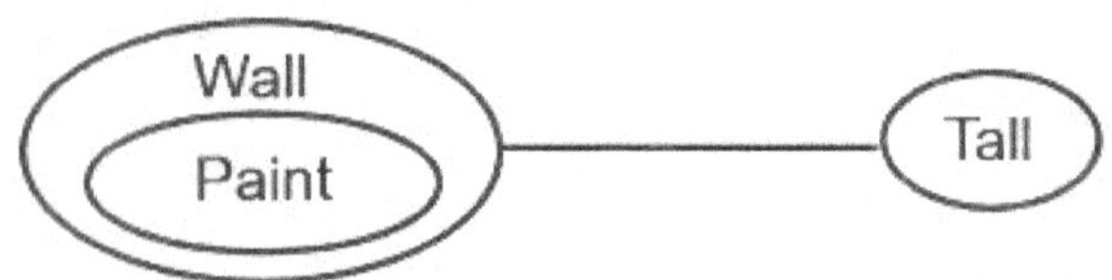

I. No Paint are Tall → True (As all paint are wall and no wall is tall. Thus, No paint are tall.)

II. Some Paint are Tall → False (This is definitely not true)

So, Only I follows.

Hence, the correct option is (A).

20. B = 25 i.e., the position number of B from the right end or in reverse order.

SUN = 8+6+13 = 27

So, CAR = 24+26+9 = 59

Hence, the correct option is (B).

21. Sarkaria Commission was set up in 1983 by the central government of India to examine the central-state relationship on various portfolios. Justice Ranjit Singh Sarkaria (Chairman of the commission), was a retired judge of the Supreme Court of India.

Hence, the correct option is (A).

22. Sukumar Sen (1899–1961) was an Indian civil servant who was the first Chief Election Commissioner of India, serving from 21 March 1950 to 19 December 1958.

Hence, the correct option is (D).

23. Under Article 370, the State of Jammu and Kashmir had a Special Status in the Indian Constitution.

Article 370 acknowledges the special status of the state of Jammu and Kashmir in terms of autonomy and its ability to formulate laws for the state's permanent residents. In the 1954 Presidential order, among other things, the Fundamental Rights in the Indian Constitution were made applicable to Kashmir with exceptions.

Hence, the correct option is (D).

24. Migration is another way by which the population size changes apart from birth and death. Migration is an integral part of redistributing population over time and space.

The pull factors make the place of destination seem more attractive than the place of origin for reasons such as:

- Better job opportunities and living conditions.
- Peace and stability.
- Security of life and property.
- Pleasant climate

Hence, the correct option is (A).

25. SBI General Insurance Company Limited has announced Paritosh Tripathi as Managing Director and Chief Executive Officer on July 2022.

He was nominated for the position by the parent company State Bank of India and has succeeded PC Kandpal.

From 2017 to 2020 he was the head of Bancassurance first with SBI Mutual Fund and then with SBI General Insurance.

Hence, the correct option is (B).

26. Indian judo player Linthoi Chanambam scripted history by winning a gold medal in the women's 57 kg category at the World Cadet Judo Championship 2022 in Sarajevo, Bosnia. 16-year-old Channambam has become the first Indian to win a gold medal at the World Judo Championships in any category.

Hence, the correct option is (B).

27. A special meeting of the UN Security Council's (UNSC) Counter-Terrorism Committee was hosted in Mumbai and Delhi on 28th and 29th of October, 2022.

Theme of the meting was 'Countering the use of new and emerging technologies for terrorist purposes'. India is currently the Chair of the UN Security Council Counter-Terrorism Committee for the year 2022.

Hence, the correct option is (D).

28. The Centre and Assam govt on 15 Sept 2022 signed a tripartite peace accord with 8 tribal outfits of Assam in the presence of Union home minister Amit Shah.

Around 1100 people have shunned the path of violence with the signing of this agreement. In January 2020, the Centre also signed a historic agreement with the Assam govt and Bodo representatives to end the over 50-year-old Bodo crisis.

Hence, the correct option is (B).

29. The Himalayas are young fold mountains in the northern part of the Indian subcontinent. The Himalayas are further grouped into four parallel longitudinal mountain belts of varying widths which are - Outer Himalaya, Lesser Himalaya, Great Himalaya, and Tibetan Himalayas. Their width varies from 400 Km in Kashmir to 150 Km in Arunachal Pradesh. The lesser Himalayas are also called Middle Himalayas. They extend from the northwest of the northern limit of the Indian Subcontinent to the southwest of the same. Sandwiched between Great Himalayas and Shivalik ranges, the lesser Himalayas run for around 2500 km. The altitudinal variations are greater in the eastern half than those in the western half.

Hence, the correct option is (C).

30. The shaded area in the map is major cotton producer states in India.

Cotton producing states in India are:

- Gujarat
- Maharashtra
- Andhra Pradesh
- Karnataka
- Tamil Nadu

Hence, the correct option is (A).

31. Neeraj Chopra has become the first Indian to win the Diamond League in 2022. Neeraj Chopra is a track and field athlete competing javelin thrower. March 2022, Neeraj Chopra has been awarded the Padma Shri. President Ram Nath Kovind honored Neeraj Chopra at a special program at Rashtrapati Bhavan.

Hence, the correct option is (A).

32. Dadabhai Naoroji, G. Subramania Iyer, R. C. Dutt were famous economic critique.

- Amongst the famous economic critique Dadabhai Naoroji, G. Subramania Iyer, R. C. Dutt who studied the economic relationship between the British Empire and India, Dadabhai Naoroji was the most prominent.
- He popularized the drain theory in his book "Poverty and Un-British Rule in India".
- They explained the colonial structure in all its three aspects of domination through trade, industry and finance.

Hence, the correct option is (D).

33. The Magadha Emperor, Ashoka invaded Kalinga in the eight year of his reign in 261 B.C. Nearly one lakh soldiers lost their lives in that war and one and half lakh soldiers were captured. The 13th rock edict of Ashoka throws light on this war.

Hence, the correct option is (C).

34. Sher Shah defeated Humayun in the battle of Chausa in 1539.

- The Battle of Chausa was a notable military engagement between the Mughal emperor, Humayun, and the Afghan, Sher Shah Suri.
- It was fought on 26 June 1539 at Chausa.
- Sher Shah was victorious and crowned himself Farid al-Din Sher Shah.

Hence, the correct option is (A).

35. PM Narendra Modi took the 1st dose of the COVID-19 vaccine at AIIMS in New Delhi on 1 March 2021.

- He has thus become the 1st beneficiary in the 2nd phase of nationwide vaccination against the coronavirus.
- He was given a dose of the home-grown Covaxin developed by Bharat Biotech and the Indian Council of Medical Research (ICMR).
- Sister P Niveda, from Puducherry, administered COVAXIN to him.

Hence, the correct option is (B).

36. Pandavani is a lyrical folk form of narration of scenes/events from Mahabharata without the use of props. It usually has a lead singer/narrator and two accompanying musicians with instruments. It is popular in tribes in Chattisgarh especially the Pardhi community. Traditionally, it was practiced only by men, but since the 1980s women have also been performing.

There are two styles of Pandavani: Vedamati and Kapalik.

In Vedamati, the artist sits on the floor and performs in a simple manner. In Kapalik, the performance is lively, where the artist enacts the scenes/characters and there is a lot of improvisation. Jhaduram Dewangan (Vedamanti style) and Teejan Bai (Kapalik style) are the most renowned performers of Pandavani. Some of the contemporary artists are Ritu Verma, Shantibai Chelak and Usha Barle.

Hence, the correct option is (B).

37. Graphite is also known as Black Lead and Plumbago. The term black lead usually refers to a powdered or processed graphite, matte black in color. Graphite is a crystalline allotrope of carbon in which carbons are arranged in hexagonal structure. It is good conductor of electricity and this makes it useful in electronic products such as electrodes, batteries, and solar panels.

Hence, the correct option is (B).

38. Invisible export means export of services.

In the balance of payment, invisible exports refer to the export of services that a domestic country exports to the outside world. As a part of international trade, invisible export is a type of export that does not involve trading of goods or commodities instead it involves the service sector like insurance, banking, consultancy, etc.

Hence, the correct option is (A).

39. The advantages of capitalist economy:

- There is more efficiency in the capitalist economy as the products are produced according to the demand of the consumers.
- There is less intervention from the government or bureaucratic interference.
- There is better scope for innovation as companies look to obtain a major part of the market with their offerings.
- It discourages any form of discrimination so that the trade can take place between two parties without any barriers.

Hence, the correct option is (C).

40. The first modern air conditioner was invented in 1902 by Willis Haviland Carrier. He was an American engineer. In 1915, he founded Carrier Corporation, a company specializing in the manufacture and distribution of heating, ventilation, and air conditioning (HVAC) systems.

Hence, the correct option is (D).

41. Given:

$(999)^2 - 2^2$

We know that,

$a^2 - b^2 = (a + b) \times (a - b)$

According to the formula used,

$(999)^2 - 2^2$

$= (999 + 2) \times (999 - 2)$

= (1001) × (997)

= (1000 + 1) × (997)

= (1000 × 997) + (1 × 997)

= 997000 + 997

= 997997

∴ The value of $(999)^2 - 2^2$ is 997997.

Hence, the correct option is (D).

42. Given,

$$\frac{4-\sqrt{0.04}}{4+\sqrt{0.4}} = \frac{4-0.2}{4+\sqrt{0.4}}$$

$$= \frac{3.8}{4+0.632} = \frac{3.8}{4.632} = 0.8$$

Hence, the correct option is (A).

43. Given:

The numbers $= 53824, 81025, 62472, 23568$

$\sqrt{53824} = 232$ ......(Which is a rational number)

$\sqrt{81025} = 284.648906549$ ......(Which is an irrational number)

$\sqrt{62472} = 249.943993726$ ......(Which is an irrational number)

$\sqrt{23568} = 153.518728499$ ......(Which is an irrational number)

∴ The required result will be 53824.

Hence, the correct option is (A).

44. Given:

Number of heads $= 48$

Number of legs $= 140$

Calculation:

Let the number of cocks $= n$

According to the question,

$$2n + 4(48 - n) = 140$$

$$\Rightarrow 192 - 2n = 140$$

$$\Rightarrow n = 26$$

∴ The number of cocks $= 26$

Hence, the correct option is (D).

45. Resolving the fractions:

$$\frac{1}{3} = 0.333$$

$$\frac{3}{4} = 0.75$$

$$\frac{2}{5} = 0.40$$

$$\frac{6}{7} = 0.857$$

Arranging in ascending order,

$$0.333 > 0.40 > 0.75 > 0.857$$

So, the correct sequence will be $\frac{1}{3}, \frac{2}{5}, \frac{3}{4}, \frac{6}{7}$.

Hence, the correct option is (C).

46. Given:

Money spend on grocery

= 30% of ₹ 2,00,000

= 60,000

Money spend on travels

= 40% of 70% of ₹ 2,00,000

= 56,000

Total money spend on grocery and travels

= 60,000+56,000

= 1,16,000

Money remaining

= 2,00,000-1,16,000

= 84,000

According to the question,

Money spend on education

= 25% of 84,000

= 21,000

Therefore, the annual saving

= 84,000-21,000

= 63,000

Hence, the correct option is (A).

47. Let the number of boys be 5x and the number of girls be 9x at the party

Given that there are 99 girls at the party,

So,

⇒ 9x = 99

⇒ x = 11

Total number of Persons at the party = Number of boys + Number of girls

⇒ Total number of Persons at the party = 5x + 9x = 14x

⇒ Total number of Persons at the party = 14 × 11

∴ Total number of Persons at the party = 154

Hence, the correct option is (D).

48. Given-

$$A:B = 7:3$$

Let $A = 7k, B = 3k$.

On putting the values of A and B,

$$\frac{AB+B^2}{A^2-B^2}$$

$$= \frac{(7k\times 3k)+(3k)^2}{(7k)^2-(3k)^2}$$

$$= \frac{21k^2+9k^2}{49k^2-9k^2}$$

$$= \frac{30k^2}{40k^2}$$

$$= \frac{3}{4}$$

Hence, the correct option is (A).

49. Given,

The average of 25 results is 18 . The average of first 12 of those is 14 and the average of last 12 is 17 .

Sum of 1st 12 results = 12 × 14

Sum of last 12 results = 12 × 17

13th result = x (let)

Now,

12 × 14 + 12 × 17 + x = 25 × 18

x = 78

Hence, the correct option is (D).

50. Given:

Time = 5 years

$$SI = \frac{PRT}{100}$$

Where P is principal, R is rate of interest and T is time.

Sum doubles itself:

So, SI = 2P – P = P

$$\Rightarrow P = \frac{P \times R \times 5}{100}$$

$$\Rightarrow R = 20\%$$

So, rate of interest = 20%

Hence, the correct option is (D).

51. Given:

Principal = Rs. 10000

Rate = 40% per annum

Compound interest earned on 3rd year = Amount received after 3 years – Amount received after 2 years

In case of compound interest:

$$\text{Amount} = P \times \left(1 + \frac{R}{100}\right)^T$$

Where,

P = Principal, R = rate of interest and T = Time

And

CI = Amount – Principal

Applying the formula:

$$\text{Amount received after 2 years} = 10000 \times \left(1 + \frac{40}{100}\right)^2$$

= Rs. 19600

And

$$\text{Amount received after 3 years} = 10000 \times \left(1 + \frac{40}{100}\right)^3$$

= Rs. 27440

∴ Interest for the 3rd year = 27440 – 19600

= Rs. 7840

Hence, the correct option is (D).

52. The ratio of the cost price to the marked price is given as ($100 -$Discount %) : ($100 +$ Profit %)

$$\Rightarrow CP : MP = (100 - 15\%) : (100 + 19\%) = 85 : 119$$

$$\therefore CP : MP = 5 : 7$$

Alternate Solution:

Let the cost price be Rs. 100.

Given that the profit $= 19\%$

So, the selling price $=$ Rs. 119

Also, the selling price $= 85\%$ of the Marked price

$$\frac{119}{85} \times 100 = \text{Marked price}$$

Marked price $=$ Rs. 140

Cost price: Marked price $= 100 : 140 = 5 : 7$

Hence, the correct option is (C).

53. According to the question,

By selling 30 articles, a man gains SP of 5 articles,

SP $=$ Selling price

CP $=$ Cost price

$$\Rightarrow 30SP - 30CP = 5SP$$

$\Rightarrow 25SP = 30CP$

$\Rightarrow CP : SP = 25 : 30 = 5 : 6$

$\therefore$ Profit percent $= \frac{1}{5} \times 100 = 20\%$

Hence, the correct option is (D).

54. Ist Discount $= 40\%$

Next effect of two successive Discounts

$36 + 4 - \frac{36 \times 4}{100} = 40 - 1.44$

Percentage Difference $= 40 - 40 + 1.44$

Difference between Discount $= 1.44\%$ of $1,00,000$

$= \frac{144}{100} \times \frac{1}{100} \times 1,00,000$

$=$ Rs. $1,440$

Hence, the correct option is (B).

55. Let the length and breadth of the rectangle be 5x and 4x respectively.

The perimeter of the rectangle = 54 cm

Perimeter of the rectangle = 2 × (l + b)

$\Rightarrow$ 2 × (5x + 4x) = 54

$\Rightarrow$ 9x = 27

$\Rightarrow$ x = 3 cm

Now, Length of the rectangle = 5 × 3 = 15 cm

Breadth of the rectangle = 4 × 3 = 12 cm

Area of the rectangle = 15 × 12

Area of the rectangle = 180 cm²

Hence, the correct option is (A).

56. Let the base of the parallelogram be x.

So, the base of the triangle $= \left(\frac{5}{7}\right) x$

Let the height of the parallelogram be P.

Let the height of the triangle be T.

Hence, we obtain the following:

The area of the triangle $= \frac{1}{2} \times [\left(\frac{5}{7}\right) x] \times 1$

The area of the parallelogram $= x \times P$

Now, both areas are equal so, we get:

$\frac{1}{2} \times [\left(\frac{5}{7}\right) x] \times T = x \times P$

$\Rightarrow \frac{T}{P} = \frac{14}{5}$

$\therefore$ The required ratio of the respective heights of the triangle and the parallelogram is 14 : 5.

Hence, the correct option is (C).

57. Let the number be $13a$ and $13b$, where a and b are co-primes.

Then, $13a \times 13b = (13 \times 273)$

$\Rightarrow ab = 21$

Two co-primes with product 21 are 3 and 7.

$\therefore$ numbers are (13×3) and (13×7) i.e, 39 and 91.

Their sum $= (39 + 91) = 130$

Hence, the correct option is (B).

58. Let's say the investment of Jalal, Amit and Firoz is x, y and z.

It has been given that Jalal has invested 4 times more than Amit and the amount invested by Firoz is $\left(\frac{3}{4}\right)^{th}$ of the amount invested by Amit.

So, $x = 4y$ and $y = \left(\frac{3}{4}\right) z$

Given that the total profit at the end of the year is Rs. 19000.

$\Rightarrow x + y + z = 19000$

$\Rightarrow 4y + y + \left(\frac{4}{3}\right) y = 19000$

$\Rightarrow 12y + 3y + 4y = 57000$

$\Rightarrow 19y = 57000$

$\Rightarrow y = 3000$

Investment of Jalal $(x) = 4y = 4 \times 3000 =$ Rs. 12000

Hence, the correct option is (B).

59. Given:

Speed of train = 72 kmph

Time = 20 seconds

Speed of car = 18 kmph

Formula used:

Speed $= \dfrac{Distance}{time}$

1 kmph $= \dfrac{5}{18}$ m/s

Calculating length of train

$\Rightarrow$ 72 kmph $= \dfrac{72 \times 5}{18}$ m/s

$\Rightarrow$ Speed of train = 20 m/s

$\Rightarrow$ length of train = Speed × Time

$\Rightarrow$ length = 20 × 20

$\Rightarrow$ Length of train = 400 m

Now, calculate relative speed

$\Rightarrow$ car is moving in opposite direction as train hence relative speed = 72 + 18

$\Rightarrow$ Relative speed = 90 kmph

$\Rightarrow$ Relative speed = 25 m/s

$\Rightarrow$ Time taken to cross car = $\dfrac{400}{25}$

$\Rightarrow$ Time taken = 16 sconds

$\therefore$ Train takes 16 seconds to cross the car.

Hence, the correct option is (B).

60. Given,

$(A + B)'$ s 1 day's work $= \dfrac{1}{20}$

$(B + C)'$ s 1 day's work $= \dfrac{1}{10}$

$(C + A)'$ s 1 day's work $= \dfrac{1}{12}$

On adding all three,

$2(A + B + C)'$ s 1 day's work $= \dfrac{1}{20} + \dfrac{1}{10} + \dfrac{1}{12}$

$= \dfrac{3+6+5}{60} = \dfrac{14}{60} = \dfrac{7}{30}$

$(A + B + C)'$ s 1 day's work $= \dfrac{7}{60}$

Hence, the work will be completed in $\dfrac{60}{7} = 8\dfrac{4}{7}$ days.

Hence, the correct option is (B).

61. The error is in part (B) of the sentence. The Superlative degree of 'strong' is 'strongest'. Hence, remove 'most'. Two superlative degrees cannot come together.

Hence, the correct option is (B).

62. The error is in part (C) of the sentence. The use of "when" is incorrect here. The correct pair of conjunction is 'No sooner - than'. See below sentence for example:

No sooner had we come out of our house than it began to rain.

The correct sentence is:

No sooner had she seen one show than she saw another.

Hence, the correct option is (C).

63. The correct answer is 'struggle'.

Struggle means a very difficult task. Example: My son is really struggling in math.

Encounter means a confrontation or unpleasant struggle. Example: The pilot told us that we might encounter turbulence during the flight.

Politics mean the activities associated with the governance of a country or area, especially the debate between parties having power. Example: Everything we understood about the world and politics changed.

Speeches (plural of 'speech') a formal talk that you give to a group of people. Example: Though not a great orator, his speeches were weighty and impressive.

The sentence talks about the task or the movement which is made successful by the policy of non-violence.

So, the most appropriate word is 'struggle'.

Hence, the correct option is (B).

64. Generally people use refined oils for their cooking.

Refined oil is a kind of oil that has been purified.

'Cleared', 'improved' and 'washed' have meanings related to the word 'refined', but they are not appropriate in the given context.

Hence, the correct option is (B).

65. The correct answer is <u>controversial</u>.

Controversial means giving rise to or likely to give rise to any controversy.

Complete sentence: The committee's suggestion was not acceptable to everyone as it was controversial.

Other options:

- Considerate means to be careful not to inconvenience or harm others.
- Concrete means existing in material or physical form.
- Convenient means fitting in well with a person's needs and activities.

Hence, the correct option is (B).

66. Mocking is the appropriate synonym of Sardonic.

The meaning of the given words:

- Threatening-Make or express a threat to do someone.
- Carelessly-It is an adverb which means 'not giving sufficient attention to someone.'
- Mocking-to laugh at somebody/something in an unkind way .

Hence, the correct option is (C).

67. Academic is the appropriate synonym of Erudite.

The meaning of the given words:

- Execute- to comply, observe
- Expanse- extension, copaciousness, copiosness
- Academic- connected with education, especially in schools and universities
- Settle- to put an end to an argument or disagreement

Hence, the correct option is (C).

68. 'To get cold feet' means to suddenly become too frightened to do something you had planned to. So, 'fear' is the most suitable response.

Hence, the correct option is (B).

69. The idiom "To pay heed" means to listen or to pay attention to someone. Therefore, 'to listen' expresses the correct meaning of the idiom.

Hence, the correct option is (B).

70. The most appropriate word for the given group of words **to try to achieve something is difficult circumstances despite setbacksis** is **persevere**.

Persevere means to try to do or continue doing something in a determined way, despite having problems.

Example: Many Black women providers have come forward to remind their Black patients that alternative treatments for severe fibroids are less invasive and can **preserve** fertility.

Hence, the correct option is (B).

71. Let's look at the options:

A renegade is a person who abandons religion.

An apostle is a vigorous and pioneering advocate or supporter of a particular policy, idea, or cause.

A charlatan is a person falsely claiming to have special knowledge or skill.

An apotheosis is the elevation of someone to a divine status.

Hence, the correct option is (A).

72. 'Curiosity' is the correct spelling. It means a strong desire to learn something.

For example, She waited a moment and then curiosity got the better of her.

Hence, the correct option is (C).

73. 'Superfluous' is the correct spelling. It means unnecessary, especially by being more than enough.

For example, In the age of technology, sending letters by mail seems rather superfluous to me.

Hence, the correct option is (D).

74. After the verb "need" an infinitive should be used. Hence, "spend" should be replaced by "to spend".

Hence, the correct option is (B).

75. There is no need to improve the sentence as the verb here is according to the second part of the subject ('either-or' case).

Hence, the correct option is (D).

76. In the context of 'affected by alcoholic drink or drugs' the phrase "under the influence" is used.

The correct statement is,

If he is under the influence of alcohol he will not be allowed to sail.

Hence, the correct option is (A).

77. According to the passage, The census points out that the anomaly in the sex ratio has been increasing. Hence, as per the data, the number of males compared to 100 girls have been on the increase since the last past decades. Though, the growth is steady (102 to 110 in 60 years). Options B and C point in the opposite direction of what the passage implies, and option D mentions the growth to be exponential (which is not the case).

Hence, the correct option is (A).

78. According to the passage, one of the startling facts brought in by analyzing the census data over the years is the positive correlation between the anomaly in sex ratio and the increasing socio-economic conditions and literacy rates. The passage goes on to mention how the urban areas have greater anomalies than the rural areas.

Hence, the correct option is (B).

79. According to the passage, though the passage hints that sex selection is more prevalent in urban areas than in rural areas, it mentions that the data contradicts any hypotheses which link sex selection to a particular or a particular set of religions.

Hence, the correct option is (D).

80. According to the passage, the law had been passed in 1994, hence there is no possibility of it still being stuck up in the parliament. Though dowry, an illegal practice, is one of the main reasons behind female foeticide, it happens only after it is known the fetus is female. Obtaining this information is what the law bans. The passage further hints that there are concerns regarding the poor enforcement of the act.

Hence, the correct option is (D).

General Intelligence and Reasoning

Q.1 Six friends, Arif, Amit, Amar, Ankit, Rohit and Aditya are sitting around a circular table but not necessarily in the same order. All of them are facing towards the center of the circle. Ankit sits second to the left of Amit who is sitting immediately to the right of Amar. One person sits between Rohit and Arif. Who is sitting second to right on Aditya?

A. Ankit   **B.** Arif   **C.** Amar   **D.** Rohit

Q.2 Direction: In the following question a number of series is given with one term missing. Choose the correct alternative that will continue the same pattern.

2,3,5,7,11, ___ 17

A. 12   **B.** 13   **C.** 14   **D.** 15

Q.3 Direction: Select the Venn diagram that best illustrates the relationship between the following classes.

Actor, Director, Male

A. 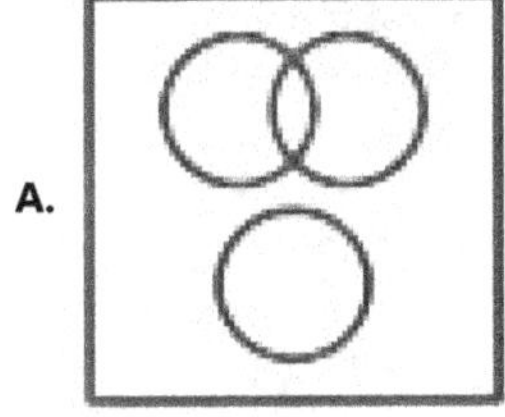   **B.** 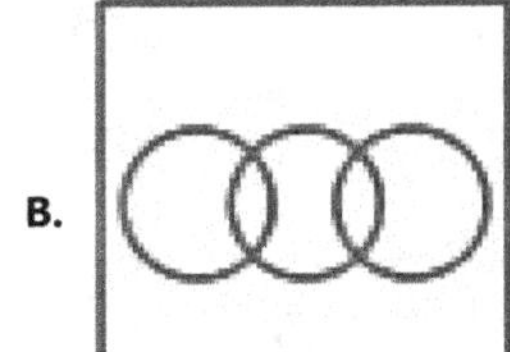

C. 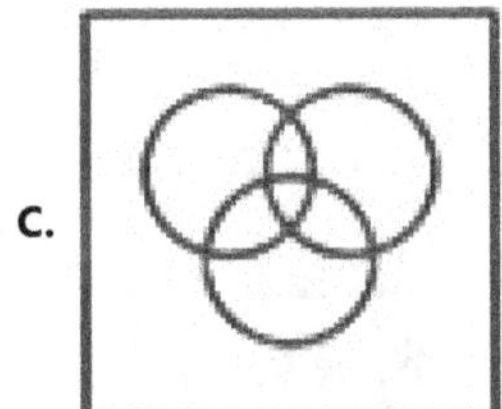   **D.** 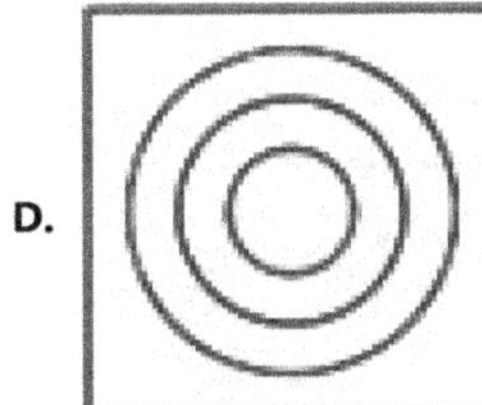

Q.4 If '+' means '×', '-' means '+', '×' means '÷' and '÷' means '-', then find the value of the given equation.

9 - 3 + 2 ÷ 16 × 2 = ?

A. 6   **B.** 5   **C.** 7   **D.** 9

Q.5 Direction: Choose the option that closely resembles the mirror image of the given figure.

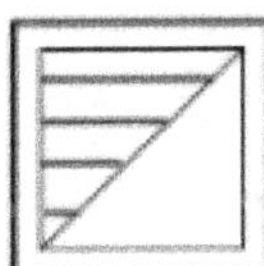

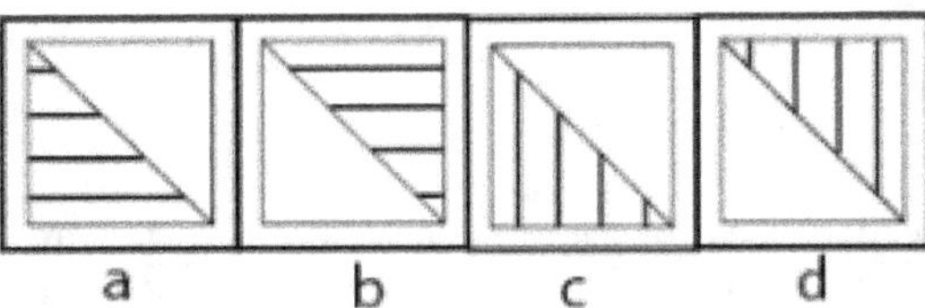

[RRB/RRC Group D, 2018]

A. a   **B.** d   **C.** c   **D.** b

Q.6 Direction: Find the next figure for the given series:

Problem Figures:

Answer Figures:

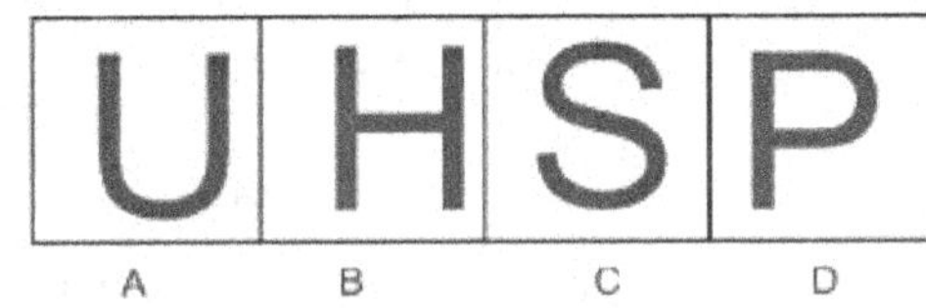

A. D   **B.** B   **C.** A   **D.** C

Q.7 Direction: In the following question, select the number which can be placed at the sign of question mark (?) from the given alternatives.

4	11	19
5	6	0
9	13	3
18	30	?

A. 20   **B.** 24   **C.** 22   **D.** 18

Q.8 Arrange the following words as per the order of dictionary-

1. Convince
2. Converge
3. Convenience
4. Convalesce
5. Converse

A. 43251   **B.** 14325   **C.** 42531   **D.** 43215

Q.9 The sum of the digits of a two digit number is 12. The difference between the first digit and the second digit of the two number is 4. What is the product of the two digits of the number?

A. 27   **B.** 32   **C.** 36   **D.** 35

Q.10 Two positions of dice are shown. Find the number of the dots on the face opposite the face bearing 3 dots.

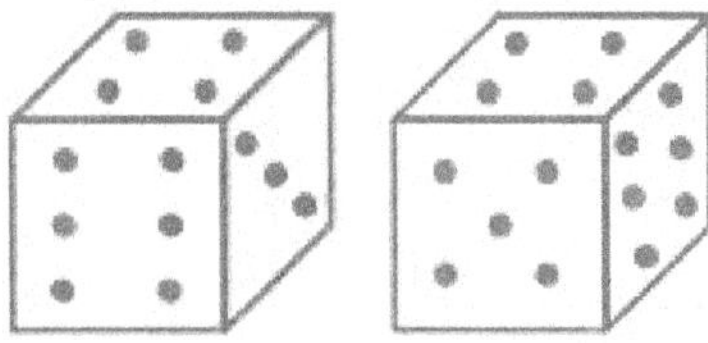

A. 1   **B.** 4
C. 2   **D.** 5

Q.11 Direction: Read the given statement(s) and conclusions carefully and select which of the conclusions logically follow(s) from the statement(s).

Statements:

No cat is a monkey.

No monkey is a cow.

Conclusions:

I. No cat is a cow.

II. Some cows are monkeys.

A.   Only conclusion I follows

B.   Only conclusion II follows

C.   Neither conclusion I nor conclusion II follows

D.   Both conclusions I and II follow

Q.12 In certain code, "LIFE" is written as "3965", then how must "FUN" be written?

A. 635   **B.** 634   **C.** 633   **D.** 629

Q.13 Direction: Select the option that is related to the third letter-cluster in the same way as the second letter-cluster is related to the first letter-cluster.

ABCD : ZYXW :: GHIJ : ?

[RRB (NTPC), 2020]

A. PQRS   **B.** TSRQ   **C.** LMNO   **D.** MLKJ

Q.14 Direction: The sequence of folding a piece of square paper and the manner in which the folded paper has been cut is shown in the figures. How would this paper look when unfolded?

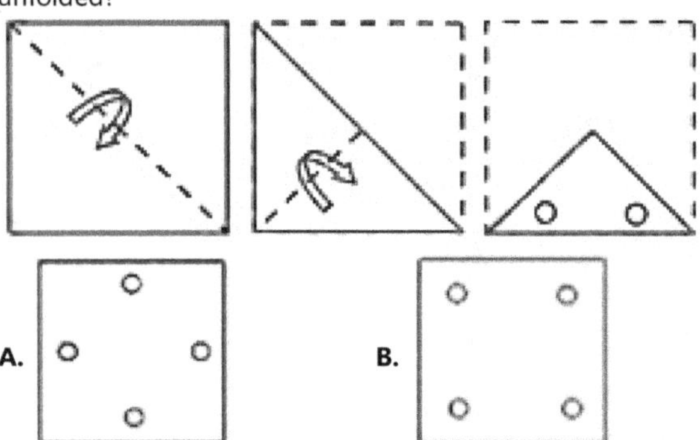

C. 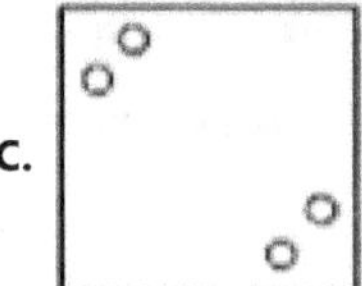   **D.** 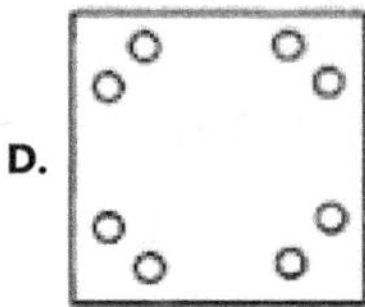

Q.15 Direction: Select the combination of letters that when sequentially placed in the blanks of the given letter series will complete the series.

ZH_ORC_ _K_R_ZH_O_C

A. K, Z, H, K, R, K, R   **B.** Z, H, K, O, C, K, R
C. K, Z, H, O, C, K, R   **D.** K, Z, O, R, C, K, R

Q.16 Select the odd letters from the given alternatives.

A. AZ   **B.** DW   **C.** GT   **D.** VR

Q.17 Direction: Choose which of the following figure is different from the rest.

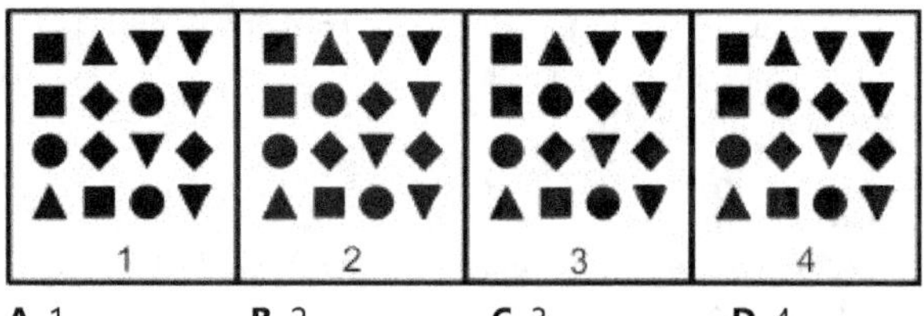

A. 1   **B.** 2   **C.** 3   **D.** 4

Q.18 Direction: From the given answer figures, select the one in which the question figure is hidden/embedded.

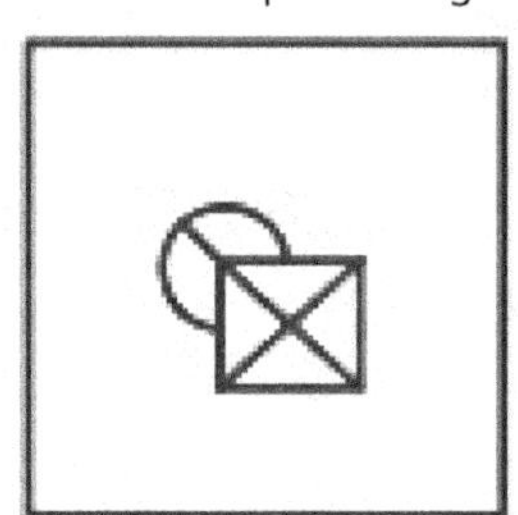

A. 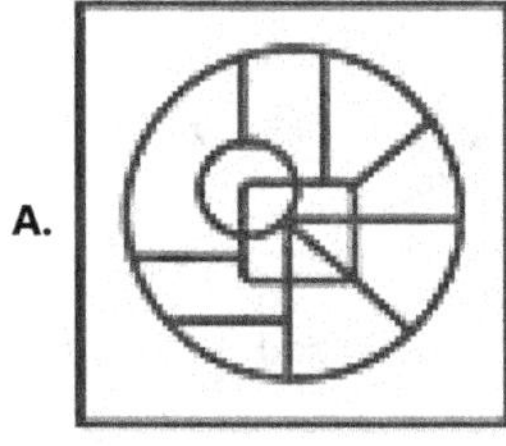   **B.** 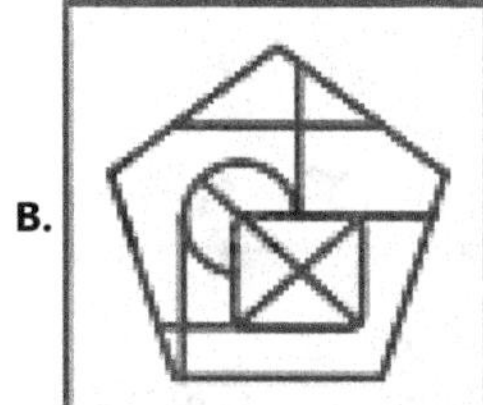

C. 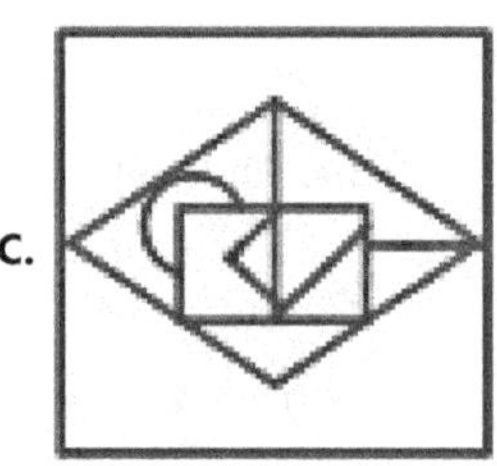   **D.** 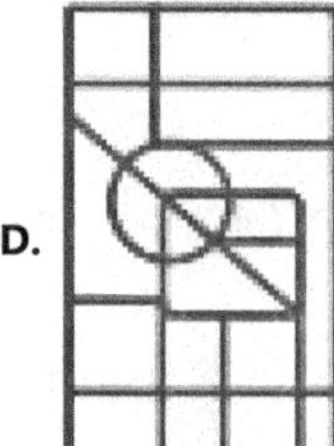

Q.19 X is the brother of Y. Y is the brother of Z. A is the father of X.

Based on these three statements, which of the following statements cannot be definitely true?

A. Y is son of A

B. X is brother of Z

C. Z is brother of X

D. Y is brother of X

Q.20 Direction: Select the option that is related to the third number in the same way as the second number is related to the first number.

2 : 54 : 4 : ?

[SSC MTS, 2021]

A. 250   **B.** 270   **C.** 201   **D.** 225

General Knowledge and General Awareness

Q.21 Which Article of the Indian Constitution gives the President the power of pardoning?

A. Article 72

B. Article 73

C. Article 74

D. Article 76

Q.22 According to the Constitution of India, the minimum age requirement for being a member of Panchayat is ______.

A. 24 years   **B.** 18 years   **C.** 21 years   **D.** 28 years

Q.23 Which one of the following categories of Fundamental Rights incorporates protection against untouchability form of discrimination?

[UPSC Prelims, 2020]

A. Right against Exploitation

B. Right to Freedom

C. Right to Constitutional Remedies (Article 32)

D. Right to Equality

Q.24 Which company has signed an MoU with the Gujarat govt to set up an IT-enabled Services (ITeS) Park in Vadodara in August 2022?

A. Aditya Birla Group

B. Reliance Industries Ltd

C. Larsen & Toubro (L&T) Ltd

D. Adani Group

Q.25 Which of the following states launched Cheerag Scheme?

A. Uttar Pradesh

B. Haryana

C. Assam

D. Jharkhand

Q.26 Abhijit Sen, who passed away on August 29, 2022, was related to which field?

A. Geography

B. Psychology

C. Biology

D. Economics

Q.27 Alluvial soil is also known as?

A. Clayey   **B.** Regular   **C.** Khadar   **D.** Laterite

Q.28 Match the pairs and choose correct option:

Rock	District
a. Gondwana series rocks	I. Yavatmal, Gadchiroli
b. Dharwar series rocks	II. Sawantwadi, Vengurla
c. Archean series rocks	III. Bhandara, Gondia
d. Vindhyan series rocks	IV. Chandrapur

[Maharashtra Public Service Commission, 2019]

A. a - III, b - II, c - IV, d - I

B. a - IV, b - I, c - II, d - III

C. a - I, b - III, c - II, d - IV

D. a - II, b - I, c - III, d - IV

Q.29 Ujali or Aneri Holi is associated with:

A. Jaunsari Tribe

B. Bhotia Tribe

C. Tharu Tribe

D. Raaji Tribe

Q.30 Which of the following physical quantities has the same unit as that of potential difference?

A. Electric field

B. Electric current

C. Electromotive force

D. Stress

Q.31 The Phillips Curve represents relationship between:

[Uttarakhand Public Service Commission (UKPSC), 2014]

A. Deflation and Unemployment

B. Inflation and Unemployment

C. Inflation and Disguised Unemployment

D. Deflation and Cyclical Unemployment

Q.32 Which of the following economists propagated the Pure Monetary Theory of Trade Cycle?

[Uttarakhand Public Service Commission (UKPSC), 2014]

A. Hawtrey   **B.** Hayek   **C.** Keynes   **D.** Hicks

Q.33 Who invented the safety break, which stop the elevator from crashing?

A. Thomas Edison

B. Eli Whitney

C. Henry Ford

D. Elisha Otis

Q.34 Who has won gold medal in Men's Rapid Fire Pistol event at the 36th National Games at Ahmedabad in Gujarat on 30 September 2022?

A. Anish

B. Ankur Goyal

C. Gurmeet

D. Satish Gupta

Q.35 The 2022 Nobel Prize in Chemistry has been jointly awarded to Carolyn Bertozzi, Morton Meldal Barry Sharpless for their work on snipping molecules. Who among these has also previously won the Noble Prize in Chemistry in 2001?

A. Carolyn Bertozzi

B. Morton Meldal

C. Barry Sharpless

D. None of these

Q.36 Who took over as the chairman and managing director of GAIL (India) Limited in October 2022?

A. Dharamveer Singh

B. Ravi Kumar Paswan

C. Kripa Shankar

D. Sandeep Kumar Gupta

Q.37 Which of the following is the oldest Vedas?

A. Atharva Veda

B. Rig Veda

C. Sama Veda

D. Yajur Veda

Q.38 Which one of the following painters was not associated with Humayun?

[Indian Military Academy (IMA), 2021], [Officers Training Academy (OTA), 2021]

A. Mir Sayyid Ali

B. Maulana Dost Musawir
C. Maulana Yosuf
D. Bihzad

Q.39 Which one of the following statements about the Colonial economy is NOT correct?

[UPSC Central Armed Police Forces AC, 2017]

A. The British presence inhibited indigenous capitalism
B. Laissez-faire actively promoted indigenous capitalism
C. The 'white collective monopoly' came earliest and remained most pronounced in Eastern India
D. The Bombay hinterland was difficult to penetrate before the construction of railways

Q.40 Who among the following has been appointed as the new CEO Of Royal Enfield in May 2022?

A. B. Govindarajan
B. Kiran Iyer
C. Mohit Goyal
D. Nishant Jain

Elementary Mathematics

Q.41 Direction: What will come in the place of the question mark $'?'$ in the following question?

$$\sqrt{324} + 9^2 - 7^2 = 2 \times (?)^2$$

A. 25 **B.** 5 **C.** 10 **D.** 20

Q.42 What is the unit digit of the expression

$$(1^1 + 2^2 + 3^3)^3?$$

A. 1 **B.** 4 **C.** 6 **D.** 8

Q.43 Sum of all the numbers between 6 and 100 which are divisible by 7?

A. 720 **B.** 710 **C.** 700 **D.** 735

Q.44 A fraction when added to $\frac{17}{3}$ gives 4. What is the fraction?

A. $-\frac{1}{3}$ **B.** $-1\frac{2}{3}$ **C.** $\frac{9}{2}$ **D.** $\frac{2}{3}$

Q.45 A number is increased first by 10% and then it is decreased by 20%. What is the percentage change in the number?

A. 12% increase **B.** 12% decrease
C. 32% increase **D.** 32% decrease

Q.46 At what rate percent per annum simple interest will a certain sum of money double itself in 15 years?

A. $6\frac{2}{3}\%$ **B.** 10% **C.** 25% **D.** 20%

Q.47 At what rate percent per annum will $Rs.\,2304$ amount to $Rs.\,2500$ in 2 years at compound interest?

A. $4\frac{1}{6}\%$ **B.** $4\frac{1}{3}\%$
C. $3\frac{1}{6}\%$ **D.** None of these

Q.48 The product of the LCM and HCF of two numbers is 48. The difference between the numbers is 8. Find the numbers?

A. 16 and 4 **B.** 8 and 16 **C.** 4 and 12 **D.** 8 and 12

Q.49 A and B invested Rs. 24000 and Rs. 8000 for a period of 2 year. After 2 year, they earned Rs. 48000. What will be the shares of A and B out of this earning?

A. Rs. 36,000, Rs. 12,000
B. Rs. 40,000, Rs. 10,000
C. Rs. 25,000, Rs. 40,000
D. Rs. 20,000, Rs. 12,000

Q.50 Two numbers are in the ratio of 5 : 6. If 8 is subtracted from them, they become in the ratio of 4 : 5. The numbers are:

A. (40, 48) **B.** (15, 16) **C.** (25, 30) **D.** (15, 18)

Q.51 The average of 20 numbers is 56. Later it was found that the number 10 was wrongly taken as 100. Find the correct average of the numbers.

A. 60.5 **B.** 59.5 **C.** 51.5 **D.** 50.5

Q.52 If a trader marks the price of articles 60% more than their cost price and allows a discount of 30%, then what is his gain percent?

A. 12% **B.** 15% **C.** 10% **D.** 20%

Q.53 The circumference of circular wire is 132 cm. Find the area of the square formed by same wire?

A. 1089 cm² **B.** 1809 cm²
C. 1890 cm² **D.** 1980 cm²

Q.54 A train crosses a pole in 16 seconds. If the length of the train is 400 m, then find the speed of the train.

A. 30 km/h **B.** 75 km/h **C.** 90 km/h **D.** 25 km/h

Q.55 12 persons can paint 10 identical rooms in 16 days. In how many days can 8 persons paint 20 such rooms?

[Indian Military Academy (IMA), 2018]

A. 12 **B.** 24 **C.** 36 **D.** 48

Q.56 Direction: What will come in the place of the question mark $'?'$ in the following question?

$$1456 \div 16 \times 14 + 22 = (?)^4$$

A. 6 **B.** 4 **C.** 16 **D.** 36

Q.57 The average of 5 quantities is 6 . The average of 3 of them is 8 . What is the average of the remaining two numbers?

A. 3 **B.** 4 **C.** 5 **D.** 6

Q.58 A Uber car can complete a certain distance in 21 hours, it covers one-third of the distance at 20 km/hr and rest at 50 km/hr. What is the total distance covered by the Uber car?

A. 800 km **B.** 700 km **C.** 950 km **D.** 620 km

Q.59 Raj can do a piece of work in 20 days. He started the work and left after some days, when 25% work was done. After it Abhijit joined and completed it working for 10 days. In how many days Raj and Abhijit can do the complete work, working together?

A. 6 **B.** 8 **C.** 10 **D.** 12

Q.60 A merchant purchases a wrist watch for Rs. 450 and fixes its price in such a way that after giving a discount of 10%, he earns a profit of 20%. Find the list price of the wrist watch.

A. Rs. 660   **B.** Rs. 480   **C.** Rs. 600   **D.** Rs. 630

<u>English</u>

Ques (61-62):Direction: In the following question, a sentence is divided into some parts. Find out which part of the sentence has an error. The number of that part is your answer. If there is no error, then choose (D) as your answer.

Q.61 Either Mohan or Rahul (A)/ are in the wrong, (B)/ both can certainly never be (C)/ No error (D).

A. A   **B.** B   **C.** C   **D.** D

Q.62 Manish was (A)/ senior to (B)/ Rohit in office (C)/. No error (D).

A. A   **B.** B   **C.** C   **D.** D

Ques (63-65):Directions: Choose the appropriate preposition for the given sentence:

Q.63 Barring strong headwinds, the plane will arrive _______ schedule.

A. during   **B.** for   **C.** by   **D.** on

Q.64 The US Open will be transmitted live _______ satellite.

A. via   **B.** throughout
C. within   **D.** towards

Q.65 Am I allowed to stay out _______ 10?

A. beside   **B.** minus   **C.** past   **D.** per

Q.66 Direction: Select the most appropriate synonym of the given word.
SPONTANEOUS

[SSC Sub Inspector (CPO), 2020]

A. planned   **B.** prejudiced
C. intended   **D.** impulsive

Q.67 Direction: In the following question, four alternatives are given for the meaning of the given idiom/Phrase. Choose the alternative which best expresses the meaning of the Idiom/Phrase.

The inspector was caught <u>red-handed</u>.

A. Found with hands tied
B. Caught with dirty hands
C. Caught in the act of committing the crime
D. Quickly

Q.68 Direction: In the following question, four alternatives are given for the meaning of the given idiom/Phrase. Choose the alternative which best expresses the meaning of the Idiom/Phrase.

Put a spoke in one's wheel

A. Tried to cause an accident
B. Helped in the execution of the plan
C. Thwarted in the execution of the plan
D. Destroyed the plan

Ques (69-70):Direction: Select the most appropriate one-word substitution for the given group of words.

Q.69 The dates when days and nights are of equal length.

[SSC Sub Inspector (CPO), 2020]

A. Equinox   **B.** Solstice   **C.** Eclipse   **D.** Stellar

Q.70 Something which is considered to be very important.
A. Cardinal   **B.** Scanty
C. Meager   **D.** Supplementary

Q.71 In the following question, a word has been written in four different ways out of which only one is correctly spelled. Select the correctly spelled word.

A. Intricate   **B.** Intrcate   **C.** Initrcate   **D.** Intarcate

Q.72 In the following question, a word has been written in four different ways out of which only one is correctly spelled. Select the correctly spelled word.

A. Rhyms   **B.** Rythm   **C.** Rhythm   **D.** Rythms

Q.73 Direction: Choose the word which best expresses the opposite meaning of the word.
TACIT
A. Order   **B.** Written
C. Oral   **D.** Understanding

Q.74 Direction: Select the most appropriate option to substitute the underlined segment. If there is no need to substitute it, select No improvement.
<u>Bulbul is honest girl</u> but she is also very rude.

[SSC MTS, 2019]

A. Bulbul is an honest girl
B. Bulbul is very honest girl
C. Bulbul is a honest girl
D. No improvement

Q.75 Direction: Select the most appropriate option to substitute the underlined segment. If there is no need to substitute it, select No improvement.
I would be eternally <u>indebted from you</u> if you could help me.

[SSC MTS, 2019]

A. indebted in you   **B.** indebted for you
C. No improvement   **D.** indebted to you

Q.76 Direction: In the following question, out of the four alternatives, select the alternative which will improve the underlined part of the sentence. In case no improvement is needed, select "No improvement".
I looked <u>anywhere</u> for my puppy but could not find it.
A. Everywhere   **B.** Somewhere
C. Nowhere   **D.** No improvement

Ques (77-80):Direction: In the following passage some words have been deleted. Fill in the blanks with the help of the alternatives given. Select the most appropriate option for each blank.

The (1)_____ of Kaziranga National Park in Assam are (2)_____ a new plan to save the endangered rhino. Nearly 50 school children from the neighbouring villages will take part in a training programme on (3)_____. The three-day programme (4)_____ trekking in the park and discussions with experts.

Q.77 Select the most appropriate option to fill in blank No.1.
[SSC Selection Post Phase IX, 2019]

A. delegation

B. people

C. government

D. authorities

Q.78 Select the most appropriate option to fill in blank No. 2
[SSC Selection Post Phase IX, 2019]

A. adapting   **B.** adopting   **C.** fostering   **D.** thinking

Q.79 Select the most appropriate option to fill in blank No. 3
[SSC Selection Post Phase IX, 2019]

A. conservation

B. endangerment

C. compensation

D. tourism

Q.80 Select the most appropriate option to fill in blank No. 4
[SSC Selection Post Phase IX, 2019]

A. inspires   **B.** includes   **C.** extends   **D.** exudes

// Smart Answer Sheet //

Correct — Percentage of students who answered correctly. **Skipped** — Percentage of students who skipped.

Q.	Ans.	Correct / Skipped	Q.	Ans.	Correct / Skipped	Q.	Ans.	Correct / Skipped	Q.	Ans.	Correct / Skipped	Q.	Ans.	Correct / Skipped
1	A	76.43 % / 10.55 %	17	A	26.37 % / 72.9 %	33	D	64.17 % / 30.01 %	49	A	61.02 % / 37.57 %	65	C	61.97 % / 35.55 %
2	B	83.28 % / 14.89 %	18	B	51.15 % / 31.75 %	34	A	55.62 % / 34.94 %	50	A	76.1 % / 23.16 %	66	D	57.68 % / 32.56 %
3	C	76.95 % / 14.93 %	19	C	60.79 % / 36.13 %	35	C	22.3 % / 73.7 %	51	C	82.58 % / 12.1 %	67	C	76.63 % / 18.61 %
4	C	78.06 % / 11.32 %	20	A	48.11 % / 36.3 %	36	D	56.53 % / 36.88 %	52	A	51.58 % / 45.83 %	68	C	11.06 % / 72.77 %
5	D	77.07 % / 17.5 %	21	A	61.08 % / 36.13 %	37	B	61.38 % / 32.15 %	53	A	77.99 % / 16.78 %	69	A	67.06 % / 30.04 %
6	D	60.21 % / 37.2 %	22	C	46.74 % / 48.8 %	38	D	64.1 % / 33.26 %	54	C	88.44 % / 10.32 %	70	A	55.83 % / 38.22 %
7	C	80.99 % / 17.99 %	23	D	43.72 % / 55.76 %	39	B	16.4 % / 75.87 %	55	D	89.13 % / 10.4 %	71	A	89.7 % / 10.16 %
8	A	42.81 % / 30.28 %	24	C	43.17 % / 52.3 %	40	A	46.5 % / 52.42 %	56	A	84.75 % / 10.3 %	72	C	87.85 % / 10.67 %
9	B	69.56 % / 30.29 %	25	B	68.98 % / 30.78 %	41	B	76.25 % / 19.97 %	57	A	85.44 % / 10.47 %	73	C	64.07 % / 35.16 %
10	D	81.28 % / 12.28 %	26	D	79.33 % / 19.53 %	42	D	77.27 % / 14.99 %	58	B	54.56 % / 45.08 %	74	A	81.6 % / 12.11 %
11	C	83.68 % / 13.85 %	27	C	51.7 % / 37.84 %	43	D	51.67 % / 41.47 %	59	B	56.57 % / 33.77 %	75	D	66.14 % / 31.87 %
12	A	84.04 % / 12.7 %	28	C	66.09 % / 30.43 %	44	B	44.03 % / 44.74 %	60	C	58.15 % / 32.41 %	76	A	47.23 % / 37.47 %
13	B	54.08 % / 31.46 %	29	C	81.3 % / 11.73 %	45	B	68.98 % / 30.46 %	61	B	49.77 % / 43.1 %	77	D	58.57 % / 32.26 %
14	D	59.82 % / 34.92 %	30	C	60.7 % / 38.23 %	46	A	49.22 % / 35.27 %	62	D	87.54 % / 11.85 %	78	B	60.39 % / 35.4 %
15	C	61.99 % / 36.74 %	31	B	16.62 % / 76.94 %	47	A	52.17 % / 38.02 %	63	D	84.81 % / 13.22 %	79	A	55.43 % / 41.25 %
16	D	53.39 % / 39.29 %	32	A	45.79 % / 37.61 %	48	C	42.22 % / 41.97 %	64	A	42.01 % / 32.88 %	80	B	62.49 % / 32.74 %

//Hints and Solutions//

1. Six Friends: Arif, Amit, Amar, Ankit, Rohit and Aditya

1. Ankit sits second to the left of Amit

2. Amit is sitting to the immediate right of Amar

3. One person sits between Rohit and Arif

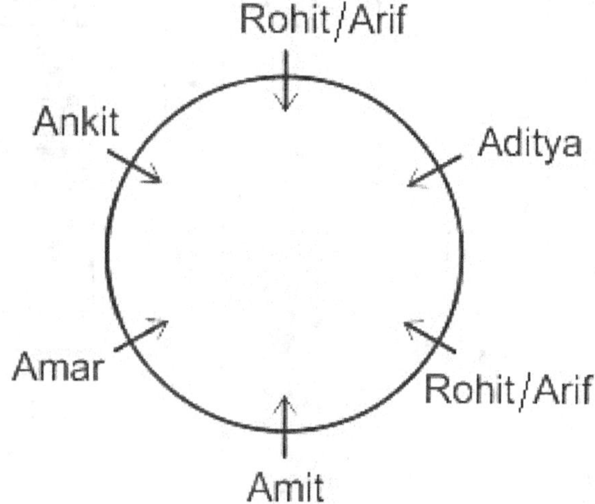

So, Ankit sits second to the right of Aditya.

Hence, the correct option is (A).

2. Given series,

2,3,5,7,11, ___ 17

The given series is of prime numbers.

The prime numbers are those which are only divisible by 1 or by itself.

Example; 2,3,5,7 etc.

After 11,13 is the next prime number.

So, 13 is the missing term.

Hence, the correct option is (B).

3. Male can be Actor as well as Director.

Therefore, the possible Venn diagram is as follows:

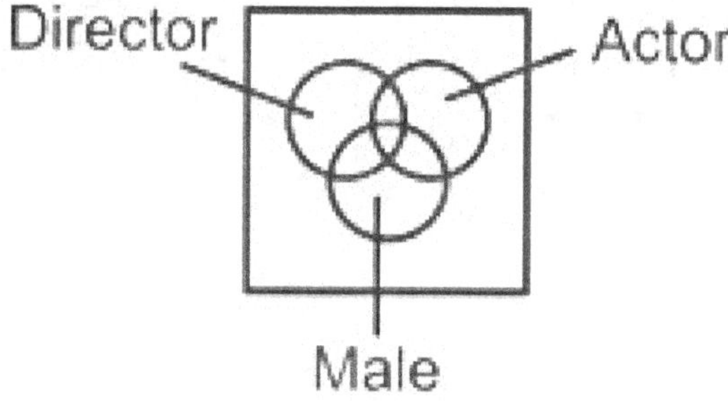

Hence, the correct option is (C).

4. The given equation is:

9 - 3 + 2 ÷ 16 × 2 = ?

After replacing the symbols by their meaning, we get:

$\Rightarrow 9 + 3 \times 2 - 16 \div 2$

$\Rightarrow 9 + 6 - 8$

$\Rightarrow 15 - 8 = 7$

Hence, the correct option is (C).

5. The mirror image is:

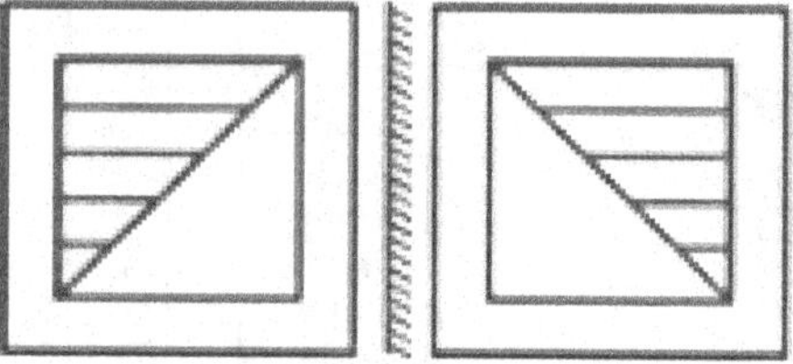

Hence, the correct option is (D).

6. We know that:

Alpha bets	A	B	C	D	E	F	G	H	I	J	K	L	M
Positional value	1	2	3	4	5	6	7	8	9	10	11	12	13
Positional value	26	25	24	23	22	21	20	19	18	17	16	15	14
Alpha bets	Z	Y	X	W	V	U	T	S	R	Q	P	O	N

The logic followed here is:

G + 4 = K;

K + 4 = O;

O + 4 = S.

So, answer figure 'C' will be the next figure for the given series.

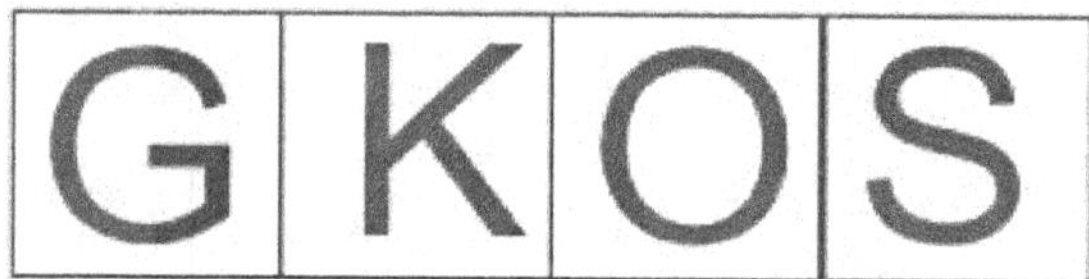

Hence, the correct option is (D).

7. The logic followed here is as follows:

4 + 5 + 9 = 18

11 + 6 + 13 = 30

Similarly,

19 + 0 + 3 = 22

Hence, the correct option is (C).

8. The correct dictionary order of the words is-

4. Convalesce

3. Convenience

2. Converge

5. Converse

1. Convince

Hence, the correct option is (A).

9. Let, the bigger digit $= x$ and smaller digit $= y$

According to the question,

$$\Rightarrow x + y = 12 \quad ...(1)$$

$$\Rightarrow x - y = 4 \quad ...(2)$$

From (1) and (2) we get, $x = 8$ and $y = 4$

∴ The product of the two digits of the number $= xy = 8 \times 4 = 32$

Hence, the correct option is (B).

10. From the given figures we can see that,

3 is adjacent to both 4 and 6.

So,

There are 5 dots on the face opposite the face bearing 3 dots.

Hence, the correct option is (D).

11. The least possible Venn Diagram for the given statements will be as follows:

I. No cat is a cow → False (This is possible but not definite)

II. Some cows are monkeys → False (This is definitely false)

So, Neither conclusion I nor conclusion II follows.

Hence, the correct option is (C).

12. According to the given coding language,

A	B	C	D	E	F	G	H	I	J	K	L	M
1	2	3	4	5	6	7	8	9	10	11	12	13
Z	Y	X	W	V	U	T	S	R	Q	P	O	N
26	25	24	23	22	21	20	19	18	17	16	15	14

L = 12 (1 + 2) = 3
I = 9
F = 6
E = 5
Similarly,
F = 6
U = 21 (2 + 1) = 3

N = 14 (1 + 4) = 5
So, FUN corresponds to 635.

Hence, the correct option is (A).

13. Letters of the word are coded according to the equivalent opposite letter of a particular letter of the word.

A	B	C	D
Z	Y	X	W

Similarly,

G	H	I	J
T	S	R	Q

Therefore, 'TSRQ' is the correct answer.

Hence, the correct option is (B).

14. When the folded paper is opened, the cuts will appear as follow:

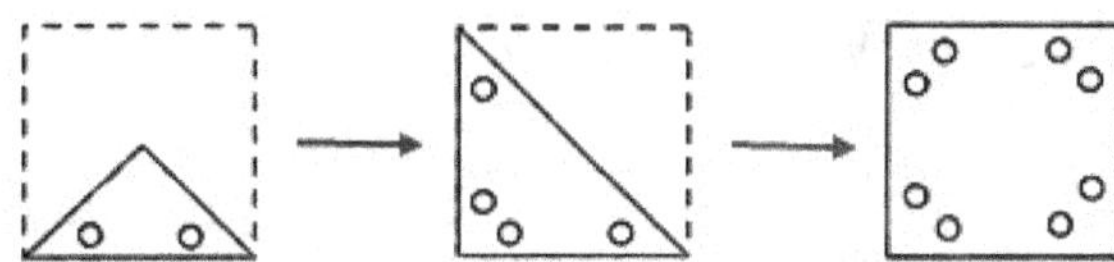

Hence, the correct option is (D).

15. Given: ZH_ORC_ _K_R_ZH_O_C

By checking options:

(A) K, Z, H, K, R, K, R → ZHKORC / ZHKKRR / ZHKORC

(B) Z, H, K, O, C, K, R → ZHZORC/ HKKORC/ ZHKORC

(C) K, Z, H, O, C, K, R → ZHKORC/ ZHKORC/ ZHKORC

(here, ZHKORC is repeating)

(D) K, Z, O, R, C, K, R → ZHKORC / ZOKRRC / ZHKORC

Option (C) gives a pattern of ZHKORC / ZHKORC / ZHKORC.

Hence, the correct option is (C).

16. All follow the same pattern except 'VR'.

The pattern followed here is,

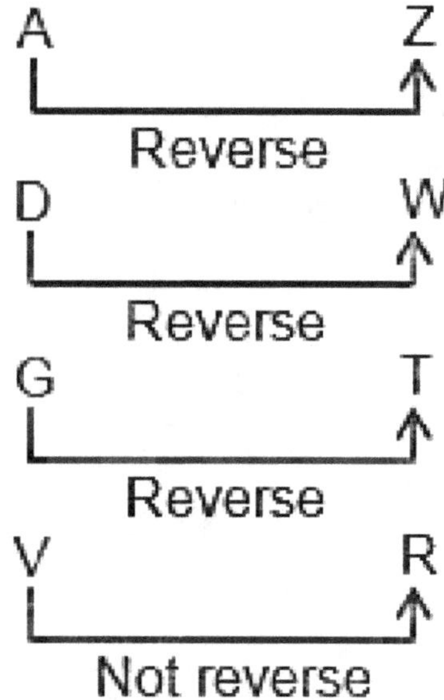

A is at 1st position, 1st position from the end is Z.

D is at 4th position, 4th position from the end is W.

G is at 7th position, 7th position from the end is T.

V is at 22nd position, 22nd position from the end is E.

∴ The odd letters from the given alternatives is 'VR'.

Hence, the correct option is (D).

17. There is circle in second row, third column which is not present in other figures.

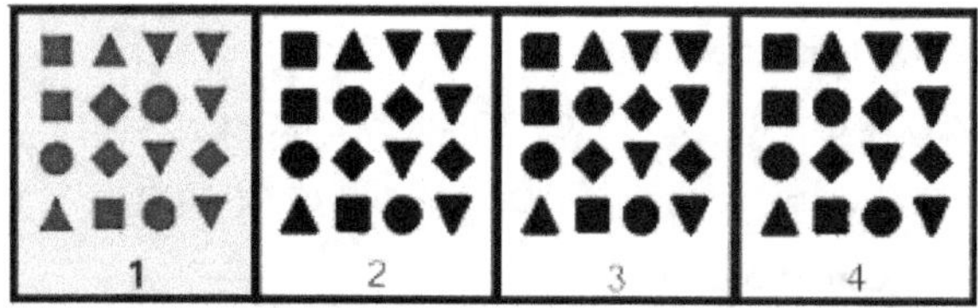

Hence, the correct option is (A).

18. The given figure is embedded in option (B) as follows:

Hence, the correct option is (B).

19. By using the symbols in the table given below, we can draw the following family tree:

Symbol in Diagram	Meaning
○	Female
□	Male
=	Married Couple
—	Siblings
|	Difference of a generation

According to the given information:

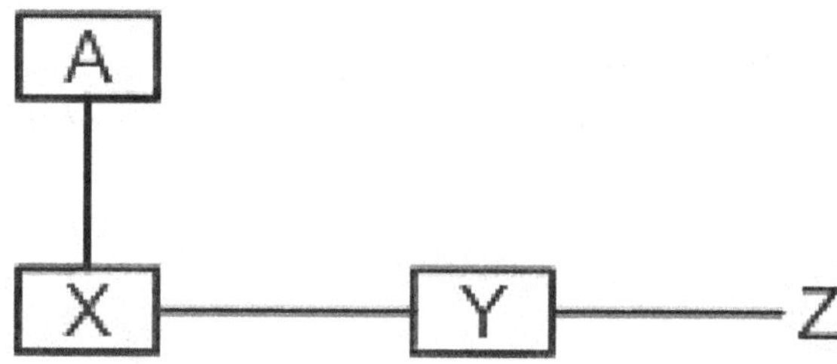

Here,

X is the brother of Y and Y is the brother of Z.

So, Z may be the brother or sister of X (As gender is not specified in the question).

Hence, the correct option is (C).

20. Given:

$$2:54::4:?$$

The logic followed here is:

$$(1\text{st number} + 1)^3 \times 2 = 2\text{nd number}$$

$$2:54 \to (2+1)^3 \times 2 = 3^3 \times 2 = 27 \times 2 = 54$$

Similarly,

$$4:? \to (4+1)^3 \times 2 = 5^3 \times 2 = 125 \times 2 = 250$$

So, 250 is the correct answer.

Hence, the correct option is (A).

21. Article 72 of the Indian Constitution gives the President the power to pardon.

Pardon means the complete release and release of an offender. Under Article 72, the President of India can grant pardon or reduce the punishment of a convicted person, especially in cases involving capital punishment. can.

Hence, the correct option is (A).

22. As per the Constitution of India, the minimum age requirement to be a member of a Panchayat is 21 years.

Member of Gram Panchayat or candidate for the seat of Sarpanch, you must be a registered voter in the electoral roll of that Gram Panchayat, and must not be less than 21 years of age. The leader of the panchayat was often called the president mukhiya, sarpanch, or pradhan, an elected or generally accepted office. Such local bodies have representatives who are elected by the local people and hence have a better understanding of the issues at the grassroots level.

Hence, the correct option is (C).

23. The right to equality has been given under Article 14-18 of the Indian Constitution.

These ensure equal treatment before the law and equal protection of the law, equal opportunities in public employment and prevent discrimination and untouchability which are social evils.

The term right to equality means that all citizens should be treated equally before the law of the land and any unfair treatment based on gender, caste, race, religion or place of birth should be discarded.

Right to equality is a fundamental element which is necessary to implement the rights given to Indian citizens. It lays the foundation of all other rights and privileges conferred by the Constitution.

Hence, the correct option is (D).

24. Larsen & Toubro (L&T) Ltd has signed an MoU with the Gujarat govt to set up an IT and IT-enabled Services (ITeS) Park in Vadodara in August 2022.

- The park is being set up under the recently announced IT/ITeS policy of the state government.
- This policy was launched in February 2022 with an aim to generate one lakh 'high-skilled jobs' in the IT sector in the next five years.

Hence, the correct option is (C).

25. Haryana Government recently launched the Haryana Cheerag Scheme.

Under the scheme, government will provide free education to Economically Weaker section (EWS) students of Government schools in private school. Cheerag Scheme stands for, "Chief Minister Equal Education Relief, Assistance and Grant".

Hence, the correct option is (B).

26. Abhijit Sen, one of India's leading agricultural economists passed away on August 29, 2022 at the age of 72. Abhijit Sen was a member of the Planning Commission of India from 2004 to 2014 during the tenure of former Prime Minister Manmohan Singh.

Hence, the correct option is (D).

27. Alluvial soil is also known as Khadar.

Alluvial soils are called transport soils because although they are formed near water bodies, these soils are carried from their origin to many other places by various natural components especially by gravity. These soils are found in the northern plains from Punjab to West Bengal and Assam. It is also found in peninsular India in the deltas of rivers like Krishna, Godavari, Kaveri and Mahanadi. The main crops cultivated are wheat, rice, maize, sugarcane, pulses and oilseeds.

Hence, the correct option is (C).

28.

Rock	District
a. Gondwana series rocks	Yavatmal, Gadchiroli
b. Dharwar series rocks	Bhandara, Gondia
c. Archean series	Sawantwadi, Vengurla
d. Vindhyan series rocks	Chandrapur

Gondwana is a region of India, named after the Gondi people who live there (though they can also be found in other parts of India). The name of the ancient continent of Gondwanaland was derived from Gondwana, because some of the earliest rock formations of this continent were first investigated in part of the region, in modern Odisha.

Dharwar Rock System is special because it is the first metamorphic sedimentary rocks in India. They are named Dharwar system because they were first studied in Dharwar region of Karnataka.

The Archean or Purana rock system in India is found in Aravallis mountains, 2/3rd of the Deccan peninsula and some parts of north east. These rocks have abundant metallic and non-metallic minerals such as iron, copper, manganese, bauxite, lead, zinc, gold, silver, tin, tungsten, mica, asbestos, graphite, etc.

The Vindhyan rocks of this area comprise sandstones, shales, limestones and conglomerates. The most persistent and well defined rock type of the Vindhyan system seen in the area are the sandstones, which show a wide range in colour, compaction and grain size.

Hence, the correct option is (C).

29. Ujali or Aneri Holi festivals are associated with Tharu Tribe. The community belongs to the Terai lowlands, amid the Shivaliks of the lower Himalayas. Most of them are forest dwellers and some practiced agriculture. The word Tharu is believed to be derived from Sthavir, meaning followers of Theravada Buddhism. The Tharus live in both India and Nepal.

Hence, the correct option is (C).

30. Electromotive force has the same unit as that of potential difference.

Electromotive force is the electric potential generated by either an electrochemical cell or a changing magnetic field. Electromotive force is commonly denoted by the acronym emf, EMF, or E. The SI unit for electromotive force is the volt (V).

Potential difference: The difference in electric potential between two points is called a potential difference. The SI unit is Volt (V).

Hence, the correct option is (C).

31. The Phillips Curve represents relationship between Inflation and Unemployment.

The Phillips curve states that inflation and unemployment have an inverse relationship. Higher inflation is associated with lower unemployment and vice versa.

Phillips conjectured that the lower the unemployment rate, the tighter the labor market and, therefore, the faster firms must raise wages to attract scarce labor. At higher rates of unemployment, the pressure abated. Phillips's "curve" represented the average relationship between unemployment and wage behavior over the business cycle. It showed the rate of wage inflation that would result if a particular level of unemployment persisted for some time.

Hence, the correct option is (B).

32. Hawtrey propagated the Pure Monetary Theory of Trade Cycle.

R.G. Hawtrey describes the trade cycle as a purely monetary phenomenon, in this sense that all changes in the level of economic activity are nothing but reflections of changes in the flow of money.

According to Hawtrey, the main factor affecting the flow of money, money supply is the credit creation by the banking system. To him, changes in income and spending are caused by changes in the volume of bank credit. The real causes of the trade cycle can be traced to variations in effective demand which occur due to changes in bank credit.

Therefore, "The trade cycle is a monetary phenomenon, because general demand is itself a monetary phenomenon."

Hence, the correct option is (A).

33. Otis invented the safety break, which would stop the elevator from crashing if it was activated by sudden falling when a rope broke.

American industrialist Elisha Otis first invented the first safe hoist in 1852. He designed this lifter when he needed to lift heavy building materials while converting a sawmill into a factory in Yonkers, New York. He invented a design that had a safety "brake". Although he did not invent the hoist, he did invent the braking safety system used in modern lifters.

Hence, the correct option is (D).

34. In the 36th National Games, Anish of Haryana won the gold medal in Men's Rapid Fire Pistol event at Ahmedabad in Gujarat on 30 Sept 2022. Ankur Goyal of Uttarakhand and Gurmeet of Punjab won silver and bronze, respectively. While in Men's 1500 Meter run, Parvez Khan won gold medal. PM Modi had inaugurated the 36th National Games in the Narendra Modi stadium in Ahmedabad, Gujarat on 29 Sept 2022.

Hence, the correct option is (A).

35. The 2022 Nobel Prize in Chemistry has been jointly awarded to Carolyn Bertozzi, Morton Meldal Barry Sharpless for their work on snipping molecules together, known as 'click chemistry'. Their work is used to explore cells track biological processes and can be applied in cancer treatment drugs. Barry Sharpless also won a Nobel Prize in 2001 for his work on chirally catalysed oxidation reactions.

Hence, the correct option is (C).

36. Seasoned finance professional Sandeep Kumar Gupta on 3rd Oct 2022 took over as the chairman and managing director of GAIL (India) Ltd, the nation's largest gas utility. Gupta, who previously was Director (Finance) at Indian Oil Corporation, replaces Manoj Jain, who superannuated on 31st Aug 2022. Gupta will have a term till Feb 2026. GAIL's natural gas pipeline network covers 21 states.

Hence, the correct option is (D).

37. The Rig Veda represents the earliest sacred book of India. It is the oldest and biggest amongst all the four Vedas.

'Rik' is the name given to those Mantras which are meant for the praise of the deities. Thus the collection (Samhita) of Riks is known as Rigveda-Samhita. The Rig Veda Samhita contains about 10552 Mantras, classified into ten books called Mandalas.

Hence, the correct option is (B).

38. Bihzad one of the following painters was not associated with Humayun.

Bihzad's name has become synonymous with the high level of artistic skill displayed by the painters under the reign of Timurids and later the dynasty of Safavids in today's Afghanistan and Iran.

- He led an entire workshop producing manuscript illuminations.
- He came up with a new style that uses geometry and architectural elements as the structural or compositional context in which the figures are arranged.

Hence, the correct option is (D).

39. During the British Rule, the Britishers used the Indian capital for their benefits and transferred the Indian capital to the England. Laissez- Faire is the system in which transaction between Private parties are free from Government intervention and during the colonial time Laissez-faire never promoted the Indigenous capitalism.

Hence, the correct option is (B).

40. Eicher Motors, the parent company of Royal Enfield, has announced appointing B Govindarajan as the motorcycle brand's Chief Executive Officer. In addition to being the CEO of Royal Enfield, Govindarajan will also serve as a Wholetime Director on the Board of Eicher Motors Limited (EML). Govindarajan has led the development & launch of several models at Royal Enfield.

Hence, the correct option is (A).

41. Given:

$$\sqrt{324} + 9^2 - 7^2 = 2 \times (?)^2$$

According to the BODMAS Rule,

$$\sqrt{324} + 9^2 - 7^2 = 2 \times (?)^2$$

$$\Rightarrow 18 + 81 - 49 = 2 \times (?)^2$$

$\Rightarrow 50 = 2 \times (?)^2$

$\Rightarrow \frac{50}{2} = (?)^2$

$\Rightarrow 25 = (?)^2$

$\Rightarrow ? = \sqrt{25}$

$\Rightarrow ? = 5$

$\therefore$ 5 will come in the place of question mark (?).

Hence, the correct option is (B).

42. Given:

The given expression is $(1^1 + 2^2 + 3^3)^3$.

Basic concept of power and number system,

$\Rightarrow (1^1 + 2^2 + 3^3)^3$

The unit digit of $1^1 = 1$

The unit digit of $2^2 = 4$

The unit digit of $3^3 = 7$

Now, sum of all digits $= 1 + 4 + 7 = 12$

$\therefore$ the unit digit of $(12)^3 = 1728$.

So, the unit digit of expression $(1^1 + 2^2 + 3^3)^3$ is 8.

Hence, the correct option is (D).

43. Numbers divisible by 7 are $7, 14, 21 + \cdots .98$

Sum $= 7 + 14 + 21 + \cdots .98$

$= 7(1 + 2 + 3 + \cdots 14)$

Sum of numbers $S_n = \frac{n}{2}[2a + (n-1)d]$

So, $S_{14} = 7\left[\frac{7}{2}\{2 \times 1 + (14 - 1) \times 1\}\right]$

$= 7[7\{2 + 13\}]$

$= 7(7 \times 15)$

$= 735$

Hence, the correct option is (D).

44. Given:

A fraction when added to $\frac{17}{3}$ gives 4.

Let the fraction be x.

According to the question,

$x + \frac{17}{3} = 4$

$\Rightarrow x = 4 - \frac{17}{3}$

$\Rightarrow x = \frac{(12 - 17)}{3}$

$\Rightarrow x = -\frac{5}{3}$

$\Rightarrow x = -1\frac{2}{3}$

$\therefore$ The fraction $-1\frac{2}{3}$.

Hence, the correct option is (B).

45. Let the number be x.

If the number is increased by 10%, then

The new number will be $= x + 10\%$ of $x = x + 0.1x = 1.1x$

Again, the number is decreased by 20%, then

The new number will be $= 1.1x - 20\%$ of $1.1x = 0.88x$

Percentage change $= (x - 0.88x) \times \frac{100}{x} = 12\%$ decrease

Hence, the correct option is (B).

46. Given:

A certain sum of money doubles itself in 15 years.

Time $T = 15$ years

Let the principal $P = Rs. X$

Amount $A = Rs. 2X$

Simple Interest $SI = A - P$

$\Rightarrow SI = Rs. (2X - X)$

$\Rightarrow SI = Rs. X$

We know that,

$R = \frac{100 \times SI}{P \times T}$ where R is rate percent per annum

$\Rightarrow R = \frac{100 \times X}{X \times 15}$

$\Rightarrow R = \frac{20}{3}$

$\Rightarrow R = 6\frac{2}{3}\%$

Hence, the correct option is (A).

47. Given-

$Rs. 2304$ amounts to $Rs. 2500$ in 2 years at compound interest.

Principal $P = Rs. 2304$

Amount $A = Rs.\,2500$

Time $T = 2$ years

According to the formula-

$$A = P\left(1 + \frac{R}{100}\right)^T \quad \text{where } R \text{ is rate percent per annum}$$

$$\Rightarrow 2500 = 2304\left(1 + \frac{R}{100}\right)^2$$

$$\Rightarrow \frac{2500}{2304} = \left(1 + \frac{R}{100}\right)^2$$

$$\Rightarrow \frac{625}{576} = \left(1 + \frac{R}{100}\right)^2$$

$$\Rightarrow \frac{25}{24} = \left(1 + \frac{R}{100}\right)$$

$$\Rightarrow \frac{1}{24} = \frac{R}{100}$$

$$\Rightarrow \frac{100}{24} = R$$

$$\Rightarrow \frac{25}{6} = R$$

$$\Rightarrow R = 4\frac{1}{6}\%$$

Hence, the correct option is (A).

48. Given:

The product of LCM and HCF $= 48$ and

Difference of two numbers $= 8$

Let the numbers be x and $(x + 8)$.

Product of numbers = HCF $\times$ LCM

$$x(x + 8) = 48$$

$$\Rightarrow x^2 + 12x - 4x - 48 = 0$$

$$\Rightarrow (x + 12)(x - 4) = 0$$

$$\Rightarrow x = 4 \text{ and } x = -12$$

Then the numbers 4 and 12.

Hence, the correct option is (C).

49. Given:

A's share : B's share = A's investment : B's investment =24000: 8000=3 : 1.

Let be A's share $= 3x$ and B's share $= 1x$

According to the question

$$3x + x = 48000$$

$$\Rightarrow 4x = 48000$$

$$\Rightarrow x = 12000$$

Put the value of x in A & B Share of B

=Rs .12000

Share of A=3 $x = 3 \times 12000$

=Rs .36000

$\therefore$ Share of A and B is Rs. 36,000 & Rs. 12,000

Hence, the correct option is (A).

50. Given:

Two numbers are in the ratio of $5:6$.

If 8 is subtracted from them, they become in the ratio of $4:5$.

Let the two number be $5x$ and $6x$

According to the question,

$$\Rightarrow \frac{(5x-8)}{(6x-8)} = \frac{4}{5}$$

$$\Rightarrow 5(5x - 8) = 4(6x - 8)$$

$$\Rightarrow 25x - 40 = 24x - 32$$

$$\Rightarrow x = 8$$

The number are $5 \times 8 = 40, 6 \times 8 = 48$.

$\therefore$ The numbers are $(40, 48)$.

Hence, the correct option is (A).

51. Given:

The average of 20 numbers is 56.

We know that,

Sum of observations = average × numbers of observations

Sum of all numbers = 56 × 20 = 1120

Later it was found that the number 10 was wrongly taken as 100

$\Rightarrow$ Correct sum = 1120 − 100 + 10 = 1030

$\therefore$ Correct Average = $\dfrac{Correct\ sum}{Number}$ = $\dfrac{1030}{20}$ = 51.5

Hence, the correct option is (C).

52. Given,

MP of the article is more than the cost price by = 60%

Discount percentage = 30%

$$SP = MP \times \frac{(100 - Discount\%)}{100}$$

Let cost price of the article be Rs. $100x$

MP of the article $= 100x \times \dfrac{160}{100} = $ Rs. $160x$

SP of the article $= 160x \times \dfrac{70}{100} = 112x$

Profit $= 112x - 100x = 12x$

$\therefore$ Profit $\% = \dfrac{12x}{100x} \times 100 = 12\%$

Hence, the correct option is (A).

53. The circumference of circular wire is 132 cm.

Now, a square is formed with the same circular wire.

∴ Circumference of circular wire = Perimeter of the square

⇒ 4 × side = 132

⇒ Side = 33 cm

Now, area of the square = side × side

= 33 × 33 = 1089 cm²

Hence, the correct option is (A).

54. Given:

Length of train = 400 m

Time taken to cross a pole = 16 sec

As we know,

$$\text{Speed} = \frac{Distance}{Time}$$

$$\text{Speed} = \frac{400}{16} \times \frac{18}{5} = 90 \text{ km/hr}$$

∴ The speed of the train is 90 km/hr.

Hence, the correct option is (C).

55. To paint 10 rooms, 12 persons take = 16 days

To paint 1 room, 12 persons will take = $\frac{16}{10} = \frac{8}{5}$ days

To paint 1 room, 1 person will take = $12 \times \frac{8}{5} = \frac{96}{5}$ days

To paint 1 room, 8 persons will take = $\frac{1}{8} \times \frac{96}{5} = \frac{12}{5}$ days

To paint 20 rooms, 8 persons will take = $20 \times \frac{12}{5}$ = 48 days

∴ 8 persons will take 48 days to paint 20 rooms.

Hence, the correct option is (D).

56. Given:

$$1456 \div 16 \times 14 + 22 = (?)^4$$

$$\Rightarrow 91 \times 14 + 22 = (?)^4$$

$$\Rightarrow 1274 + 22 = (?)^4$$

$$\Rightarrow (?)^4 = 1296$$

$$\Rightarrow ? = 6$$

∴ The value of ? is 6

Hence, the correct option is (A).

57. Given,

The average of 5 quantities $= 6$

Therefore, the sum of the 5 quantities $= 5 \times 6 = 30$

The average of three of these 5 quantities $= 8$

Therefore, the sum of these three quantities $= 3 \times 8 = 24$

Sum of the remaining two quantities $= 30 - 24 = 6$

Average of these two quantities $= \frac{6}{2} = 3$

Hence, the correct option is (A).

58. Given:

Uber car complete a certain distance in $= 21$ hours

One-third part of the distance cover by Uber car in $20 km/hr.$

Rest part of the distance cover by Uber car in $50 km/hr.$

Formula:

$$\text{Speed} = \frac{Distance}{Time}$$

Calculation:

Let, the distance $= x km$

According to the question,

$$\Rightarrow \left[\frac{x}{3} \times \frac{1}{20}\right] + \left[\frac{2x}{3} \times \frac{1}{50}\right] = 21$$

$$\Rightarrow \frac{x}{60} + \frac{x}{75} = 21$$

$$\Rightarrow \frac{9x}{300} = 21$$

$$\Rightarrow x = \frac{21 \times 300}{9}$$

$$\Rightarrow x = 700 km$$

∴ Total distance is $700 km.$

Hence, the correct option is (B).

59. Given,

Efficiency of Raj $= \frac{100}{20} = 5\%$

Work completed by Raj $= 25\%$

Rest work $= 75\%$

Efficiency of Abhijit $= \frac{75}{10} = 7.5\%$

Combined efficiency $= 5 + 7.5 = 12.5\%$

They will complete the whole work by working together in, $= \frac{100}{12.5}$

$= 8$ days

Hence, the correct option is (B).

60. Given:

Cost price of the wrist watch $CP =$ Rs. 450

Profit $P = 20\%$

Selling price of the wrist watch $SP = 120\% \times$ Rs. 450

$$\Rightarrow SP = \frac{120}{100} \times 450$$

$$\Rightarrow SP = \text{Rs. } 540$$

Discount given $d = 10\%$

List price of the wrist watch $LP = \frac{100 \times SP}{100 - \%d}$

$$\Rightarrow LP = \frac{100 \times 540}{100 - 10}$$

$$\Rightarrow LP = \frac{100 \times 540}{90}$$

$$\Rightarrow LP = \text{Rs. } 600$$

Hence, the correct option is (C).

61. In the given sentence, "are" should be replaced by "is". If the subjects are both singular and are connected by the words "or," "nor," "neither/nor," "either/or," and "not only/but also" the verb is singular.

Hence, the correct option is (B).

62. There is no error in the given sentence.

As some adjectives like "junior, senior, prior, prefer, inferior" don't take "than" after them in the comparative degree. Rather they take "to" after them.

Hence, the correct option is (D).

63. Let us explore the given options:

- The preposition 'on' means at the time of.
- The preposition 'during' means throughout the course or duration of a period of time.
- The preposition 'for' is used for saying the particular time or date that something is planned to happen.
- The preposition 'by' is used for indicating a deadline or the end of a particular time period.

Correct Sentence: Barring strong headwinds, the plane will arrive on schedule.

Hence, the correct option is (D).

64. Let us explore the given options:

- The preposition 'via' means travelling through a place en route to a destination.
- The preposition 'throughout' means in every part of a place or object.
- The preposition 'within' means inside something.
- The preposition 'towards' means in the direction of.

Correct Sentence: The US Open will be transmitted live via satellite.

Hence, the correct option is (A).

65. Let us explore the given options:

- The preposition 'past' means beyond in time; later than.
- The preposition 'beside' means at the side of; next to.
- The preposition 'minus' means of temperature below zero by.
- The preposition 'per' means for each (used with units to express a rate).

Correct Sentence: Am I allowed to stay out past 10?

Hence, the correct option is (C).

66. The correct answer is 'impulsive'.

The word 'Spontaneous' means done instantly and without conscious thought or decision.

Example: His jokes seemed spontaneous, but were in fact carefully prepared beforehand.

The synonyms of the word 'Spontaneous' are "impulsive, random, instinctive".

From the synonym of the given word, we can say that the word 'impulsive' is the same in meaning.

The word 'impulsive' means acting or done without forethought.

Example: He needs to learn to control his impulsive behavior.

Hence, the correct option is (D).

67. Red-handed: caught in the act of doing something wrong or illegal.

In a sentence: He was caught red-handed taking money from the cash register.

Hence, the correct option is (C).

68. Put a spoke in somebody's wheel: to prevent somebody from putting their plans into operation.

His letter really put a spoke in our wheel. The best option is thwarted in the execution of the plan.

Hence, the correct option is (C).

69. Let's look at the meaning of the marked option:

- Equinox- the time or date (twice each year) at which the sun crosses the celestial equator, when day and night are of approximately equal length (about September 22 and March 20)

Let's look at the meanings of the other given options:

- Solstice- the time or date (twice each year) at which the sun reaches its maximum or minimum declination, marked by the longest and shortest days (about June 21 and December 22)
- Eclipse- an obscuring of the light from one celestial body by the passage of another between it and the observer or between it and its source of illumination
- Stellar- relating to a star or stars

So, from the given meanings, we find that equinox is the correct one-word substitute.

Hence, the correct option is (A).

70. The most appropriate one-word for the given group of words is 'Cardinal'.

Word	Meaning	Example
Cardinal	of great importance	Finding food was a cardinal concern.
Scanty	smaller in size or amount than is considered necessary or is hoped for	Evidence of such an association is, however, scanty in children of pre-school age.
Meager	(of amounts or numbers) very small or not enough	The prisoners existed on a meager diet.
Supplementary	added to something else in order to improve it or complete it	Teachers often create supplementary materials for their classes.

Hence, the correct option is (A).

71. Intricate is the correct spelling.

Intricate means very complicated or detailed.

Hence, the correct option is (A).

72. Rhythm is correctly spelled.

Rhythm means a strong, regular repeated pattern of movement or sound.

Hence, the correct option is (C).

73. The meaning of the given words:

Tacit: he word 'Tacit' means understood or implied without being stated.

Oral: the word 'Oral' means relating to the transmission of information or literature by word of mouth.

Order: an authoritative command or instruction.

Written: mark (letters, words, or other symbols) on a surface, typically paper, with a pen, pencil, or similar implement.

Understanding: the power of abstract thought; intellect.

So, from the given meanings, we find that tacit is the antonym for understanding.

Hence, the correct option is (C).

74. 'an' and 'a' are definite articles whereas 'the' is an indefinite article.'an' is used when the word starts with a vowel sound - that is, 'a', 'e', 'i', 'o', 'u' and 'a' is used for words starting with a consonant sound. Here, 'honest', when pronounced, has a sound of 'o' which is a vowel. So, 'an' must be used before 'honest'.

So, the correct sentence is "Bulbul is an honest girl but she is also very rude".

Hence, the correct option is (A).

75. In the given sentence, there is an inappropriate use of prepositions.

Here, to will be used after indebted which is an appropriate preposition. To is used after adjectives and it also denotes destination.

Example: We are deeply indebted to you for your help.

We use from to refer to the place where someone or something starts or originates.

Example: The wind is coming from the north.

So, the correct sentence is "I would be eternally indebted to you if you could help me".

Hence, the correct option is (D).

76. The correct answer is 'everywhere'

The adverb 'everywhere' means in or to all places.

The adverb 'anywhere' means in or to any place.

The adverb 'somewhere' means in or to someplace.

The adverb 'nowhere' means not in or to any place; not anywhere.

So the correct sentence is-

I looked everywhere for my puppy but could not find it.

Hence, the correct option is (A).

77. The given sentence talks about the people who have administrative power or control of the park.

- The word 'delegation' cannot be chosen because it means a body of delegates (delegate - a person sent or authorized to represent others, in particular, an elected representative sent to a conference).
- The word 'people' is clearly not relevant here.
- The word 'government' cannot be chosen.
- The word 'authorities', which means 'the people who have administrative power or control', is the best fit.

Hence, the correct option is (D).

78. It is clear from the sentence that a new plan was chosen.

- The word 'adapting', which means 'to modify', cannot be used here.
- The word 'fostering', which means 'to encourage', is not the best fit for the sentence.
- The word 'thinking' cannot be chosen because the plan was being chosen.
- The word 'adopting', which means 'to embrace' or 'to choose', is the best fit.

Hence, the correct option is (B).

79. The word 'Conservation', which means 'preservation', is the right answer as the passage suggests that the government is organizing training programs to spread awareness.

- The word 'endangerment', which means 'to put someone in danger', is irrelevant for the sentence.
- The word 'tourism' cannot be used here as the plan is to protect the rhino.
- The word 'Compensation', which means 'money awarded to someone'

Hence, the correct option is (A).

80. It is about a training programme and the word 'trekking' is mentioned here. It can be said that 'trekking' is a part of the programme.

- The word 'inspire', which means 'to motivate', cannot be the answer.
- The word 'extends', which means 'to expand', is not relevant. So, it cannot be chosen.
- The word 'exudes', which means 'to discharge' or 'to release', is not relevant for the sentence.
- The word 'includes', which means 'comprise', is the best fit.

Hence, the correct option is (B).

General Intelligence and Reasoning

Q.1 Direction: In the following question, select the related number from the given alternatives.

$1511 : 2 : : 6554 : ?$

A. 3   **B.** 4   **C.** 5   **D.** 6

Q.2 Rohit, Kyra, Suraj, Laila and Diya are sitting on a bench. Kyra is sitting to the right of Suraj, who is not sitting at extreme corners. Laila is sitting in between Kyra and Rohit. Diya is sitting at extreme left. Who is to the left of Kyra?

A. Rohit   **B.** Diya   **C.** Suraj   **D.** Laila

Q.3 Find the missing number in the series given below.

10, 21, 43, 87, ?

A. 175   **B.** 185   **C.** 202   **D.** 165

Q.4 After folding, punching and opening the paper as shown in the question figures below, which answer figure will it look like?

Question figure

  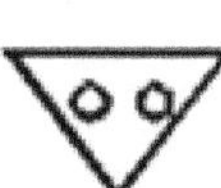

Answer figure

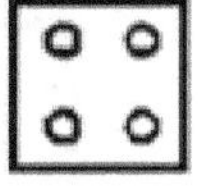 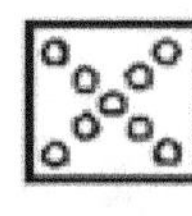

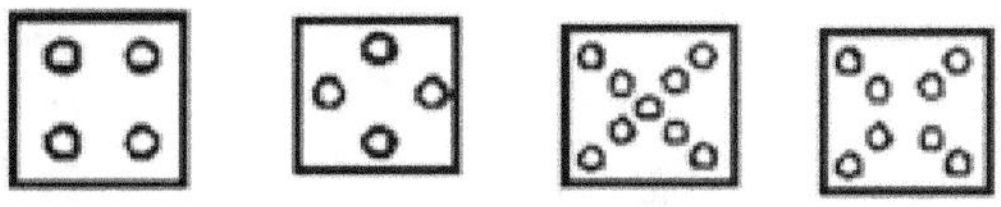

(A)   (B)   (C)   (D)

A. (A)   **B.** (B)   **C.** (C)   **D.** (D)

Q.5 Direction: Choose the correct alternatives from the given ones that will complete the series?

V, S, P, M, ?, G

A. T   **B.** P   **C.** L   **D.** J

Q.6 From the given options, find the ODD one out.

A. PV   **B.** TW   **C.** LO   **D.** EH

Q.7 W introduced herself to U by saying that you are the daughter-in-law of my husband's father's wife. How are U and W related to each other?

A. U is W' s husband's brother's wife.

B. U is W's husband's sister.

C. W is U's husband's sister.

D. W is U's brother's wife.

Q.8 Direction: In the following question, you are given a figure (X) followed by four alternative figures (1), (2), (3), and (4) such that figure (X) is embedded in one of them. Trace out the alternative figure which contains fig. (X) as its part.

Find out the alternative figure which contains figure (X) as its part.

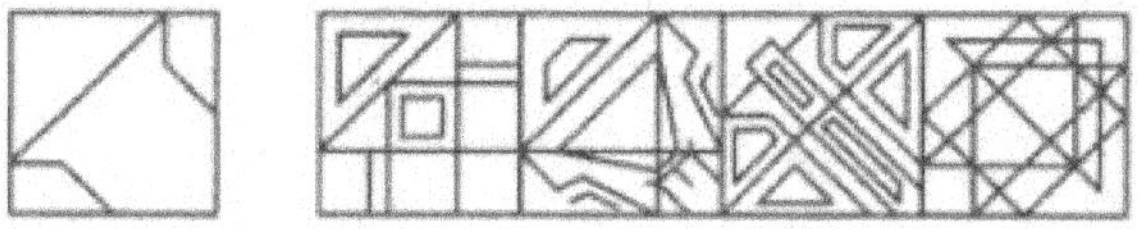

(X)   (1)   (2)   (3)   (4)

A. (1)   **B.** (2)   **C.** (3)   **D.** (4)

Q.9 Direction: Identify the diagram which best represents the relationship among the classes given below.

Surat, Gujarat, India

A. 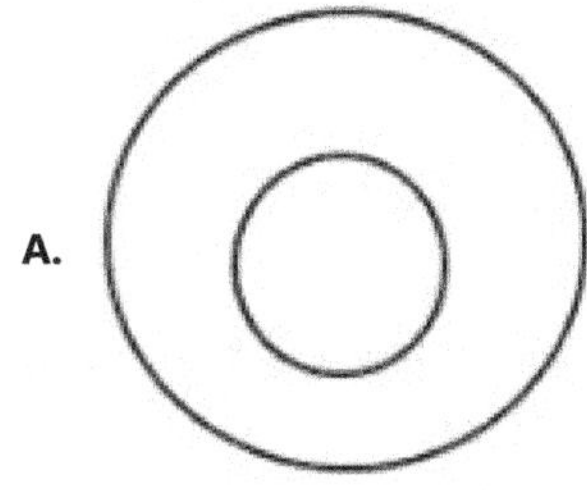

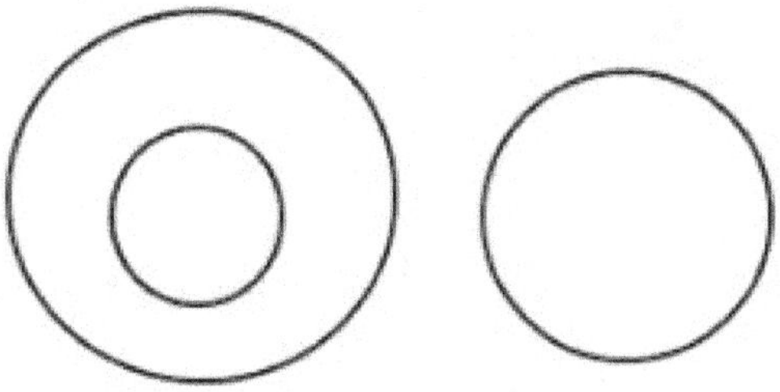

B. 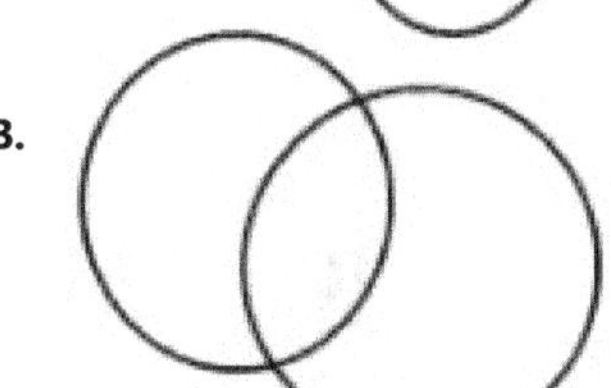

C. 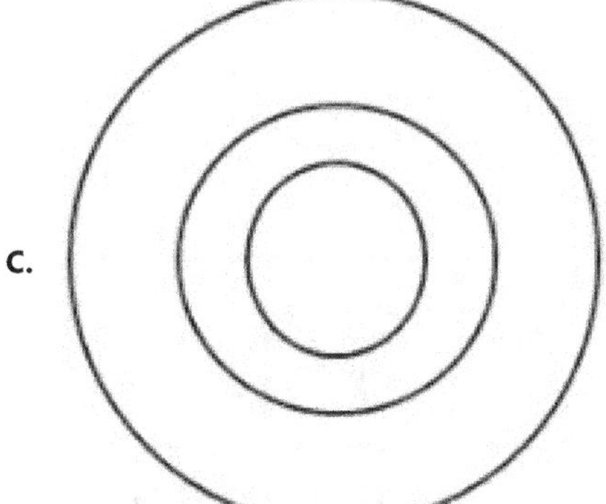

D. 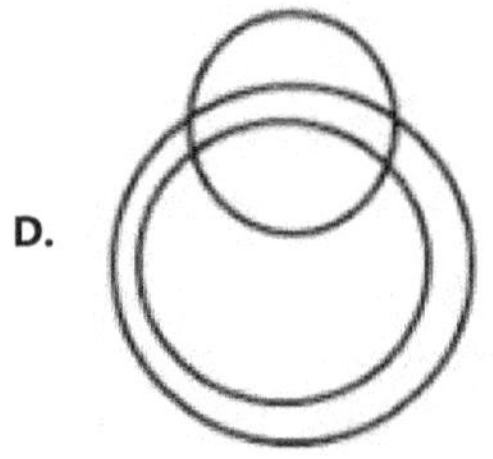

Q.10 If ' − ' means addition, ' + ' means division, ' ÷ ' means multiplication, ' × ' means is subtraction, then,

$$34 - 25 + 5 \times 8 \div 4 + 2 - 7 = ?$$

A. 27   **B.** 30   **C.** 14   **D.** 12

Q.11 Direction: Choose the mirror image of the following figure.

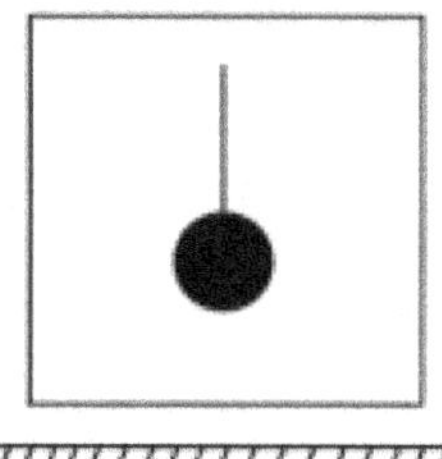

[RRB/RRC Group D, 2018]

A.   **B.**   **C.**   **D.**

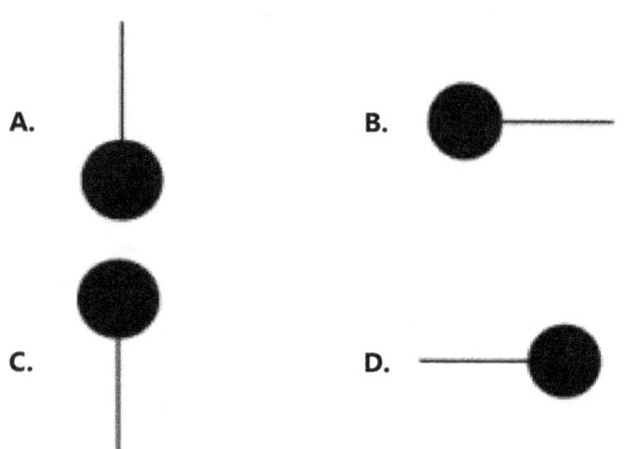

Q.12 Direction: Which answer figure will complete the pattern in the question figure?

Question figure

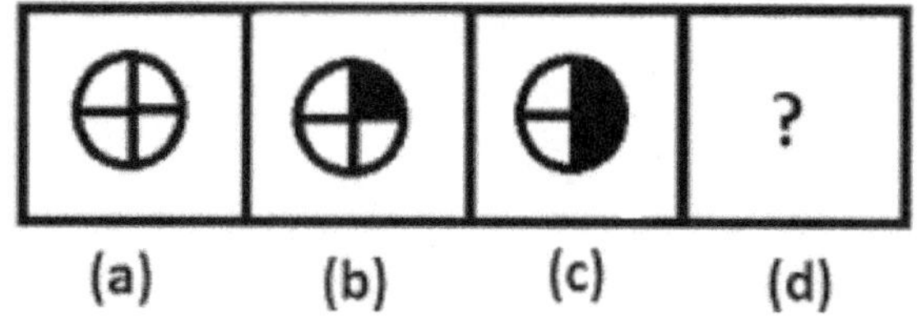

(a)   **(b)**   **(c)**   **(d)**

answer figure

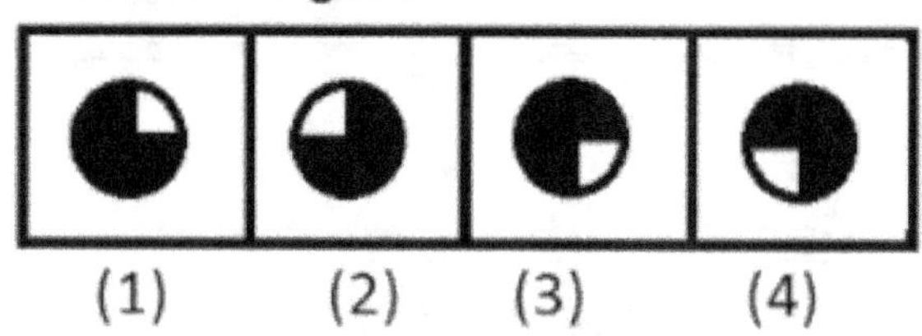

(1)   **(2)**   **(3)**   **(4)**

A. (1)   **B.** (2)   **C.** (3)   **D.** (4)

Q.13 Assuming that the characters in the given figure follow similar pattern, find the missing number.

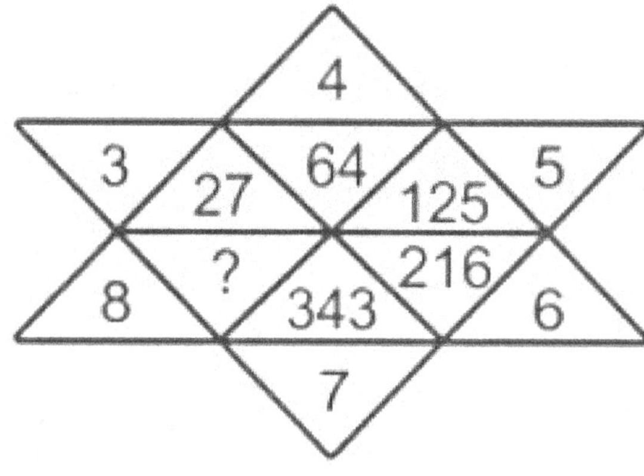

A. 64   **B.** 512   **C.** 16   **D.** 24

Q.14 Arrange the given words in reverse order in which they occur in the dictionary.

1) Resign
2) Respect
3) Response
4) Resonance
5) Resolve

A. 1, 5, 4, 2, 3   **B.** 3, 2, 4, 5, 1
C. 5, 4, 3, 2, 1   **D.** 1, 2, 3, 4, 5

Q.15 Direction: Which of the following interchange of signs would make the given equation correct?

64 − 8 × 9 ÷ 8 = 64

A. + and −   **B.** ÷ and ×   **C.** + and ÷   **D.** − and ÷

Q.16 In each of the number-pairs, the second number is obtained by performing a certain mathematical operation on the first number. Three of the following pairs follow the same pattern and thus form a group. Select the number-pair that does NOT belong to that group.

A. 125 : 512
B. 64 : 1331
C. 343 : 1000
D. 216 : 729

Q.17 An unfold dice is given below. If we fold these dice then how many dots will appear on the opposite side of six dots?

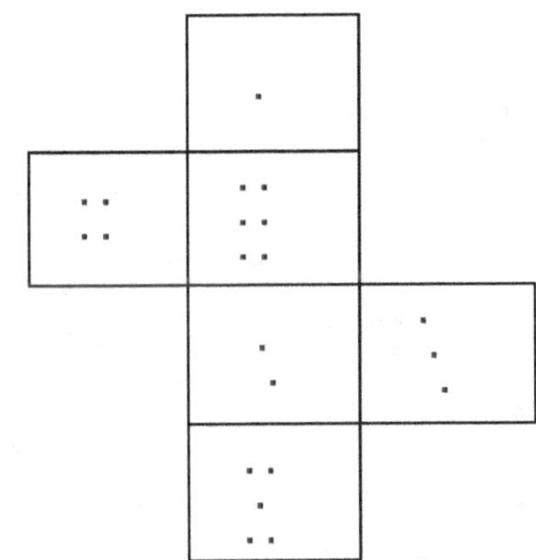

A. 5 dots   **B.** 6 dots   **C.** 7 dots   **D.** 5 dots

Q.18 Direction: Read the given statement(s) and conclusions carefully and select which of the conclusions logically follow(s) from the statement(s).

Statements:

Some pens are erasers.

No eraser is a pencil.

Conclusions:

I. All pencils can be pens.

II. Some pens are neither erasers nor pencils.

A. Only I follow

B. Only II follow

C. Either I or II follows

D. Neither I nor II follows

Q.19 In a code language, if CLOSURE is written as 312151921185, then how will INFLUENCE be written in the same language?

[SSC Selection Post Phase IX, 2020]

A. 9146122151435   **B.** 9136122151335

C. 8146122051435   **D.** 1847122151435

Q.20 Select the option that is related to the fifth letter-cluster in the same way as the second letter-cluster is related to the first letter-cluster and the fourth letter-cluster is related to the third letter-cluster.

VTZX : NLRP :: MJVQ : EBNI :: PNTR : ?

A. FGJL   **B.** HFLJ   **C.** GFLJ   **D.** FHJL

General Knowledge and General Awareness

Q.21 Who has the authority to decide in the event of a dispute in the election of the President of India?

[RRB (NTPC), 2017]

A. Lok Sabha

B. Election Commissioner

C. Prime Minister

D. Supreme Court

Q.22 How much the government has announced to spend on the 'Jal Jeevan Mission' in the next five years?

A. 4.2 lakh crore rupees

B. 7.9 lakh crore rupees

C. 11.5 lakh crore rupees

D. 3.6 lakh crore rupees

Q.23 Council of Minister is collectively responsible to whom?

[Uttarakhand Public Service Commission (UKPSC), 2014]

A. Prime Minister   **B.** President

C. Rajya Sabha   **D.** Lok Sabha

Q.24 _______ has become the first major port of the country to become 100% Landlord port.

A. Kolkata Port

B. Kandla Port

C. New Mangalore Port

D. Jawaharlal Nehru Port

Q.25 Who has won the gold medal at the 12th International Jumping Meeting in Greece in May 2022?

A. Satish Kumar

B. Saurabh Desai

C. Murali Sreeshankar

D. Soumyapada Mohanty

Q.26 Pradeep Kumar Rawat assumed charge as India's new ambassador to_____ in March 2022.

A. China   **B.** Malaysia   **C.** Poland   **D.** USA

Q.27 44th International Chess Olympiad was held in which of the following Indian state?

A. Karnataka   **B.** Kerala

C. Tamil Nadu   **D.** Telangana

Q.28 Indian Institute of Science (IISc) and the ___________ have signed an MoU to collaborate on aviation research and development in August 2022.

A. Indian Navy   **B.** Indian Army

C. Indian Air Force   **D.** Indian Coast Guard

Q.29 Which one of the following rivers takes a 'U' turn at Namcha Barwa and enters India?

[Indian Military Academy (IMA), 2019], [Officers Training Academy (OTA), 2019]

A. Ganga   **B.** Tista

C. Barak   **D.** Brahmaputra

Q.30 Where are Jhumri Telaiya situated?

[Indian Military Academy (IMA), 2019], [Officers Training Academy (OTA), 2019]

A. Jharkhand   **B.** Bihar

C. Assam   **D.** West Bengal

Q.31 Who among the following is the author of the novel 'Burnt Sugar'?

A. Sree Iyer   **B.** Avni Doshi

C. Tenzin Priyadarshi   **D.** Zara Houshmand

Q.32 Pattachitra style of painting is one of the oldest and most popular art forms of _____.

A. Karnataka   **B.** Odisha

C. Kerala   **D.** Tamil Nadu

Q.33 What are the main components of Brass Alloy?

A. Copper and Zinc

B. Copper and Strontium

C. Copper, Zinc and Nickel

D. Copper and Nickel

Q.34 How many countries does India share its land borders with?

A. Four   **B.** Five   **C.** Seven   **D.** Nine

Q.35 Which State had won maximum gold medal in the Khelo India Youth Games 2021?

A. Maharashtra   **B.** Manipur

C. Haryana   **D.** Karnataka

Q.36 Which of the following is a rock-cut-sculpture of the Mauryan period?

A. Dhauli Elephant

B. Parkham Yaksha

C. Rampurwa Bull

D. The Lion from Sanchi

Q.37 ISRO's first launch mission of 2022 was done by which of the following Launch Vehicle?

A. PSLV-C50   **B.** PSLV-C51

C. PSLV-C52   **D.** PSLV-C55

Q.38 Under the Maratha administration, the title for the Prime Minister was:

[SSC Selection Post Phase IX, 2020]

A. Peshwa   **B.** Sumant

C. Pundit Rao   **D.** Sar-i-Naubat

Q.39 Who among the following granted 'Diwani' to the East India Company ?

A. Farrukh Siyar   **B.** Shah Alam II

C. Shah Alam I   **D.** Shuja-Ud-Daulah

Q.40 As per the report of The International Labour Organisation, what is the projected number of global unemployment in 2022?

A. 207 million   **B.** 307 million

C. 107 million   **D.** 507 million

Elementary Mathematics

Q.41 The value of $0.9 \div (0.3 \times 0.3)$ is:

[Jawahar Navodaya Entrance Class VI, 2020]

A. 0.01   **B.** 0.1   **C.** 1   **D.** 10

Q.42 Which of the following is not equal to 25?

[Jawahar Navodaya Entrance Class VI, 2020]

A. $50 - (100 \div 4)$

B. $20 + (20 \div 4)$

C. $10 + (5 \times 2) + (10 - 5)$

D. $24 + (2 \times 1)$

Q.43 Find the greatest number of five digits, which is exactly divisible by 468.

[RRB (NTPC), 2021]

A. 99468   **B.** 99486   **C.** 99864   **D.** 99684

Q.44 Find the sum of the numbers between 400 and 500 such that when 8, 12 and 16 divide them, it leaves 5 as remainder in each case.

[RRB (NTPC), 2021]

A. 922   **B.** 932   **C.** 942   **D.** 912

Q.45 Express 0.875 and 0.375 as a Fraction:

A. $\frac{3}{11}$ and $\frac{7}{11}$ **B.** $\frac{7}{9}$ and $\frac{9}{13}$

C. $\frac{7}{8}$ and $\frac{3}{8}$ **D.** $\frac{7}{9}$ and $\frac{9}{11}$

Q.46

Two students appeared at an examination. One of them secured 9 marks more than the other and his marks was 56% of the sum of their marks. The marks obtained by them are:

A. 39, 30   **B.** 41, 32   **C.** 42, 33   **D.** 43, 34

Q.47 Two positive numbers are in the ratio 3 : 4. The difference of their squares is 63. Find the sum of the numbers.

A. 21   **B.** 28   **C.** 35   **D.** 42

Q.48 Seats for Mathematics, Physics, and Biology in a school are in the ratio 5 : 7 : 8. There is a proposal to increase these seats by 40%, 50%, and 75% respectively. What will be the ratio of increased seats?

A. 2 : 3 : 4   **B.** 6 : 7 : 8   **C.** 6 : 8 : 9   **D.** 6 : 3 : 9

Q.49 Nine persons went to a hotel for taking their meals. Eight of them spent Rs. 12 each of their meals and the ninth spent Rs. 8 more than the average expending of all the nine. Total money spent by them was?

A. 104   **B.** 105   **C.** 116   **D.** 117

Q.50 What is the ratio of simple interest obtained on a sum of money at a certain rate of interest for 5 years to the simple interest obtained on the same sum of money at the same rate of interest for 20 years?

A. 2 : 1   **B.** 1 : 2   **C.** 4 : 1   **D.** 1 : 4

Q.51 At what rate percent per annum does a certain sum invested at compound interest amount to 27 times of itself in 3 years?

A. 75%   **B.** 100%   **C.** 200%   **D.** 250%

Q.52 A shopkeeper purchased an item for Rs. ' x ' and he marked up the price by Rs. 220. He finally sold the item to a customer after a 25% discount at Rs. ' y ' and earns a profit of Rs. 40. Find the value of x.

A. 400   **B.** 450   **C.** 500   **D.** 600

Q.53 A dealer sold a bicycle at a profit of 10%. Had he bought the bicycle at 10% less price and sold it at a price Rs 60 more, he would have gained 25%. The cost price of the bicycle was:

A. 2,400　　**B.** 2,200　　**C.** 2,000　　**D.** 2,600

Q.54 A bike dealer sold a bike at two successive discounts of 30% and 40%. If the selling price of the bike is Rs. 44100, then what is the marked price?

A. Rs. 105000　　　　**B.** Rs. 110000
C. Rs. 108000　　　　**D.** Rs. 100000

Q.55 The area of a circular field is 124.74 hectares. The cost of fencing it at the rate of 80 paise per metre is:

A. Rs. 3168　　　　**B.** Rs. 1584
C. Rs. 1729　　　　**D.** None of these

Q.56 The perimeter of a rectangular field is 84 m. If the length of the field is 3 m more than twice the breadth, then what is the length of the filed?

A. 23 m　　　　**B.** 25 m
C. 27 m　　　　**D.** None of these

Q.57 Find the sum of digits of the least square number which can be divided by 4, 9, 10 and 12.

A. 7　　**B.** 8　　**C.** 9　　**D.** 6

Q.58 Sonu invented 10% more than the investment of Mona and Mona invested 10% less than the investment of Raghu. If the total investment of all the three persons is 5780, find the investment of Raghu.

A. Rs 2010　　**B.** Rs 2000　　**C.** Rs 2100　　**D.** Rs 2210

Q.59 A is twice as fast as B and B is thrice as fast as C. If some distance is covered by C in 54 minutes, then in how much time will B cover?

A. 9 minutes　　　　**B.** 18 minutes
C. 12 minutes　　　　**D.** 15 minutes

Q.60 A and B together can do a piece of work in 20 days and A alone can do it in 30 days. B alone can do the work in how many days?

A. 45　　**B.** 60　　**C.** 75　　**D.** 90

English

Q.61 Direction: In the following question, some parts of the sentence may have errors. Find out which part of the sentence has an error and select the appropriate option. If a sentence is free from error, select 'No Error'.

He believed that so (1)/ societies create the best conditions for (2)/ individual development and social improvement. (3)/ No error (4)

A. (1)　　**B.** (2)　　**C.** (3)　　**D.** (4)

Q.62 Direction: In the following question, some parts of the sentence may have errors. Find out which part of the sentence has an error and select the appropriate option. If a sentence is free from error, select 'No Error'.

One of the great challenge (1)/ with Indian history is (2)/ that there is just so much of it. (3) No error (4)

A. (1)　　**B.** (2)　　**C.** (3)　　**D.** (4)

Q.63 Direction: Choose the most suitable determiner for the given sentence.

The president gave _______ soldier a medal.

A. Another　　**B.** All　　**C.** Other　　**D.** Each

Q.64 Direction: Fill in the blank with the correct option.

______ noise would frighten the animal away.

A. Few　　**B.** A little　　**C.** The little　　**D.** A few

Q.65 Direction: Fill in the blank with the correct conjunction.

_______ I had seen him, I would have greeted him.

A. That　　**B.** If　　**C.** So　　**D.** When

Q.66 Which of the following words is the most opposite in meaning to the word 'Effective'?

A. Efficacious　　　　**B.** Credible
C. Operative　　　　**D.** Incompetent

Ques (67-70):Direction: In the following question, out of the four given alternatives, select the alternative which best expresses the meaning of the Idiom/Phrase.

Q.67 Call it a day

A. To declare the end of time
B. To declare the end of a task
C. Call someone daily
D. Call someone today

Q.68 Couch potato

A. To be lazy
B. To sit on a couch
C. To eat potatoes
D. To become a potato on a couch

Q.69 The killing of a race

A. Homicide　　　　**B.** Genocide
C. Suicide　　　　**D.** Murder

Q.70 One who is blamed for wrongdoings or mistakes of others

A. Assailant　　　　**B.** Mugger
C. Scapegoat　　　　**D.** Slasher

Q.71 In the following question, a word has been spelt in four different ways out of which only one is correctly spelt. Select the correctly spelt word.

A. Ambivalent　　　　**B.** Ambivelent
C. Ambyvelent　　　　**D.** Ambyvalent

Q.72 In the following question, a word has been spelt in four different ways out of which only one is correctly spelt. Select the correctly spelt word.

A. Decksterity　　　　**B.** Dexterity
C. Deksterity　　　　**D.** Dextarity

Ques (73-75):Direction: Select the most appropriate option to improve the underlined segment in the given sentence. If there is no need to improve it, select 'No improvement required'.

Q.73 Many a <u>politician was</u> involved in the scam.

A. politicians is   **B.** politicians were
C. politician were   **D.** No Improvement

Q.74 Ramesh is <u>as tall if not,</u> taller than Mahesh.

A. not as tall but   **B.** not so tall but as
C. as tall as, if not   **D.** No improvement

Q.75 He bought a very expensive <u>piece of furniture</u> for his new apartment.

A. furnitures   **B.** piece of furnitures
C. pieces of furnitures   **D.** No Improvement

Ques (76-79):Direction: In the following passage there are blanks, each of which has been numbered. Find out the appropriate words.

In 2006 the International Astronomical Union (IAU) voted to remove Pluto's planetary status. Now some researchers are _____ (1) _____ this decision, citing the manner in which scientific tradition has dealt with the taxonomy of planets. The IAU, in 2006, designated Pluto a 'dwarf planet' along with Ceres in the asteroid belt and Xena, an object in the Kuiper belt, which is an icy ring of frozen objects that circle the solar system beyond Neptune's orbit. It was a bid to overcome sentiment and go by a scientific rationale. The meeting defined three conditions for a celestial object to be called a planet: one, it must orbit the Sun; two, it should be massive enough to acquire an approximately spherical shape; three, it has to 'clear its orbit', that is, be the object that _____ (2) _____ the maximum gravitational pull within its orbit. Owing to this third property, if an object ventures close to a planet's orbit, it will either collide with it and be accreted, or be ejected out. However, Pluto is affected _____ (3) _____ Neptune's gravity. It also shares its orbit with the frozen objects in the Kuiper belt. Based on this, the IAU _____ (4) _____ that Pluto did not 'clear its orbit'. Dwarf planets, on the other hand, need only satisfy the first two conditions.

Q.76 Select the most appropriate option to fill in the blank No. (1).

A. Agreeing   **B.** Bound
C. Rejecting   **D.** Challenging

Q.77 Select the most appropriate option to fill in the blank No. (2).

A. Exerts   **B.** Pulls   **C.** Donates   **D.** Ushers

Q.78 Select the most appropriate option to fill in the blank No. (3).

A. to   **B.** for   **C.** at   **D.** by

Q.79 Select the most appropriate option to fill in the blank No. (4).

A. was deem   **B.** deemed
C. will be deeming   **D.** will deem

Q.80 Direction: Select the most appropriate synonym of the given word.

BENIGN

A. Severe   **B.** Malignant

C. Favourable   **D.** Harsh

// Smart Answer Sheet //

Correct — Percentage of students who answered correctly. **Skipped** — Percentage of students who skipped.

Q.	Ans.	Correct	Skipped
1	C	24.23 %	73.57 %
2	C	86.49 %	13.12 %
3	A	60.87 %	35.8 %
4	D	20.32 %	70.36 %
5	D	51.77 %	35.63 %
6	A	87.56 %	12.11 %
7	A	52.41 %	32.0 %
8	D	88.89 %	10.6 %
9	C	82.69 %	16.94 %
10	B	84.1 %	15.65 %
11	C	76.01 %	23.91 %
12	B	89.93 %	10.04 %
13	B	77.4 %	10.8 %
14	B	40.76 %	57.1 %
15	D	66.36 %	30.51 %
16	B	78.28 %	15.1 %
17	A	52.74 %	35.47 %
18	A	81.51 %	11.72 %
19	A	77.09 %	13.61 %
20	C	62.34 %	32.5 %
21	D	62.4 %	33.2 %
22	D	51.19 %	43.28 %
23	D	88.4 %	10.49 %
24	D	45.38 %	41.18 %
25	C	87.62 %	11.06 %
26	A	53.98 %	36.46 %
27	C	59.61 %	38.91 %
28	A	40.32 %	39.69 %
29	D	61.36 %	31.64 %
30	A	47.05 %	30.66 %
31	B	30.99 %	67.04 %
32	B	58.16 %	41.41 %
33	A	41.43 %	35.17 %
34	C	50.71 %	44.99 %
35	C	47.94 %	34.45 %
36	A	89.19 %	10.5 %
37	C	51.83 %	44.2 %
38	A	67.63 %	30.27 %
39	B	55.58 %	39.02 %
40	A	88.6 %	10.53 %
41	D	82.87 %	16.19 %
42	D	80.2 %	16.75 %
43	D	48.34 %	43.73 %
44	A	87.18 %	12.56 %
45	C	61.58 %	30.55 %
46	C	54.06 %	40.92 %
47	A	81.16 %	16.93 %
48	A	81.03 %	10.67 %
49	D	89.74 %	10.14 %
50	D	78.17 %	20.5 %
51	C	44.58 %	48.21 %
52	C	67.44 %	30.81 %
53	A	27.32 %	70.08 %
54	A	76.87 %	21.92 %
55	A	82.29 %	14.25 %
56	D	85.75 %	12.91 %
57	C	69.29 %	30.47 %
58	B	30.05 %	68.38 %
59	B	79.71 %	13.19 %
60	B	76.24 %	13.73 %
61	A	57.62 %	37.47 %
62	A	83.67 %	14.73 %
63	D	63.79 %	32.41 %
64	B	44.0 %	46.82 %
65	B	78.44 %	17.94 %
66	D	63.19 %	36.48 %
67	B	60.21 %	35.06 %
68	A	44.7 %	54.68 %
69	B	85.75 %	14.09 %
70	C	89.05 %	10.86 %
71	A	42.39 %	33.9 %
72	B	67.69 %	30.4 %
73	D	60.39 %	34.74 %
74	C	67.09 %	30.98 %
75	D	11.48 %	84.02 %
76	D	41.79 %	37.37 %
77	A	62.24 %	35.2 %
78	D	51.61 %	39.92 %
79	B	77.95 %	16.19 %
80	C	56.08 %	42.16 %

//Hints and Solutions//

1. Here, the second number can be represented as the Average of digits of the first number.

In $1511:2 \Rightarrow \dfrac{(1+5+1+1)}{4} = 2$

In a similar way,

In $6554 \Rightarrow$ Average of $\dfrac{(6+5+5+4)}{4} = 5$

Hence, the correct option is (C).

2. 1. Rohit, Kyra, Suraj, Laila and Diya are sitting on a bench.

2. Diya is sitting at extreme left.

3. Kyra is sitting to the right of Suraj, who is not sitting at extreme corners.

4. Laila is sitting in between Kyra and Rohit.

Two cases are possible according to the given connditions:

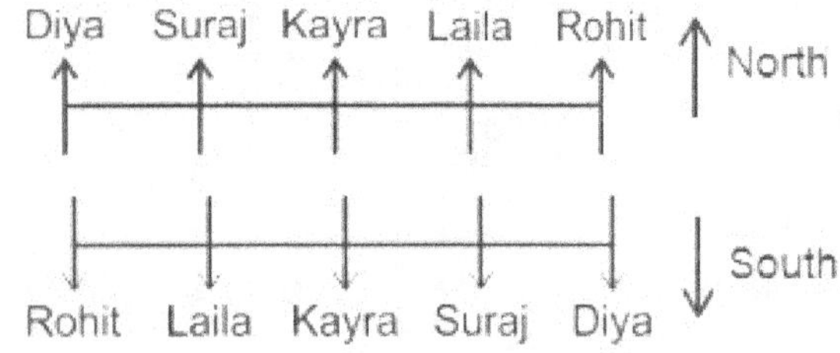

In both the cases, Suraj is to the left of Kayra.

Hence, the correct option is (C).

3. The pattern followed is:

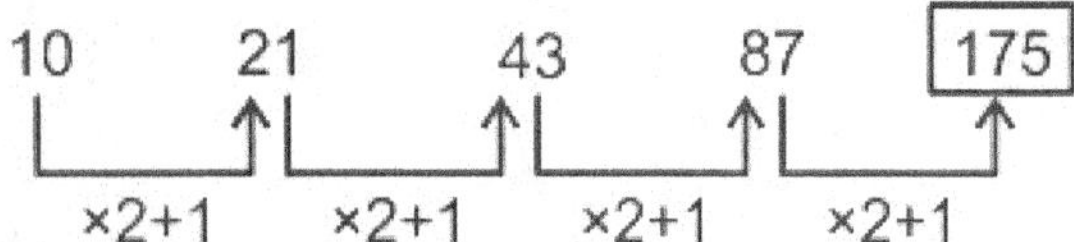

Hence, the correct option is (A).

4. When the piece of paper is opened the unfolded form appears as shown in the figure (D).

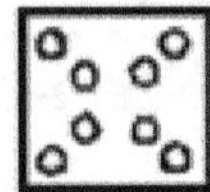

Hence, the correct option is (D).

5. The logic followed here is as follows:

$$V \xrightarrow{-3} S \xrightarrow{-3} P \xrightarrow{-3} M \xrightarrow{-3} J \xrightarrow{-3} G$$

Thus, "J" is the correct answer.

Hence, the correct option is (D).

6.

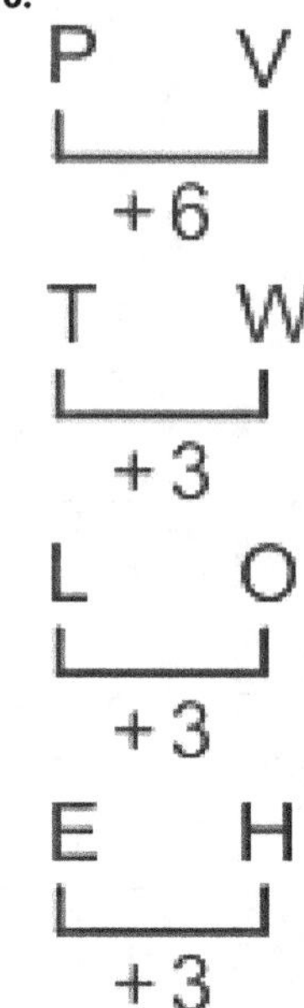

All follow the same pattern, except 'PV'.

Hence, the correct option is (A).

7. The best possible diagram from the given information is,

Symbol in Diagram	Meaning
◯	Female
▢	Male
─────	Married Couple
─────	Siblings
│	Difference of A Generation

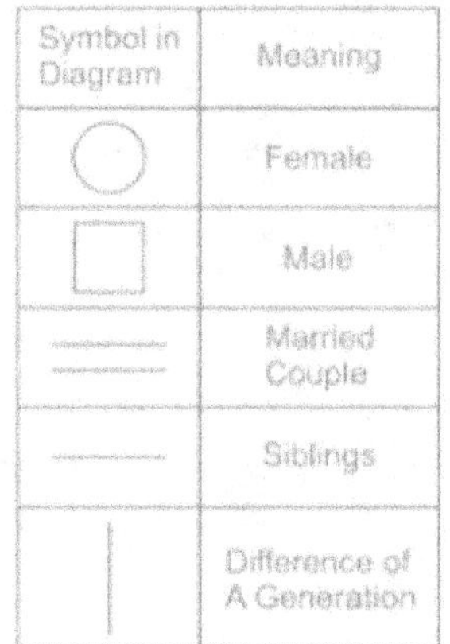

'U is W's husband's brother's wife' is the correct answer.

Hence, the correct option is (A).

8. On observation, we find that X is embedded in Fig. (4).

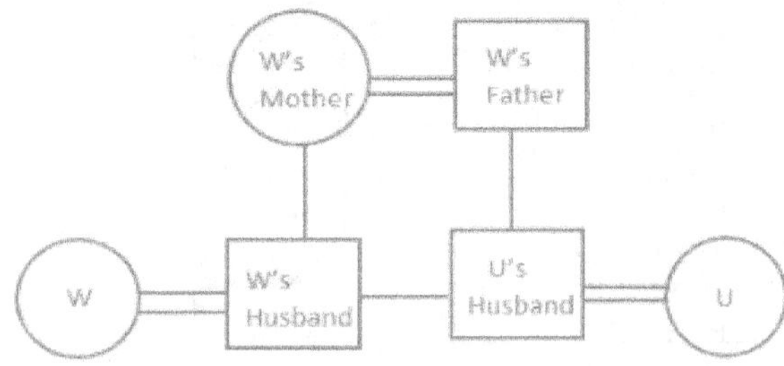

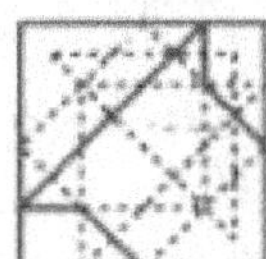

Hence, the correct option is (D).

9. Surat is a city in Gujarat and Gujarat is a state in India.

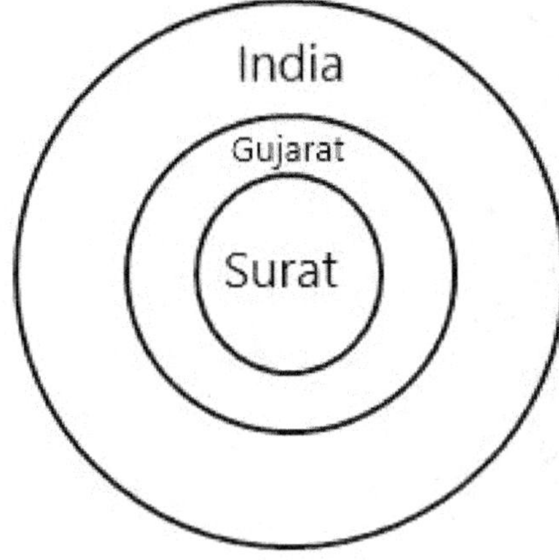

Hence, the correct option is (C).

10. Given,

$$34 - 25 + 5 \times 8 \div 4 + 2 - 7 = ?$$

After changing the signs-

$$34 + 25 \div 5 - 8 \times 4 \div 2 + 7$$

$$= 34 + 5 - 8 \times 2 + 7$$

$$= 39 - 16 + 7 = 30$$

Hence, the correct option is (B).

11. The mirror image of the given image is:

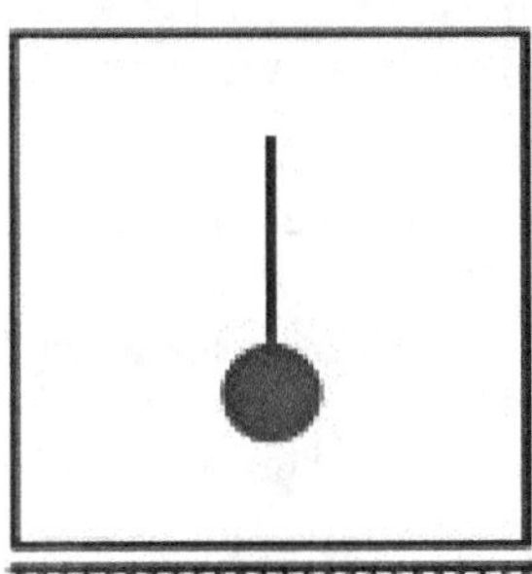

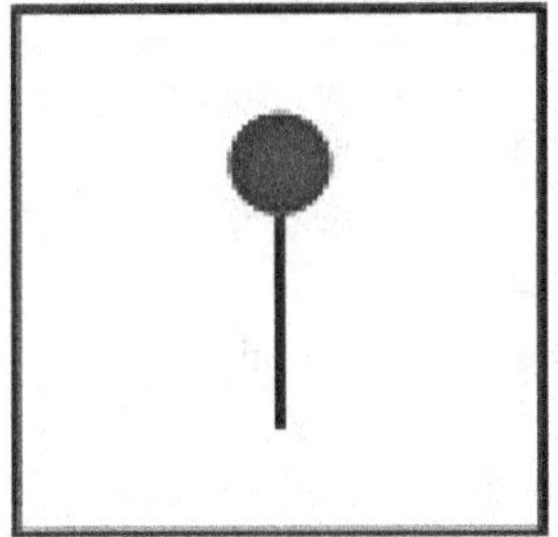

Hence, the correct option is (C).

12. In each step one quarter of the figure is shaded in clockwise direction.

Hence, the correct option is (B).

13. The logic follows here is:

$$3^3 = 27$$

$$4^3 = 64$$

$$5^3 = 125$$

$$6^3 = 216$$

$$7^3 = 343$$

Similarly,

$$8^3 = \text{" } 512 \text{"}$$

Hence, the correct option is (B).

14. On arranging the words in reverse order as per the dictionary we get,

3) Response

2) Respect

4) Resonance

5) Resolve

1) Resign

So, the correct reverse order is "3, 2, 4, 5, 1" as per dictionary.

Hence, the correct option is (B).

15. $64 - 8 \times 9 \div 8 = 64$

Putting ($-$ & $\div$) in the equation,

$$\Rightarrow 64 \div 8 \times 9 - 8 = 64$$

$$\Rightarrow 8 \times 9 - 8 = 64$$

$$\Rightarrow 72 - 8 = 64$$

$$\Rightarrow 64 = 64$$

Hence, the correct option is (D).

16. LOGIC: (First Number)3 : (First Number + 3)³

(A) $125 : 512 = 5^3 : 8^3$

$= 5 : (5 + 3)^3$

(B) $64 : 1331 = 4^3 : 11^3$

$= 4 : (4 + 7)^3$

(C) $343 : 1000 = 7^3 : 10^3$

$= 7 : (7 + 3)^3$

(D) $216 : 729 = 6^3 : 9^3$

$= 6 : (6 + 3)^3$

Hence, the correct option is (B).

17. If we fold the given dice and put the face with six dots on top then the face with five dots will be at the bottom.

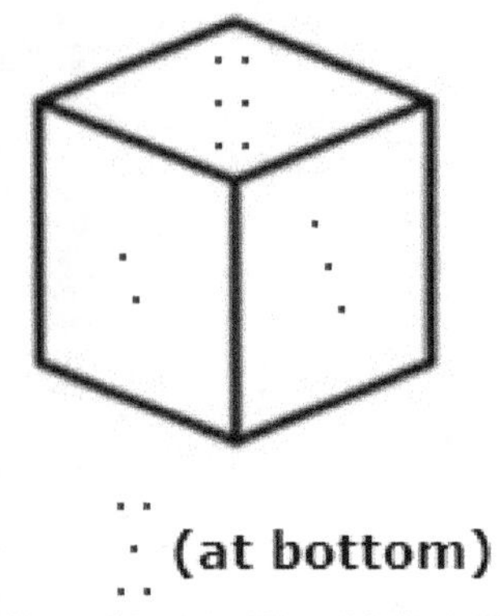

(at bottom)

Hence, the correct option is (A).

18. The least possible Venn Diagram for the given statements will be as follows:

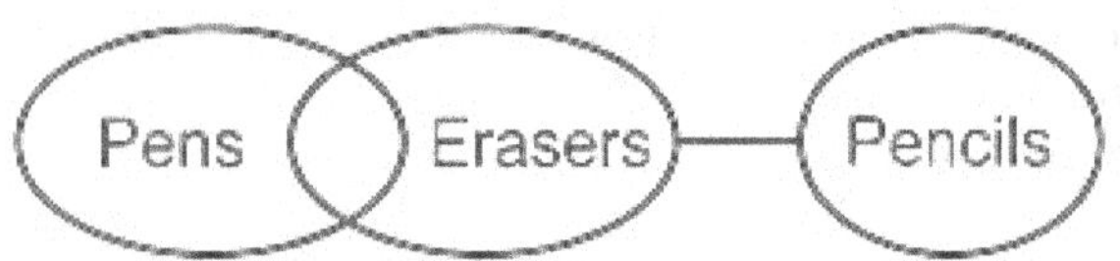

I. All pencils can be pens → True (Pencil can be a subset of Pen so this possibility is true)

II. Some pens are neither erasers nor pencils → False (Some pens are neither eraser nor pencil we cannot say that definitely This conclusion is a possible not a definite conclusion so, it is false)

So, only I follow.

Hence, the correct option is (A).

19. Logic: Each letter of the word 'CLOSURE' is coded as its respective numerical position in alphabetical order.

Position of each letter of the word 'CLOSURE' is -

C → 3, L → 12, O → 15, S → 19, U → 21, R → 18, E → 5

Therefore code of CLOSURE is- 312151921185

Similarly, the word 'INFLUENCE' will be coded as-

I → 9, N → 14, F → 6, L → 12, U → 21, E → 5, N → 14, C → 3, E → 5

Thus, INFLUENCE will be written as- 9146122151435.

Hence, the correct option is (A).

Q.20

Alpha bets	A	B	C	D	E	F	G	H	I	J	K	L	M
Positional value	1	2	3	4	5	6	7	8	9	10	11	12	13
Positional value	26	25	24	23	22	21	20	19	18	17	16	15	14

Alpha bets	Z	Y	X	W	V	U	T	S	R	Q	P	O	N

According to the alphabetical positions of the letters,

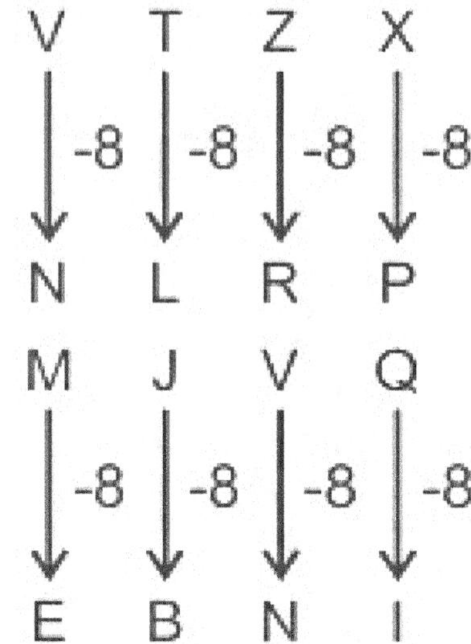

Similarly,

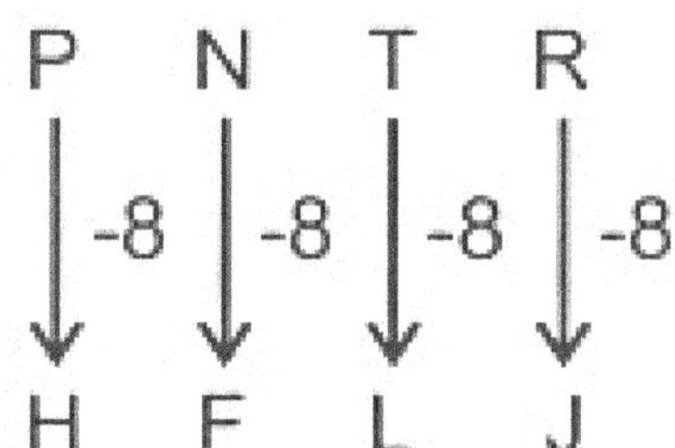

So, 'HFLJ' is the correct answer.

Hence, the correct option is (C).

21. The Supreme court of India decides the disputes regarding the election of the President of India and the election of the Vice President of India. It is incubated in Article 71(1) of our Indian constitution. The judges of the Supreme Court are appointed by the President.

- Supreme Court came into existence on 26 January 1950 and is the apex court in India.

- The legislature of the Union, which is called Parliament, consists of the President and two Houses, known as the Council of States (Rajya Sabha) and the House of the People (Lok Sabha).

- The Lok Sabha (House of the People) is the lower house of the Parliament of India.

  - Members of the Lok Sabha are elected by direct election under the universal adult franchise.

  - Qualifications for a member of Lok Sabha:
    - A person must be a citizen of India.
    - Not less than 25 years of age.

  - The normal term of Lok Sabha is 5 years.

- The 'Council of States' is also known as Rajya Sabha.
    - The constitution lays down 250 as the maximum strength of the Rajya Sabha, out of which 12 are nominated by the President from among persons who have achieved distinction in literature, art, science, and social services.
    - Qualifications for a member of Rajya sabha:
        - A person must be not less than 30 years of age.

Hence, the correct option is (D).

22. The Modi government already approved the allocation of Rs 3.60 lakh crore for the Jal Jeevan Mission over the next five years. The mission is aimed at providing piped water supply to all rural households by 2020-24.

Hence, the correct option is (D).

23. According to Article 75 clause 3 , the Council of Minister is collectively responsible to Lok Sabha.

Council of Ministers:

- Prime Minister and other Ministers are collectively known as Council of Ministers.
- Three categories of the Ministers viz Cabinet Ministers, Minister of State and Deputy Ministers.
- All of them are appointed by the President of India.
- The total number of ministers cannot exceed 15% of the total strength of the Lok Sabha.
- Every Minister is responsible for the acts of the officers of his department.
- He has to answer questions regarding the affair of his department in Parliament.
- Council of Ministers rarely meets so the driving wheel of the government is the Cabinet.

Hence, the correct option is (D).

24. Jawaharlal Nehru Port has become the first major port of the country to become 100% Landlord port. JNP is one of the leading container ports of the country and is ranked 26th among the top 100 global ports (as per Lloyds List Top 100 Ports 2021 Report). Currently, five container terminals are operated at JNP, of which only one is port owned.

Hence, the correct option is (D).

25. Murali Sreeshankar has won the gold medal at the 12th International Jumping Meeting in Greece in May 2022.

India's ace long jumper Murali Sreeshankar, on 26 May 2022, won the gold medal at the 12 th International Jumping Meeting in Greece with an effort of 8.31 m. Thobias Montler of Sweden & Jules Pommery of France claimed silver with 8.27 m & bronze with 8.17 m respectively. Sreesankar also created a record last month with a jump of 8.36 m and is currently the national record holder.

Hence, the correct option is (C).

26. India's new ambassador to China Pradeep Kumar Rawat assumed charge on 14 March 2022.

He succeeds Vikram Misri, who was appointed as Deputy National Security Advisor. Mr. Rawat, a 1990 batch Indian Foreign Service (IFS) officer, was India's ambassador to the Netherlands. He also served as the ambassador of India to Indonesia and Timor-Leste from September 2017-December 2020.

Hence, the correct option is (A).

27. 44th International Chess Olympiad, the world's biggest chess event, was held at Poonjeri Village in Mamallapuram, Chennai, Tamil Nadu, from July 28 to August 10, 2022. PM Modi and Chief Minister of Tamil Nadu M K Stalin attended the grand inaugural ceremony. The official mascot is 'Thambi', a horse clad in the traditional Veshti -Sattai'. The Olympiad was originally scheduled to take place in Russia, but the event did not happen in Russia due to the ongoing Russian-Ukraine war.

Hence, the correct option is (C).

28. Bengaluru-based Indian Institute of Science (IISc) and the Indian Navy have signed an MoU to collaborate on aviation research and development. The areas of collaboration under the MoU will fall under the domain of aerospace/aeronautical engineering, including design and education technology.

Hence, the correct option is (A).

29. The river Brahmaputra originates on the Angsi Glacier which is located on the Northern Side of the Himalayas in Burang, Tibet.

- It flows as Yarlung Tsangpo River flowing into Southern Tibet, breaking through the Himalayas creating great gorges.
- Tsangpo or Brahmaputra takes a U-turn at Namcha Barwa before entering Arunachal Pradesh, where it is called Dihang or Siang River.
- Further, the Dihang river meets Dibang and Lohit Rivers at the front of the Assam Valley flowing southwest through it.
- It is here that the river is called the Brahmaputra River.
- Right Bank Tributaries of Brahmaputra - Subansiri, Kameng, Manas and Sankosh.
- Left Bank Tributaries of Brahmaputra - Burhi Dihing, Dhansari (South) and Kalang.
- Subansiri which with its origin in Tibet is an antecedent river, meaning it maintains its original pattern and course despite any changes in the underlying rock topography.

Hence, the correct option is (D).

30. Jhumri Telaiya situated in Jharkhand.

- The place has micacious soil, i.e soil containing Mica.
- Jharkhand is the 28th state of the Indian Union.
- It was established on 15th November 2000.
- Ranchi is the capital of the State.
- State Animal - Elephant.

- State Bird - Koel
- State Tree - Sal
- State Flower - Palash

Hence, the correct option is (A).

31. Avni Doshi is an author of the novel 'Burnt Sugar' which has been longlisted for the Booker Prize 2020.

- It is her debut book which is a feminist novel set in modern-day India that ponders motherhood and the change of roles from being a daughter to becoming a caregiver for an elderly mother.
- The Booker Prize for Fiction, formerly known as the Booker–McConnell Prize (1969–2001) and the Man Booker Prize (2002–2019), is a literary prize awarded each year for the best original novel written in the English language and published in the United Kingdom.

Hence, the correct option is (B).

32. Pattachitra style of painting is one of the oldest and most popular art forms of Odisha. Pattachitra artform is known for its intricate details as well as mythological narratives and folktales inscribed in it.

Hence, the correct option is (B).

33. Brass is a metallic alloy that is made of Copper and Zinc. Brass has been used in many musical instruments. It is an ideal alloy for the transport of water through pipes and fittings. It is also appropriate for use in marine engines and pump parts.

Hence, the correct option is (A).

34. India shares its land borders with seven countries namely Myanmar, Pakistan, Nepal, Afghanistan, Bhutan, China, and Bangladesh. Across the sea to the south, lie our island neighbours- Sri Lanka and the Maldives.

- India Pakistan border is called the line of control.
- The Indian states of Punjab, Rajasthan, Jammu, and Kashmir, and Gujarat have the India-Pakistan border.
- Manipur, Mizoram, Arunachal Pradesh, and Nagaland share the land border with Myanmar.
- Arunachal Pradesh and Sikkim share the border with China.
- Assam, Mizoram, Meghalaya, Tripura, and West Bengal share their border with Bangladesh.
- Uttarakhand, Uttar Pradesh, West Bengal, Bihar, and Sikkim share a border with Nepal.

Hence, the correct option is (C).

35. Haryana has topped the table with a total of 137 medals in the Khelo India Youth Games 2021.

- Maharashtra managed 125 medals to come in the second position.
- Karnataka finished third with 67 medals.
- Khelo India Youth Games 2021 was organized in Panchkula by the Haryana state government.

- Khelo India Scheme is the flagship Central Sector Scheme of the Ministry of Youth Affairs & Sports.
- Order of States with maximum medals: Haryana> Maharashtra> karnataka> Manipur.

Hence, the correct option is (C).

36. The **rock-cut sculpture** of the Mauryan Period is **Dhauli Elephant.**

- Dhauli is located in the ancient territory of Kalinga, now the state of Orissa, which the emperor Ashoka Maurya conquered with appalling loss of life in about 260 BC.
- Rock cut elephant at Dhauli is one of the oldest monument which sculpted elephant faces east.

Hence, the correct option is (A).

37. Recently the Indian Space Research Organisation's first launched mission of 2022 **PSLV-C52** is designed to orbit the Earth Observation Satellite EOS-04.

- The launch of Polar Satellite Launch Vehicle (PSLV-C52) is scheduled from the First Launch Pad of Satish Dhawan Space Centre, Sriharikota.
- EOS-04 is a Radar Imaging Satellite designed to provide high quality images under all weather conditions for agriculture, forestry, hydrology and flood mapping etc.

Hence, the correct option is (C).

38. The peshwa, also known as the Mukhya pradhan, originally headed the advisory council of the Raja Shivaji.

- After Shivaji's death the council broke up and the office lost its primacy, but it was revived when Shivaji's grandson Shahu appointed Balaji Vishvanath Bhat, a Chitpavan Brahman, as peshwa in 1714.
- Balaji's son Baji Rao I secured the hereditary succession to the peshwa ship.
- Peshwas were the loyal ministers of Marathas state who were appointed to assist the king in different administrative as well as political affairs.
- The Peshwas named their secretariat as Huzur Daftar which was situated in Poona.

Hence, the correct option is (A).

39. The Mughal Emperor Shah Alam II granted the Diwani rights to the East India Company after the defeat in the Battle of Buxar (1764).

- Emperor Shah Alam II granted the Diwani rights of Bengal in the year 1765.
- Diwani rights mean the right to collect the land revenue.
- Shah Alam II, (25 June 1728 – 19 November 1806) was the eighteenth Mughal Emperor and the son of Alamgir II.
- He fought the famous Battle of Buxar in 1764 along with his allies Mir Qasim and Shuja-ud Daula against the East India Company.

Hence, the correct option is (B).

40. The International Labour Organisation has projected global unemployment at 207 million in 2022, almost 21 million more than in 2019.

- The total hours worked in 2022 have been projected to be almost 2% below their pre-pandemic level or a deficit of 52 mn full-time equivalent jobs.
- This was stated in its latest report on World Employment and Social Outlook, which was released on 17 Jan 2022.

Hence, the correct option is (A).

41. Given:

$$0.9 \div (0.3 \times 0.3)$$

$$= 0.9 \div (0.09)$$

$$= \frac{0.9}{0.09} = \frac{0.90}{0.09} = \frac{90}{9} = 10$$

The value of $0.9 \div (0.3 \times 0.3)$ is 10

Hence, the correct option is (D).

42. By checking option one by one:

Option (A) $50 - (100 \div 4) = 50 - 25 = 25$

Option (B) $20 + (20 \div 4) = 20 + 5 = 25$

Option (C) $10 + (5 \times 2) + (10 - 5)$

$$= 10 + 10 + 5 = 25$$

Option (D) $24 + (2 \times 1) = 24 + 2 = 26$

So, we can see that Option (D) is not equal to 25.

Hence, the correct option is (D).

43. Let the number be 99999 in this case

Number $=$ Division $\times$ Quotient $+$ Remainder

$$99999 = 468 \times 213 + 315$$

$$99999 - 315 = 468 \times 213$$

So,

Highest 5 digit number divisible by $468 = 99999 - 315$

$$= 99684$$

Hence, the correct option is (D).

44. Given,

Numbers are $8, 12$ and 16 that must divide numbers between 400 and 500 and get remainder 5.

To find the multiple of different numbers, we need to find out the LCM

LCM of $8, 12, 16$

$$8 = 2^3, 12 = 2^2 \times 3, 16 = 2^4$$

$$\text{LCM} = 2^4 \times 3 = 48$$

Number pattern $= 48k + 5$ (Remainder)

Number between 400 and 500

Smallest number $= 48 \times 9 + 5 = 437$

Largest number $= 48 \times 10 + 5 = 485$

So,

Sum of numbers $= 437 + 485$

$$= 922$$

Hence, the correct option is (A).

45. Given:

0.875 and 0.375

Now,

Multiply and divide 0.875 with 1000,

$$0.875 \times \frac{1000}{1000} = \frac{875}{1000}$$

After simplifying this, it gives fraction $\frac{7}{8}$

Therefore, 0.875 as fraction $= \frac{7}{8}$

Similarly,

Mutiply and divide 0.375 with 1000,

$$0.375 \times \frac{1000}{1000} = \frac{375}{1000}$$

Now, this can be resulted after simplifying fraction $\frac{3}{8}$.

Therefore,

0.375 as fraction $= \frac{3}{8}$

Hence, the correct option is (C).

46. Let one of the students secure x marks.

Then, the other student secures $(x + 9)$ marks.

From the given condition, we have

$$(x + 9) = 56\% \text{ of } (x + x + 9) = \frac{56}{100} \times (2x + 9)$$

$$\Rightarrow 100x + 900 = 112x + 504$$

$$\Rightarrow 12x = 900 - 504 = 396$$

$$\Rightarrow x = \frac{396}{12} = 33$$

Therefore, marks obtained by other student $x + 9 = 33 + 9 = 42$.

Marks obtained by both students are 33 and 42.

Hence, the correct option is (C).

47. Given:

Two positive numbers are in the ratio 3 : 4.

Let the numbers are 3x, 4x.

The difference of their squares is 63.

$\Rightarrow$ (4x)^2 - (3x)^2 = 63

$\Rightarrow$ 16x^2 - 9x^2 = 63

$\Rightarrow$ 7x^2 = 63

$\Rightarrow$ x^2 = 9

$\Rightarrow$ x = ±3

Since the numbers are positive,

$\Rightarrow$ x = 3

First number = 3x

= 3 × 3

= 9

Second number = 4x

= 4 × 3

= 12

Sum of the numbers = 9 + 12 = 21

Hence, the correct option is (A).

48. Let the number of seats for Mathematics, Physics and Biology be $5x, 7x$ and $8x$ respectively.

Number of increased seats are $(140\%$ of $5x), (150\%$ of $7x)$ and $(175\%$ of $8x)$

$$\Rightarrow \left(\frac{140}{100} \times 5x\right), \left(\frac{150}{100} \times 7x\right) \text{ and } \left(\frac{175}{100} \times 8x\right)$$

$$\Rightarrow 7x, \frac{21x}{2} \text{ and } 14x$$

$$\therefore \text{ The required ratio } = 7x : \frac{21x}{2} : 14x$$

$$\Rightarrow 14x : 21x : 28x$$

$$\Rightarrow 2 : 3 : 4$$

Hence, the correct option is (A).

49. We know that the average money spent is given by the formula-

$$Avgerage = \frac{\text{Sum of money}}{\text{Number of persons}}$$

Now, let us find the average of nine persons spent money as:

$$y = \frac{12+12+12+12+12+12+12+x}{9}$$

$$y = \frac{96+x}{9}$$

We are given that the money spent by a ninth person is Rs. 8 more than the average of nine persons.

In mathematical equation this statement can be written as:

$$x = y + 8$$

Now, by substituting the value of $'y'$ we got in above equation we get

$$x = \frac{96+x}{9} + 8$$

$$9x = 96 + x + 72$$

$$8x = 168$$

$$x = 21$$

So, the amount spent by the ninth person is Rs. 21 .

But we are asked to find the total amount spent by 9 persons.

So, by adding the amount spent by each person we get

$$T = 12 + 12 + 12 + 12 + 12 + 12 + 12 + 12 + 21$$

$$T = 117$$

Therefore, the total amount spent by the nine persons is Rs. 117.

Hence, the correct option is (D).

50. Let the sum of money $P = Rs. A$

Let the rate of interest $R = r\%$

Case 1:

Time $T_1 = 5$ years

Simple Interest $SI_1 = \frac{A \times r \times 5}{100}$

$$\Rightarrow SI_1 = Rs. \frac{Ar}{20}$$

Case 2:

Time $T_2 = 20$ years

Simple Interest $SI_2 = \frac{A \times r \times 20}{100}$

$$\Rightarrow SI_2 = Rs. \frac{Ar}{5}$$

Required ratio $= SI_1 : SI_2$

$$= \frac{Ar}{20} : \frac{Ar}{5}$$

$$= 1 : 4$$

Hence, the correct option is (D).

51. Given:

A certain sum amounts to 27 times of itself in 3 years.

Let the sum = Rs. P

Amount A = Rs. 27P

Time T = 3 years

According to the formula:

$A = P\left(1 + \dfrac{R}{100}\right)^T$ where R is rate percent per annum

$\Rightarrow 27P = P\left(1 + \dfrac{R}{100}\right)^3$

$\Rightarrow 27 = \left(1 + \dfrac{R}{100}\right)^3$

$\Rightarrow 3^3 = \left(1 + \dfrac{R}{100}\right)^3$

On equating the bases,

$\Rightarrow 3 = 1 + \dfrac{R}{100}$

$\Rightarrow \dfrac{R}{100} = 2$

$\Rightarrow R = 200\%$

Hence, the correct option is (C).

52. GIVEN:

Mark up amount $=$ Rs. 220

Discount $= 25\%$ and Profit $=$ Rs. 40

Marked price $=$ Cost price $+$ Markup

Selling Price $=$ Marked price $-$ Discount

Marked price $= \left(1 + \dfrac{Markuppercentage}{100}\right) \times CP$

$SP = \left(1 - \dfrac{Discountpercentage}{100}\right) \times MP$ Cost price of item $= 'X'$

$\Rightarrow$ Marked price of item $= (x + 220)$

$\Rightarrow$ Selling price of item $= 75\%$ of $(x + 220) = y$

$0.75x + 165 = y$

According to the question,

$(0.75x + 165) - x = 40$

$\Rightarrow 0.25x = 125$

$\Rightarrow x = 500$

Hence, the correct option is (C).

53. Let the CP of bicycle = Rs x

Old SP of bicycle $= x \times 110\%$ ....(i)

Now, new $CP = x \times 90\%$

And new $SP = x \times 90\% \times 125\%$ ...(ii)

Difference between new SP and old SP = 60 Rs

$x \times 90\% \times 125\% - x \times 110\% = 60$

$\Rightarrow \dfrac{x \times 11250}{10000} - \dfrac{x \times 110}{100} = 60$

$\Rightarrow x\left[\dfrac{1125 - 1100}{1000}\right] = 60$

$\Rightarrow x\left[\dfrac{60000}{25}\right]$

$\Rightarrow x = 2400$ Rs

Hence, the correct option is (A).

54. Given:

Discounts = 30% and 40%

SP = Rs. 44100

Let the marked price be x.

30% = $\dfrac{3}{10}$

40% = $\dfrac{2}{5}$

$\Rightarrow x \times \left(\dfrac{7}{10}\right) \times \left(\dfrac{3}{5}\right) = 44100$

$\Rightarrow x = 2100 \times 50$

$\Rightarrow x = 105000$

$\therefore$ The marked price of the bike is Rs. 105000.

Hence, the correct option is (A).

55. Given,

$\pi r^2 = 124.74$ hectare

$\pi r^2 = 1247400 \ m^2$

$r = 630 \ m$

$2\pi r = 3960$

Cost $= 3960 \times 0.8 = 3168$

Hence, the correct option is (A).

56. Let the length and breadth of the field be 'l' m and 'b' m respectively.

According to the question, the length of the field is 3 m more than twice the breadth

$\Rightarrow$ l = (2b + 3) m

We know that,

Perimeter of a rectangular field = 2(l + b)

$\Rightarrow$ 84 = 2(2b + 3 + b)

$\Rightarrow \dfrac{84}{2} = 3b + 3$

$\Rightarrow b = \dfrac{39}{3} = 13$ m

$\therefore b = 13$ m

$l = 2b + 3 = 2 \times 13 + 3 = 29$ m

$\therefore l = 29$ m

Hence, the correct option is (D).

57. Given:

Numbers 4, 9, 10 and 12

We know that for a number to be square, it has factors in pairs.

To get the least square number which can be divided by 4, 9, 10 and 12 we find it by taking their LCM and making the factors in pairs.

LCM [4, 9, 10, 12]

$\Rightarrow 2 \times 2 \times 3 \times 3 \times 5$

$\Rightarrow (2)^2 \times (3)^2 \times 5$

Since the above number doesn't contains factors in pairs

To get least square number we multiply it by 5

$\Rightarrow (2)^2 \times (3)^2 \times 5 \times 5$

$\Rightarrow (2)^2 \times (3)^2 \times (5)^2$

$\Rightarrow 4 \times 9 \times 25$

$\Rightarrow 900$

$\therefore$ Sum of digits $= 9 + 0 + 0 = 9$

Hence, the correct option is (C).

58. Let Mona's investment $=$ Rs 100

Sonu's investment = Rs 110 and Raghu's investment $= \dfrac{100}{90} \times 100 = $ Rs $\dfrac{1000}{9}$

Ratio of Mona's, Sonu's and Raghu's investments $= 100 : 110 : \dfrac{1000}{9}$

$= 90 : 99 : 100$

Sum of ratios $= 90 + 99 + 100 = 289$

Raghu's investment $=$ Rs $\left(\dfrac{100}{289} \times 5870\right)$

$=$ Rs 2000

Hence, the correct option is (B).

59. Given:

A is twice as fast as B and B is thrice as fast as C.

C covered some distance in 54 min.

Formula used:

Speed $= \dfrac{Distance}{Time}$

Let the time taken by B be t min.

$\Rightarrow A : B = 2 : 1, B : C = 3 : 1$

$\Rightarrow A : B : C = (2 \times 3) : (1 \times 3) : (1 \times 1)$

$\Rightarrow A : B : C = 6 : 3 : 1$

$\Rightarrow$ Ratio of speed between A, B and C = 6 : 3 : 1

$\Rightarrow$ Ratio of time $= \left(\dfrac{1}{6}\right) : \left(\dfrac{1}{3}\right) : 1$

$\Rightarrow$ Ratio of time between A, B and C = 1 : 2 : 6

$\Rightarrow$ 6 unit = 54 min

$\Rightarrow$ 1 unit = 9 min

$\Rightarrow$ 2 unit = 18 min

$\Rightarrow$ So, time taken by B = t = 18 min

Hence, the correct option is (B).

60. Given:

A and B together can do a piece of work in 20 days.

Part of work A and B can do in 1 day $= \dfrac{1}{20}$

A alone can do the work in 30 days.

Part of work A can do in 1 day $= \dfrac{1}{30}$

$\therefore$ Part of work B alone can do in a day $= \dfrac{1}{20} - \dfrac{1}{30} = \dfrac{1}{60}$

$\therefore$ B alone can do the work in 60 days.

Hence, the correct option is (B).

61. The error lies in the incorrect usage of a preposition. Structures using "such" and "so" are similar in meaning and different in construction. The main difference is that "such" takes a noun phrase, while "so" takes an adjective. As per the above segment, "societies" is the noun, and "such" is the correct preposition.

The correct sentence would be:

He believed that such societies create the best conditions for individual development and social improvement.

Hence, the correct option is (A).

62. The word "challenge" should be replaced by its plural "challenges" as the general rule for the usage of the phrase "one of the" is: "One of the + PLURAL NOUN + that/who etc. + SINGULAR/PLURAL VERB". So, the noun following the phrase "one of the" is always a plural noun, whereas the use of verbs as singular or plural will entirely depend upon the subject of the statement, i.e. singular verb for singular subject and plural verb for the plural subject.

The correct sentence is:

"One of the great challenges with Indian history is that there is just so much of it".

Hence, the correct option is (A).

63. Each: We use each to refer to the individual things or persons in a group of two or more, Each is followed by a singular subject.

- We spent five days on the coast and each day we swam in the ocean.

The correct sentence is: The president gave each soldier a medal.

Hence, the correct option is (D).

64. The term 'a little' means some or a small quantity. It is used as an adverb. If one uses 'a little' in a sentence, it means some or a small quantity. So, if we use 'a little' in the same example, i.e., 'There is a little hope that the patient will survive' then, it means there's some chance or a small chance that the patient might survive.

Example: There's a little chance that the boy will win.

The correct sentence is: A little noise would frighten the animal away.

Hence, the correct option is (B).

65. The given sentence is an example of subordinating conjunction. The Conjunction introducing the dependent or subordinate clause is called a Subordinating Conjunction.

These are: After, Because, If, That Though, Although, Till, Before, Unless, As, When, While.

- Example: He ran away because the police were after him.

Correct Sentence: If I had seen him, I would have greeted him.

Hence, the correct option is (B).

66. 'Incompetent' means 'unskilled' or 'inadequate'.

'Effective' means 'to be successful'.

'Efficacious' means 'to be able to produce the desired result'.

'Credible' means 'acceptable'.

'Operative' means 'valid'.

The word that carries the most opposite meaning is 'incompetent'.

Hence, the correct option is (D).

67. Call it a day means to finish a task or decide or agree to stop doing something.

For example, I think we have done enough work today, I am feeling tired now, let's call it a day.

Hence, the correct option is (B).

68. To be a couch potato means a person who takes little or no exercise and watches a lot of television.

For example, My brother is so lazy that he does nothing the whole day, but sits on the couch and watches television and now I call him a couch potato.

Hence, the correct option is (A).

69. Genocide- The deliberate killing of a large group of people, especially those of a particular nation or ethnic group. The killing of a race.

Homicide- The killing of one person by another.

Suicide- Killing oneself.

Murder- The crime of killing a person illegally and on purpose.

Hence, the correct option is (B).

70. Scapegoat means "a person who is blamed for wrongdoings or mistakes of others."

Assailant: a person who physically attacks another.

Mugger: a person who attacks and robs another in a public place.

Slasher: a sporting competitor who is quick and agile.

Hence, the correct option is (C).

71. 'Ambivalent' is the correct spelling. It means having mixed feelings towards someone/something.

Hence, the correct option is (A).

72. 'Dexterity' is the correct spelling. It means being skilled in performing tasks using the hand.

Hence, the correct option is (B).

73. **'Many a'** is always followed by **a singular noun** and a singular verb. 'Many a' is used to refer to a large number of things or people

Examples:

- **Many a student was** drowned in the river.
- **Many a tale was** told.
- **Many a man has** tried but few men have succeeded.

According to the rule and examples that are given above, the given sentence is correct.

Therefore, option (D) is the correct answer.

Hence, the correct option is (D).

74. Correct Sentence: Ramesh is **as tall as if not**, taller than Mahesh.

Some conjunctions given below are used in a pair known as correlative conjunctions:

- Whether...or, either...or, so/as...as, so...that, neither...nor, not only...but also, though...yet, etc.

The conjunction 'so/as...as' is used to compare different things.

Whereas the sentence compares the height of two subjects.

According to the rule and the example given above, **'as tall as, if not'** will be used in the **underlined part** of the sentence.

Hence, the correct option is (C).

75. **"Furniture"** is an **uncountable noun.**

Uncountable nouns are the nouns that **cannot** be counted or separated.

- **E.g.** furniture, equipment, machinery, information, work, bread, etc.

Uncountable nouns are not used in plural forms.

Examples:

- I need new equipment to complete this project.

- The information that you gave was very useful.

If we have to use uncountable nouns in the plural sense, we use **certain words** with them. E.g. a piece of information, a slice of bread, etc.

According to the rule and example that are given above, the given sentence is grammatically correct and needs **no improvement.**

Hence, the correct option is (D).

76. Correct sentence: Now some researchers are **challenging** this decision, citing the manner in which scientific tradition has dealt with the taxonomy of planets.

Let us discuss the meanings of the given options:

- **Challenging**: to question if something is true, right, etc., or not.

- **Agreeing**: to have the same opinion as somebody/something.

- **Rejecting**: to refuse to accept somebody/something.

- **Bound**: to run quickly with long steps.

Here, the passage is talking about the validation of researchers over the decision.

Hence, the correct option is (D).

77. Correct sentence: be the object that **exerts** the maximum gravitational pull within its orbit.

Let us discuss the meanings of the given options:

- **Exerts**: to make use of something, for example influence, strength, etc., to affect somebody/something.

- **Pulls**: to use force to move somebody/something towards yourself.

- **Donates:** to give money or goods to an organization, especially one for people or animals who need help.

- **Ushers**: to take or show somebody where to go.

Here, the passage is talking about the application of the maximum gravitational pull by the object.

Hence, the correct option is (A).

78. Correct sentence: However, Pluto is affected **by** Neptune's gravity.

We can use to as a preposition **to** indicate a destination or direction.

- **Example**: We're going **to** Liverpool next week.

We use **for** to talk about a purpose or a reason for something.

- **Example**: I'm going for some breakfast. I'm really hungry.

We use **at** to talk about points in time, ages and some periods of time.

- **Example**: I was up **at** 6 am this morning.

When we use the passive voice, we can use a phrase with **by** to say who did the action.

- **Example**: The wedding cake was made **by** Henry's mother.

As per the statement, Neptune's gravity affects Pluto.

Thus, the correct answer is '**by**.'

Hence, the correct option is (D).

79. Correct sentence: Based on this, the IAU **deemed** that Pluto did not 'clear its orbit'. Dwarf planets, on the other hand, need only satisfy the first two conditions.

- The second part of the sentence is in the Past Tense, therefore the first part of the sentence must be in the Past Tense.

- Thus, '**deemed**' is the correct construction.

Hence, the correct option is (B).

80. The word 'Benign' means not harsh or stern, especially in nature or effect.

The synonyms of the word 'Benign' are "favourable, gentle, peaceful".

From the synonym of the given word, we can say that the word 'favourable' is the same in meaning.

The word 'favourable' means promoting or contributing to personal or social well-being.

Let's see the meaning of other given options-

WORDS	MEANING
severe	strict or harsh
malignant	evil in nature or effect
harsh	cruel or severe

Hence, the correct option is (C).

General Intelligence and Reasoning

Q.1 Direction: Select the combination of letters which, when sequentially placed in the blanks of the given series, will complete the series.

D Q _ R _ D _ M R _ D _ M _ T

A. MQTTQR

B. MTQRQT

C. MTQTRQ

D. MTQTQR

Q.2 Four letter clusters are given. Out of which three are alike in some way and one is irrelevant. Select the irrelevant letter cluster.

A. NRV **B.** QVB **C.** SXD **D.** YDJ

Q.3 Direction: Select the option which has the same relation with the third term as the second term is related to the first term.

BEGIN : EBGNI :: CADET : ?

A. ACTDE **B.** TEDCA **C.** ADFTE **D.** ACDTE

Q.4 In a certain code language, PLAN is written as OBMQ, and NOT is written as UPO. How will MOTHER be written in the same code language?

A. SFIUQM

B. SFIUPN

C. SFIVQN

D. SGIURN

Q.5 If ' A ' denotes 'addition', ' B ' denotes 'multiplication', ' C ' denotes 'subtraction', and ' D ' denotes 'division', then what will be the value of the following expression?

$82\ A\ 126\ B\ 16\ D\ 112\ C\ 73$

A. 52 **B.** 27 **C.** 72 **D.** 25

Q.6 An amount of ₹ 870 is divided between Urmi and Kripa in the ratio of $18:11$, respectively, whereas an amount of ₹ 960 is divided between Poorvi and Mrinal in the ratio of $5:7$, respectively. Who gets the maximum amount of money among all four?

A. Urmi **B.** Mrinal **C.** Kripa **D.** Poorvi

Q.7 Direction: Select the option in which the given figure is embedded (rotation of the figure is not allowed).

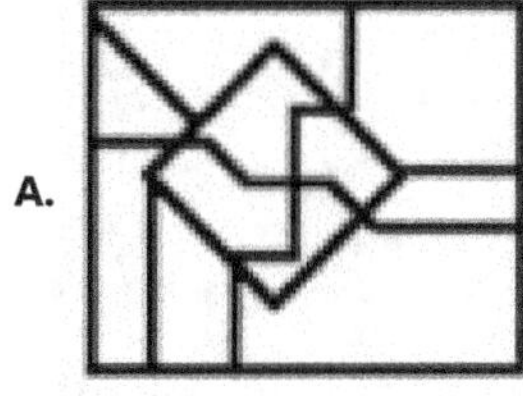

A.

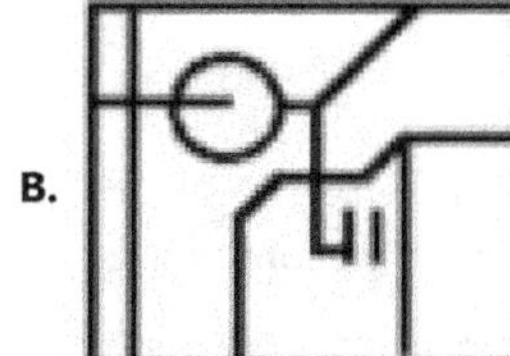

B.

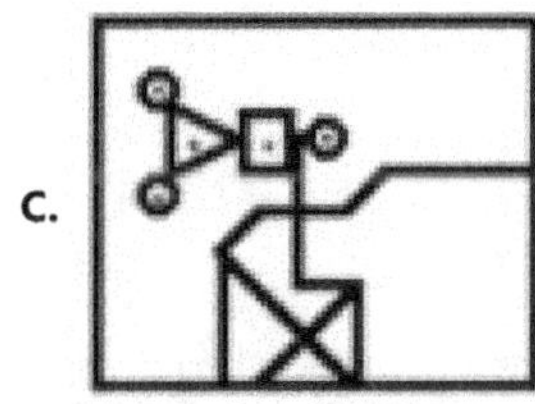

C.

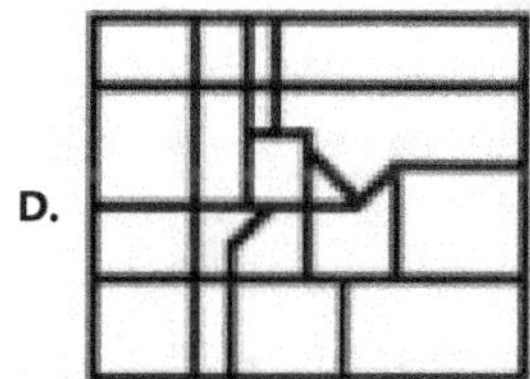

D.

Q.8 The given sheet is folded to form a cube. In the cube so formed, select the letter which will be on the opposite of face representing the letter ' D '.

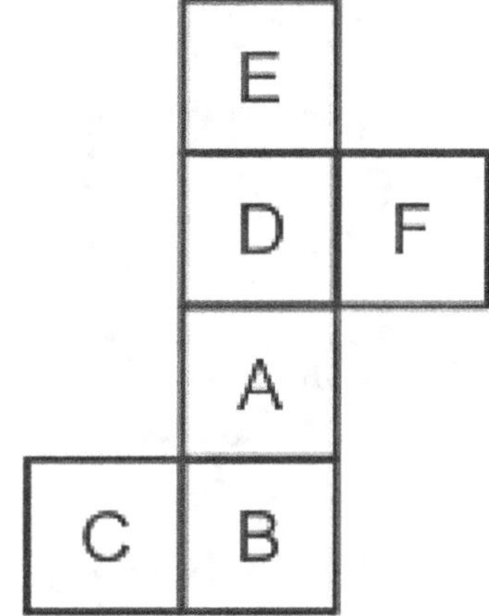

A. E **B.** B **C.** C **D.** F

Q.9 Direction: Select the correct option that shows the order of the given words in the order in which they appear in the English dictionary.

1. Carpet, 2. Caring, 3. Carrot, 4. Creamy, 5. Creek

A. 2, 1, 3, 5, 4

B. 1, 2, 3, 4, 5

C. 2, 1, 3, 4, 5

D. 2, 3, 1, 4, 5

Q.10 In a cafeteria, seven customers (B, G, H, K, L, M and N) sit on three different benches $(X, Y$ and $Z)$. Each bench must have at least two customers sitting on it. Customer G does not sit with customers K, L and M. Customer B sits only with customer N. Customer K sits on Bench X with his best friends. Customer H sits on Bench Z. On which bench are there three customers?

A. Only Bench X

B. Bench X or Bench Y

C. Only Bench Z

D. Only Bench Y

Q.11 Direction: Select the set of classes whose relationship between them is best represented by the given Venn diagram.

A. Grandfather, mother, pharmacist
B. Cardiologist, lawyer, professor
C. Mothers, women, lawyers
D. Daughters, brothers, engineers

Q.12 Direction: From the given alternatives, select the figure which can come in place of the question mark (?) in the following series.

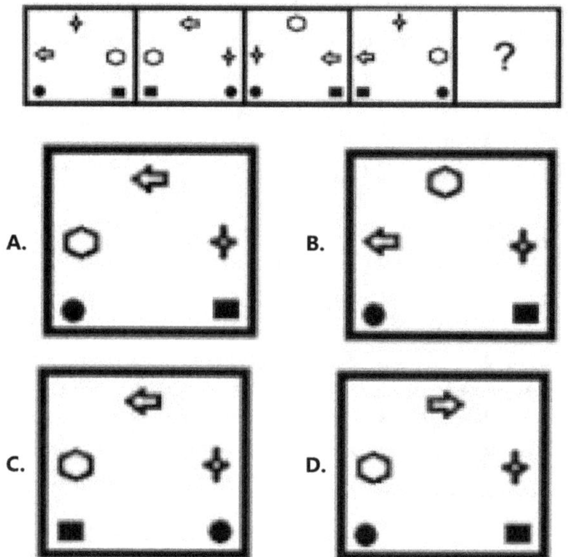

Q.13 Direction: Read the given statements and conclusions carefully. Assuming that the information given in the statements is true, even if it appears to be at variance with commonly known facts, decide which of the given conclusions logically follow(s) from the statements.

Statements:

1. All gardens are resorts.

2. No resort is a court.

3. All parks are courts.

Conclusions:

I. No court is a garden.

II. No garden is a park.

A. None of the conclusions follow
B. Only conclusion I follows
C. Only conclusion II follows
D. Both the conclusions follow

Q.14 Direction: The sequence of folding a piece of paper and the manner in which the folded paper has been cut is shown in the following figures. How would this paper look when unfolded?

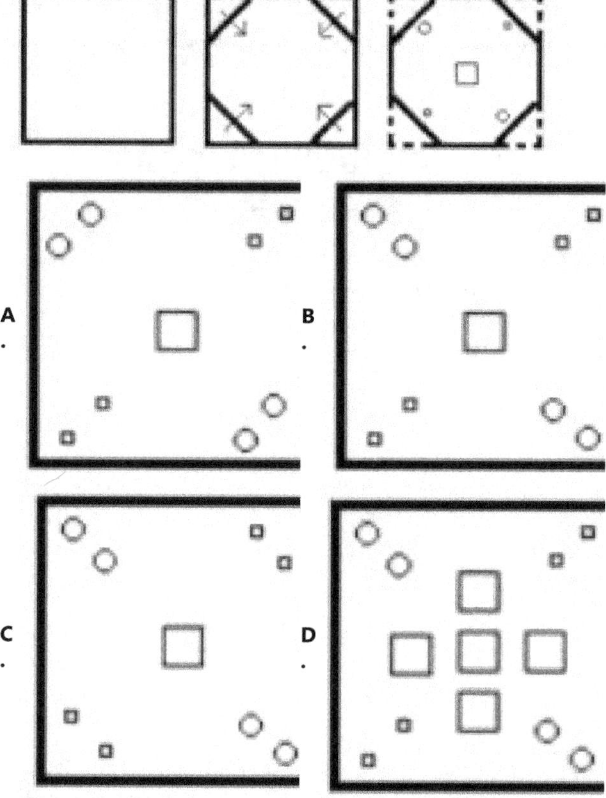

Q.15 Direction: Select the number from the given alternatives which can replace the question mark (?) in the following series.

$27, 41, 57, 76, 99, ?$

A. 152   B. 114   C. 136   D. 127

Q.16 Direction: Select the option which has the same relation with the third number as the second number with the first number and the sixth number with the fifth number.

$6 : 4 : : 11 : ? : : 16 : 8$

A. 6   B. 5   C. 8   D. 7

Q.17 In a certain code language, 'NAUSEA' is coded as '236943' and 'SYRUP' is coded as '97165'. In the same language, How 'SUPPRESS' will be coded as?

A. 96552599   B. 86552489
C. 96441499   D. 96551499

Q.18 Six friends, Govardan, Sarayu, Rekha, Shyamala, Hema and Ganesh, are standing in a queue at a ticket counter. There are two persons between Sarayu and Hema. Rekha is between Hema and Shyamala. Only one person is standing ahead of Govardan. Ganesh who is third from the back end of the row, is between Govardan and Hema. Which two persons are standing between Sarayu and Hema?

A. Govardan and Rekha
B. Shyamala and Rekha
C. Govardan and Ganesh
D. Ganesh and Shyamala

Q.19 Direction: Select the number from the given alternatives which can replace the question mark (?) in the following series.

23,40,74,125,193, ?

A. 270   **B.** 278   **C.** 290   **D.** 225

Q.20 In a certain code language, 'POUR' is written as 'OPRU' and 'TACKLE' as 'ATKCEL'. How will 'FORMATIONS' be written in the same language?

A. OFNRTAONSI   **B.** OFMTRAOISO
C. MFPRTAOKSN   **D.** OFMRTAOISN

Q.21 Direction: Select the number from the given alternatives in which the given numbers are related to each other in the same way as the numbers in the given set are related to each other.

(12,14,56)

A. (16,18,96)   **B.** (24,16,214)
C. (10,16,82)   **D.** (14,20,145)

Q.22 Direction: From the given alternatives, select the set of letters that can come in place of the question mark (?) in the following series.

BEI, EHL, HKO, KNR, ?

A. NPS   **B.** NRU   **C.** NQU   **D.** NQT

Q.23 Roshan is the brother of Kripa, who is the son of Pranjal. Vaishnavi is the wife of Ayush. Pramila is the daughter of Devika. Devika is the grandmother of Aayush, who is the son of Roshan. How is Roshan related to Pramila?

A. Father-in-law   **B.** Father
C. Brother   **D.** Nephew

Q.24 Direction: Select the correct mirror image of the five combination when the mirror is placed at the right side.

D. Wind Speed and Direction

General Knowledge and General Awareness

Q.26 The Forest (Conservation) Act in India was passed in the year ________.

A. 1976   **B.** 1988   **C.** 1980   **D.** 1974

Q.27 In which year 'Pradhan Mantri Jeevan Jyoti Bima Yojana' was launched?

A. 2018   **B.** 2014   **C.** 2015   **D.** 2017

Q.28 Which of the following web series won the Best Drama Series award at the 48th International Emmy Awards 2020?

A. Ashram   **B.** Made in Heaven
C. Delhi Crime   **D.** Mirjapur

Q.29 Which of the following functions is not controlled by the medulla oblongata?

A. Sneezing   **B.** Vomit   **C.** To clap   **D.** Cough

Q.30 Which of the following lakes was formed by meteorite impact during the Neolithic era?

A. Vembanad Lake, Kerala
B. Chilka Lake, Odisha
C. Loktak Lake, Manipur
D. Lonar Lake, Maharashtra

Q.31 Which of the following country chaired the G7 Leaders' Summit held in June 2021?

A. Republic of Korea   **B.** United Kingdom
C. India   **D.** Australia

Q.32 Which committee was appointed by the Standing Committee of the Non-Party Conference in November to examine the communal matter in a judicial framework after the break-up of the Gandhi-Jinnah talks on communal problems?

A. Zakir Hussain Committee
B. Sapru Committee
C. Sardar Patel Committee
D. Balwant Rai Mehta Committee

Q.33 On 17th September, 2020, The International Tennis Federation (ITF) announced that the Federation or 'Fed' Cup will now be known as ________ in honor of the great female tennis player.

A. Martina Navratilova Cup
B. Billy Jin King Cup
C. Chris Evert Cup
D. Steffi Graf Cup

Q.34 Emperor _____ awarded the title Zarin Qalam or Golden Pen to Muhammad Hussein al-Qatib Kashmiri for his beautiful handwriting.

A. Shahjahan   **B.** Jahangir
C. Aurangzeb   **D.** Akbar

Q.35 Who among the following was the captain of Nepal's cricket team till November 2020?

Q.25 'Ammeter' is related to 'Current' in the same way as 'Anemometer' is related to '________'.

A. Temperature
B. Potential Difference
C. Water

A. Gyanendra Malla
B. Rohit Poudel
C. Sandeep Lamichhane
D. Deepender Singh Eri

Q.36 In October 2020, what was the name of the initiative launched by Indian Railways for the safety of its women passengers?

A. Naari Seva   **B.** Meri Saheli
C. Naari Sahayak   **D.** Naari Shakti

Q.37 When the Constitution of India was being drafted, the Constituent Assembly had to take into account the unrest that India was going through. Which of the following was not relevant in that scenario?

A. The socio-economic condition of the people was very favorable.
B. The princely state was uncertain about its future.
C. The country was made up of many different communities.
D. The partition of India and Pakistan was confirmed.

Q.38 Kadamai was a form of land revenue under the ______ dynasty.
A. Chola   **B.** Kushan
C. Chalukya   **D.** Gupta

Q.39 The filmmaker from Arunachal had received the prestigious Dada Saheb Phalke Award for a documentary on ______ in 2020.
A. boat ride   **B.** honey hunting
C. animal hunting   **D.** bird watching

Q.40 Which of the following is not a characteristic of 'solid'?
A. A solid has a fixed volume.
B. Solids can be compressed easily.
C. Solids can break when subjected to force.
D. It is difficult to change the shape of solids, so they are hard.

Q.41 On 7 September 2021, NASA announced that the Perseverance rover has completed the collection of the first sample of ______ Mars.
A. soil   **B.** dust   **C.** rock   **D.** snow

Q.42 On which day do we celebrate the festival of 'Holi' according to the Hindu calendar?
A. A day after the full moon
B. New moon day
C. A day before full moon
D. Full moon day

Q.43 As on 27 November 2020, India's foreign exchange reserves stood at around ______ billion.
A. $774   **B.** $574   **C.** $474   **D.** $374

Q.44 Which of the following events took place in the year 1856?
A. Tantya Tope was captured, tried to escape and was put to death.
B. Awadh was captured by the British East India Company.
C. Mangal Pandey was hanged.
D. Bahadur Shah Zafar was sent to Rangoon jail.

Q.45 Which of the following is the oldest Joint Stock Bank of India established in 1865?
A. State Bank Of Travancore
B. Dena Bank
C. Canara Bank
D. Allahabad Bank (now Indian Bank)

Q.46 Which of the following is a unicellular organism?
A. Red algae   **B.** Muscle cells
C. Fungus   **D.** Bacteria

Q.47 The classical singer, Girija Devi was proficient in which form of Hindustani classical music?
A. Tarana   **B.** Dhrupad   **C.** Thumri   **D.** Khayal

Q.48 Which one of the following states of India had the highest density of population as per 2011 census?
A. Sikkim   **B.** Bihar
C. Madhya Pradesh   **D.** Uttar Pradesh

Q.49 Who among the following is the first Indian woman cricketer to play 200 One Day International (ODI) matches?
A. Anuja Patil   **B.** Mithali Raj
C. Poonam Yadav   **D.** Deepti Sharma

Q.50 Which of the following rivers flows through Tibet, India and Bangladesh?
A. Brahmaputra   **B.** Yamuna
C. Narmada   **D.** Ganga

Elementary Mathematics

Q.51 Varun bought a curtain cloth from a wholesaler at 20% discount on the marked price. He then marked the cloth at 20% higher than the original marked price and allowed 10% discount. What is his percentage profit?
A. 25   **B.** 20   **C.** 30   **D.** 35

Q.52 Find the value of $85 \div 17$ of $4 - [65 \div 13$ of $2 - 14 \times (19 - 25) \div 12 - 10]$ of $\frac{2}{3}$.
A. $\frac{11}{12}$ **B.** $\frac{3}{2}$ **C.** $\frac{7}{6}$ **D.** $\frac{19}{12}$

Q.53 One-fifth of three-eighths of two-thirds of a number is 20. What is 60% of that number?
A. 120   **B.** 156   **C.** 365   **D.** 240

Q.54 The ratio of the number of girls and boys in a school is $2:7$. If the number of girls and boys are increased by 15% and 20% respectively, then what will be the new ratio?
A. $23:84$ **B.** $19:14$ **C.** $24:71$ **D.** $21:22$

Q.55 A trader allows a discount of 10% on the marked price and still gains 8% on the whole. At what percentage above the cost price does he mark his goods?
A. 35%   **B.** 25%   **C.** 18%   **D.** 20%

Q.56 Rohit can complete a piece of work in 32 days, while Raj can complete it by himself in 48 days. They started the work together, but Rohit left 8 days before the work got over. For how many days did they work together?
A. 18   B. 12   C. 15   D. 16

Q.57 The average monthly income of A and B is ₹ $4,500$, the average monthly income of B and C is ₹ $5,600$, and the average monthly income of A and C is ₹ $4,800$. Find the monthly income of B.
A. ₹ 6,900   B. ₹ 4,750   C. ₹ 3,700   D. ₹ 5,300

Q.58 A person saves 12% of his income. One year later, his income shoots up by 25% but he still saves the same amount of money. What is the percentage hike in his expenditure?
A. 27.4%   B. 28.4%   C. 25.4%   D. 33%

Q.59 Two friends, A and B, invested in a business in the ratio of $3:4$. A withdrew his share two months early. At the end of one year, the total profit was ₹ $2,600$. A's share of profit will be:
A. ₹ 750   B. ₹ 1,000   C. ₹ 800   D. ₹ 1,110

Q.60 Find the single discount equivalent to two successive discounts of 25% and 10%.
A. 28%   B. 40.25%   C. 32.5%   D. 45.5%

Q.61 The ratio of the radii of two right circular cones, C and D, is $2:3$ and their heights are in the ratio $3:2$. The ratio of the volume of cone D to that of cone C is:
A. $4:3$ B. $2:3$ C. $3:4$ D. $3:2$

Q.62 Find the value of $\dfrac{\frac{2}{5}\text{ of }7\frac{1}{2}\div\frac{3}{4}-\frac{3}{4}\times1\frac{1}{2}\div2\frac{1}{4}}{5\frac{1}{2}\div3\frac{2}{3}\text{ of }\frac{3}{8}}$.
A. $\frac{3}{4}$ B. $\frac{1}{2}$ C. $\frac{7}{8}$ D. $\frac{5}{3}$

Q.63 In a family 5 people spend 10% on the purchase of sugar. The price of sugar increased by 10%. What should be the percentage decrease in the consumption of sugar so as not to increase the expenditure?
A. 11%   B. $9\frac{1}{11}\%$ C. 10%   D. 9%

Q.64 A sum of money at compound interest amounts to seven times of itself in 3 years. In how many years will it be 2401 times of itself?
A. 9   B. 12   C. 18   D. 15

Q.65 How many maximum litres of milk can a hemispherical bowl of diameter 9 cm hold approximately?
A. 0.191 litres   B. 0.90 litres
C. 0.0191 litres   D. 1.90 litres

Q.66 Karthik invested an amount of ₹ $9,000$ in a fixed deposit scheme for 3 years at compound interest at the rate of 2% p.a. How much amount (correct to two decimal places) will he get on maturity of the fixed deposit?
A. ₹ 9,650   B. ₹ 10,255.25
C. ₹ 9,525.50   D. ₹ 9,550.87

Q.67 By selling 90 pens for ₹ $1,575$, a shopkeeper loses 30%. How many pens should he sell for ₹ 708 so as to earn a profit of 18%?
A. 30   B. 20   C. 24   D. 25

Q.68 Find the least number which is a perfect square and is divisible by each of the following numbers.
$15, 24$ and 36
A. 3600   B. 1600   C. 900   D. 6400

Q.69 Pipes A and B can fill a tank in 18 hours and 27 hours, respectively. If both the pipes are opened on alternate hours, one at a time, and pipe A is opened for the first hour, then in how many hours will the tank be filled completely?
A. 21   B. $20\frac{1}{2}$ C. 20   D. $21\frac{1}{2}$

Q.70 For a certain sum, in 2 years, the simple interest is ₹ 80 and the compound interest for the same period and at the same rate of interest is ₹ 85. The rate of interest per annum is:
A. 7.5%   B. 8.5%   C. 12.5%   D. 5.5%

Q.71 The average weight of 6 persons is increased by 1.5 kg when a new person replaces the one whose weight is 45 kg. How much should a new person weight?
A. 54 kg   B. 55 kg   C. 50 kg   D. 48 kg

Q.72 If $0.35:x::5:6$, then what is the value of x?
A. 0.48   B. 0.42   C. 0.34   D. 0.44

Q.73 A motorcar started with a speed of 60 km/hr, and its speed is increased by 20 km/hr every 3 hour. How many hours will it take to cover a distance of 470 km?
A. $6\frac{1}{4}$ B. $5\frac{2}{3}$ C. 7   D. $6\frac{1}{2}$

Q.74 If $9987693\times6432\times7695$ is divided by 10, then what will be the remainder?
A. 6   B. 0   C. 1   D. 9

Q.75 A man covers two-third of a certain distance at the speed of 70 km/hr and the rest at the speed of 50 km/hr. It takes him $6\frac{4}{5}$ hours for the whole journey. At a speed of 56 km/hr, in what time will he be able to cover the entire distance?
A. 7 hours   B. $8\frac{1}{3}$ hours
C. $7\frac{1}{2}$ hours   D. 8 hours

English

Q.76 Direction: Select the most appropriate meaning of the given idiom.
To get out of hand
A. To get out of control
B. To get an award
C. To get angry

D. To get in a trouble

Ques (77-78):Direction: The following sentence has been split into four segments. Identify the segment that contains a grammatical error.

Q.77 The visitors / were being showed / a collection of / old manuscripts.

A. a collection of

B. old manuscripts

C. The visitors

D. were being showed

Q.78 Mohit is expecting / a huge profit / at his / recent investment.

A. at his

B. a huge profit

C. Mohit is expecting

D. recent investment

Ques (79-80):Direction: Select the most appropriate option to fill in the blank.

Q.79 When his mother was away, he took the _____ of his little brother.

A. management

B. power

C. charge

D. duty

Q.80 Mere classroom teaching-learning is boring and _____ for students.

A. varied

B. monotonous

C. exciting

D. interesting

Q.81 Direction: Select the most appropriate synonym of the given word.

Maintain

A. Care

B. Ignore

C. Release

D. Neglect

Q.82 Direction: Select the most appropriate ANTONYM of the given word.

Beneficial

A. Careful

B. Fearful

C. Hopeful

D. Harmful

Q.83 Direction: Select the option that can be used as a one-word substitute for the given group ofwords.

The sound of owls

A. Hoot

B. Caw

C. Cluck

D. Moo

Q.84 Direction: Select the most appropriate option to fill in the blank.

He _____ an important question in the meeting.

A. rose

B. risen

C. rise

D. raised

Q.85 Select the INCORRECTLY spelt word.

A. Brilliant

B. Illusion

C. Scrutiny

D. Abandan

Q.86 Direction: Select the option that can be used as a one-word substitute for the given group ofwords.

Able to be harmed easily

A. Vulnerable

B. Available

C. Accessible

D. Flexible

Q.87 Direction: The following sentence has been divided into parts. One of them may contain an error.Select the part that contains the error from the given options. If you don't find anyerror, mark 'No error' as your answer.

May I / please borrow / yours book?

A. No error

B. yours book

C. May I

D. please borrow

Q.88 Direction: Select the most appropriate option that can substitute the underlined segment in thegiven sentence. If there is no need to substitute it, select 'No substitution required'.

The task our English teacher gave us <u>was both challenging</u> and entertaining.

A. No substitution required

B. was together challenged

C. was both challenge

D. is additionally challenging

Q.89 Select the INCORRECTLY spelt word.

A. Pretanse

B. Reliance

C. Alliance

D. Defiance

Q.90 Direction: Select the most appropriate SYNONYM of the given word.

Compose

A. Clutch

B. Confuse

C. Collect

D. Cuddle

Q.91 Direction: Select the most appropriate meaning of the given idiom.

To take stock of

A. To measure

B. To think carefully

C. To count

D. To discuss

Q.92 Direction: Select the option that can be used as a one-word substitute for the given group ofwords.

A large number of things placed one on top of another

A. Batch

B. Group

C. Pile

D. Load

Ques (93-94):Direction: Select the option that will improve the underlined part of the given sentence. In case no improvement is needed, select 'No improvement required'.

Q.93 The children <u>were been drove</u> to the picnic spot in the school bus.

A. were been driving

B. were being driven

C. were been driven

D. No improvement required

Q.94 Aphrodite vowed that Paris <u>would had</u> the most beautiful woman as his wife

A. will be having

B. would have

C. No improvement required

D. would be having

Q.95 Direction: Select the most appropriate ANTONYM of the given word.

Stout

A. Obese

B. Heavy

C. Thin

D. Bulky

Ques (96-100):Direction: In the following passage, some words have been deleted. Read the passage carefully and select the most appropriate option to fill in each blank.

Football legend Diego Maradona was buried in a private ceremony after a day of (1) _____scenes in the Argentine capital Buenos Aires. Only (2) _____ two dozen relatives and closefriends (3) _____ the final ceremony on Thursday. But (4) _____ huge crowds turned out topay (5) _____ respects, with many weeping, blowing kisses and praying as they filed pasthis coffin.

Q.96 Select the most appropriate option to fill in blank no. 1.

A. impressive

B. exciting

C. emotional

D. expressive

Q.97 Select the most appropriate option to fill in blank no. 2.

A. around

B. more or less

C. roughly

D. just

Q.98 Select the most appropriate option to fill in blank no. 3.

A. attending

B. attended

C. have attended

D. attend

Q.99 Select the most appropriate option to fill in blank no. 4.

A. early
B. earliest
C. earlier
D. as early

Q.100 Select the most appropriate option to fill in blank no. 5.

A. their
B. his
C. them
D. its

// Smart Answer Sheet //

Correct — Percentage of students who answered correctly. **Skipped** — Percentage of students who skipped.

Q.	Ans.	Correct / Skipped
1	D	54.72 % / 18.86 %
2	A	52.83 % / 20.75 %
3	D	66.04 % / 22.64 %
4	B	26.42 % / 24.52 %
5	B	32.08 % / 16.98 %
6	B	32.08 % / 22.64 %
7	D	32.08 % / 24.52 %
8	B	56.6 % / 20.76 %
9	C	41.51 % / 22.64 %
10	A	20.75 % / 20.76 %
11	C	45.28 % / 15.1 %
12	A	37.74 % / 20.75 %
13	D	39.62 % / 20.76 %
14	B	47.17 % / 22.64 %
15	D	52.83 % / 18.87 %
16	A	24.53 % / 22.64 %
17	D	58.49 % / 26.42 %
18	C	18.87 % / 22.64 %
19	B	47.17 % / 20.75 %
20	D	69.81 % / 20.76 %
21	A	41.51 % / 24.53 %
22	C	58.49 % / 22.64 %
23	C	24.53 % / 22.64 %
24	A	62.26 % / 22.65 %
25	D	35.85 % / 22.64 %
26	C	7.55 % / 32.07 %
27	C	15.09 % / 30.19 %
28	C	5.66 % / 32.08 %
29	C	13.21 % / 30.19 %
30	D	13.21 % / 30.19 %
31	B	13.21 % / 30.19 %
32	B	11.32 % / 32.08 %
33	B	7.55 % / 32.07 %
34	D	5.66 % / 32.08 %
35	A	9.43 % / 30.19 %
36	B	9.43 % / 30.19 %
37	A	13.21 % / 30.19 %
38	A	15.09 % / 30.19 %
39	B	5.66 % / 30.19 %
40	B	30.19 % / 30.19 %
41	C	11.32 % / 30.19 %
42	D	20.75 % / 30.19 %
43	B	18.87 % / 30.19 %
44	B	15.09 % / 32.08 %
45	D	24.53 % / 30.19 %
46	D	16.98 % / 32.08 %
47	C	9.43 % / 30.19 %
48	B	26.42 % / 30.18 %
49	B	47.17 % / 30.19 %
50	A	33.96 % / 30.19 %
51	D	9.43 % / 41.51 %
52	D	1.89 % / 43.39 %
53	D	20.75 % / 43.4 %
54	A	18.87 % / 47.17 %
55	D	5.66 % / 41.51 %
56	D	5.66 % / 43.4 %
57	D	9.43 % / 47.17 %
58	B	11.32 % / 47.17 %
59	B	3.77 % / 47.17 %
60	C	22.64 % / 45.28 %
61	D	5.66 % / 43.4 %
62	C	11.32 % / 45.28 %
63	B	15.09 % / 39.63 %
64	B	9.43 % / 45.29 %
65	A	7.55 % / 43.39 %
66	D	9.43 % / 45.29 %
67	C	9.43 % / 45.29 %
68	A	28.3 % / 45.28 %
69	D	9.43 % / 39.63 %
70	C	15.09 % / 39.63 %
71	A	11.32 % / 41.51 %
72	B	26.42 % / 47.16 %
73	D	15.09 % / 37.74 %
74	B	24.53 % / 45.28 %
75	C	7.55 % / 45.28 %
76	A	15.09 % / 81.14 %
77	D	9.43 % / 81.14 %
78	A	7.55 % / 81.13 %
79	C	0 % / 100 %
80	B	11.32 % / 83.02 %

Q.	Ans.	Correct		Q.	Ans.	Correct		Q.	Ans.	Correct		Q.	Ans.	Correct		Q.	Ans.	Correct
		Skipped				Skipped				Skipped				Skipped				Skipped
81	A	15.09 % 83.02 %		85	D	9.43 % 83.02 %		89	A	9.43 % 83.02 %		93	B	7.55 % 83.02 %		97	A	11.32 % 83.02 %
82	D	11.32 % 83.02 %		86	A	11.32 % 83.02 %		90	C	9.43 % 83.02 %		94	B	11.32 % 83.02 %		98	B	5.66 % 83.02 %
83	A	11.32 % 83.02 %		87	B	9.43 % 83.02 %		91	B	3.77 % 83.02 %		95	C	3.77 % 83.02 %		99	C	7.55 % 83.02 %
84	D	11.32 % 83.02 %		88	A	9.43 % 83.02 %		92	C	7.55 % 83.02 %		96	C	9.43 % 83.02 %		100	A	11.32 % 83.02 %

//Hints and Solutions//

1. Given sequence: D Q _ R _ D _ M R _ D _ M _ T

Option (A): M Q T T Q R → D Q M R Q - D T M R T - D Q M R T

Option (B): M T Q R Q T → D Q M R T - D Q M R R - D Q M T T

Option (C): M T Q T R Q → D Q M R T - D Q M R T - D R M Q T

Option (D): M T Q T Q R → D Q M R T - D Q M R T - D Q M R T

In option (D), DQMRT is repeated.

Hence, the correct option is (D).

2. The logic followed here is:

Option (A): NRV → N + 4 = R; R + 4 = V

Option (B): QVB → Q + 5 = V; V + 6 = B

Option (C): SXD → S + 5 = X; X + 6 = D

Option (D): YDJ → Y + 5 = D; D + 6 = J

Hence, the correct option is (A).

3. The logic followed here is:

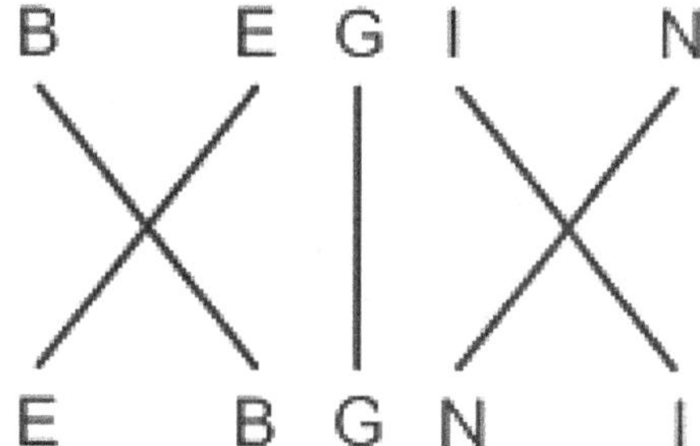

Similarly,

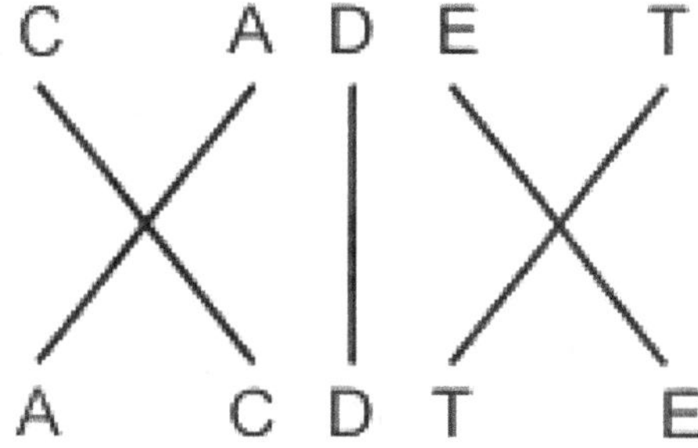

Hence, the correct option is (D).

4. The logic followed here is:

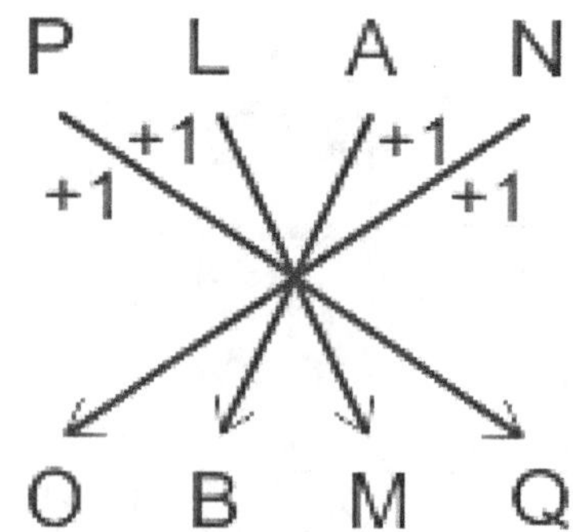

And,

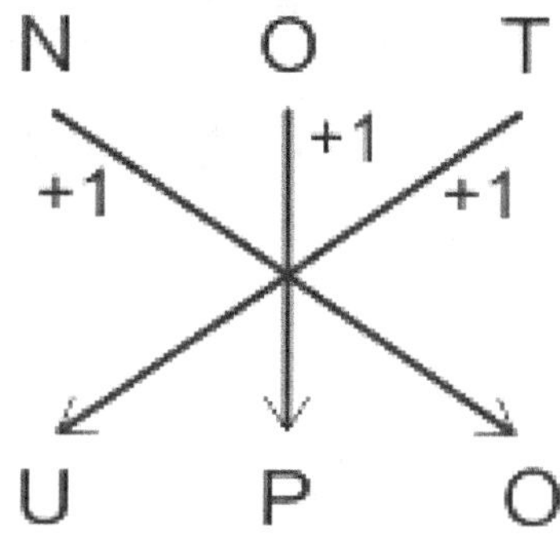

Similarly,

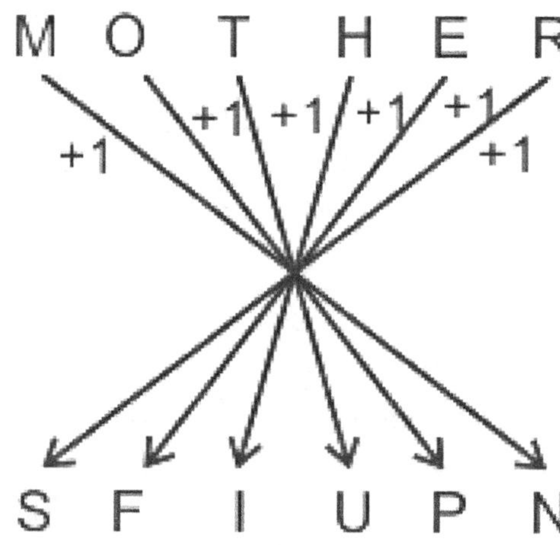

Hence, the correct option is (B).

5. Given,

$A \rightarrow +, \ B \rightarrow \times, \ C \rightarrow -, \ D \rightarrow \div,$

82 A 126 B 16 D 112 C 73

After replacing the letters by their meaning, we get:

$82 + (126 \times 16) \div 112 - 73$

$82 + 2016 \div 112 - 73$

$= 82 + 18 - 73$

$= 100 - 73$

$= 27$

Hence, the correct option is (B).

6. Given,

An amount of ₹ 870 is divided between Urmi and Kripa in the ratio of $18:11$, respectively.

Amount of money Urmi got = $\dfrac{18}{(18+11)} \times 870$

$= \dfrac{18}{29} \times 870$

$= 540$

Amount of money Kripa got $= 870 - 540$

$= 330$

An amount of ₹ 960 is divided between Poorvi and Mrinal in the ratio of $5:7$.

Amount of money Poorvi got $= \dfrac{5}{(5+7)} \times 960$

$= \dfrac{5}{12} \times 960$

$= 400$

Amount of money Mrinal got $= 960 - 400$

$= 560$

Thus, Mrinal gets the maximum amount of money among all four.

Hence, the correct option is (B).

7. The image embedded in the given figure is shown below:

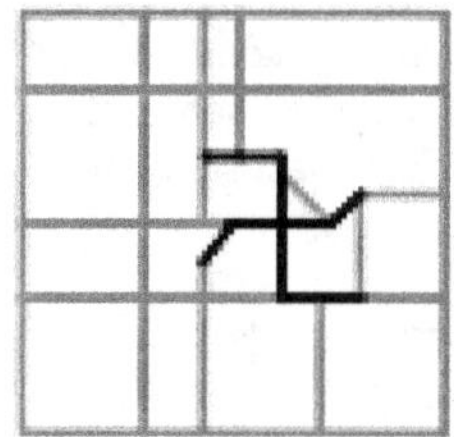

Hence, the correct option is (D).

8. The paper when folded to form a dice, the faces that will be opposite to each other is shown below:

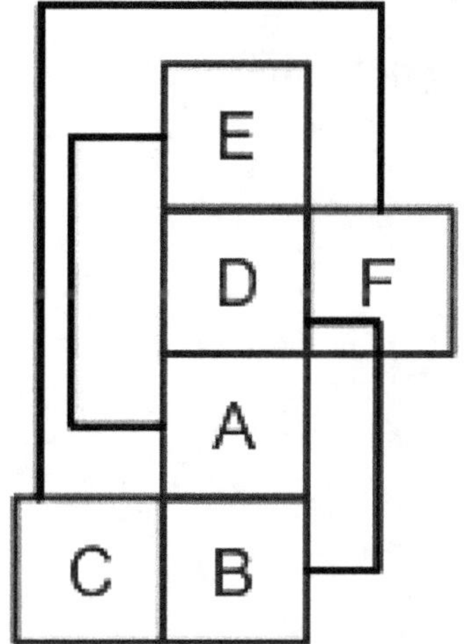

Clearly, B will be the face opposite to D.

Hence, the correct option is (B).

9. The correct option that indicates the arrangement of the given words in the order in which they appear in an English dictionary is:

2. Caring, 1. Carpet, 3. Carrot, 4. Creamy, 5. Creek

Hence, the correct option is (C).

10. Given,

In a cafeteria, seven customers (B, G, H, K, L, M and N) sit on three different benches $(X, Y$ and $Z)$.

Each bench must have at least two customers sitting on it.

- Customer K sits on Bench X with his best friends.
- Customer H sits on Bench Z.

Bench	Customers
X	K
Y	
Z	H

Customer B sits only with customer N.

As B sits only with N, they are sitting on bench Y as bench Y is vacant and no one else sits on it.

Bench	Customers
X	K
Y	B, N
Z	H

Customer G does not sit with customers K, L and M.

- Customer G sits with H on bench Z as G does not sit with customers K, L and M.

- Also, L and M sits on bench X with K.

Bench	Customers
X	K, L, M
Y	B, N
Z	H, G

Clearly, on bench X, there are three customers.

Hence, the correct option is (A).

11. The set of classes whose relationship between them is best represented by the given Venn diagram is shown below:

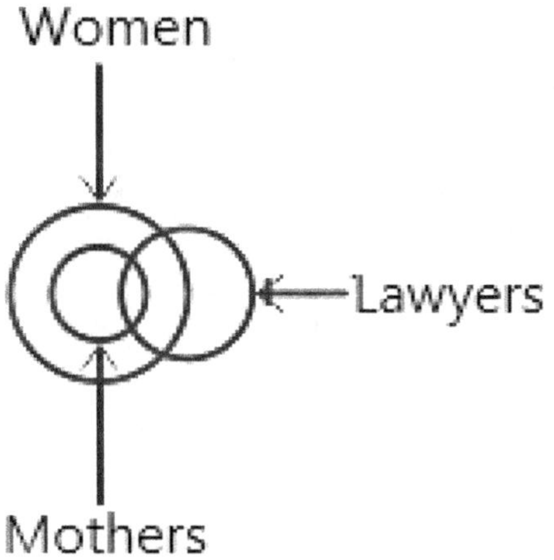

All mothers are women.

Some mothers and women are lawyers.

Hence, the correct option is (C).

12. The pattern followed here is:

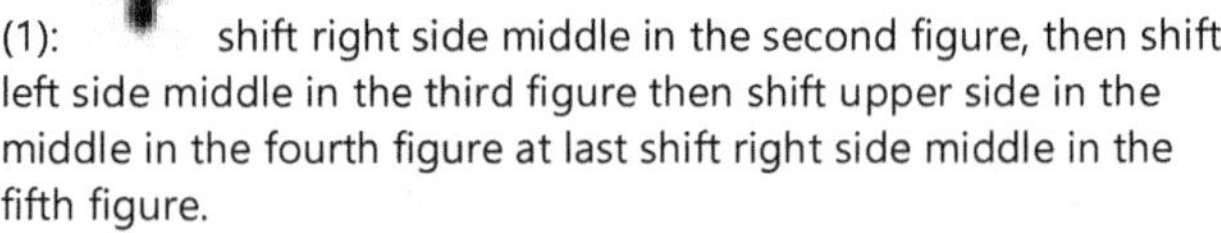

(1): shift right side middle in the second figure, then shift left side middle in the third figure then shift upper side in the middle in the fourth figure at last shift right side middle in the fifth figure.

(2) Square and circle interchange their position in every figure.

(3) Arrow shift upper side in the middle in second figure, then shift right side middle in the third figure, then shift left side in the fourth figure at last shift upper side in the middle of the figure.

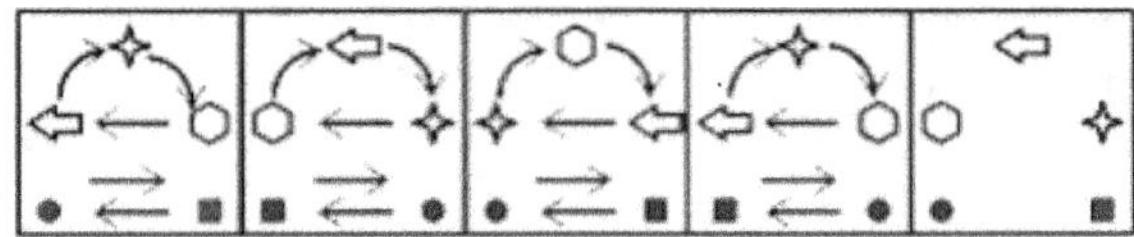

(4) shift left side middle of the figure in second figure, then shift upper middle of the figure in third figure, then shift right side middle in the figure in fourth figure, at last shift left side middle of the figure.

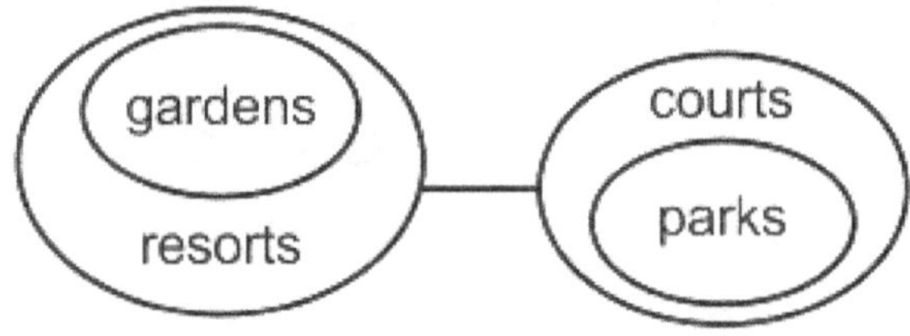

Hence, the correct option is (A).

13. The least possible Venn diagram is:

Conclusions:

I. No court is a garden. → Follow (As, All gardens are resorts and No resort is a court)

II. No garden is a park. → Follow (As, All gardens are resorts, No resort is a court and All parks are courts)

Therefore, Both the conclusions follow.

Hence, the correct option is (D).

14. The paper when unfolded will appear as shown below:

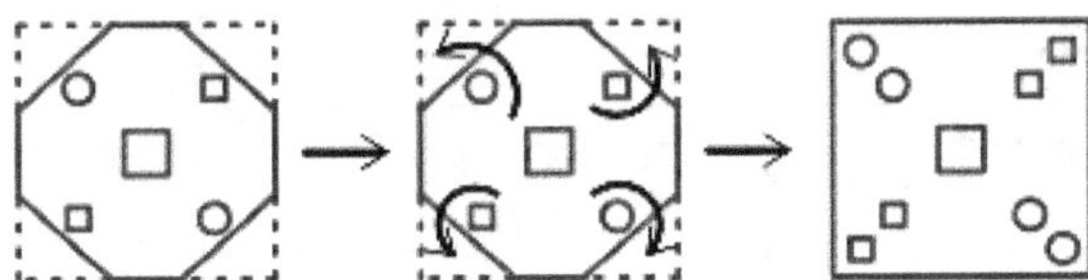

Hence, the correct option is (B).

15. The logic followed here is:

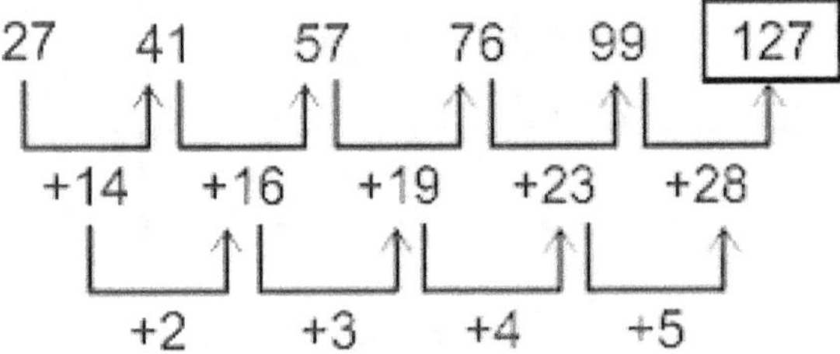

Hence, the correct option is (D).

16. Given,

$$6:4::11:?::16:8$$

The logic followed here is

$$(\text{First number } +4) \times \left(\frac{2}{5}\right) = \text{Second number}$$

$$6:4 \Rightarrow (6+4) \times \left(\frac{2}{5}\right) = 10 \times \left(\frac{2}{5}\right)$$

$$= 2 \times 2$$

$$= 4$$

And,

$$16:8 \Rightarrow (16+4) \times \left(\frac{2}{5}\right) (= 20 \times \left(\frac{2}{5}\right)$$

$$= 4 \times 2$$

$$= 8$$

Similarly,

$$11:? \Rightarrow (11+4) \times \left(\frac{2}{5}\right) = 15 \times \left(\frac{2}{5}\right)$$

$$= 3 \times 2$$

$$= 6$$

Hence, the correct option is (A).

17. The logic followed here is:

$$N \to 2, A \to 3, U \to 6, S \to 9, E \to 4, A \to 3$$

And,

$$S \to 9, Y \to 7, R \to 1, U \to 6, P \to 5$$

Similarly,

$$S \to 9, U \to 6, P \to 5, P \to 5, R \to 1, E \to 4, S \to 9, S \to 9$$

SUPPRESS will be coded as 96551499.

Hence, the correct option is (D).

18. Given,

Six friends, Govardan, Sarayu, Rekha, Shyamala, Hema and Ganesh, are standing in a queue at a ticket counter.

1. Only one person is standing ahead of Govardan.

___ > Govardan > ___ > ___ > ___ > ___

2. Ganesh who is fourth from the back end of the row, is between Govardan and Hema.

___ > Govardan > Ganesh > Hema > ___ > ___

3. There are two persons between Sarayu and Hema.

Sarayu > Govardan > Ganesh > Hema > ___ > ___

4. Rekha is between Hema and Shyamala.

Sarayu > Govardan > Ganesh > Hema > Rekha > Shyamala

Clearly, Govardan and Ganesh are the two persons standing between Sarayu and Hema.

Hence, the correct option is (C).

19. The logic followed here is:

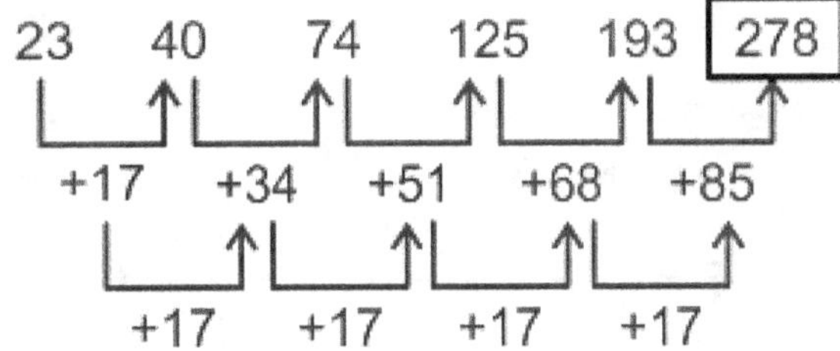

Hence, the correct option is (B).

20. The logic followed here is:

And,

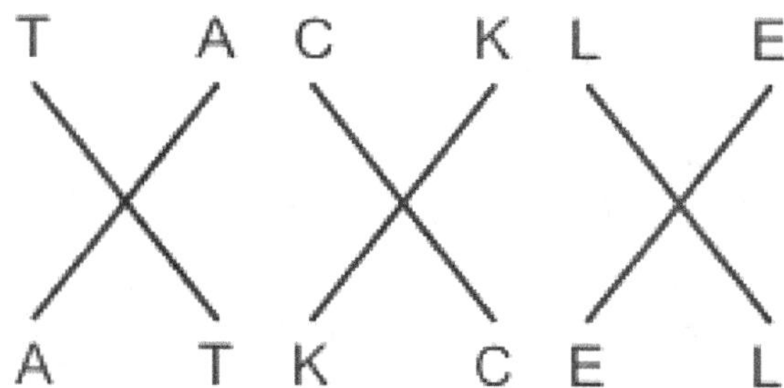

Similarly,

Hence, the correct option is (D).

21. Given,

$(12,14,56)$

Logic: $\dfrac{(First\ number \times Second\ number)}{3} = $ Third number

$(12,14,56) = \dfrac{(12 \times 14)}{3} = 4 \times 14 = 56$

Now, from option (A),

$(16,18,96) = \dfrac{(16 \times 18)}{3}$

$= 16 \times 6$

$= 96$

Hence, the correct option is (A).

22. The logic followed here is:

$$B \xrightarrow{+3} E \xrightarrow{+3} H \xrightarrow{+3} K \xrightarrow{+3} N$$
$$E \xrightarrow{+3} H \xrightarrow{+3} K \xrightarrow{+3} N \xrightarrow{+3} Q$$
$$I \xrightarrow{+3} L \xrightarrow{+3} O \xrightarrow{+3} R \xrightarrow{+3} U$$

Hence, the correct option is (C).

23. By using the symbols in the table given below, we can draw the following family tree:

Symbol in Diagram	Meaning
○	Female
□	Male
═	Married Couple
—	Siblings
│	Difference of A Generation

Graphing of the family tree as per given information:

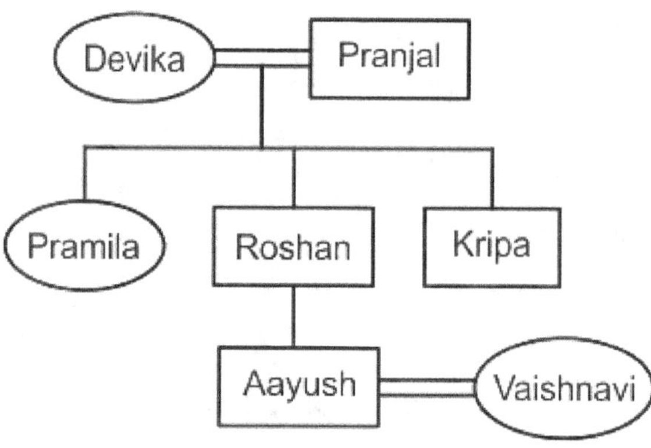

Thus, Roshan is the brother of Pramila.

Hence, the correct option is (C).

24. The mirror image of the given combination when the mirror is placed on the right side is as shown below:

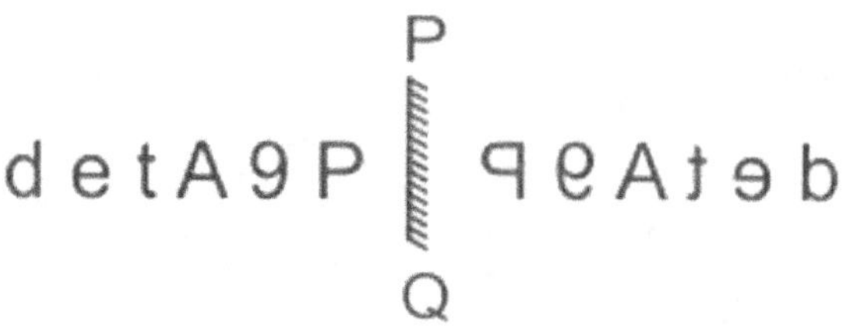

Hence, the correct option is (A).

25. The logic followed here is:

Ammeter' is related to 'Current' → An ammeter is a measuring instrument used to measure the current in a circuit.

Similarly,

'Anemometer' is related to 'Wind Speed and Direction' → An anemometer is an instrument that measures wind speed and direction.

Hence, the correct option is (D).

26. The Forest (Conservation) Act in India was passed in the year 1980.

The Forest (Conservation) Act in India was enacted by the parliament for the conservation and protection of forest resources. It limits the state government, except for prior permission from the central government to take any decisions. The objective of these acts is to protect its flora, and fauna and prevent deforestation for cultivation, grazing, and other purposes.

Hence, the correct option is (C).

27. 'Pradhan Mantri Jeevan Jyoti Bima Yojana' was launched in 2015.

It is a one-year life insurance scheme offering coverage for death for any reason. It provides 2 Lakh life cover against a premium of Rs 330 per year. The age group between 18-50 years is covered under this scheme.

Hence, the correct option is (C).

28. Delhi Crime web series won the Best Drama Series award at the 48th International Emmy Awards 2020.

The 48th International Emmy Awards 2020 was held in Hammerstein Ballroom, New York City. International Emmy Awards was formed in 1946 and in 1949 presented the first Emmys. The awards were made by the National Academy of Television Arts and Sciences. The awards are given in the following categories which are dramatic series, comedy series, special drama, limited series, and variety, music, or comedy. Delhi Crime became the 1st Indian web series to receive an award in Drama-Series.

Hence, the correct option is (C).

29. To clap functions is not controlled by the medulla oblongata.

The medulla oblongata is the lower part of the brain. It is tube or funnel-shaped. Its function is to regulate breathing, heartbeat, and digestion. It connects our brain with the spinal cord, pons, and cerebral cortex.

Hence, the correct option is (C).

30. Lonar Lake, Maharashtra was formed by meteorite impact during the Neolithic era.

Lonar lake is a saline lake located in Buldhana district, Maharashtra. It is formed after a meteorite impact led to crater formation. It has been designated as a Ramsar site by wetland international in the year 2020. The colour of the lake is pink due to the presence of Haloarchaea microbes. It is a notified National Geo-heritage Monument due to its culturally significant offering insight into earth's evolution.

Hence, the correct option is (D).

31. United Kingdom chaired the G7 Leaders' Summit held in June 2021.

Indian Prime Minister addressed the 47th G7 Summit 2021 through video conferencing. The last G7 summit was in France in 2019.

About G7: It is an intergovernmental organisation that was formed in 1975. The country meets annually to discuss issues of common interest like global economic governance, international security and energy policy. India is not part of the G7 country. India was invited to G7 because its agenda is 'deep and diverse.

The G7 countries: UK, Canada, France, Germany, Italy, Japan and the US.

Hence, the correct option is (B).

32. Sapru committee was appointed by the Standing Committee of the Non-Party Conference in November to examine the communal matter in a judicial framework after the break-up of the Gandhi-Jinnah talks on communal problems.

The Sapru Committee Report was published in 1945. The Sapru Committee consisted of thirty members. The Sapru Committee 21 recommendations pertaining to constitutional questions that concerned the governance and politics of India. The Sapru Committee Report rejected the proposal for the division of the Indian sub-continent into the two states of India and Pakistan.

Hence, the correct option is (B).

33. On 17th September, 2020, The International Tennis Federation (ITF) announced that the Federation or 'Fed' Cup will now be known as Billy Jin King Cup in honor of the great female tennis player.

It is the first major Team tournament to be named after a woman. Changed name in September 2020 in honour of former World No,1 Billie Jean King.

Hence, the correct option is (B).

34. Emperor Akbar awarded the title Zarin Qalam or Golden Pen to Muhammad Hussein al-Qatib Kashmiri for his beautiful handwriting.

Akbar was born on October 15, 1542, in Umarkot (now in Sindh Province, Pakistan). Akbar was the son of Humayun and the grandson of Babur. Akbar got enthroned at a very early stage of 14 years. Akbar ruled from 1556 to 1605.

Hence, the correct option is (D).

35. Gyanendra Malla was the captain of Nepal's cricket team till November 2020.

Gyanendra Malla born 16 September 1990. Gyanendra Malla is an Nepali right-handed batsman. Gyanendra Malla was a part of the Nepal Under-15 and Under-19 squads before joining the senior side.

Hence, the correct option is (A).

36. In October 2020, Meri Saheli was the name of the initiative launched by Indian Railways for the safety of its women passengers.

Meri Saheli Initiative was launched to provide safety and security to lady passengers travelling by trains for their entire journey from originating station to the terminating station. Section 58 of the Railways Act, 1989 provides for the earmarking of accommodation for female passengers in trains.

Hence, the correct option is (B).

37. When the Constitution of India was being drafted, the Constituent Assembly had to take into account the unrest that India was going through. The socio-economic condition of the people was very favorable was not relevant in that scenario.

On 29th August 1947, the Constituent Assembly through a resolution appointed a Drafting Committee. The Drafting Committee had seven members: Alladi Krishnaswami Ayyar, N. Gopalaswami; B.R. Ambedkar, K.M Munshi, Mohammad Saadulla, B.L. Mitter and D.P. Khaitan. At its first meeting on 30th August 1947, the Drafting Committee elected B.R Ambedkar as its Chairman.

Hence, the correct option is (A).

38. Kadamai was a form of land revenue under the Chola dynasty.

The Kadamai tax was a type of land revenue that the peasants had to pay to their landlords or king. During the Chola administration, there were around 400 different types of taxes. Vetti also called forced labour and Kadamai also called land revenue. Land revenue and trade tax were the main source of income, The Chola rulers. The Chola Empire was a Southern Indian Tamil family and is one of the longest-ruling dynasties in the history of the world.

Hence, the correct option is (A).

39. The filmmaker from Arunachal had received the prestigious Dada Saheb Phalke Award for a documentary on "honey hunting" in 2020.

Honey hunting has an integral part of the Arunachal Pradesh, Sherdukpen community. The documentary is made by independent filmmaker Kezang D Thongdok.

The Dadasaheb Phalke Award is India's highest award in the field of cinema. It is presented annually at the National Film Awards ceremony by the Directorate of Film Festivals. Presented first in 1969, the award was introduced by the Government of India. The award comprises a Swarna Kamal (Golden Lotus) medallion, a shawl, and a cash prize of ₹ 10 lakh.

Hence, the correct option is (B).

40. Solids can be compressed easily, is not a characteristic of 'solid'. Solid is a form of matter that has structural rigidity and a firm shape which cannot be changed easily.

It has a fixed shape and volume. The intermolecular force of attraction is strong as molecules of particles are closely attached. There is less Intermolecular space between particles. They are not easily compressible. It is difficult to change the shape of solids, so they are hard.

Hence, the correct option is (B).

41. On 7 September 2021, NASA announced that the Perseverance rover has completed the collection of the first sample of rock Mars.

The Perseverance rover has collected 11 scientifically-compelling rock core samples and one atmospheric sample. NASA, or the National Aeronautics and Space Administration, was created by President Dwight Eisenhower in 1958.

Hence, the correct option is (C).

42. On full moon day, we celebrate the festival of 'Holi' according to the Hindu calendar.

Holi marks the arrival of spring after a long winter and is symbolic of the triumph of good over evil. It is the festival of colours where people play with water and powder colours. It falls in the Hindu calendar month of Phalgun on the full-moon day, which is in March. It is the second biggest Hindu festival after Diwali.

Hence, the correct option is (D).

43. As on 27 November 2020, India's foreign exchange reserves stood at around $574 billion.

India's foreign reserve includes Foreign assets, Gold reserve, Special drawing rights, and Reserve with IMF. It helps in managing crises, and rupee appreciation and boosts the confidence of investors. As of October 2022, India's Foreign reserve is $532.838 billion.

Hence, the correct option is (B).

44. Awadh was captured by the British East India Company in the year 1856.

The Company annexed the state of Awadh in 1856 on the charges of misgovernance by the Nawab of Awadh. It was captured on the order of Lord Dalhousie under the Doctrine of lapse. Wajid Ali Shah was the ruler of Awadh during the annexation and was later deported to Garden Reach in Metiabruz, Kolkata.

Hence, the correct option is (B).

45. Allahabad Bank (now Indian Bank) is the oldest Joint Stock Bank of India established in 1865.

A joint stock bank is a bank with more than one shareholder. Allahabad, established in the year 1865, is the oldest Joint Stock Bank. The first type of joint-stock banks was the Bank of Bombay, established in Bombay in 1720.

Hence, the correct option is (D).

46. Bacteria is a unicellular organism.

Unicellular organisms are made up of single cells. They may be eukaryotic or prokaryotic. They can survive in any environment. They are so small cannot be seen with the naked eye. They reproduce asexually. Some unicellular organisms are bacteria, protists, and yeast.

Hence, the correct option is (D).

47. The classical singer, Girija Devi was proficient in the Thumri form of Hindustani classical music.

Girija Devi is a classical singer and represents Banaras Gharana. She was born on 8 May 1929, in Varanasi, Uttar Pradesh. She is also called Queen of Thumri. She has won Padma Shree (1972), Padma Bhushan (1989), and Padma Vibhushan (2016) for her contribution to classical music.

Hence, the correct option is (C).

48. Bihar states of India had the highest density of population as per the 2011 census.

Population density is the number of people per square km in a geographical area. Bihar has a population density of 1,106 persons per square kilometer as per the census 2011.

Hence, the correct option is (B).

49. Mithali Raj is the first Indian woman cricketer to play 200 One Day International (ODI) matches.

Mithali Raj was born on 3 December 1982, in Jodhpur district, Rajasthan. She is also the 1st and only woman cricketer to participate in the 6 world cup. She is the all-time leading run-scorer for India in Test, ODI, and T20. As of August 2022. She has received many awards for her contribution and performance in cricket. Wisden Leading Woman Cricketer in the World in 2017, Arjuna Award in 2003, the Padma Shri in 2015, and Major Dhyan Chand Khel Ratna in 2021. She has taken retirement from all forms of cricket in June 2022.

Hence, the correct option is (B).

50. Brahmaputra river flows through Tibet, India and Bangladesh.

Brahmaputra river originates in the Chemayungdung glacier of the Kailash range near Mansarovar lake. In Tibet it is known as Tsangpo while entering India in Arunachal Pradesh it is called the Dihang river, it came to know as Bramhaputra in Assam and in Bangladesh its name is Jamuna. It is well known for floods, channel shifting and bank erosion. While flowing from the slope of Namcha Barwa mountains in Arunachal Pradesh it has the highest Hydroelectric Potential. Majuli the largest riverine island in the world is created by it. Its major tributaries are Dibang, Lohit, Subansiri, Kameng and Manas.

Hence, the correct option is (A).

51. As we know,

$$\text{Profit } \% = \left(\frac{P}{CP}\right) \times 100$$

Where,

CP = Cost price

P = Profit

Let the Marked Price set by the Wholesaler be 100.

$$\text{Cost price } (CP) \text{ for Varun} = \frac{100-20}{100} \times 100 \quad (\because 20\% \text{ discount })$$

$$= 80$$

$$\text{Marked Price } (MP) \text{ set by Varun} = \frac{100+20}{100} \times 100$$

$$= 120 \quad (\because 20\% \text{ higher than the original marked price })$$

$$\text{Selling Price } (SP) \text{ of Varun} = \frac{100-10}{100} \times 120$$

$$= 108 \quad (\because 10\% \text{ discount })$$

$$\text{Profit } \% \text{ of Varun} = \frac{(108-80)}{80} \times 100$$

$$= 35\%$$

Hence, the correct option is (D).

52. Given:

$$85 \div 17 \text{ of } 4 - [65 \div 13 \text{ of } 2 - 14 \times (19 - 25) \div 12 - 10] \text{ of } \frac{2}{3}.$$

$$= 85 \div 68 - [65 \div 26 - 14 \times (-6) \div 12 - 10] \text{ of } \frac{2}{3}$$

$$= \frac{85}{68} - [\frac{65}{26} - 14 \times \frac{(-6)}{12} - 10] \text{of } \frac{2}{3}$$

$$= \frac{5}{4} - [\frac{5}{2} + 7 - 10] \text{ of } \frac{2}{3}$$

$$= \frac{5}{4} - [\frac{5}{2} - 3] \text{ of } \frac{2}{3}$$

$$= \frac{5}{4} + \frac{1}{2} \text{ of } \frac{2}{3}$$

$$= \frac{5}{4} + \frac{1}{3}$$

$$= \frac{19}{12}$$

Hence, the correct option is (D).

53. Given,

One-fifth of three-eighths of two-thirds of a number $= 20$

Let the required number be X.

Then according to question,

$$\frac{1}{5} \times \frac{3}{8} \times \frac{2}{3} \times X = 20$$

$$\Rightarrow \frac{X}{20} = 20$$

$$\Rightarrow X = 400$$

Now,

$$60\% \text{ of } X = \frac{60}{100} \times 400$$

$$= 240$$

Hence, the correct option is (D).

54. Given,

The ratio of the number of girls and boys $= 2:7$

Let number of Girls be $2X$.

And number of Boys be $7X$.

Increased number of Girls $= 2X \times \frac{115}{100}$ (15% increase)

$= 2X \times \frac{23}{20}$

$= \frac{23X}{10}$

Increased number of Boys $= 7X \times \frac{120}{100}$ (20% increase)

$= 7X \times \frac{6}{5}$

$= \frac{42X}{5}$

New ratio will be,

Girls : Boys $= \frac{23X}{10} : \frac{42X}{5}$

$= 23:84$

Hence, the correct option is (A).

55. Given:

Discount $= 10\%$

Profit $= 8\%$

As we know,

Markup $\% = \frac{(MP-CP)}{CP} \times 100$

Let Mark Price (MP) be 100.

According to Question,

Selling price $(SP) = \frac{90}{100} \times 100$

$= 0.9 \times 100$

$= 90$

Cost price $\times \frac{108}{100} = 90$

$= \frac{90 \times 100}{108}$

$\Rightarrow$ Cost price $(CP) = \frac{250}{3}$

Markup $\% = \frac{100 - \frac{250}{3}}{\frac{250}{3}} \times 100$

Markup $\% = 20\%$

Hence, the correct option is (D).

56. Given,

Time taken by Rohit to complete work alone $= 32$ days

Time taken by Raj to complete work alone $= 48$ days

As we know,

Efficiency $= \frac{\text{Total work done}}{\text{Total time taken}}$

Let the Total work be the LCM of 32 and $48 = 96$

Now, Efficiency of Rohit $= \frac{96}{32}$

$= 3$

Efficiency of Raj $= \frac{96}{48}$

$= 2$

Rohit left the work 8 days before the work got over, which means that Raj worked alone during the last 8 days before the completion of the work.

Work done by Raj during the last 8 days $= 8 \times 2$

$= 16$

Remaining work $= 96 - 16$

$= 80$

This remaining work was done by Raj and Rohit together,

Time taken by Rohit and Raj to complete this work together $= \frac{80}{(3+2)}$

$= 16$

Hence, the correct option is (D).

57. Given:

Average monthly income of A and $B = ₹ \ 4500$

Average monthly income of B and $C = ₹ \ 5600$

Average monthly income of A and $C = ₹ \ 4800$

As we know,

Average of N terms $= \frac{\text{Sum of N terms}}{\text{Total number of terms}}$

$\Rightarrow$ Total monthly income of A and $B = 2 \times 4500$

$= 9000$

$\Rightarrow$ Total monthly income of B and $C = 2 \times 5600$

$= 11200$

$\Rightarrow$ Total monthly income of C and $A = 2 \times 4800$

$= 9600 \quad ...(1)$

$\Rightarrow$ Total monthly income of A, B and C

$= (A + B) + (B + C) + (C + A) = 9000 + 11200 + 9600$

$A + B + C = \frac{29800}{2}$

$A + B + C = 14900 \quad \dots (2)$

$\Rightarrow$ Subtracting (1) from equation (2)

$\Rightarrow B = 14900 - 9600$

$= 5300$

Hence, the correct option is (D).

58. Given,

Savings $= 12\%$

As we know,

Income $=$ Savings $+$ Expenditure

Let the income be 100.

Savings $= \frac{112}{100} \times 100 - 100$

$= 12 \quad (\because 12\% \text{ of income })$

Expenditure $= 100 - 12$

$= 88$

Increased Income $= \frac{125}{100} \times 100$

$= 125 \quad (\because 25\% \text{ increase })$

Still he saves the same amount i.e. 12

New Expenditure $= 125 - 12$

$= 113$

Percentage hike in expenditure $= \frac{(\text{New expenditure - Initial expenditure})}{\text{Initial Expenditure}}$

$\Rightarrow$ Percentage hike in expenditure $= \frac{(113-88)}{88} \times 100$

$\Rightarrow \frac{25}{88} \times 100$

$= 28.4\%$

Hence, the correct option is (B).

59. Given:

Total Profit $= ₹ \, 2600$

The ratio of investment of A and $B = 3:4$

A invested for 10 months

B invested for 12 months

As we know,

Profit of Investment $=$ Investment Amount $\times$ Time of Investment

Let the investment of A is $3X$.

And the investment of B is $4X$.

Profit of $A = 10 \times 3X$

Profit of $B = 12 \times 4X$

Total Profit $= 30X + 48X$

$= 78X$

Now, according to question,

$78X = 2600$

$\Rightarrow X = \frac{2600}{78}$

Profit of $A = 10 \times 3 \times \frac{2600}{78}$

$= 1000$

Hence, the correct option is (B).

60. Given:

The two successive discounts are 25% and 10%.

Let the Mark Price be 100.

Selling Price after two discounts $= 100 \times \frac{100-25}{100} \times \frac{100-10}{100}$

$= 100 \times \frac{75}{100} \times \frac{90}{100}$

$= \frac{9 \times 75}{10}$

$= 67.5$

Equivalent Single Discount $= 100 - 67.5$

$= 32.5$

Hence, the correct option is (C).

61. Given:

Ratio of radii of cones C and D is $2:3$.

Ratio of Heights of cones C and D is $3:2$.

As we know,

Volume of cone $= \frac{1}{3} \times \pi \times r^2 \times h$

$\Rightarrow$ Volume $\propto r^2 \times h$

where, $r =$ radius of cone

$h =$ height of cone

Let radius of cone $C = 2x$, Height of cone C $= 3y$

$\Rightarrow$ Volume of cone $C \propto (2x)^2 \times (3x)$

Radius of cone $D = 3x$, height of cone $D = 2y$

$\Rightarrow$ Volume of cone $D \propto (3x)^2 \times (2x)$

$\Rightarrow$ Volume of cone D : Volume of cone $C =$
$18x^2 y : 12x^2 y$

$= 3:2$

Hence, the correct option is (D).

62. Given,

$$\frac{\frac{2}{5} \text{ of } 7\frac{1}{2} \div \frac{3}{4} - \frac{3}{4} \times 1\frac{1}{2} \div 2\frac{1}{4}}{5\frac{1}{2} \div 3\frac{2}{3} \text{ of } \frac{3}{8}}$$

$$= \frac{\frac{2}{5} \text{ of } \frac{15}{2} \div \frac{3}{4} - \frac{3}{4} \times \frac{3}{2} \div \frac{9}{4}}{\frac{11}{2} \div \frac{11}{3} \text{ of } \frac{3}{8}}$$

$$= \frac{3 \div \frac{3}{4} - \frac{3}{4} \times \frac{3}{2} \div \frac{9}{4}}{\frac{11}{2} \div \frac{11}{8}}$$

$$= \frac{4 - \frac{3}{4} \times \frac{2}{3}}{4}$$

$$= \frac{4 - \frac{1}{2}}{4}$$

$$= \frac{8-1}{2 \times 4}$$

$$= \frac{7}{2 \times 4}$$

$$= \frac{7}{8}$$

Hence, the correct option is (C).

63. Given:

The price of sugar is increased by 10%.

As we know,

Expenditure $=$ Price $\times$ Quantity

Percentage reduction in a Quantity $=$
$$\frac{\text{(Old quantity - New quantity)}}{\text{Old quantity}} \times 100$$

If Price is increased in ratio $a : b$

Then, to keep the expenditure same

The quantity should be reduced in the ratio $b : a$

Here, price is increaseby 10%.

Ratio of price change $= 10 : 11$

$\Rightarrow$ Ratio of quantity $= 11 : 10$

Reduction in quantity $= \dfrac{(11-10)}{11}$

$$= \frac{1}{11}$$

Percentage reduction in consumption $= \dfrac{1}{11} \times 100$

$$= 9\frac{1}{11}\%$$

Hence, the correct option is (B).

64. Given:

A sum amounts to 7 times itself in 3 years.

As we know,

Amount $=$ Principal $\times \left(1 + \dfrac{\text{Rate}}{100}\right)^t$

Where $t =$ number of years

Let P be the sum of money and $R =$ rate $\%$

Amount after 3 years,

$$7P = P\left(1 + \frac{R}{100}\right)^3$$

$$\Rightarrow 7 = \left(1 + \frac{R}{100}\right)^3 \quad \cdots (1)$$

Let after 't' years amount becomes 2401 times of sum

$$2401 \times P = P\left(1 + \frac{R}{100}\right)^t$$

$$\Rightarrow 2401 = \left(1 + \frac{R}{100}\right)^t$$

$$\Rightarrow 7^4 = \left(1 + \frac{R}{100}\right)^t \quad \cdots (2)$$

On comparing (1) and (2) we get,

$$\left(1 + \frac{R}{100}\right)^{12} = \left(1 + \frac{R}{100}\right)^t$$

$$\Rightarrow t = 12$$

$\therefore$ After 12 years the principal will become 2401 times of itself.

Hence, the correct option is (B).

65. Given:

Diameter of hemisphere $= 9$ cm

Radius $= \dfrac{9}{2}$ cm

As we know,

Volume of hemisphere $= \dfrac{2}{3} \times \pi \times r^3$

Where $r =$ radius of hemisphere

Volume $(V) = \dfrac{2}{3} \times \pi \times \left(\dfrac{9}{2}\right)^3$

$$= \frac{2}{3} \times \frac{22}{7} \times \left(\frac{9}{2}\right)^3$$

$$= 190.92 \text{ cm}^3$$

$$= 0.191 \text{ litres } (\because 1 \text{ litre} = 1000 \text{ cm}^3)$$

Hence, the correct option is (A).

66. Given:

Investment amount $= ₹ 9000$

Time $= 3$ years

Rate of compound interest $= 2\%$

As we know,

Compound rate of interest for 3 years if Rate $\%$ is same for each year $= 3R + \frac{3R^2}{100} + \frac{R^3}{10000}$

Where $R =$ Rate $\%$ for each year

Amount $=$ Principal $\left(1 + \frac{\text{Rate}}{100}\right)^n$

Where $n =$ time period

Compound rate of interest for 3 years $= (3 \times 2) + \frac{\left(3 \times 2^2\right)}{100} + \frac{2^3}{10000}$

$$\Rightarrow 6 + 0.12 + 0.0008$$

$$\Rightarrow 6.1208$$

$\therefore$ Compound rate of interest for 3 years $= 6.1208$

Amount $= 9000 \times \left(1 + \frac{6.1208}{100}\right)$

$$= 9000 \times \frac{106.1208}{100}$$

$$= 9550.87$$

Hence, the correct option is (D).

67. Given:

The selling price of 90 pens $= ₹ 1557$

Loss $\% = 30\%$

Selling price (SP) of 90 pens $= 1557$

Loss $\% = 30\%$

$\therefore$ Cost Price (CP) of 90 pens $= \frac{(1557 \times 100)}{(100 - 30)}$

$$\Rightarrow CP \text{ of } 90 \text{ pens} = \frac{15570}{7}$$

$$\Rightarrow CP \text{ of } 1 \text{ pen} = \frac{15570}{(7 \times 90)}$$

$$\Rightarrow CP \text{ of } 90 \text{ pen} = ₹ \frac{173}{7}$$

Let P pens be sold to earn a profit of 18%

CP of P pens $= \frac{173P}{7}$

SP of P pens $= ₹ 708$

$$\Rightarrow \text{Profit } \% \text{ of } P \text{ pens} = \frac{(\text{SP of P pens - CP of P pens})}{(\text{CP of P pens})} \times 100$$

$$\Rightarrow 18 = \frac{\left(708 - \frac{173P}{7}\right)}{\left(\frac{173P}{7}\right)} \times 100$$

$$\Rightarrow 18 = \left(\frac{708 \times 7}{173P - 1}\right) \times 100$$

$$\Rightarrow 118 = \frac{708 \times 7 \times 100}{173P}$$

$$\Rightarrow P = \frac{(708 \times 7 \times 100)}{(173 \times 118)}$$

$$\Rightarrow P = 24.27$$

$\because$ The number of Pens cannot be in decimal, we take the value of P as the nearest integer i.e. $P = 24$

Hence, the correct option is (C).

68. Given numbers are $15, 24$ and 36.

As we know,

The Least common multiple (LCM) of two or more numbers is the least number which is exactly divisible by each of those numbers.

The least number which is divisible by each of $15, 24$ and 36 will be the LCM of $15, 24$ and 36.

$$15 = 3 \times 5$$

$$24 = 3 \times 2 \times 2 \times 2$$

$$36 = 2 \times 2 \times 3 \times 3$$

LCM of $15, 24$ and $36 = 2 \times 2 \times 2 \times 3 \times 3 \times 5$

$$= 360$$

Clearly, we can see that to make 360 a perfect square number we have to multiply it by 2 and 5, then we get

$$\Rightarrow 360 \times 2 \times 5 = 3600$$

$\therefore$ The smallest number is 3600 which is a perfect square and is divisible by each of $15, 24$ and 36.

Hence, the correct option is (A).

69. Given,

Pipes A and B can fill a tank in 18 hours and 27 hours, respectively.

As we know,

$$\text{Efficiency} = \frac{Total\ work\ done}{Total\ time\ taken}$$

Let the total volume of the tank be the LCM of 18 and 27 i.e., 54 unit.

The efficiency of $A = \frac{54}{18} = 3$

Efficiency of $B = \frac{54}{27} = 2$

Tank filled by both pipes together in 2 days (A starts the work) $= 3 + 2 = 5$ unit

Tank filled by both pipes together in 20 days $= 50$ unit

Now, on the 21st day, A will fill 3 units of tank

Total tank filled till now $= 53$ unit

On the 22nd day, B will work and will fill 2 units of the tank, but we need only 1 unit of more work.

Therefore B will work only half a day.

Total number of days taken $= 21\frac{1}{2}$ days

$\therefore$ The total number of days taken by A and B together to fill the tank completely is $21\frac{1}{2}$ days.

Hence, the correct option is (D).

70. Given,

Compound interest for two years $= ₹\ 85$

Simple interest for two years $= ₹\ 80$

As we know,

Simple interest $(SI) = \frac{(P \times R \times T)}{100}$

Where $P =$ Principal amount, $R =$ Rate, $T =$ Time

Simple interest (SI) is the rate percent of the principal amount

In compound interest, the principal modifies every year. The interest of the previous year becomes the principal for the following year.

For example,

Let $(SI)(\text{for } 1 \text{ year }) ₹\ X$, Rate $\% = R$

Then, $CI(\text{for } 2 \text{ years }) = X + X + R\%$ of X

Or, $CI\ (\text{for 2 years }) = S \text{ for } 2 \text{ years } + R\% \times SI \text{ for } 1$ year

$SI \text{ for } 1 \text{ year} = \frac{80}{2}$

$= ₹\ 40$

$CI(\text{for } 2 \text{ years }) = SI \text{ for } 2 \text{ years } + R\% \times SI \text{ for } 1 \text{ year}$

$85 = 80 + R\% \times 40$

$\Rightarrow R\% \times 40 = 5$

$\Rightarrow R \times \frac{40}{100} = 5$

$\Rightarrow R = \frac{25}{2}$

$\Rightarrow R = 12.5\%$

Hence, the correct option is (C).

71. Given,

The average weight of 6 persons is increased by 1.5 kg.

The person with a weight of 45 kg is replaced by a new person.

As we know,

$$\text{Average of } N \text{ terms} = \frac{\text{Sum of N terms}}{\text{Total number of terms}}$$

Let the average of the 6 persons be ' A '

And the weight of the new person be ' x kg'

Now, equating the sum of weights before and after leaving the person,

$\Rightarrow 6 \times A - 45 + x = 6 \times (A + 1.5)$

$\Rightarrow x = 45 + 9$

$\Rightarrow x = 54$ kg

Hence, the correct option is (A).

72. Given,

$0.35 : x : : 5 : 6$

The given proportion can also be written as,

$\frac{0.35}{x} : \frac{5}{6}$

On cross multiplying, we get

$\Rightarrow x = \frac{(6 \times 0.35)}{5}$

$\Rightarrow x = 0.42$

Hence, the correct option is (B).

73. As we know,

Distance $=$ Speed $\times$ Time

According to the question,

For 3 hours, Speed $= 60$ km/hr

Distance covered in two hours $= 60 \times 3$

$= 180$ km

For next 3 hours, Speed $= 60$ km/hr $+20$ km/hr

$= 80$ km/hr

Distance covered in next 3 hours $= 80 \times 3$

$= 240$ km

Distance covered in 6 hours $= 180$ km $+240$ km

$= 240$ km

Remaining Distance $= 470 - 420$

$= 50$ km

Now, speed $= 80 + 20$

$= 100$ km/hr

Now, Time $= \dfrac{50}{100}$

$= \dfrac{1}{2}$ hr

Total Time $= 3$ hr $+3$ hr $+\dfrac{1}{2}$ hr

$= 6\dfrac{1}{2}$ hr

Hence, the correct option is (D).

74. Given,

$$\dfrac{(9987693 \times 6432 \times 7695)}{10}$$

As we know,

If a Product is divided by ' 10 ' then the unit digit of the product will be the remainder. Similarly, if it is divided by ' 100 ', then the last two digits will be the remainder.

Unit digit of the given product will be,

Unit digit $= 3 \times 2 \times 5 = 0$

Hence, the correct option is (B).

75. Given,

Total time $= 6\dfrac{4}{5} = \dfrac{34}{5}$ hrs

As we know,

Time $= \dfrac{Distance}{Speed}$

Let the distance between the two points be ' $3X$ '.

The person travels $2X$ distance with a speed of 70 km/hr

He travels the remaining X distance with a speed of 50 km/hr

Using the formula, for the whole journey,

$$\dfrac{34}{5} = \dfrac{2X}{70} + \dfrac{X}{50}$$

$\Rightarrow \dfrac{34}{5} = \dfrac{17X}{350}$

$\Rightarrow X = 2 \times 70$

$= 140$ km

$\therefore$ Distance $(3X) = 140 \times 3$

$= 420$ km

Time taken to travel this distance with a speed of 56 km/hr,

Time $= \dfrac{420}{56} = \dfrac{15}{2}$

Or Time $= 7\dfrac{1}{2}$ hrs

Hence, the correct option is (C).

76. The meaning of the given idiom is "to get out of control".

We use the given idiom to refer to a situation where a scenario becomes difficult to manage.

Example: We knew things were about to get out of hand when we saw the armed robbers shoot the security guard at the bank.

Hence, the correct option is (A).

77. The given sentence is an example of past continuous passive tense.
The structure of past continuous passive tense is "was or were" + being + past participle.
We use "were" in the sentence as the subject of the sentence i.e., visitors are plural.
We also need to use the past participle form of the main verb 'show' that is "shown".

The correct sentence is: The visitors were being shown a collection of old manuscripts.

Hence, the correct option is (D).

78. The usage of the preposition is incorrect in the given sentence.
We need to use the preposition "from".
We use the preposition "from" to give a reason for something.
Example: Rohit was on sick leave last week as he was recovering from Covid-19.
In the given sentence we are being told the reason for his huge profit so we need to use the preposition "from".

The correct sentence is: Mohit is expecting a huge profit from his recent investment.

Hence, the correct option is (A).

79. Let's look at the meaning of the given words.

- Management: the process of dealing with or controlling things or people.

- Power: the ability or capacity to do something or act in a particular way.

- Charge: entrust (someone) with a task as a responsibility.

- Duty: a task or action that one is required to perform as part of one's job.

As per the meaning of the given words, "charge" is the appropriate word choice for the blank. In the given sentence, the implied meaning is that in the absence of his mother, he took the responsibility of caring for his brother. So, the charge is the correct word choice.

The correct sentence is: When his mother was away, he took the charge of his little brother.

Hence, the correct option is (C).

80. Let's look at the meaning of given words.

- Varied: incorporating a number of different types of elements; showing variation or variety.

- Monotonous: dull, tedious, and repetitious; lacking in variety and interest.

- Exciting: causing great enthusiasm and eagerness.

- Interesting: arousing curiosity or interest; holding or catching the attention.

As per the meaning of the given words, "monotonous" is the appropriate word choice. In the given sentence, the implied meaning is that mere classroom teaching becomes boring and tedious for the students. So, monotonous is the correct word choice for the blank.

The complete sentence is: Mere classroom teaching-learning is boring and monotonous for students.

Hence, the correct option is (B).

81. Care is the most appropriate synonym of the Maintain word.

Maintain: Cause or enable (a condition or situation) to continue.

Example: She was finding it hard to maintain her balance.

Care: The provision of what is necessary for the health, welfare, maintenance, and protection of someone or something.

Example: She cares about the dogs in her neighborhood as she is an animal lover.

Hence, the correct option is (A).

82. Harmful is the most appropriate antonym of the given word Beneficial.

Beneficial: Resulting in good; favourable or advantageous.

Example: Regular exercise has many beneficial health effects.

Harmful: Causing or likely to cause harm.

Example: Watching TV for long hours without maintaining an adequate distance from the screen is harmful to our eyes.

Hence, the correct option is (D).

83. Let's look at the meaning of the given words.

Hoot: a low, wavering musical sound that is the typical call of many kinds of owls.

Caw: the harsh cry of a rook, crow, or similar bird.

Cluck: (of a hen) make a short, low sound.

Moo: make the characteristic deep resonant vocal sound of cattle.

As per the meaning of the given words, "hoot" is the one-word substitute for the given group of words.

Hence, the correct option is (A).

84. He raised an important question in the meeting.

Raised: To elevate something to a higher level/position.

In the given sentence the phrase "raised a question" means to start talking about a subject that you want other people to consider.

Hence, the correct option is (D).

85. Let's look at the correct spelling and meaning of the word.

Abandon: Cease to support or look after (someone); desert.

Example: She was abandoned by her mother in childhood due to poverty and drug abuse.

All the other words are spelled correctly.

Hence, the correct option is (D).

86. Let's look at the meaning of given words.

Vulnerable: exposed to the possibility of being attacked or harmed, either physically or emotionally.

Available: able to be used or obtained; at someone's disposal.

Accessible: (of a place) able to be reached or entered.

Flexible: able to be easily modified to respond to altered circumstances.

As per the meaning of the given words, "vulnerable" is the one-word substitute for the given group of words.

Example: After his chemotherapy, his body became vulnerable to all sorts of ailments.

Hence, the correct option is (A).

87. In the given sentence, the usage of the possessive pronoun "yours" is wrong. We need to use the possessive adjective "your" in the given sentence.

The main difference between the two is that "your" always has an object whereas yours is usually the object in a sentence.

Example: May I borrow your car? (possessive adjective).

We have told you everything about the pros and cons of marriage but the decision is yours. (possessive pronoun)

The correct sentence is: May I please borrow your book?

Hence, the correct option is (B).

88. The given sentence is grammatically correct so we don't need to change anything.

The given sentence is in the past continuous tense with the auxiliary verb 'to be' in the past tense form "was" with both the verbs in present participle forms.

The usage of both to refer to the two verbs is also correct.

Hence, the correct option is (A).

89. Let's look at the meaning of the given words.
Pretense: an attempt to make something that is not the case appear true.Example: Ranjith said, "You know there is no pretense with me when it comes to financial matters"

All the other words are spelled correctly.

Hence, the correct option is (A).

90. Collect the most appropriate synonym of the given word compose.

Compose: Form (a whole) by ordering or arranging the parts, especially in an artistic way.

Example: Ten rooms and three baths compose the house.

Collect: Bring or gather together (a number of things).

Example: I want to collect some historical records of the Siraiki community for my research work.

Hence, the correct option is (C).

91. To think carefully is the most appropriate meaning of the given idiom to take stock of.

The meaning of the given idiom is "make an overall assessment of a particular situation, typically before making a decision."

We use the given idiom to refer to a situation where one is taking into account all the pros and cons of the situation at hand.

Example: The cops were quick to take stock of the situation at the neighbor's house in the aftermath of a burglary.

Hence, the correct option is (B).

92. Let's look at the meaning of the given words.

- Batch: a quantity or consignment of goods produced at one time.
- Group: a number of people or things that are located, gathered, or classed together.
- Pile: a heap of things laid or lying one on top of another.
- Load: a heavy or bulky thing that is being carried or is about to be carried.

As per the meaning of the given words, "pile" is the one-word substitute for the given group of words.

Example: Her mother shouted at her after finding the pile of smelly clothes lying on the floor.

Hence, the correct option is (C).

93. The given sentence is in the past continuous tense. The action that started in the past was happening for some time.

So we need the present participle of "be" which is "being" in the given sentence.

We also need to use the past participle form of the verb." drive" which is "driven".

The correct sentence is: The children were being driven to the picnic spot in the school bus.

Hence, the correct option is (B).

94. In the given sentence the usage of the auxiliary verb "had" after the modal verb would is incorrect.
We commonly use the "would have" as it is the conditional perfect.
We use the modal auxiliary would have to refer to a situation to express a missed opportunity in the past.

The correct sentence is: Aphrodite vowed that Paris would have the most beautiful woman as his wife.

Hence, the correct option is (B).

95. 'Thin' is the most appropriate antonym of the given word 'Stout'.

Stout: (of a person) rather fat or of heavy build.

Example: She is getting too stout for her dresses.

Thin: Having little, or too little, flesh or fat on the body.

Example: Abhishek used to be such a thin and lanky fellow in his teenage years.

Hence, the correct option is (C).

96. Let's look at the meaning of the given words:

Impressive: evoking admiration through size, quality, or skill; grand, imposing, or awesome.

Exciting: causing great enthusiasm and eagerness.

Emotional: arousing or characterized by intense feeling.

Expressive: effectively conveying thought or feeling.

As per the meaning of the given words, "emotional" is the appropriate word choice for the blank.

In the given sentence, the implied meaning of the given sentence is that the crowd was feeling intense emotion at the demise of the footballing legend. So, "emotional" is the correct word choice.

Hence, the correct option is (C).

97. Let's look at the meaning of the given words.

Around: approximately. it is an adverb.

More or less: mostly or nearly.

Roughly: in a violent or angry way.

Just: now, very soon, or very recently.

As per the meaning of the given words, "around" is the appropriate word choice for the blank.

In the given sentence, the speaker is trying to give an approximate estimate of the number of relatives. So "around" is the correct word choice.

Hence, the correct option is (A).

98. The given sentence is in the past tense as it is describing an event that has already taken place.

We need to use the past tense form of the verb in the given sentence.

The past tense form of the verb "attend" is attended".

Hence, the correct option is (B).

99. In the given sentence, we need to use the comparative adjective of the adjective "early".

We need to use the comparative adjective as the speaker is comparing the size of the crowd before and during the final ceremony.

The comparative adjective form of early is "earlier".

Hence, the correct option is (C).

100. In the given sentence, we need to use the possessive pronoun "their".

We use the possessive pronoun "their" to show a thing that belongs to someone or an action or deed they have done.

In the given sentence, "their" highlights the actions of the people i.e., paying respects in this context.

Hence, the correct option is (A).

General Intelligence and Reasoning

Q.1 Four letter-clusters have been given, out of which three are alike in some manner andone is different. Select the letter-cluster that is different.

A. NPLR **B.** YAWD **C.** SUQW **D.** PRNT

Q.2 Presently Suman is four times as old as her son. Five years ago, she was seven timesas old as her son. What is the age of her son?

A. 11 years **B.** 10 years **C.** 16 years **D.** 12 years

Q.3 Direction: Select the set of classes the relationship among which is best illustrated by the given Venn diagram.

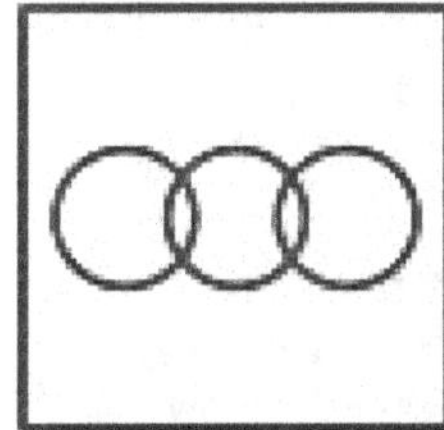

A. Mercury, Planets, Venus
B. Businessmen, Scientists, Singers
C. Spinach, Vegetables, Peach
D. Women, Swimmers, Men

Q.4 A cube is made by folding the given sheet. In the cube so formed, select the number that will be on the face opposite the face showing the number '4'.

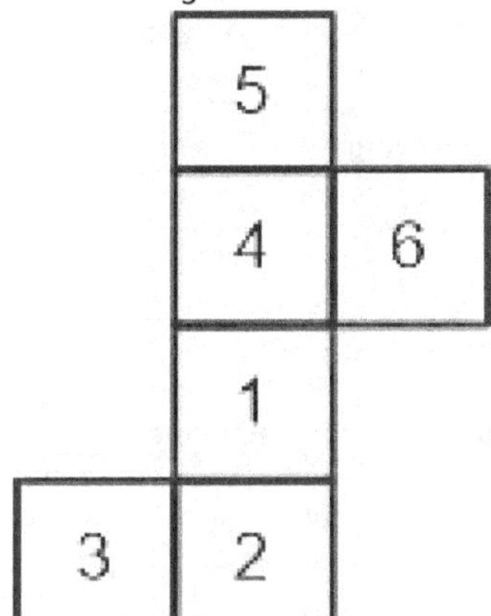

A. 2 **B.** 3 **C.** 6 **D.** 5

Q.5 Direction: Select the figure that will replace the question mark (?) in the following figure series.

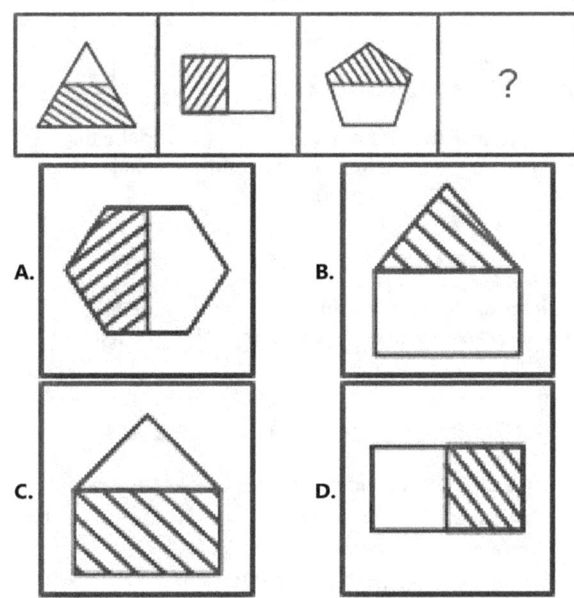

Q.6 Direction: Select the correct option that indicates the arrangement of the given words in theorder in which they appear in an English dictionary.

1. Nervous, 2. Nobility, 3. Nebulizer, 4. Nominate, 5. Nitrogen

A. 3, 4, 2, 5, 1 **B.** 3, 1, 5, 2, 4
C. 3, 5, 1, 2, 4 **D.** 3, 1, 2, 5, 4

Q.7 The sequence of folding a piece of paper and the manner in which the folded paper has been cut is shown in the following figures. How would this paper look when unfolded?

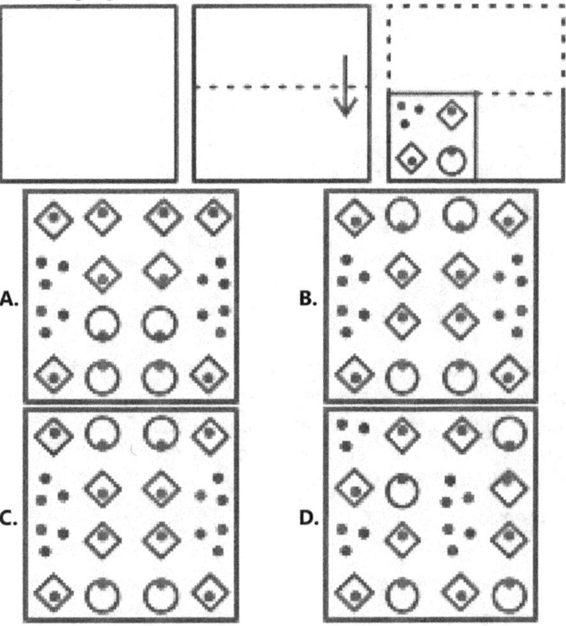

Q.8 In a certain code language, 'FALSE' is coded as '2141588'.How will 'CHOICE' be codedin that language?

A. 24191812248   **B.** 6181921288
C. 24181924128   **D.** 6191812822

Q.9 Direction: Select the number from among the given options that can replace the question mark(?) in the following series.

1, 8, 81, ?, 15625

A. 1015   **B.** 1225   **C.** 1227   **D.** 1024

Q.10 Direction: Select the option that is related to the third letter-cluster in the same way as thesecond letter-cluster is related to the first letter-cluster.

CNK : JUR :: FJL : ?

A. NPR   **B.** MQS   **C.** OSU   **D.** KOQ

Q.11 Direction: Select the number from among the given options that can replace the question mark(?) in the following series.

2, 10, 30, ?, 130

A. 68   **B.** 65   **C.** 70   **D.** 75

Q.12 If 'A' denotes 'addition', 'B' denotes 'multiplication', 'C' denotes 'subtraction', and 'D' denotes 'division', then what will be the value of the following expression?

$$483 D 23 A 93 C 16 B 4 C (15 B 2)$$

A. 30   **B.** 78   **C.** 20   **D.** 55

Q.13 Direction: Select the correct mirror image of the given combination when the mirror is placed at PQ as shown.

Q.14 Direction: Read the given statements and conclusions carefully. Assuming that the informationgiven in the statements is true, even if it appears to be at variance with commonlyknown facts, decide which of the given conclusions logically follow(s) from thestatements.

Statements:

All pens are pencils.

Some markers are pencils.

Conclusions:

I. All pens are markers.

II. Some pens are markers.

A. Only conclusion II follows
B. None of the conclusions follow
C. Only conclusion I follows
D. Both the conclusions follow

Q.15 Direction: Select the option in which the given figure is embedded (rotation is NOT allowed).

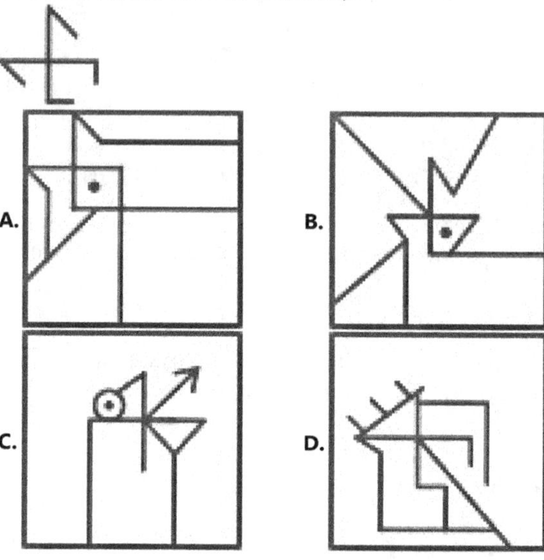

Q.16 In a certain code language, 'LUCKNOW' is written as 'CULKWON' and 'UDAIPUR' iswritten as 'ADUIRUP'. How will 'GWALIOR' be written in that language?

A. WGLAROI   **B.** AGWLRIO
C. AWGROIL   **D.** AWGLROI

Q.17 Direction: Select the letter-cluster from among the given options that can replace the questionmark (?) in the following series.

EIM, QUY, CGK, ?

A. DHL   **B.** LPT   **C.** SWA   **D.** OSW

Q.18 Direction: Study the given pattern carefully and select the number that can replace the question mark (?) in it.

34	18	43
47	?	28
71	33	61

A. 42   **B.** 25   **C.** 35   **D.** 19

Q.19 Direction: Select the option that is related to the third number in the same way as the secondnumber is related to the first number and the sixth number is related to the fifthnumber.

$$11 : 77 :: 12 : ? :: 14 : 119$$

A. 90   **B.** 97   **C.** 83   **D.** 79

Q.20 Nisha, who is Dileep's daughter, says to Deveshi, "Your mother Ritu is the youngersister of my father, who is the second child of Krishna". How is Krishna related toDeveshi?

A. Paternal grandfather
B. Father-in-law
C. Father

D. Maternal grandfather

Q.21 Seven doctors, S, T, U, V, X, Y and Z, are sitting around a round table, facing towardsthe centre, for a case study. Y is sitting third to the right of Z and between S and X. Z issitting second to the right of U. V is sitting third to the left of X. Two doctors are sittingbetween Y and V. Based on the given information, which of the following statements iscorrect?

A. Z is sitting between T and X.
B. S is sitting fourth to the left of T.
C. U is sitting to the immediate right of V.
D. Four doctors are sitting between Y and Z.

Q.22 Direction: Study the given pattern carefully and select the letter that can replace the question mark (?) in it.

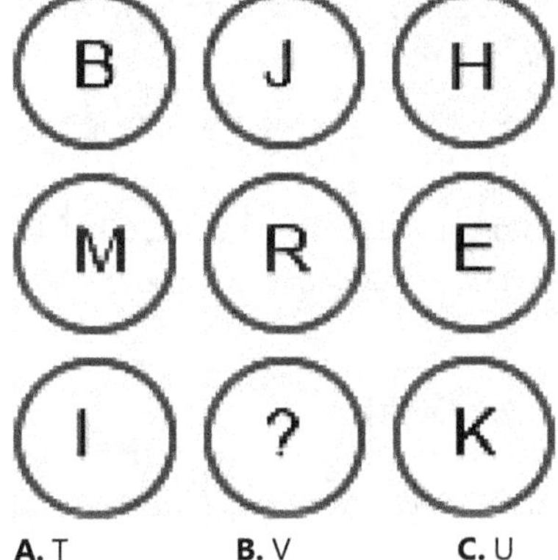

A. T   **B.** V   **C.** U   **D.** S

Q.23 M, N, L, O, Q and H are sitting in a row. Q and H are in the centre. M and N are at theends. L is sitting to the left of N. Who is to the right of M?

A. N   **B.** O   **C.** L   **D.** Q

Q.24 In a certain code language,'nuk me xil' means 'lit this light', 'ki me to' means 'thebright light', and 'nuk ki yun' means' this is bright'. What will be the code for 'lit' in thatlanguage?

A. nuk   **B.** yun   **C.** xil   **D.** me

Q.25 Cataract is related to 'Eye' in the same way as Meniere's disease is related to'_______'.

A. Nose   **B.** Mouth   **C.** Teeth   **D.** Ear

General Knowledge and General Awareness

Q.26 The difference between the total revenue and total expenditure of the government is called ______.
A. fiscal deficit   **B.** budgetary deficit
C. deflation   **D.** primary deficit

Q.27 Who among the following is NOT a hockey player?
A. Ajit Singh   **B.** Manu Bhaker
C. Deepika Thakur   **D.** Akashdeep Singh

Q.28 In which macaronic language was a fourteenth-century text, the Lilatilakam, written?
A. Rekhta   **B.** Brahmi
C. Manipravalam   **D.** Mozakhraf

Q.29 According to the Public Affairs Index 2020, which among the following has been adjudged the best governed state in the country in the large states category?
A. Kerala   **B.** Uttar Pradesh
C. Odisha   **D.** Rajasthan

Q.30 Which of the following books is NOT authored by Shashi Tharoor?
A. The Hindu Way: An Introduction to Hinduism (2019)
B. An Era of Darkness: The British Empire in India (2016)
C. Making India Awesome (2015)
D. The Paradoxical Prime Minister (2018)

Q.31 The human eye is like a camera. Its lens system forms an image on a light sensitive screen called the ______.
A. cornea   **B.** iris   **C.** retina   **D.** pupil

Q.32 Which of the following is an example of primary activity of the economic sector of India?
A. Forestry   **B.** Transport
C. Communication   **D.** Cloth weaving

Q.33 Federalism is one of the key features of the Constitution of India, under which:
A. The head of the government is also head of the state
B. States draw their authority from the Parliament
C. All persons in India are governed by laws and policies made by the Judiciary only
D. States are agents of the Federal government

Q.34 In India, National Epilepsy Day 2020 was celebrated on:
A. 17 November   **B.** 28 November
C. 25 November   **D.** 1 November

Q.35 _______ is the science that studies the structure of the body.
A. Anatomy   **B.** Cytology
C. Palynology   **D.** Palaeobotany

Q.36 Who among the following was PETA India's Person of the year 2019?
A. Virat Kohli   **B.** Sonam Kapoor
C. Anushka Sharma   **D.** PV Sindhu

Q.37 Which of the following countries will host the 2022 Asian Games?
A. Indonesia   **B.** China
C. Japan   **D.** South Korea

Q.38 Anopheles is a ______ which carries the parasite of malaria.
A. female mosquito   **B.** housefly
C. male mosquito   **D.** spider

Q.39 Which of the following countries hosted the 13th BRICS Summit in 2021?
A. India   **B.** China   **C.** Russia   **D.** Brazil

Q.40 The ______ is the final authority of making laws in any democratic country.
A. Prime Minister   **B.** Parliament
C. Law Minister   **D.** President

Q.41 Kulik Bird Sanctuary is located in which of the following states?

A. Andhra Pradesh   **B.** Maharashtra
C. Madhya Pradesh   **D.** West Bengal

Q.42 Holt Mackenzie and Robert Merttins Bird introduced:

A. The Mahalwari System
B. The Ryotwari System
C. The Doctrine of Lapse
D. The Permanent Settlement

Q.43 During which of the following national movements in Bengal was a tricolour flag designed?

A. Khilafat Movement
B. Civil Disobedience Movement
C. Swadeshi Movement
D. Quit India Movement

Q.44 As of July 2021, the Ayushman Bharat Pradhan Mantri Jan Arogya Yojana (AB-PM-JAY) was NOT implemented in the state of __________.

A. West Bengal   **B.** Karnataka
C. Punjab   **D.** Gujarat

Q.45 Which of the following festivals is celebrated during the Amavasya of the Kartik month?

A. Govardhan puja   **B.** Dhanteras
C. Raksha Bandhan   **D.** Diwali

Q.46 When a good is produced by exploiting natural resources, it falls in the category of:

A. Mining industry   **B.** Service sector
C. Agriculture sector   **D.** Industrial sector

Q.47 What is NOT a specific feature of commercial farming as against subsistence farming?

A. It is mainly practiced in lesser developed countries
B. Most of the work is done by machines
C. The amount of capital used is large
D. Crops are grown for sale in the market

Q.48 How many times have Mumbai Indians won the IPL title till its 2020 edition?

A. 4   **B.** 2   **C.** 3   **D.** 5

Q.49 The Bengal tiger was adopted as 'The national animal of India' in the year _____.

A. 1978   **B.** 1974   **C.** 1976   **D.** 1972

Q.50 Who among the following was the last Mughal Emperor?

A. Shah Jahan   **B.** Aurangzeb
C. Akbar   **D.** Bahadur Shah II

Elementary Mathematics

Q.51 P and Q can together finish a work in 21 days. They worked together for 12 days and Q left. After that, P finished the remaining work in 15 days. In how many days P alone can finish the work?

A. 28 days   **B.** 35 days   **C.** 19 days   **D.** 24 days

Q.52 The average height of 23 boys is 1.2 m. When 3 boys leave the group, then the average height increases by 0.15 m. What is the average height of the 3 boys who leave?

A. 0.5 m   **B.** 0.2 m   **C.** 0.45 m   **D.** 0.6 m

Q.53 A shopkeeper gives 10% discount on the cost of rice. A buyer could purchase $5\ kg$ more rice for ₹ 720. Find the selling price of rice per kg.

A. ₹ 19   **B.** ₹ 12   **C.** ₹ 16   **D.** ₹ 18

Q.54 An express train travelled at an average speed of $120\ km/h$, stopping for 4min after every $80\ km$. How long did it take to reach its destination at the distance of $720\ km$ from the starting point?

A. $5\ h45$ min   **B.** $7\ h15$ min
C. $6\ h32$ min   **D.** $5\ h24$ min

Q.55 The cost of levelling a circular park at ₹ 6.50 per m^2 is ₹ $36,036$. What is the cost (in Rs.) of putting a fence around it at ₹ 18 per m? (Take $\pi = \dfrac{22}{7}$)

A. 3960   **B.** 4752   **C.** 4644   **D.** 7416

Q.56 The value of $20 - [7 - \{4 - (8 - \overline{6 + 3})\}]$ is:

A. 20   **B.** 2   **C.** 16   **D.** 18

Q.57 An article was sold at $\dfrac{5}{8}$ of its cost price. The loss per cent is:

A. 1.35   **B.** 27.5   **C.** 37.5   **D.** 32

Q.58 By what percentage is one-third of 90 lesser that three-eights of 160?

A. 45%   **B.** 50%   **C.** 60%   **D.** 25%

Q.59 The sum of three numbers is 172. If the ratio of the first number to the second number is $3:5$ and that of the second number to the third number is $7:6$, then find the first number.

A. 42   **B.** 30   **C.** 40   **D.** 58

Q.60 What is the least five-digit number that is exactly divisible by $21, 35,$ and 56?

A. 10000   **B.** 10040   **C.** 10920   **D.** 10080

Q.61 A, B and C can complete a piece of work individually in $7\dfrac{1}{2}$ days, 15 days and 30 days, respectively. A and B start working but A quits the job after 3 days. Then C joined B and both did the work till the completion of the work. In how many days will the whole work be completed?

A. 12 days   **B.** 7 days   **C.** 8 days   **D.** 6 days

Q.62 Two numbers are in the ratio $8:5$. If 17 is subtracted from the first number and 25 is added to the second number, then the ratio becomes $1:3$, What is the sum of the two numbers?

A. 13 **B.** 39 **C.** 52 **D.** 65

Q.63 If the two numbers are, respectively, 20% and 30% less than a third number, then what percentage of the first number is the second number?

A. 87.5% **B.** 90.5% **C.** 85.5% **D.** 101.5%

Q.64 The amount obtained by investing a certain sum in $4\frac{3}{4}$ years at 12% p.a. at simple interest is ₹ $2,175$ more than the simple interest on the same sum in 11 years at the same rate. The sum (in ₹) is:

A. 8,400 **B.** 8,700 **C.** 8,000 **D.** 8,500

Q.65 The value of $\frac{5}{14} \div 5\frac{3}{7}$ of $\frac{7}{19} - \left(\frac{3}{4} - \frac{4}{7}\right)$ is:

A. 0 **B.** 5 **C.** 10 **D.** 1

Q.66 23 oranges were bought for ₹ 193.20 and sold at the rate of ₹ 108 per dozen. Find the profit percentage correct to one decimal place.

A. 5.9% **B.** 8.4% **C.** 7.1% **D.** 4.5%

Q.67 A cyclist covers a distance of 17 km in 2 h. His speed (in km/h) is:

A. 8 **B.** 8.5 **C.** 7.5 **D.** 6.5

Q.68 A sum of ₹ $1,800$ gives a simple interest of ₹ 360 in 3 years 4 months. The rate of interest per annum is:

A. 8% **B.** 10% **C.** 6% **D.** 12%

Q.69 A wall clock is listed at ₹ $1,200$ and the discount offered is 10%. What additional discount must be given to bring the net selling price to ₹ 945?

A. 10% **B.** 12.5% **C.** 9.25% **D.** 15%

Q.70 The average salary of all the workers in an organisation is ₹ $9,000$. The average salary of 8 technicians is ₹ $14,000$ and the average salary of the rest is ₹ $5,000$. Find the total number of workers in the organisation.

A. 18 **B.** 15 **C.** 20 **D.** 23

Q.71 A person bought a table and a chair for ₹ $2,200$. He sold the table at a gain of 15% and the chair at a loss of 5%, thereby gaining 4% on the whole. Find the cost of the table.

A. ₹ 1,125 **B.** ₹ 1,050 **C.** ₹ 1,200 **D.** ₹ 990

Q.72 A certain sum amounts to ₹ $9,900$ in 4 years and to ₹ $11,700$ in 7 years at the same rate per cent per annum at simple interest. What will be the amount (in ₹) of the same sum at $9\frac{2}{3}\%$ for $2\frac{1}{4}$ years at simple interest?

A. 9541.50 **B.** 9165.75
C. 10000.00 **D.** 9131.25

Q.73 The ratio of two numbers a and b is $5:8$. If 5 is subtracted from a and 3 is added to b, then the ratio becomes $8:15$. What is the difference between the two original numbers?

A. 24 **B.** 36 **C.** 30 **D.** 27

Q.74 The sum of two numbers is 35 and the HCF and LCM of these numbers are 5 and 60, respectively. Find the sum of the reciprocals of the numbers.

A. $\frac{3}{25}$ **B.** $\frac{4}{15}$ **C.** $\frac{7}{60}$ **D.** $\frac{5}{60}$

Q.75 A cylindrical tank is $80\ cm$ in diameter and $5.6\ m$ in height. The cost (in ₹) of painting the curved surface of the tank at the rate of ₹ $20/m^2$ is:

(Take $\pi = \frac{22}{7}$)

A. 281.60 **B.** 301.80 **C.** 321.20 **D.** 261.40

English

Q.76 Direction: Select the option that can be used as a one-word substitute for the given group of words.

The branch of biology that deals with the relations of organisms to one another and to their physical surroundings.

A. Anthropology **B.** Ecology
C. Gerontology **D.** Morphology

Q.77 Direction: Select the most appropriate option to fill in the blank.

It is a disorder that manifests usually in middle _____.

A. ages **B.** age **C.** life **D.** year

Q.78 Direction: Parts of the given sentence have been given as options. One of them contains a grammatical error. Select the option that has the error.

Lack of calcium in human body usually leads against several health complications.

A. leads against
B. several health complications
C. Lack of calcium
D. in human body

Q.79 Direction: The following sentence has been split into four segments. Identify the segment that contains a grammatical error.

Sharada was cooking lunch / when I am going / to give her / the mobile phone.

A. Sharada was cooking lunch
B. to give
C. the mobile phone
D. when I am going

Q.80 Direction: Select the most appropriate meaning of the given idiom.

Having a soft spot for

A. Being too ridiculous **B.** Having soft skin
C. Being fond of **D.** Being angry

Q.81 Direction: Select the most appropriate ANTONYM of the given word.

Ignorance

A. Knowledge

B. Truth

C. Innocence

D. Virtue

Q.82 Direction: Select the option that can be used as a one-word substitute for the given group of words.

Someone who buys and sells goods in large amounts to shops and businesses

A. Wholesaler

B. Merchant

C. Supplier

D. Dealer

Q.83 Direction: Select the most appropriate synonym of the given word.

Coincidence

A. Extent   **B.** Accent   **C.** Chance   **D.** Incident

Q.84 Direction: Select the most appropriate option that can substitute the underlined segment in the given sentence. If there is no need to substitute it, select 'No substitution required'.

Leopards and cats <u>are belong</u> to the same family of animals.

A. No substitution required

B. belong

C. belongs

D. belonging

Q.85 Direction: Select the option that will improve the underlined part of the sentence. In case no improvement is needed, select 'No improvement required'.

<u>Neglected for a long time</u>, the ancient monument needs immediate restoration.

A. Neglecting from a long time

B. No improvement required

C. Having neglect for a long time

D. Neglected in the long time

Q.86 Direction: Select the most appropriate option to fill in the blank.

An important _____ of education is to develop character.

A. scheme   **B.** purpose   **C.** means   **D.** image

Q.87 Direction: Select the most appropriate meaning of the given idiom.

To be on pins and needles

A. To be in an agitated state of suspense

B. To sit on a box of pins

C. To be attacked from both sides

D. To avoid making a decision

Q.88 Direction: Select the most appropriate option that can substitute the underlined segment in the given sentence. If there is no need to substitute it, select 'No substitution required'.

Mala's voice is <u>much more melodious to Gita.</u>

A. much more melodious than Gita's

B. much melodious to Gita's

C. much more melodious to Gita's

D. No substitution required

Q.89 Direcction: The following sentence has been split into four segments. Identify the segment that contains a grammatical error.

The eldest / prince is / the heir / of the throne.

A. of the throne

B. The eldest

C. the heir

D. prince is

Q.90 Direction: Select the most appropriate option to fill in the blank.

He was in _____ of the costumes for the play.

A. charge

B. care

C. duty

D. responsibility

Q.91 Direction: Select the most appropriate ANTONYM of the given word.

Damage

A. Hurt   **B.** Ruin   **C.** Harm   **D.** Mend

Q.92 Direction: Select the option that can be used as a one-word substitute for the given group of words.

One who cannot be changed or reformed

A. Invincible

B. Inevitable

C. Incapable

D. Incorrigible

Q.93 Direction: Select the INCORRECTLY spelt word.

A. Magnificant

B. Gregarious

C. Commitment

D. Persuasion

Q.94 Direction: Select the INCORRECTLY spelt word

A. Unassuming

B. Unflappable

C. Unruffled

D. Unannimous

Q.95 Direction: Select the most appropriate synonym of the given word.

Mirth

A. Delight   **B.** Joint   **C.** Scene   **D.** View

Ques (96-100):Direction: In the following passage, some words have been deleted. Read the passage carefully and select the most appropriate option to fill in each blank.

A tic is a repeated, impulsive action, which an actor feels powerless (1)_____ or avoid. Only when the individual performs the tic, is tension and anxiety (2)_____, within the individual with a tic disorder. Tics can be (3)_____ by an emotional state or sensation, and can happen for no obvious reason. General types of tics (4)_____ verbal tics, facial tics and (5)_____ muscular tics.

Q.96 Select the most appropriate option to fill in blank number (1).

A. controls

B. controlling

C. to control

D. controlled

Q.97 Select the most appropriate option to fill in blank number (2).

A. modified   **B.** stored   **C.** added   **D.** released

Q.98 Select the most appropriate option to fill in blank number (3).

A. done   **B.** began   **C.** triggered   **D.** elicited

Q.99 Select the most appropriate option to fill in blank number (4).

A. include   **B.** included

C. including   **D.** includes

Q.100 Select the most appropriate option to fill in blank number (5).

A. the other   **B.** others   **C.** another   **D.** other

// Smart Answer Sheet //

Correct Percentage of students who answered correctly. **Skipped** Percentage of students who skipped.

Q.	Ans.	Correct / Skipped
1	B	81.25 % / 11.46 %
2	B	50.53 % / 42.21 %
3	D	58.8 % / 40.06 %
4	A	47.35 % / 32.63 %
5	A	79.97 % / 13.54 %
6	B	81.44 % / 16.12 %
7	C	11.65 % / 84.09 %
8	A	46.68 % / 43.91 %
9	D	78.5 % / 15.03 %
10	B	65.0 % / 34.47 %
11	A	54.12 % / 42.92 %
12	C	76.03 % / 16.77 %
13	B	87.55 % / 12.15 %
14	B	57.23 % / 39.34 %
15	A	63.61 % / 36.35 %
16	D	84.56 % / 10.41 %
17	D	50.74 % / 44.09 %
18	B	49.09 % / 40.62 %
19	A	43.57 % / 45.76 %
20	D	30.13 % / 68.2 %
21	B	68.17 % / 31.23 %
22	A	84.61 % / 13.6 %
23	B	40.15 % / 44.77 %
24	C	67.64 % / 30.1 %
25	D	61.18 % / 38.46 %
26	A	41.36 % / 37.23 %
27	B	14.27 % / 82.05 %
28	C	54.69 % / 31.53 %
29	A	30.63 % / 67.82 %
30	C	59.27 % / 31.58 %
31	C	89.24 % / 10.15 %
32	A	26.63 % / 70.56 %
33	D	41.45 % / 44.55 %
34	A	52.94 % / 33.08 %
35	A	86.89 % / 11.99 %
36	A	53.61 % / 34.67 %
37	B	54.71 % / 45.18 %
38	A	83.68 % / 12.57 %
39	A	66.6 % / 31.19 %
40	B	40.16 % / 36.19 %
41	D	54.23 % / 41.81 %
42	A	59.92 % / 36.1 %
43	C	20.9 % / 75.98 %
44	A	69.58 % / 30.23 %
45	D	82.4 % / 14.8 %
46	C	56.8 % / 35.44 %
47	A	49.95 % / 34.85 %
48	D	85.35 % / 13.79 %
49	D	51.7 % / 41.46 %
50	D	62.14 % / 36.34 %
51	B	66.23 % / 31.24 %
52	B	28.03 % / 69.28 %
53	C	51.2 % / 37.23 %
54	C	40.76 % / 38.99 %
55	B	84.5 % / 13.74 %
56	D	83.67 % / 12.28 %
57	C	83.1 % / 12.16 %
58	B	83.51 % / 11.65 %
59	A	87.92 % / 10.51 %
60	D	87.95 % / 11.67 %
61	B	55.14 % / 33.01 %
62	C	67.12 % / 32.77 %
63	A	82.08 % / 16.89 %
64	B	63.89 % / 33.13 %
65	A	87.16 % / 10.42 %
66	C	40.8 % / 31.34 %
67	B	76.66 % / 12.28 %
68	C	41.05 % / 56.52 %
69	B	45.17 % / 33.19 %
70	A	53.26 % / 40.28 %
71	D	42.09 % / 43.64 %
72	D	69.58 % / 30.09 %
73	D	67.53 % / 30.55 %
74	C	80.97 % / 12.09 %
75	A	48.14 % / 30.88 %
76	B	81.71 % / 10.27 %
77	B	55.34 % / 37.04 %
78	A	32.77 % / 67.22 %
79	D	63.67 % / 30.51 %
80	C	83.89 % / 15.77 %

Q.	Ans.	Correct / Skipped
81	A	63.18 %
		36.16 %
82	A	83.24 %
		14.93 %
83	C	50.29 %
		31.72 %
84	B	77.71 %
		12.01 %

Q.	Ans.	Correct / Skipped
85	B	40.77 %
		30.48 %
86	B	82.6 %
		16.76 %
87	A	64.7 %
		33.83 %
88	A	88.82 %
		10.3 %

Q.	Ans.	Correct / Skipped
89	A	41.85 %
		32.8 %
90	A	81.64 %
		11.77 %
91	D	54.44 %
		37.8 %
92	D	87.5 %
		12.2 %

Q.	Ans.	Correct / Skipped
93	A	87.15 %
		10.24 %
94	D	81.48 %
		18.29 %
95	A	45.42 %
		42.67 %
96	C	63.47 %
		31.52 %

Q.	Ans.	Correct / Skipped
97	D	79.63 %
		14.59 %
98	C	55.9 %
		33.91 %
99	A	53.9 %
		43.35 %
100	D	84.69 %
		12.24 %

//Hints and Solutions//

1. The pattern followed here is:

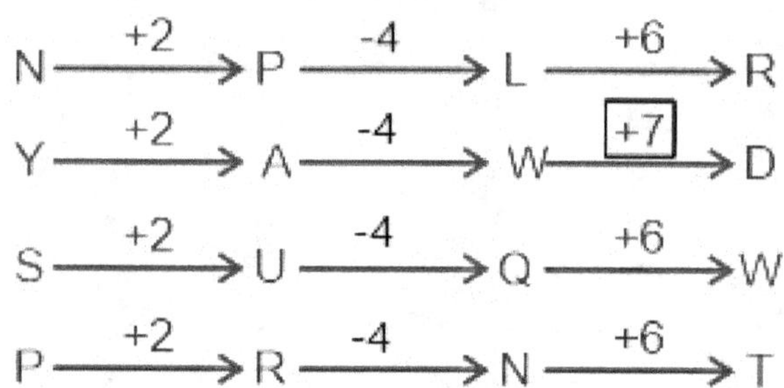

Thus YAWD is different from other words.

Hence, the correct option is (B).

2. Given: Suman is four times as old as her son. Five years ago, she was seven times as old as her son.

Let the present age or Suman be $'S'$ and that of her son be $'p'$.

According to the question,

$$S = 4 \times p \,...\text{(i)}$$

$$S - 5 = 7 \times (p - 5)$$

Putting the value of S from equation (i);

$$4p - 5 = 7p - 35$$

$$\Rightarrow 7p - 4p = 35 - 5$$

$$\Rightarrow 3p = 30$$

$$\Rightarrow p = 10$$

So, the age of the son of Suman is 10 years.

Hence, the correct option is (B).

3. Some women are swimmers, and some men are swimmers, as shown below:

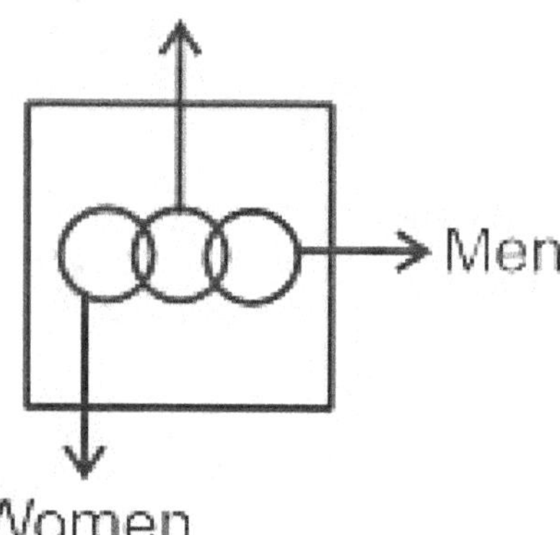

So, "women, swimmers, men" is the correct answer.

Hence, the correct option is (D).

4. In this question, We will use the opposite face relation of cube which is shown below:

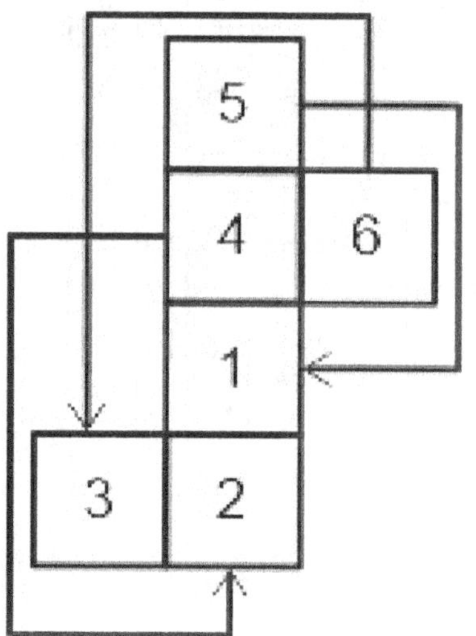

The opposite faces are:

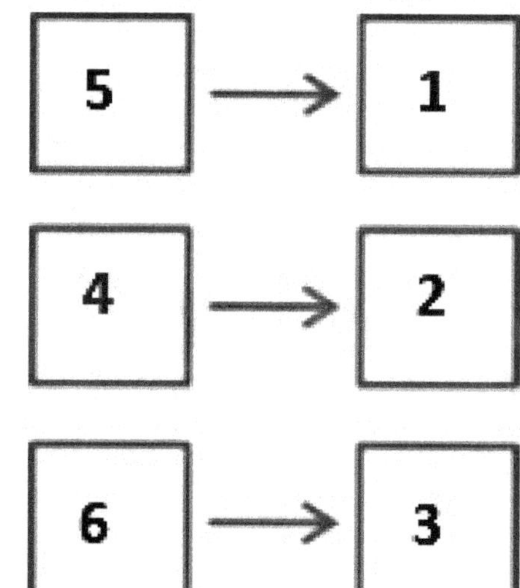

So, 2 is the number that will be on the opposite the face showing the number '4'.

Hence, the correct option is (A).

5. The logic followed here is:

The number of lines of the polygon increases by 1 in each step and half of the polygon is shaded, thus the final series is as follows;

- Figure (1) → Triangle (3 sides)
- Figure (2) → Rectangle (4 sides)
- Figure (3) → Pentagon (5 sides)
- Figure (4) → Hexagon (6 sides)

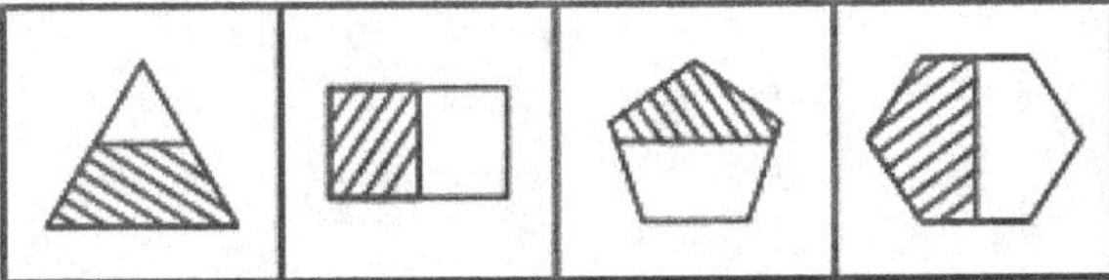

Hence, the correct option is (A).

6. By arranging the given words in dictionary order;

3. Nebulizer

1. Nervous

5. Nitrogen

2. Nobility

4. Nominate

So, 3, 1, 5, 2, 4 is the correct order.

Hence, the correct option is (B).

7. The logic followed here is:

The paper when unfolded will look like this:

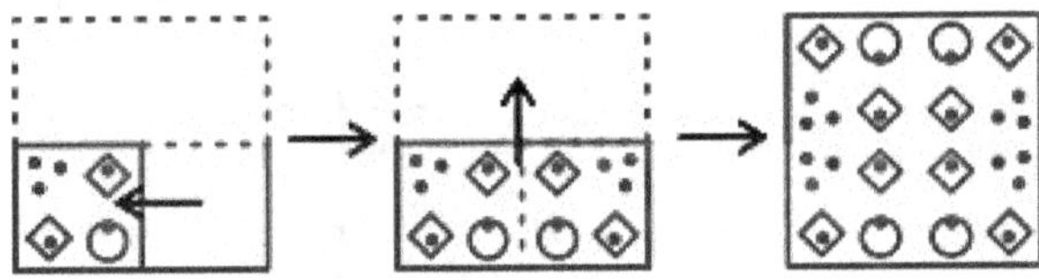

Hence, the correct option is (C).

8. Given: 'FALSE' is coded as '2141588'.

The logic followed here is:

The opposite positional value of consonant and add 3 to the positional values of vowels, as shown below,

- Consonants ⇔ Opposite letter positional value
- Vowel + 3

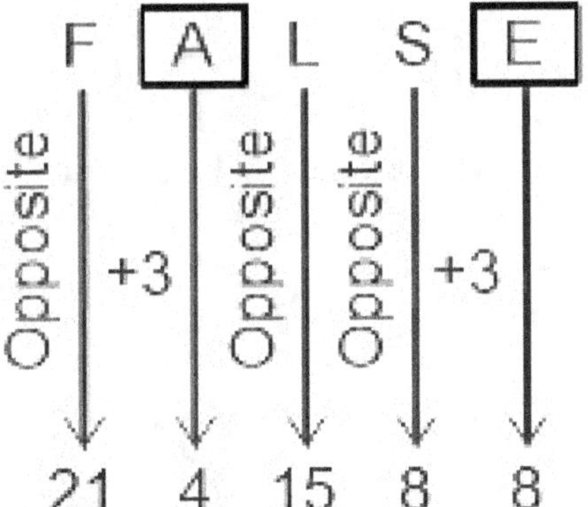

Similarly,

- Consonants ⇔ Opposite letter positional value
- Vowel + 3

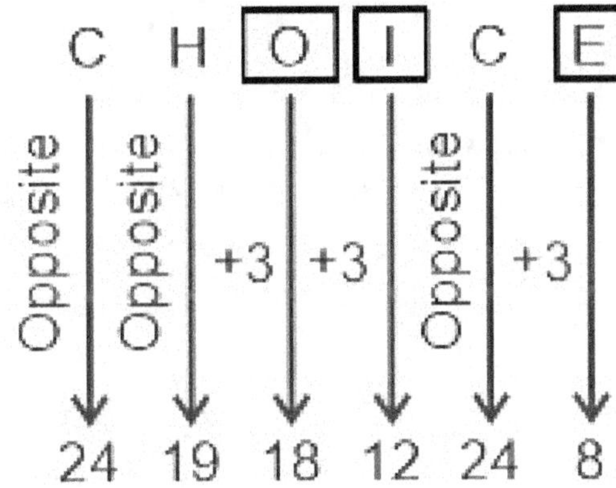

So, 24191812248 is the correct answer.

Hence, the correct option is (A).

9. The logic followed here is:

$$1 \quad 8 \quad 81 \quad \boxed{1024} \quad 15625$$

$$(1^2) \quad (2^3) \quad (3^4) \quad (4^5) \quad (5^6)$$

So, 1024 is the correct answer.

Hence, the correct option is (D).

10. The logic followed here is:

$$C \xrightarrow{+7} J$$
$$N \xrightarrow{+7} U$$
$$K \xrightarrow{+7} R$$

Similarly,

$$F \xrightarrow{+7} M$$
$$J \xrightarrow{+7} Q$$
$$L \xrightarrow{+7} S$$

So, MQS is the correct answer.

Hence, the correct option is (B).

11. The logic followed here is:

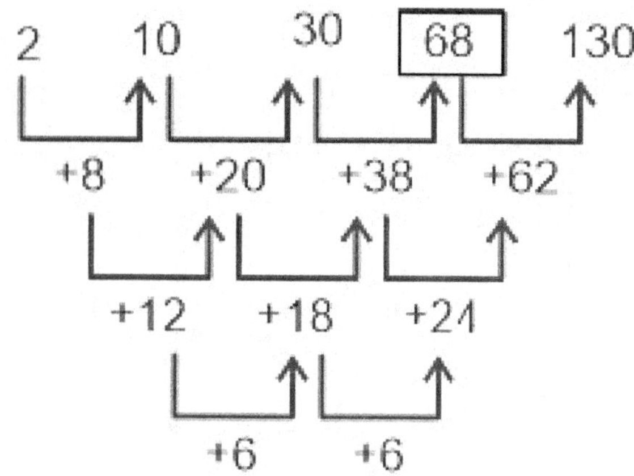

So, the missing number is 68.

Hence, the correct option is (A).

12. Given:

$$483D23A93C16B4C(15B2)$$

By substituting symbols according to question,

$$483 \div 23 + 93 - 16 \times 4 - (15 \times 2)$$
$$= 483 \div 23 + 93 - 16 \times 4 - 30$$
$$= 21 + 93 - 16 \times 4 - 30$$
$$= 21 + 93 - 64 - 30$$
$$= 114 - 6 - 30$$
$$= 50 - 30$$
$$= 20$$

Hence, the correct option is (C).

13. The given word "CONTINUITY" ends with Y. So the mirror image will start with 'Y'.

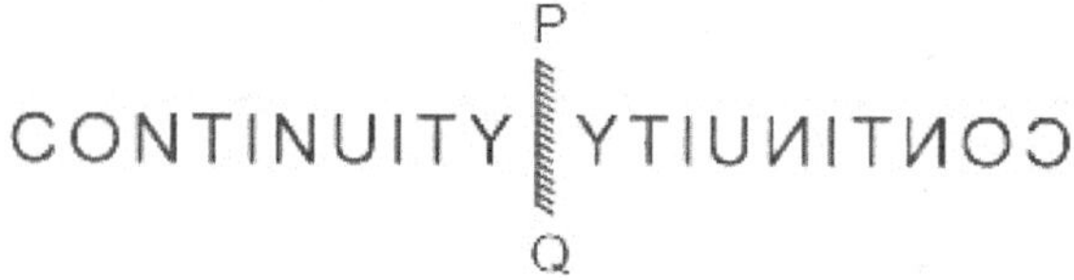

Hence, the correct option is (B).

14. The least possible diagram is as follows:

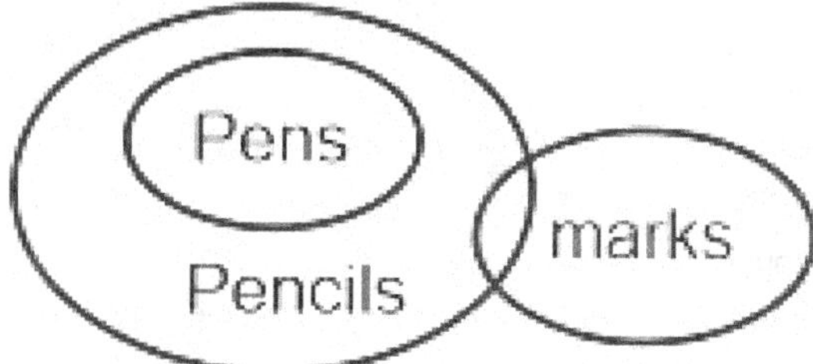

Conclusions:

I. All pens are markers → False (it is possible but not definite as shown in the diagram above)

II. Some pens are markers → False (it is possible but definite as shown in the diagram above)

So, none of the conclusions follow.

Hence, the correct option is (B).

15. The logic followed here is:

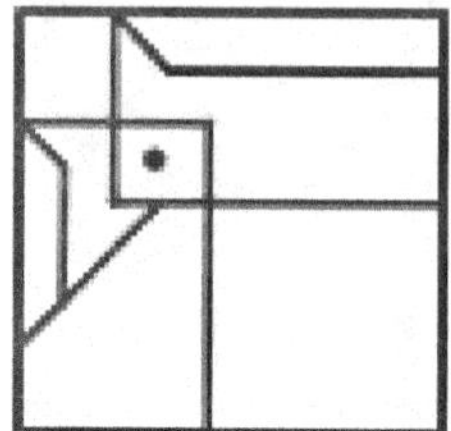

Hence, the correct option is (A).

16. The logic followed here is:

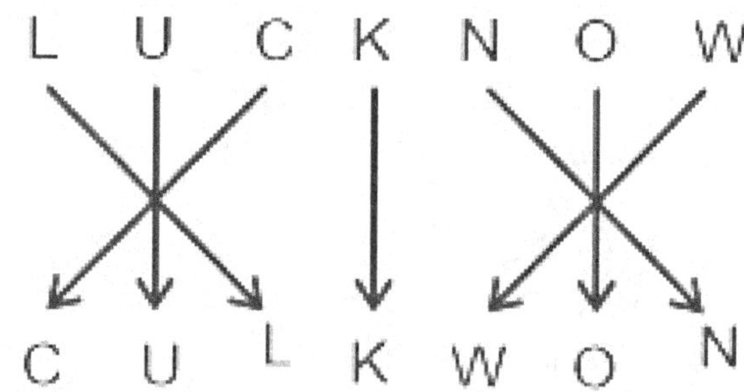

And,

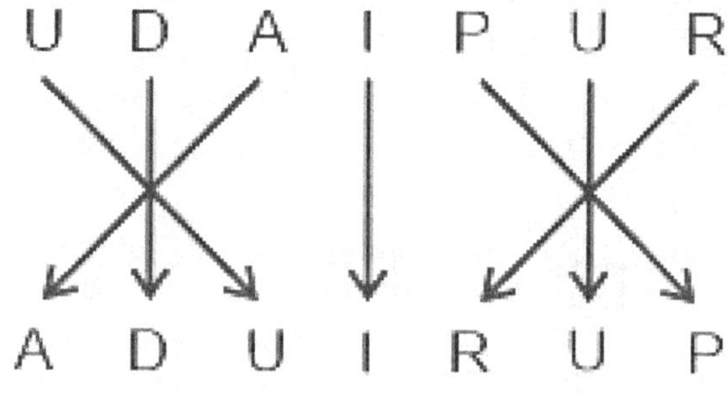

Similarly,

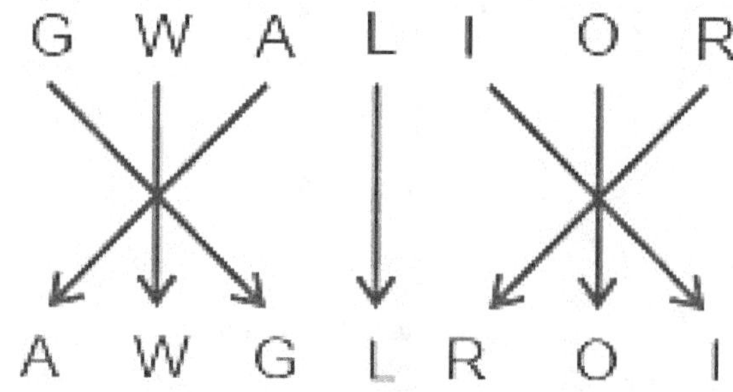

So, AWGLROI is the correct answer.

Hence, the correct option is (D).

17. The logic followed here is:

$$E \xrightarrow{+12} Q \xrightarrow{+12} C \xrightarrow{+12} O$$
$$I \xrightarrow{+12} U \xrightarrow{+12} G \xrightarrow{+12} S$$
$$M \xrightarrow{+12} Y \xrightarrow{+12} K \xrightarrow{+12} W$$

So, OSW is the correct answer.

Hence, the correct option is (D).

18. The logic followed here is:

Column wise,

$$(3^{rd} \text{ number} - 1^{st} \text{ number}) + 10 = 2^{nd} \text{ number.}$$

Column (1): $71 - 34 + 10 = 47$

Column (3): $61 - 43 + 10 = 28$

Similarly,

Column (2): $33 - 18 + 10 = 25$

So, 25 is the correct answer.

Hence, the correct option is (B).

19. The logic followed here is:

$(\text{First number} + 3) \times (\text{First number} \div 2) = \text{Second number}$

$11:77 \Rightarrow$

$(11 + 3) \times (11 \div 2)$

$= 14 \times (11 \div 2)$

$= 7 \times 11 = 77$

Similarly,

$12:?$

$(12 + 3) \times (12 \div 2)$

$= 15 \times 6$

$= 90$

And

$14:119 \Rightarrow$

$(14 + 3) \times (14 \div 2)$

$= 17 \times 7$

$= 119$

So, the correct answer is 90.

Hence, the correct option is (A).

20. Possible tree diagram will be:

Symbol in Diagram	Meaning
◯	Female
▢	Male
═	Married Couple
—	Siblings
│	Difference of a generation

Your (Deveshi) mother Ritu is the younger sister of my (Nisha) father (Dileep), who is the second child of Krishna. Thus, the final family tree is as follows:

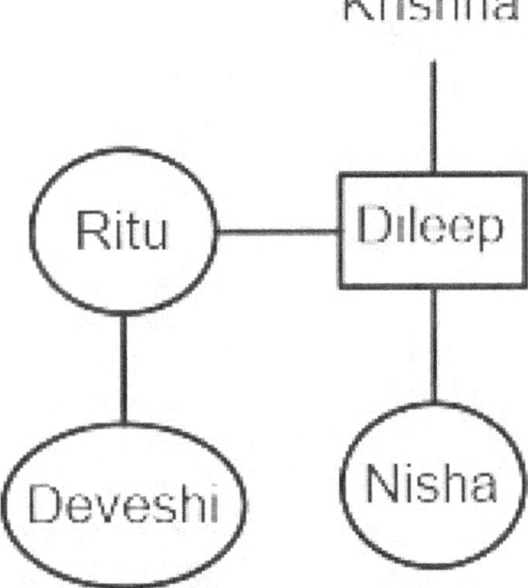

Since, the gender of Krishna is not specified here, thus, Krishna can be maternal grandmother or the maternal grandfather of Devashi.

Therefore, from given options we can say that Krishna is the maternal grandfather of Deveshi.

So, Krishna is the maternal grandfather of Deveshi.

Hence, the correct option is (D).

21. Seven doctors: S, T, U, V, X, Y, and Z are sitting around a round table, facing the center.

(1) Y is sitting third to the right of Z and between S and X.

(2) Z is sitting second to the right of U.

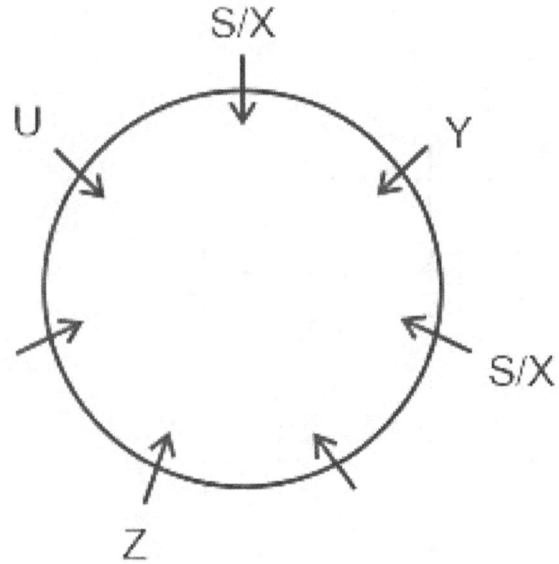

(3) V is sitting third to the left of X.

(4) Two doctors are sitting between Y and V. Therefore, the final seating arrangement is as follows:

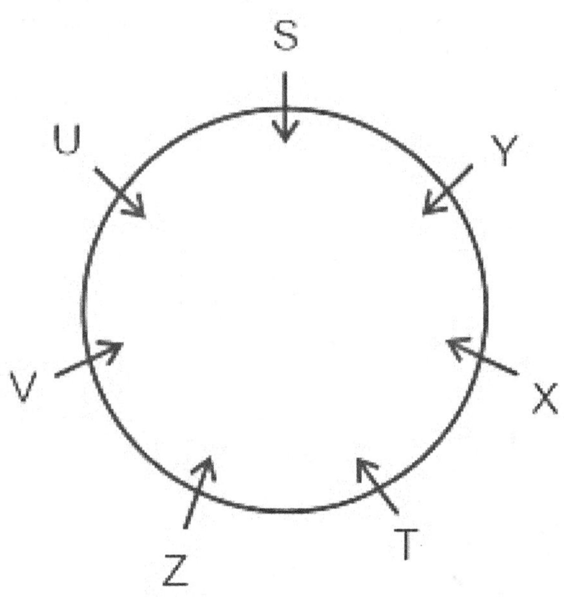

Now, we can check the options:

(1) Z is sitting between T and X → False (T is sitting between Z and X)

(2) S is sitting fourth to the left of T → True

(3) U is sitting to the immediate right of V → False (U is sitting immediate left of V)

(4) Four doctors are sitting between Y and Z → False (either two or three doctors are sitting between Y and Z)

So, S is sitting fourth to the left of T is correct.

Hence, the correct option is (B).

22. The logic followed here is:

J (10) - B (2) = H (8)

R (18) - M (13) = E (5)

Similarly,

? - I (9) = K (11)

? = I (11) + K (9)

? = T (20)

So, T is the correct answer.

Hence, the correct option is (A).

23. People: M, N, L, O, Q, and H are sitting in a row.

(1) M and N are at the ends.

(2) L is sitting to the left of N.

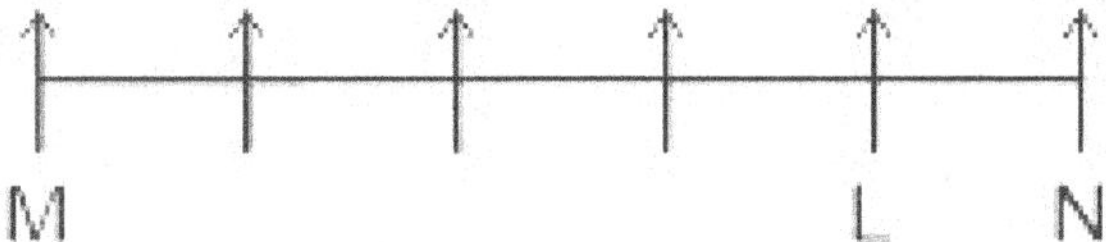

(3) Q and H are in the center. Therefore, the final seating arrangement is as follows:

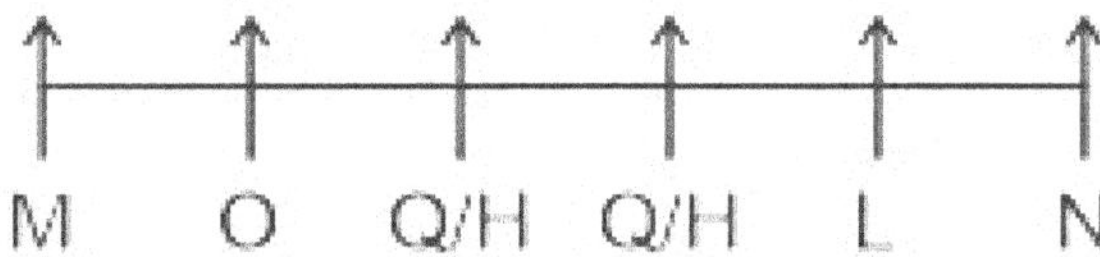

Thus O is sitting to the right of M.

So, O is the correct answer.

Hence, the correct option is (B).

24. The logic followed here is:

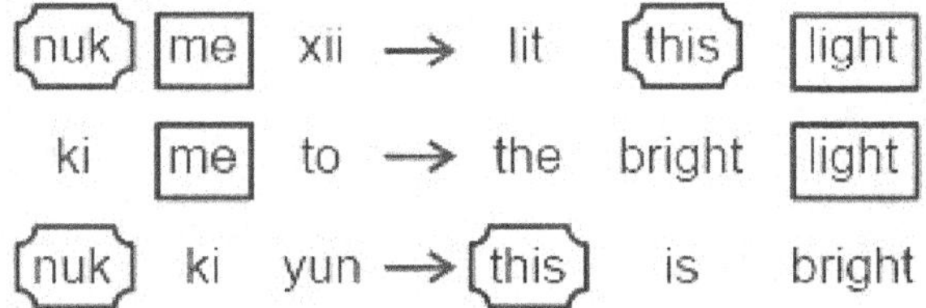

Hence, the correct option is (C).

25. The logic followed here is:

A cataract is a disease related to 'Eye'.

Similarly,

Meniere's disease is related to 'Ear'.

So, "Ear" the is the correct answer.

Hence, the correct option is (D).

26. The difference between the total revenue and total expenditure of the government is called fiscal deficit.

A fiscal Deficit is a difference between the total income of the government (total taxes and non-debt capital receipts) and its total expenditure. A recurring high fiscal deficit means that the government has been spending beyond its means. The government meets the fiscal deficit by borrowing money. In a way, the total borrowing requirements of the government in a financial year are equal to the fiscal deficit in that year. A fiscal deficit situation occurs when the government's expenditure exceeds its income. This difference is calculated both in absolute terms and also as a percentage of the Gross Domestic Product (GDP) of the country.

Fiscal Deficit formula:

Fiscal Deficit = Total expenditure of the government (capital and revenue expenditure) - Total income of the government (Revenue receipts + recovery of loans + other receipts).

Hence, the correct option is (A).

27. Manu Bhaker is not a hockey player.

Manu Bhaker is an Olympian from India who competes in airgun shooting. She earned two gold medals for India at the 2018 ISSF World Cup. She is the youngest Indian to earn an ISSF World Cup gold medal. In her first Commonwealth Games debut, she won the gold medal in the women's 10 m air pistol event at the age of 16. She qualified for the finals after scoring 388/400 points in the women's 10m air pistol qualification round at the 2018 Commonwealth Games.

Hence, the correct option is (B).

28. The Lilatilakam was written in the Manipravalam language and was a fourteenth-century text.

Manipravalami is a South Indian macaronic language documented in some texts. It is a hybrid language that blends Sanskrit vocabulary with Tamil morpho-syntax and is commonly written in the Grantha script. However, the Sanskrit text Lilatilakam, written in the 14th century, claims that Manipravalam is a hybrid of Tamil and Sanskrit.

Hence, the correct option is (C).

29. According to the Public Affairs Index 2020, Kerala has been adjudged the best governed state in the country in the large states category.

Public Affairs Index-2020 was released by the Public Affairs Centre (PAC), a non profit organisation, headed by former ISRO chairman K Kasturirangan. The states were ranked on governance performance based on a composite index in the context of sustainable development. According to the PAC rankings, Kerala (1.388 PAI Index point), Tamil Nadu (0.912), Andhra Pradesh (0.531) and Karnataka (0.468) occupied the top four slots in large state category in terms of governance.

Hence, the correct option is (A).

30. Making India Awesome (2015) books is not authored by Shashi Tharoor.

'Making India Awesome: New Essays and Columns' by renowned Indian author Chetan Bhagat is a book that showers light on India's most obstinate snags-unemployment, violence, poverty, discrimination against women, religious fundamentalism, illiteracy and communal violence.

Shashi Tharoor is an Indian former international civil servant, diplomat, Bureaucrat and politician, writer and public intellectual who has been serving as Member of Parliament for Thiruvananthapuram, Kerala, since 2009. He is the Chairman of the Standing Committee on Chemicals and Fertilizers. Some books by Shashi Tharoor: Reasons of State (1985), India: From Midnight to the Millennium (1997), Nehru: The Invention of India, Bookless in Baghdad (2005) etc.

Hence, the correct option is (C).

31. The human eye is like a camera. Its lens system forms an image on a light sensitive screen called the retina.

The retina is the light-sensitive surface of an eye on which the image is formed. It generates signals which are transmitted to the brain through optical nerves.

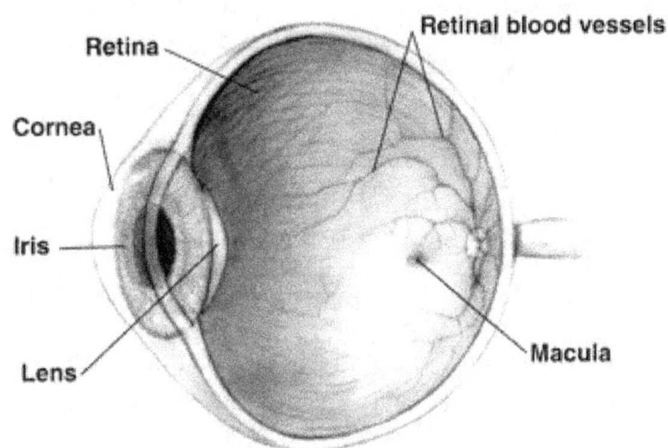

Hence, the correct option is (C).

32. Forestry is an example of primary activity of the economic sector of India.

Primary Sector- sources of raw materials (agriculture and allied sector services). They are the sources of production of raw materials for secondary and tertiary sectors, it includes: Agriculture and forestry, Fishing and poultry farming, Animal Husbandry

Hence, the correct option is (A).

33. Federalism is one of the key features of the Constitution of India, under which states are agents of the Federal government.

Federalism is part of the basic structure of the Indian constitution which cannot be altered or destroyed through constitutional amendments under the constituent powers of the Parliament without undergoing judicial review by the Supreme Court.

Federal features of the Indian constitution: Written constitution, Supremacy of constitution, Division of powers, Independent judiciary, Bicameralism, Rigidity of constitution, Two governments

Hence, the correct option is (D).

34. In India, National Epilepsy Day 2020 was celebrated on 17 November.

Epilepsy is a chronic disorder of brain characterized by recurrent 'seizures' or 'fits'. The seizures are caused as a result of sudden, excessive electrical discharges in the neurons (brain cells). The condition can affect people at any age and each age group has unique concerns and problems.

Hence, the correct option is (A).

35. Anatomy is the science that studies the structure of the body. There are several branches or types of anatomy including gross anatomy, microscopic anatomy, human anatomy, phytotomy, zootomy, embryology, and comparative anatomy. Each branch is focused on a specific part of the study of anatomy.

Hence, the correct option is (A).

36. India captain Virat Kohli was named People for the Ethical Treatment of Animals (PETA) India's 'Person of the Year for 2019' for his animal advocacy efforts. The PETA awards are given to people or organizations that take initiative in the welfare of animals and violence against animals. Past recipients of the award include Shashi Tharoor, Anushka Sharma, R Madhavan, and Jacqueline Fernandez.

Hence, the correct option is (A).

37. Asian Games, 2022 will be a multi-sport event celebrated in Hangzhou, Zhejiang, China.

Hangzhou will be the third Chinese city to host the Asian Games, after Beijing in 1990 and Guangzhou in 2010. On 8 April 2019, the Olympic Council of Asia initially announced that the Games would feature 37 sports, including the 28 mandatory Olympic sports to be contested at the 2024 Summer Olympics in Paris.

Hence, the correct option is (B).

38. Anopheles is a female mosquito which carries the parasite of malaria.

Malaria is an acute febrile disease caused by the Plasmodium parasite that is transmitted to people by the bite of a female Anopheles mosquito. Plasmodium groups are single-celled microorganisms. The disease is widespread in tropical and sub-tropical regions around the equator.

Hence, the correct option is (A).

39. India hosted the 13th BRICS Summit in 2021.

Prime Minister Narendra Modi chaired the 13th BRICS Summit on 9 September 2021 in a virtual format. The meeting was attended by the President of Brazil Jair Bolsanaro, the President of Russia Vladimir Putin, the President of China Xi Jinping and the President of South Africa Cyril Ramaphosa. The theme for the Summit is BRICS@15: Intra-BRICS cooperation for continuity, consolidation and consensus.

Hence, the correct option is (A).

40. The Parliament is the final authority of making laws in any democratic country.

The law proposals which are passed by the parliament should be approved by the President and similarly, the law proposals which are passed by state legislatures should be approved by Governor. Parliament has also the power to amend the laws in India. Prime Minister is the head of the council of ministers and also heads the cabinet and acts as the chief advisor to the President. Parliament is the supreme law-making institution in India. It has two houses, the Lok Sabha and the Rajya Sabha.

Hence, the correct option is (B).

41. Raiganj Wildlife sanctuary also popularly known as Kulik bird sanctuary. It is located near Raiganj in Uttar Dinajpur district in the state of West Bengal. The bird sanctuary is home to 164 species of birds and some 90,000 to 1,00,000 migratory birds visit the sanctuary every year.

Hence, the correct option is (D).

42. Holt Mackenzie and Robert Merttins Bird introduced the Mahalwari System.

In 1822, Englishman Holt Mackenzie and Robert Merttins Bird devised this system. The land revenue was collected from the farmers by the village headmen on behalf of the whole village (and not the zamindar). The entire village was converted into one bigger unit called 'Mahal' and was treated as one unit for the payment of land revenue. It was the first to have concluded with the village community.

Hence, the correct option is (A).

43. During Swadeshi Movement in Bengal was a tricolour flag designed.

Pingali Venkayya is the freedom fighter who designed and handed over the tricolour (which later became the national flag) to Mohandas Karamchand Gandhi. Venkayya was educated at Cambridge and grew up to become a polymath with interests in geology, agriculture, education and languages.

Hence, the correct option is (C).

44. As of July 2021, the Ayushman Bharat Pradhan Mantri Jan Arogya Yojana (AB-PM-JAY) was not implemented in the state of West Bengal.

AB-PMJAY is the world's largest Government funded health assurance scheme. AB-PMJAY provides health assurance of up to Rs.5 Lakh per family per year for secondary and tertiary healthcare hospitalizations. AB-PMJAY is a completely cashless and paperless scheme. The benefits under AB-PMJAY are portable across the country. There is no cap on family size, or age or gender.

Hence, the correct option is (A).

45. Diwali festivals is celebrated during the Amavasya of the Kartik month. Diwali symbolizes the spiritual victory of light over darkness, good over evil, and knowledge over ignorance. The festival usually lasts five days and is celebrated during the Hindu lunisolar month Kartika (between mid-October and mid-November).

Hence, the correct option is (D).

46. When a good is produced by exploiting natural resources, it falls in the category of agriculture sector.

When we produce goods by exploiting natural resources it comes under the primary sector as these economic activities are directly tied to the extraction of resources from the earth.

Hence, the correct option is (C).

47. "It is mainly practiced in lesser developed countries" is not a specific feature of commercial farming as against subsistence farming.

Subsistence Farming is characterised by small and scattered land holdings and the use of primitive tools. As the farmers are poor, they do not use fertilisers and high yielding variety of seeds in their fields to the extent they should do. Shifting cultivation is a type/ example of subsistence farming in which the farmers clear a patch of forest land by cutting and burning trees and then crops are grown. This type of farming is practised to meet the needs of the farmer's family. Traditionally, low levels of technology and household labour are used to produce small output. Facilities like electricity and irrigation are generally not available to them. So It is mainly practiced in lesser developed countries.

Hence, the correct option is (A).

48. 5 times have Mumbai Indians won the IPL title till its 2020 edition.

Indian Premier League (IPL) is a Twenty20 cricket league that is contested by ten teams based out of 10 cities/states of India. The tournament follows a double round-robin and playoffs format. It was founded in 2007 by the Board of Control for Cricket in India (BCCI).

Hence, the correct option is (D).

49. The Bengal tiger was adopted as 'The national animal of India' in the year 1972. The Bengal Tiger was declared as the national animal of India in April 1973, with the initiation of Project Tiger. It was a step to protect the tigers in India.

Hence, the correct option is (D).

50. Bahadur Shah II was the last Mughal Emperor.

Bahadur Shah Zafar was born on 24 October 1775 and was the twentieth and last Mughal Emperor of India and Urdu poet. He was the second son and the successor to his father, Akbar II, who died on 28 September 1837. He was a titular Emperor, as the Mughal Empire existed in name only, and his authority was limited only to the walled city of Old Delhi (Shahjahanabad). After the Indian Rebellion of 1857, the British exiled him from Delhi. Zafar died on Friday, 7 November 1862 during his exile in Rangoon, Burma.

Hence, the correct option is (D).

51. Given:

P and Q can together finish a work in 21 days.

As we know,

Total work $=$ Efficiency of the workers $\times$ time taken by them

Let the efficiency of P and Q be p and q

According to the question,

$$21(p + q) = 12(p + q) + 15p$$

$$\Rightarrow 21p + 21q = 12p + 12q + 15p$$

$$\Rightarrow 21q - 12q = 27p - 21p$$

$$\Rightarrow 9q = 6p$$

$$\Rightarrow 3q = 2p$$

$$\Rightarrow \frac{q}{p} = \frac{2}{3}$$

So, ratio of efficiency of P and Q is $3:2$

Let the efficiency of P and Q be $3x$ and $2x$

Now,

Total work $= 21 \times 5x$

$= 105x$

Required time taken by P $= \dfrac{105x}{3x}$

$= 35$ days

$\therefore$ P alone can finish the work in 35 days.

Hence, the correct option is (B).

52. Given:

The average height of 23 boys is 1.2 m.

When 3 boys leave the group, then the average height increases by 0.15 m.

As we know,

$$\text{Average} = \frac{\text{Sum of elements}}{\text{Number of elements}}$$

Total height of the 23 boys $= 23 \times 1.2 \; m$

$= 27.6$ m

Total height of the 20 boys $= 20(1.2 + 0.15)$

$= 20 \times 1.35$

$= 27$ m

So, the height of 3 boys $= 27.6 - 27$

$= 0.6$

Average height of the 3 boys $= \dfrac{0.6}{3}$

0.2 m

$\therefore$ The average height of the 3 boys who leave was 0.2 m.

Hence, the correct option is (B).

53. Given:

A shopkeeper gives 10% discount on the cost of rice. A buyer could purchase $5\ kg$ more rice for ₹ 720.

Let the price of the rice/ kg be $10x$.

So, the reduced price $= 10x \times 90\%$

$= 9x$

According to the question,

$$\frac{720}{9x} - \frac{720}{10x} = 5$$

$$\Rightarrow \frac{80}{x} - \frac{72}{x} = 5$$

$$\Rightarrow \frac{80-72}{x} = 5$$

$$\Rightarrow \frac{8}{x} = 5$$

$$\Rightarrow 5x = 8$$

$$\Rightarrow x = \frac{8}{5}$$

$$= 1.6$$

So, selling price $= 10 \times 1.6$

$$= 16$$

$\therefore$ The selling price of rice per kg is ₹ 16.

Hence, the correct option is (C).

54. Given:

The average speed of train $= 120\ km/hr$

Distance $= 720\ km$

Train stopping for 4 minutes after every $80\ km$

As we know,

Distance $=$ Speed $\times$ Time

where d is Distance s is Speed t is Time

According to the question, we have

The time taken by train is $t = \frac{720}{120}$

$$\Rightarrow t = 6\ hr$$

Number of stops in $720\ km = \left(\frac{720}{80}\right) - 1$

$\Rightarrow$ Number of stops $= 9 - 1$

$\Rightarrow$ Number of stops $= 8$

Total time of stopping $= 8 \times 4$

$\Rightarrow$ Total time of stopping $= 32\ min$

$\therefore$ The total time to cover $720\ km$ is $6\ hr\ 32$ min.

Hence, the correct option is (C).

55. Given:

The cost of leveling a circular park at ₹ 6.50 per m^2 is ₹ $36,036$.

As we know,

Area of a circle $= \pi r^2$

Perimeter of a circle $= 2\pi r$

Let the radius of the circular park be r.

According to the question,

$$\frac{22}{7} \times r^2 \times 6.5 = 36036$$

$$\Rightarrow r^2 = 5544 \times \frac{7}{22}$$

$$\Rightarrow r^2 = 1764$$

$$\Rightarrow r = 42$$

Now,

Required cost $= 2 \times \frac{22}{7} \times 42 \times 18$

$$= 2 \times 22 \times 6 \times 18$$

$$= 4752$$

$\therefore$ The cost (in ₹) of putting a fence around it at ₹ 18 per m is 4752.

Hence, the correct option is (B).

56. Given:

$$20 - [7 - \{4 - \left(8 - 6 \overline{+ 3}\right)\}]$$

Using the BODMAS rule to solve the above expression, we get

$$20 - [7 - \{4 - \left(8 - 6 \overline{+ 3}\right)\}]$$

$$= 20 - [7 - \{4 - (8 - 9)\}]$$

$$= 20 - [7 - \{4 - (-1)\}]$$

$$= 20 - [7 - \{4 + 1\}]$$

$$= 20 - [7 - 5]$$

$$= 20 - 2$$

$$= 18$$

$\therefore$ Required answer is 18.

Hence, the correct option is (D).

57. Given:

An article was sold at $\frac{5}{8}$ of its cost price.

As we know,

$$\text{Loss } \% = \left(\frac{\text{Loss}}{\text{Cost price}}\right) \times 100$$

Let the cost price of the article be $8x$

So, selling price $= 8x \times \dfrac{5}{8}$

$= 5x$

Loss $= 8x - 5x$

$= 3x$

Loss $\% = \left(\dfrac{3x}{8x}\right) \times 100$

$= 37.5$

$\therefore$ The loss percent is 37.5.

Hence, the correct option is (C).

58. Given:

Numbers are 90 and 160

$\dfrac{1}{3}^{rd}$ of $90 = 90 \times \left(\dfrac{1}{3}\right)$

$= 30$

$\dfrac{3}{8}^{th}$ of $160 = 160 \times \left(\dfrac{3}{8}\right)$

$= 60$

Difference $= 60 - 30$

$= 30$

Required $\% = \left(\dfrac{30}{60}\right) \times 100$

$= 50\%$

$\therefore$ Required answer is 50%.

Hence, the correct option is (B).

59. Given:

The sum of three numbers is 172.

Ratio of the first number to the second number is $3:5$ and that of the second number to the third number is $7:6$

Let three numbers are a, b and c

$\Rightarrow a:b = 3:5 = 21:35$

$\Rightarrow b:c = 7:6 = 35:30$

$\Rightarrow a:b:c = 21:35:30$

Now,

$a + b + c = 172$

$\Rightarrow 21k + 35k + 30k = 172$

$\Rightarrow 86k = 172$

$\Rightarrow k = 2$

So, $a = 21 \times 2 = 42$

$\therefore$ The first number is 42.

Hence, the correct option is (A).

60. Given:

Numbers are $21, 35, 56$

LCM of $21, 35,$ and 56 is 840

So, the five digit number must be $840x$ where x is a real number,

Now.

For $x = 10$

Number is 8400

For $x = 11$

Number is 9240

For $x = 12$

Number is 10080 which is a five digit number.

$\therefore$ The required number is 10080.

Hence, the correct option is (D).

61. Given:

A, B and C can complete a piece of work individually in $7\dfrac{1}{2}$ days, 15 days and 30 days.

As we know,

Total work = Efficiency of the workers $\times$ Time taken by them

LCM of $7\dfrac{1}{2}, 15, 30$ is 30 units i.e total work

The efficiency of A $= \dfrac{30}{7\frac{1}{2}}$

$= 4$ units/day

The efficiency of B $= \dfrac{30}{15}$

$= 2$ units/day

The efficiency of C $= \dfrac{30}{30}$

$= 1$ unit/day

Let C and B together work for x days

According to the question,

$3 \times 6 + 3x = 30$

$\Rightarrow 18 + 3x = 30$

$\Rightarrow 3x = 30 - 18$

$\Rightarrow 3x = 12$

$\Rightarrow x = 4$

So, C and B together work for 4 days

Total time $= 3 + 4$

$= 7$ days

$\therefore$ The whole work will be completed in 7 days.

Hence, the correct option is (B).

62. Given:

Ratio of two numbers a and b is $8:5$

Let numbers be $8x$ and $5x$.

According to the question,

$\frac{(8x-17)}{(5x+25)} = \frac{1}{3}$

$\Rightarrow 24x - 51 = 5x + 25$

$\Rightarrow 19x = 25 + 51$

$\Rightarrow 19x = 76$

$\Rightarrow x = 4$

So, the numbers are:

$8 \times 4 = 32$

$5 \times 4 = 20$

Sum $= 32 + 20$

$= 52$

$\therefore$ The sum of the two numbers is 52.

Hence, the correct option is (C).

63. Given:

Two numbers are, respectively, 20% and 30% less than a third number

Let the third number be $100x$.

So, the 1st number $= 100x - 100x \times 20\%$

$= 80x$

And 2nd number $= 100x - 100x \times 30\%$

$= 70x$

Required $\% = \left(\frac{70x}{80x}\right) \times 100$

$= 87.5\%$

$\therefore$ Required answer is 87.5%.

Hence, the correct option is (A).

64. Given:

The amount obtained by investing a certain sum in $4\frac{3}{4}$ years at 12% p.a. at simple interest is ₹ $2,175$ more than the simple interest on the same sum in 11 years at the same rate.

As we know,

$S.I. = \frac{(P \times T \times R)}{100}$

Amount $= P + S.I.$

Here,

$P =$ Sum

$T =$ Time

$R =$ Rate

Let the sum be ₹ P.

According to the question,

$P + P \times \left(\frac{19}{4}\right) \times \left(\frac{12}{100}\right) - P \times 11 \times \left(\frac{12}{100}\right) = 2175$

$\Rightarrow P + \frac{57P}{100} - \frac{132P}{100} = 2175$

$\Rightarrow \frac{(100P+57P-132P)}{100} = 2175$

$\Rightarrow \frac{25P}{100} = 2175$

$\Rightarrow \frac{P}{4} = 2175$

$P = 8700$

$\therefore$ The sum (in ₹) is 8700.

Hence, the correct option is (B).

65. Given:

$\frac{5}{14} \div 5\frac{3}{7}$ of $\frac{7}{19} - \left(\frac{3}{4} - \frac{4}{7}\right)$

Using the BODMAS rule to solve the above expression, we get

$\frac{5}{14} \div 5\frac{3}{7}$ of $\frac{7}{19} - \left(\frac{21-16}{28}\right)$

$= \frac{5}{14} \div 5\frac{3}{7}$ of $\frac{7}{19} - \frac{5}{28}$

$= \frac{5}{14} \div \frac{38}{7}$ of $\frac{7}{19} - \frac{5}{28}$

$$= \frac{5}{14} \div 2 - \frac{5}{28}$$

$$= \frac{5}{14} \times \frac{1}{2} - \frac{5}{28}$$

$$= \frac{5}{28} - \frac{5}{28}$$

$$= 0$$

$\therefore$ Required answer is 0.

Hence, the correct option is (A).

66. Given:

23 oranges were bought for ₹ 193.20 and sold at the rate of ₹ 108 per dozen.

Cost of 23 oranges $= 193.20$

Cost of 1 orange $= \frac{193.20}{23}$

$= 8.4$

Cost of 12 orange or 1 dozen $= 8.4 \times 12$

$= 100.8$

Profit $= 108 - 100.8$

$= 7.2$

Profit $\% = \left(\frac{7.2}{100.8}\right) \times 100$

$= 7.14\% \approx 7.1\%$

$\therefore$ The profit percentage correct to one decimal place is 7.1%.

Hence, the correct option is (C).

67. Given:

A cyclist covers a distance of 17 km in 2 h.

As we know,

$$\text{Speed} = \frac{Distance}{time}$$

Speed of the cyclist $= \frac{17}{2}$

$= 8.5$ km/h

$\therefore$ His speed (in km/h) is 8.5.

Hence, the correct option is (B).

68. Given:

A sum of ₹ $1,800$ gives a simple interest of ₹ 360 in 3 years 4 months.

As we know,

$$S.I = \frac{(P \times T \times R)}{100}$$

Here,

$P = $ Sum

$T = $ Time

$R = $ Rate

3 years and 4 months $= \left(3 + \frac{4}{12}\right)$ years or $3\frac{1}{3}$ years

Now,

Let the rate of interest be R

So,

$$360 = \frac{\left(1800 \times \frac{10}{3} \times R\right)}{100}$$

$$\Rightarrow 360 = \frac{6000R}{100}$$

$$\Rightarrow 360 = 60R$$

$$\Rightarrow R = \frac{360}{60}$$

$$= 6$$

$\therefore$ The rate of interest per annum is 6%.

Hence, the correct option is (C).

69. Given:

Marked price $= $ ₹ 1200

Discount offered $= 10\%$

Net selling price $= $ ₹ 945

As we know,

Additional Discount $\% = $
$$\frac{\text{(Amount after first Discount - Net selling Price)}}{\text{(Amount after first Discount)}} \times 100$$

After first Discount $= 1200 \times 90\%$

$= 1080$

Additional Discount $\% = \left[\frac{(1080 - 945)}{1080}\right] \times 100$

$= \left(\frac{135}{1080}\right) \times 100$

$= 12.5\%$

$\therefore$ Required answer is 12.5%.

Hence, the correct option is (B).

70. Given:

The average salary of workers in an organisation is ₹ $9,000$.

The average salary of 8 workers is ₹ $14,000$ and the average salary of the rest is ₹ $5,000$.

As we know,

Sum of observation $=$ average $\times$ number of observation

Let the number of workers be x.

According to the question,

$9000 \times x = 14000 \times 8 + 5000(x - 8)$

$\Rightarrow 9000x = 112000 + 5000x - 40000$

$\Rightarrow 9000x - 5000x = 112000 - 40000$

$\Rightarrow 4000x = 72000$

$\Rightarrow x = \dfrac{72000}{4000}$

$\Rightarrow x = 18$

$\therefore$ The total number of employees is 18.

Hence, the correct option is (A).

71. Given:

The cost price of the table and chair is 2200.

Let be assume the cost price of the chair is x and the cost price of the table is y.

$\Rightarrow x + y = 2200 \ldots$(i)

Now,

$0.95x + 1.15y = 1.04 \times 2200$

$\Rightarrow 95x + 115y = 228800$

$\Rightarrow 19x + 23y = 45760 \ldots$(ii)

By solving both the equation we get,

$x = 1210, y = 990$

$\therefore$ The cost of the table is ₹ 990.

Hence, the correct option is (D).

72. Given:

The amount of 4 years is ₹ 9900 and amount of 7 years is ₹ 11700 at simple interest The rate for $2\frac{1}{4}$ is $9\frac{2}{3}\%$

As we know,

Simple interest $= \dfrac{P \times R \times T}{100}$

Amount of 4 year $= P\left(1 + \dfrac{4R}{100}\right)$

Amount of 7 year $= P\left(1 + \dfrac{7R}{100}\right)$

$P\left(1 + \dfrac{4R}{100}\right) = 9900 \ldots$(i)

$P\left(1 + \dfrac{7R}{100}\right) = 11700 \ldots$(ii)

Subtract equation (i) from (ii)

We get,

$\Rightarrow \dfrac{3PR}{100} = 1800$

$\Rightarrow \dfrac{PR}{100} = 600$

We put the value of $\dfrac{PR}{100}$ in equation (i)

$\Rightarrow P + 4 \times 600 = 9900$

$\Rightarrow P = 9900 - 2400$

$= 7500$

So, the principle we get is 7500

The amount $= 7500 + 7500 \times \dfrac{9}{4} \times \dfrac{29}{300}$

$= 7500 + 1631.25$

$= 9131.25$

$\therefore$ The amount is ₹ 9131.25.

Hence, the correct option is (D).

73. Given:

Ratio of two numbers a and b is $5 : 8$

Let numbers be $5x$ and $8x$.

According to the question,

$\dfrac{(5x - 5)}{(8x + 3)} = \dfrac{8}{15}$

$\Rightarrow 75x - 75 = 64x + 24$

$\Rightarrow 75x - 64x = 24 + 75$

$\Rightarrow 11x = 99$

$\Rightarrow x = 9$

So, the numbers are

$5 \times 9 = 45$

$8 \times 9 = 72$

Difference $= 72 - 45$

$= 27$

$\therefore$ The difference between the two original numbers is 27.

Hence, the correct option is (D).

74. Given:

Sum of two numbers $= 35$

HCF of the given numbers $= 5$

LCM of the given numbers $= 60$

Let the two numbers be $5x$ and $5y$.

According to the questions,

$5x + 5y = 35$

$\Rightarrow x + y = 7$....(i)

LCM $= 5xy = 60$

$\Rightarrow xy = \dfrac{60}{5}$

$\Rightarrow xy = 12$....(ii)

From equation (i) and equation (ii),

$x = 3, y = 4$

So, the numbers are $15, 20$

Now,

Reciprocal $= \dfrac{1}{15}, \dfrac{1}{20}$

Now,

$\left(\dfrac{1}{15}\right) + \left(\dfrac{1}{20}\right)$

$= \dfrac{7}{60}$

$\therefore$ The sum of the reciprocal of the given numbers is $\dfrac{7}{60}$.

Hence, the correct option is (C).

75. Given:

A cylindrical tank is $80\ cm$ in diameter and $5.6\ m$ in height

As we know,

Curved surface area $= 2\pi rh$

Here,

$r =$ radius

$h =$ height

$80\ cm = 0.8\ cm$ $\left[\text{As } 1\ m = 100\ cm\right]$

Curved surface area $= 2 \times \dfrac{22}{7} \times 0.4 \times 5.6$

$= 14.08\ m^2$

Required cost $= 14.08 \times 20$

$= 281.60$

$\therefore$ The cost (in ₹) of painting the curved surface of the tank at the rate of ₹ $20/m^2$ is 281.60.

Hence, the correct option is (A).

76. Ecology: the branch of biology that deals with the relations of organisms to one another and to their physical surroundings.

Anthropology: the study of human societies and cultures and their development.

Gerontology: the scientific study of old age, the process of aging, and the particular problems of old people.

Morphology: the study of the forms of things.

Hence, the correct option is (B).

77. Correct sentence: It is a disorder that manifests usually in middle age.

Here most suitable word is 'age'.

Age: the period of time that a person, animal, or plant has lived or is expected to live.

Example: What age was he when he died?

Hence, the correct option is (B).

78. The error lies incorrect usage of the preposition 'against' in place of preposition 'to'.

Against: in opposition to.

- Example: We played football against a school from another district.

To: approaching or reaching (a particular condition).

- Example: The meat was cooked to perfection.

Thus, 'to' will be used in place of 'against'.

Correct sentence: Lack of calcium in human body usually leads to several health complications.

Hence, the correct option is (A).

79. The given sentence is a hybrid sentence where it is using two tenses simulateneously.

The given sentence depicted that during an action of a past at a particular time a different action happened. Thus, to show the second action, since it also happened in past it will be written in simple past because it doesn't have any relation with present or future.

Therefore, 'am going' needs to be replaced with 'went'.

Correct sentence: Sharada was cooking lunch when I went to give her the mobile phone.

Hence, the correct option is (D).

80. Being fond of is the most appropriate meaning of the given idiom.

Having a soft spot for: It is an idiomatic phrase that means a strong liking for someone or something.

Example: They both have a soft spot for puppies.

Hence, the correct option is (C).

81. Knowledge is the most appropriate antonym of the given word.

Ignorance: lack of knowledge or information.

- Example: We can no longer claim ignorance of the effects of plastic use.

Knowledge: facts, information, and skills acquired by a person through experience or education; the theoretical or practical understanding of a subject.

- Example: A surgeon, for example, would need to show that he or she had the right technical skills rather than simply demonstrate abstract knowledge.

Hence, the correct option is (A).

82. Someone who buys and sells goods in large amounts to shops and businesses. - Wholesaler

Wholesaler: An individual who buy or sell goods in relatively large quantities or in bulk.

Merchant: a business or an individual that sells directly to the public either from a store or through the internet.

Supplier: a person or organization that provides something needed such as a product or service.

Dealer: a person who trades in something.

Hence, the correct option is (A).

83. Chance is the most appropriate synonym of the given word.

Coincidence: an occasion when two or more similar things happen at the same time, especially in a way that is unlikely and surprising.

- Example: You chose exactly the same wallpaper as us - what a coincidence!

Chance: the unknown and unpredictable element that causes an event to result in a certain way rather than another, spoken of as a real force.

- Example: They once holidayed in Rome and chanced upon a bar called The Seamus Heaney.

Hence, the correct option is (C).

84. The error lies incorrect usage of 'are'.

The sentence is giving an information or fact about Leopards and cats. It isn't stating any action.

Thus, 'belong' will be used in place of 'are belong'.

Correct sentence: Leopards and cats belong to the same family of animals.

Hence, the correct option is (B).

85. The word 'neglected' expresses that somebody/something to fail to take care of somebody/something.

The expression 'a long time' will be used with the preposition 'for' because as a preposition it is used to express 'over a span of (time or distance)'.

Thus, the given sentence is correct and required no improvement.

Correct sentence: Neglected for a long time, the ancient monument needs immediate restoration.

Hence, the correct option is (B).

86. Correct sentence: An important purpose of education is to develop character.

Purpose: the reason for which anything is done, created, or exists.

Example: The purpose of the occasion was to raise money for medical supplies.

Hence, the correct option is (B).

87. "To be in an agitated state of suspense" is the most appropriate meaning of the given idiom.

To be on pins and needles: It is an idiomatic phrase that means in a nervous or jumpy state of anticipation.

Example: These days, the economy seems to be on pins and needles.

Hence, the correct option is (A).

88. In the given sentence a comparison is being done between the voice of Mala and Gita. Thus, to show the possession apostrophe will be used with both the nouns and to show comparison comparative degree of adjective will be used.

Thus, 'than Gita's' will be used in place of ' to Gita'.

Correct sentence: Mala's voice is much more melodious than Gita's.

Hence, the correct option is (A).

89. The error lies incorrect usage of the preposition 'of' in place of preposition 'to'.

- Let's take a look at the word 'heir' it means a person who has legal claim to a title or a throne when the person holding it dies.
- In monarchies the phrase i.e. used to show it is 'heir to the throne'.
- Thus, 'to' will be used in place of 'of'.

Correct sentence: The eldest prince is the heir to the throne.

Hence, the correct option is (A).

90. Correct sentence: He was in charge of the costumes for the play.

Charge: entrust (someone) with a task as a duty or responsibility.

Example: I have been given charge of this class.

Hence, the correct option is (A).

91. Mend is the most appropriate antoynm of the given word.

Damage: physical harm caused to something in such a way as to impair its value, usefulness, or normal function.

- Example: He maliciously damaged a car with a baseball bat.

Mend: repair (something that is broken or damaged).

- Example: They took a long time to mend the roof.

Hence, the correct option is (D).

92. Incorrigible can be used as a one-word substitute for the given group of words.

Incorrigible: (of a person or their tendencies) not able to be corrected, improved, or reformed.

Hence, the correct option is (D).

93. 'Magnificant' is the incorrectly spelt word.

Magnificant: There is no such word in the dictionary, the correct spelling is 'Magnificent' which means impressively beautiful, elaborate, or extravagant; striking.

Hence, the correct option is (A).

94. 'Unannimous', is the incorrectly spelt word.

Unannimous: There is no such word in the dictionary, the correct spelling is 'Unanimous' which means (of an opinion, decision, or vote) held or carried by everyone involved.

Hence, the correct option is (D).

95. Delight is the most appropriate synonym of the given word.

Mirth: joyfulness, gaiety, or merriment, esp. when characterized by laughter

- Example: It was at this point I rolled off the sofa with helpless mirth.

Delight: a high degree of gratification or pleasure : joy

- Example: She laughed with delight as she opened the present.

Hence, the correct option is (A).

96. 'A tic is a repeated, impulsive action, which an actor feels powerless (1)_____ or avoid.'

- Preposition: a word governing, and usually preceding, a noun or pronoun and expressing a relation to another word or element in the clause.

- To connect the adjective 'powerless' with the verb 'avoid' preposition will be used.

Correct sentence: A tic is a repeated, impulsive action, which an actor feels powerless (1)to control or avoid.

Hence, the correct option is (C).

97. Correct sentence: Only when the individual performs the tic, is tension and anxiety (2)released, within the individual with a tic disorder.

Released: allow (something) to move, act, or flow freely.

Hence, the correct option is (D).

98. Correct sentence: Tics can be (3)triggered by an emotional state or sensation, and can happen for no obvious reason.

Here most suitable word is 'triggered'. This sentence need a word which defines the breakout of emotions. So, we choose triggered in this blank.

Triggered: cause (an event or situation) to happen or exist.

Hence, the correct option is (C).

99. In the sentence, 'General types of tics (4)_____ verbal tics, '.

In the sentence, noun 'general types' is a plural noun and thus require plural verb according to the subject-verb agreement.

Include: comprise or contain as part of a whole.

Correct sentence: General types of tics (4)include verbal tics,

Hence, the correct option is (A).

100. The sentence is expressing the general types of tics.

- Tic: a habitual spasmodic contraction of the muscles, most often in the face.

- It mentions two tics i.e. verbal and facial and remaining tics under the category of muscular tics.

- Therefore, to specify it 'other' will be used in the blank.

Correct sentence: verbal tics, facial tics and (5)other muscular tics.

Hence, the correct option is (D).

General Intelligence and Reasoning

Q.1 Five friends, P, Q, R, S and T are sitting in a row facing south. Q is sitting in the centre position. P is sitting at the west end. T and R are sitting on one side of Q. Two persons are sitting between P and R. Who is sitting between Q and P?

A. Q   **B.** T   **C.** S   **D.** R

Q.2 Direction: Select the option that is related to the third term in the same way as the second term isrelated to the first term.

Bhubaneswar : Odisha :: Aizawl : ?

A. Mizoram   **B.** Meghalaya
C. Manipur   **D.** Tripura

Q.3 Direction: Select the number from among the given options that can replace the question mark(?) in the following series.

19, 23, 32, 48, 73, ?

A. 109   **B.** 108   **C.** 111   **D.** 103

Q.4 Direction: Study the given pattern carefully and select the number that can replace the question mark (?) in it.

13	26	39
30	42	?
17	16	15

A. 40   **B.** 45   **C.** 54   **D.** 60

Q.5 In a certain code language, 'ARROW' is written as 'FOOSE' and 'GERM' is written as'THOR'. How will 'MOWER' be written in that language?

A. SHORE   **B.** ROSHE   **C.** RSEHO   **D.** HORSE

Q.6 Direction: Select the combination of letters that when sequentially placed in the blanks of the given series will complete the series.

C 2 _ X 2 C C _ X X 2 _ C 2 _ X _ C

A. C2X2X   **B.** X2CX2   **C.** AXX2C   **D.** XCX2C

Q.7 The sequence of folding a piece of paper and the manner in which the folded paper has been cut is shown in the following figures. How would this paper look when unfolded?

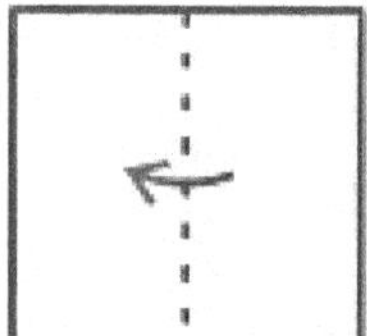 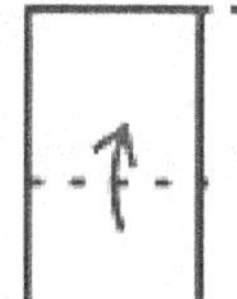 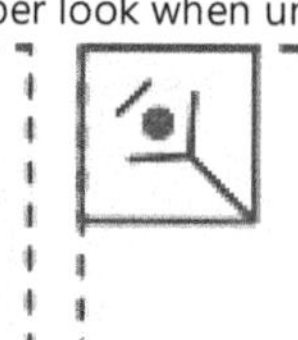

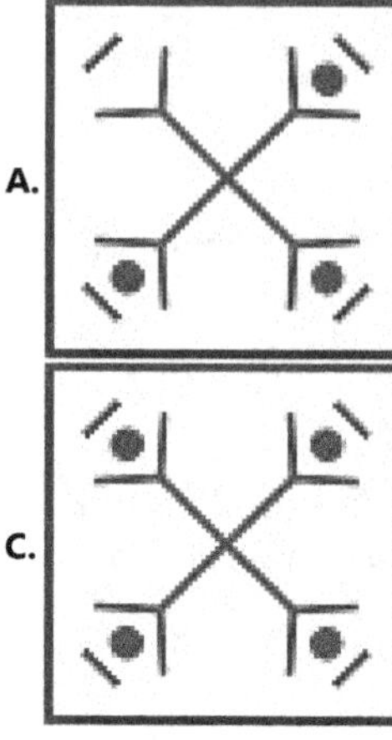 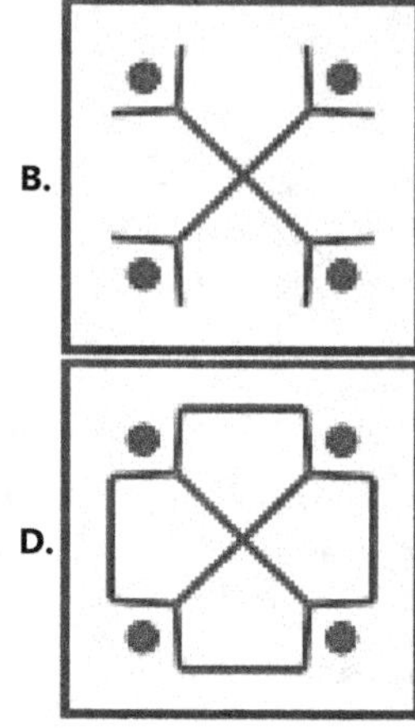

Q.8 Direction: Select the letter-cluster from among the given options that can replace the questionmark (?) in the following series.

SKH, PMG, MOF, JQE, ?

A. GSD   **B.** SDF   **C.** GTD   **D.** HSD

Q.9 Four letter-clusters have been given, out of which three are alike in some manner andone is different. Select the letter-cluster that is different.

A. HIJ   **B.** QRS   **C.** DEF   **D.** NMP

Q.10 Eight friends, A, B, C, D, E, F, G and H, are sitting in a straight line, all facing the north.F is sitting between D and G. B is sitting between H and A. E is third to the left of G. Gis sitting at one of the corners. H is third to the left of C. Who is sitting between A andE?

A. B   **B.** H   **C.** D   **D.** C

Q.11 Two different positions of the same dice marked with the letters/symbols X, $, Y, &, Z and @ are shown.

Select the letter/symbol that will be on the face opposite to the face having the symbol $.

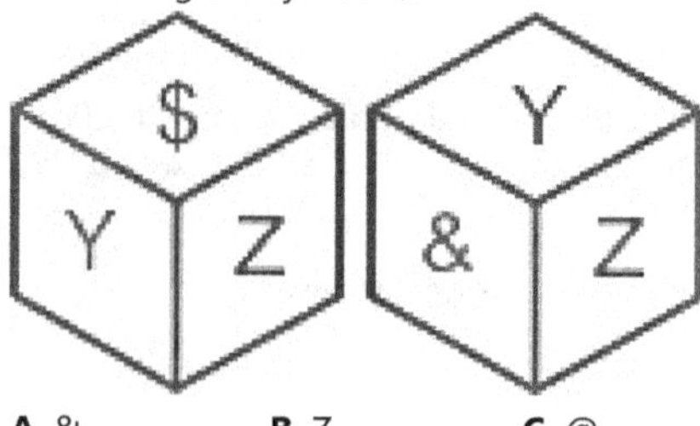

A. &   **B.** Z   **C.** @   **D.** X

Q.12 In a certain code language, 'India is my country' means '8573', 'Sam is my friend'means '8634', 'My country' means '73' and 'Team India' means '59'. What number is thecode for 'Country'?

A. 5   **B.** 7   **C.** 8   **D.** 3

Q.13 'R+S' means 'R is the daughter of S'. 'R–S' means 'R is the husband of S'.'R × S'means 'R is the brother of S'. If 'T × V + Z', then which of the following options is true?

A. T is the uncle of Z.

B. T is the father of Z.

C. T is the son of Z.

D. T is the brother of Z.

Q.14 Direction: Select the correct option that indicates the arrangement of the given words in theorder in which they appear in an English dictionary.

1. Prestige, 2. Pristine, 3. Prescribe, 4. Prepaid, 5. Premium

A. 4, 5, 3, 2, 1   **B.** 5, 3, 4, 1, 2

C. 5, 4, 3, 1, 2   **D.** 4, 5, 3, 1, 2

Q.15 Direction: Select the option that is related to the third term in the same way as the second term isrelated to the first term.

BLOCK : LBPKC :: MARGIN : ?

A. OHQHBL   **B.** OHBHQL

C. OBHQHL   **D.** OHHQBL

Q.16 Direction: Select the option in which the given figure is embedded (rotation is NOT allowed).

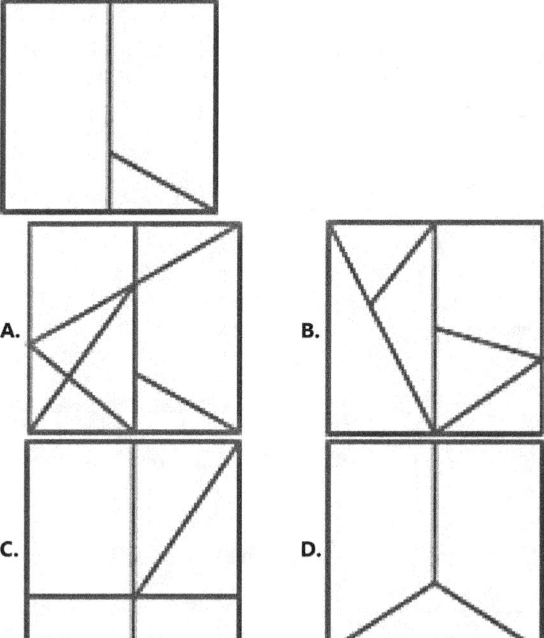

Q.17 Direction: Select the number from among the given options that can replace the question mark(?) in the following series.

$$24, 40, 64, 104, ?, 312$$

A. 228   **B.** 176   **C.** 154   **D.** 168

Q.18 In the following Venn diagram, the circle represents 'vegetables', the triangle represents 'roots', the square represents 'hard soil', and the rectangle represents 'summer'. Which of the following letters represents root vegetables that grow in summer but NOT in hard soil?

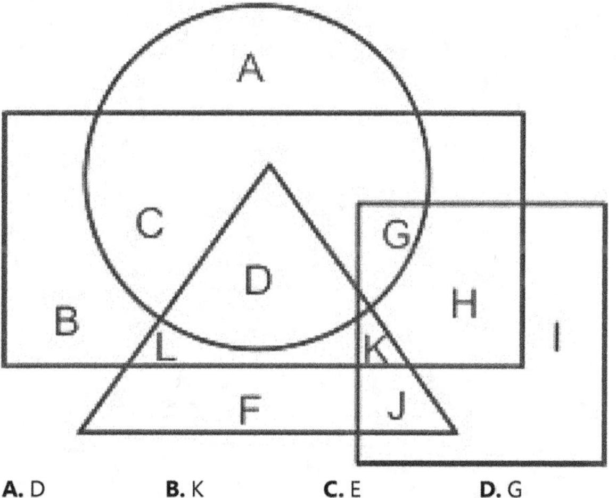

A. D   **B.** K   **C.** E   **D.** G

Q.19 Direction: Select the option that is related to the third number in the same way as the secondnumber is related to the first number.

$$31 : 90 : : 43 : ?$$

A. 130   **B.** 125   **C.** 102   **D.** 75

Q.20 Direction: Read the given statements and conclusions carefully. Assuming that the informationgiven in the statements is true, even if it appears to be at variance with commonlyknown facts, decide which of the given conclusions logically follow(s) from thestatements.

Statements:

All blues are whites.

Some whites are greys.

Conclusions:

I. All greys are whites.

II. All greys are blues.

A. Neither conclusion I nor conclusion II follows

B. Only conclusion I follows

C. Only conclusion II follows

D. Both the conclusions follow

Q.21 When a number is added to its multiple of 5 and its square, the sum of these threenumbers is 91. Find the number.

A. 9   **B.** 11   **C.** 7   **D.** 6

Q.22 In a certain code language, 'CIRCLE' is written as 'DLWAHY'. How will 'SQUARE' bewritten in that language?

A. TTPNKY   **B.** TNZYVY

C. TTZYNY   **D.** TNPYVY

Q.23 In an imaginary mathematical system, symbol ' − ' stands for addition, symbol ' + ' standsfor division, symbol ' × ' stands for subtraction, and symbol ' ÷ ' stands for multiplication.All other rules of mathematics are the same as in the existing system. What is thevalue of the following expression?

$$240 \times 72 + 8 \div 24 - 6$$

A. 30   **B.** 36   **C.** 26   **D.** 19

Q.24 Direction: Select the correct mirror image of the given combination when the mirror is placed at 'PQ' as shown.

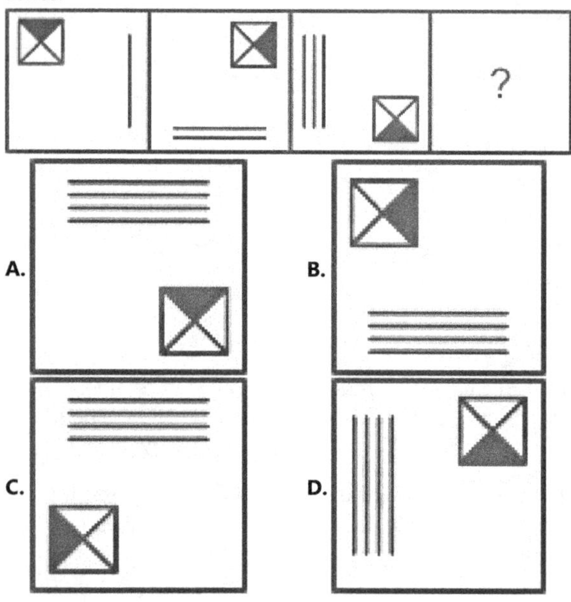

Q.25 Direction: Select the figure from among the given options that can replace the question mark (?) in the following series.

General Knowledge and General Awareness

Q.26 Which of the following articles of the Constitution of India is related to the promotion of co-operative societies?

A. 43A   **B.** 43B   **C.** 31A   **D.** 31B

Q.27 Which of the following nations was India's top trading partner in the financial year 2019-20?

A. China   **B.** The US

C. Mauritius   **D.** Japan

Q.28 After the death of Guru Gobind Singh in 1708, the Khalsa revolted against the Mughal authority under the leadership of ____.

A. Guru Angad   **B.** Guru Amar Das
C. Banda Bahadur   **D.** Guru Nanak Dev

Q.29 Who among the following founded the newspaper 'Sambad Kaumudi'?

A. Rash Bihari Bose
B. Raja Ram Mohan Roy
C. Shishir Kumar Ghosh
D. Ishwar Chandra Vidyasagar

Q.30 Which of the following set of countries participated in the Malabar Naval Exercise 2020?

A. India, Japan and the US
B. India, Israel and the US
C. India, Australia, Israel and the US
D. India, Australia, Japan and the US

Q.31 Sarayu river is a tributary of which river?

A. Pindar   **B.** Bhagirathi
C. Tons   **D.** Sharda

Q.32 On 26 January 2019, the Constitution of India completed 69 years of its existence. In these years, it was amended ____________ times (as on 12 January 2019).

A. 100   **B.** 103   **C.** 109   **D.** 106

Q.33 Which year marks the beginning of phase 2 of the Swachh Bharat Mission (Grameen)?

A. 2020-21   **B.** 2019-20   **C.** 2018-19   **D.** 2021-22

Q.34 Who among the following represents India in archery?

A. Deepika Kumari   **B.** Soumyajit Ghosh
C. Neeraj Chopra   **D.** Manika Batra

Q.35 ______ represents the high point of an eclectic art, which, in the 7th and 8th centuries under the Chalukya dynasty, achieved a harmonious blend of architectural forms from northern and southern India.

A. Kochi   **B.** Pattadakal
C. Konark   **D.** Bhimbetka

Q.36 ____________ is known as viticulture.

A. Growing vegetables, flowers and fruits
B. Cultivation of grapes
C. Breeding of fish
D. Rearing of silkworms

Q.37 Who among the following is best known for his plays 'Yayati' and 'Tughlaq'?

A. Viju Khote
B. Shreeram Lagoo
C. Girish Karnad
D. Mohammed Zahur Khayyam

Q.38 Faqir Chand Kohli, who passed away in November 2020, was known as the '____'.

A. Father of Indian Civil Services
B. Father of Indian Space Programme
C. Father of Indian Prehistory
D. Father of Indian Software (IT) Industry

Q.39 In a molecule of water, the ratio of the mass of hydrogen to that of oxygen is:

A. $1:8$ **B.** $1:4$ **C.** $1:2$ **D.** $1:16$

Q.40 Union Minister of Education launched a free mobile app called _____ , on 5September 2020.

A. EnglishPro **B.** Beelinguapp
C. Duolingo **D.** Hello Talk

Q.41 α particles are doubly charged ions of _______.
A. lithium **B.** beryllium
C. helium **D.** hydrogen

Q.42 Which of the following institutions started the 'Team Halo' initiative in November 2020?
A. World Bank
B. United Nations
C. World Health Organization
D. World Trade Organization

Q.43 With which of the following sports would you associate the team 'Kerala Blasters'?
A. Football **B.** Badminton
C. Kabaddi **D.** Cricket

Q.44 Which of the following is the traditional bamboo dance of the Mizos?
A. Moyashai **B.** Udoho
C. Cheraw **D.** Aaluyattu

Q.45 The Third Battle of Panipat between the Marathas and Ahmad Shah Durrani , the rulerof Afghanistan was fought in the year:
A. 1781 **B.** 1851 **C.** 1761 **D.** 1831

Q.46 In November 2020, the Board of Control for Cricket in India (BCCI) announced _____as Team India's kit sponsor till 2023.
A. Byju's **B.** Nike
C. MPL Sports **D.** Oppo

Q.47 Raja Todar Mal was the Revenue Minister during the reign of which of the followingMughal emperors?
A. Humayun **B.** Shah Jahan
C. Jahangir **D.** Akbar

Q.48 As per calculations done in 2011-2012, the poverty line for a person of rural India gotfixed at ___ per month.
A. ₹816 **B.** ₹752 **C.** ₹1,000 **D.** ₹687

Q.49 Five rivers from Punjab (India) enter the river _____ at Mithankot in Pakistan
A. Indus **B.** Yamuna
C. Ganga **D.** Brahmaputra

Q.50 _______ is a simple device that is used to either break the electric circuit, or tocomplete it.
A. Transistor **B.** Switch
C. Capacitor **D.** Resistor

Elementary Mathematics

Q.51 The perimeter of an equilateral triangle is $36\sqrt{3}\ cm$. Find its height.
A. $18\ cm$ **B.** $9\ cm$ **C.** $10\ cm$ **D.** $6\ cm$

Q.52 A person crosses a $1600\ m$ long street in $4\ \min$. What is his speed (in km/h)?
A. 22 **B.** 14 **C.** 20 **D.** 24

Q.53 A chair is sold for ₹ 720 after giving a discount of 10% on its marked price. The cost price of the chair is ₹ 640. If it is sold at the marked price, then the profit percentage will be:
A. 30% **B.** 20% **C.** 18% **D.** 25%

Q.54 What is 12% of 4% of 7% of 2×10^6?
A. 386 **B.** 583 **C.** 672 **D.** 121

Q.55 A solid metallic rectangular block of dimensions $112\ cm \times 44\ cm \times 25\ cm$ is melted and recast into a cylinder of radius $35\ cm$. The curved surface area (in cm^2) of the cylinder is: (Take $\pi = \dfrac{22}{7}$)
A. 7260 **B.** 6600 **C.** 7040 **D.** 6160

Q.56 Find the value of $45 - 3 \times (4\ \text{of}\ 6 + 12 \div 3 \times 6 - 4 \times 5) + 6$
A. -45 **B.** -135 **C.** -33 **D.** -30

Q.57 By selling $36\ m$ of jute, a shopkeeper gains an amount equal to the selling price of $12\ m$ of jute. Find the gain percentage.
A. 50% **B.** 40% **C.** 45% **D.** 55%

Q.58 Divide ₹ 2760 in to two parts such that when these are invested for 2 and 4 years, respectively, at the rate of 5% per annum simple interest, the amounts received are equal. What is the second part (in ₹) invested?
A. 1100 **B.** 1500 **C.** 1320 **D.** 1440

Q.59 A $725\ m$ long train passes a tunnel $235\ m$ long in 48 seconds. Find the speed of the train.
A. $42\ km/h$ **B.** $72\ km/h$
C. $36\ km/h$ **D.** $100\ km/h$

Q.60 A batsman scored 124 runs, which included 6 boundaries and 10 sixes. What percentage of his total score did he make by running between the wickets?
A. $28\frac{19}{31}\%$ **B.** $24\frac{1}{31}\%$ **C.** $32\frac{8}{31}\%$ **D.** $35\frac{3}{31}\%$

Q.61 The salaries of Ravi and Sumit are in the ratio $4:5$. If the salary of each is increased by ₹ 6000 the new ratio becomes $35:40$. What will be Sumit's increased salary?

A. ₹ 26000   **B.** ₹ 36000

C. ₹ 16000   **D.** ₹ 160000

Q.62 Anu is four times as good as Binni in completing a task. Together they finish the same task in 7 hours. In how many hours will Anu alone complete the task?

A. 22   **B.** $\frac{35}{4}$ **C.** $\frac{31}{4}$ **D.** 24

Q.63 The number of students in class IX and class X is 42 and 45, respectively. The ratio of the number of boys to girls in classes is IX and X is $9:5$ and $8:7$, respectively. What is the difference between the total number of boys and the total number of girls in both the classes taken together?

A. 11   **B.** 12   **C.** 17   **D.** 15

Q.64 P, Q and R can complete a work in 10 days, 20 days and 30 days, respectively, working alone. How soon can the work be completed if P is assisted by Q and R on alternate days?

A. 7 days   **B.** 9 days   **C.** 5 days   **D.** $6\frac{1}{2}$ days

Q.65 A loss of $10\frac{1}{2}\%$ gets converted into a profit of $11\frac{3}{5}\%$ when the selling price is increased by ₹ 132.60. The cost price (in ₹) the article is:

A. 750   **B.** 800   **C.** 600   **D.** 500

Q.66 The greatest number that will divide $398,437$ and 5425 leaving $7,12$ and 2 as remainders, respectively, is:

A. 11   **B.** 15   **C.** 17   **D.** 19

Q.67 If the average of two numbers is 13 and the square root of their product is 12, then the difference between the numbers is:

A. 10   **B.** 18   **C.** 8   **D.** 12

Q.68 The average of 10 observations is 46. It was realised later that an observation was misread as 42 in place of 142. The correct average is:

A. 52   **B.** 46   **C.** 58   **D.** 56

Q.69 The ratio of A's and B's salary is $6:7$. If B's salary is increased by $5\frac{1}{2}\%$. then his total salary becomes ₹ $1,47,700$. The salary (in ₹) of A is:

A. 1,10,000   **B.** 1,20,000

C. 1,40,000   **D.** 1,35,000

Q.70 The certain sum amounts to ₹ $9,982.50$ in $2\frac{1}{2}$ years at 12% p.a., interest compounded 10-monthly. The sum (in ₹) is:

A. 8500   **B.** 7800   **C.** 8000   **D.** 7500

Q.71 As nine-digit number $89563x87y$ is divisible by 72. What is the value of $\sqrt{7x - 3y}$?

A. 8   **B.** 5   **C.** 6   **D.** 4

Q.72 The value of $3 \times 7 + 5 - 6 \div 3 - 9 + 45 \div 5 \times 4 - 45$ is:

A. 9   **B.** 6   **C.** 7   **D.** 36

Q.73 A TV was available for ₹ $14,500$. The price came down to ₹ $11,890$ during the Diwali sale. What is the percentage discount?

A. 19.56%   **B.** 19%   **C.** 18%   **D.** 17.6%

Q.74 A shopkeeper sold an article at a gain of 20%. Had he bought it for 20% less than the original cost and sold it for ₹ 10 less, he would have gained 25%. Then the Cost Price of the article is:

A. ₹ 50   **B.** ₹ 40   **C.** ₹ 60   **D.** ₹ 45

Q.75 A certain sum amounts to ₹ 13200 after 4 years and to ₹ 16400 after 8 years at the same rate per cent p.a. at simple interest. The simple interest (in ₹) on the same sum at 10% p.a. for $3\frac{1}{5}$ years will be:

A. 4000   **B.** 3200   **C.** 2500   **D.** 3500

English

Q.76 Direction: Select the most appropriate synonym of the given word.

Visible

A. Secret   **B.** Apparent

C. Vague   **D.** Hidden

Q.77 Direction: Select the most appropriate option that can substitute the underlined word in the given sentence.

Microwave ovens heat food quickly, <u>anxiously</u> and safely, but do not brown or bake food in the way that conventional ovens do.

A. Angrily   **B.** Efficiently

C. Beautifully   **D.** Accidently

Q.78 Direction: Select the most appropriate option to fill in the blank.

A _____ mind rarely meets a dead end; it continues the search for the answers.

A. peculiar   **B.** weird   **C.** curious   **D.** strange

Q.79 Direction: The following sentence has been divided into parts. One of them may contain an error. Select the part that contains the error from the given options. If you don't find any error, mark 'No error' as your answer.

She left / hers umbrella / at the office.

A. No error   **B.** hers umbrella

C. She left   **D.** at the office

Q.80 Direction: Select the option that can be used as a one-word substitute for the given group of words.

A person who knows everything:

A. Naive
B. Omniscient
C. Intelligent
D. Omnipresent

Q.81 Direction: The following sentence has been split into four segments. Identify the segment that contains a grammatical error.

Mohan told to / Sagar that he / was looking / very pale.

A. very pale
B. Sagar that he
C. Mohan told to
D. was looking

Q.82 Direction: Select the most appropriate option that can substitute the underlined segment in the given sentence. If there is no need to substitute it, select 'No substitution required'.

I'm sure he will grab the chance <u>to earn</u> some extra money.

A. No substitution required
B. of earns
C. to earned
D. to earns

Q.83 Direction: Select the option that can be used as a one-word substitute for the given group of words.

One who examines a company's financial records

A. Conductor
B. Author
C. Auditor
D. Instructor

Q.84 Direction: Select the most appropriate option to fill in the blank.

The doctor _____ her to stop eating fried food.

A. advised
B. considered
C. arranged
D. expressed

Q.85 Direction: Select the most appropriate option that can substitute the underlined segment in the given sentence. If there is no need to substitute it, select 'No substitution required'.

You need to get the cholesterol <u>from out of your system.</u>

A. out of your system
B. No substitution required
C. out your system
D. from out off your system

Q.86 Direction: Select the most appropriate option to fill in the blank.

A dialogue is a _____ between two or more people.

A. conversation
B. commission
C. convertible
D. conversion

Q.87 Direction: Select the most appropriate meaning of the given idiom.

Play for time

A. To do something in the stipulated time
B. To make excuses or do things to gain time
C. To play something for the sake of old times
D. To play music in the time provided

Q.88 Direction: Select the INCORRECTLY spelt word.

A. Aniversary
B. Felicitate
C. Congratulations
D. Response

Q.89 Direction: Select the most appropriate meaning of the given idiom.

To breathe one's last

A. To take a major decision
B. To give final verdict
C. To make a plot
D. To die

Q.90 Direction: Select the INCORRECTLY spelt word.

A. Delivery
B. Stationary
C. Dictionery
D. Voluntary

Q.91 Direction: The following sentence has been split into four segments. Identify the segment that contains a grammatical error.

Neither the manager / nor the employees was / aware of the / shortage of raw materials

A. Neither the manager
B. shortage of raw materials
C. nor the employees was
D. aware of the

Q.92 Direction: Select the option that can be used as a one-word substitute for the given group of words.

Anything that leads to death

A. Scary
B. Serious
C. Fatal
D. Ominous

Q.93 Direction: Select the most appropriate ANTONYM of the given word.

Vital

A. Critical
B. Trivial
C. Manual
D. Crucial

Q.94 Direction: Select the most appropriate ANTONYM of the given word.

Precarious

A. Safe
B. Dangerous
C. Uncertain
D. Perilous

Q.95 Direction: Select the most appropriate SYNONYM of the given word.

Threat

A. Suggestion
B. Proof
C. Attention
D. Risk

Ques (96-100):Direction: In the following passage, some words have been deleted. Read the passage carefully and select the most appropriate option to fill in each blank.

When the air is clear, the sunset (1)_____ yellow, because the light from the sun has passed a long distance through the air and the blue light (2)_____ scattered away. If the air is polluted with small particles, natural (3)_____ otherwise, the sunset will be more red. Sunsets over the sea may also be orange, (4)_____ salt particles in the air. The sky (5)_____ the sun is seen reddened, as well as the light coming directly from the sun.

Q.96 Select the most appropriate option to fill in blank no. (1).

A. is
B. appears
C. has appeared
D. appeared

Q.97 Select the most appropriate option to fill in blank no. (2).

A. has   **B.** was   **C.** will be   **D.** has been

Q.98 Select the most appropriate option to fill in blank no. (3).

A. if   **B.** but   **C.** or   **D.** and

Q.99 Select the most appropriate option to fill in blank no. (4).

A. for   **B.** due to   **C.** because   **D.** as

Q.100 Select the most appropriate option to fill in blank no. (5).

A. across   **B.** through   **C.** along   **D.** around

// Smart Answer Sheet //

Correct — Percentage of students who answered correctly. **Skipped** — Percentage of students who skipped.

Q.	Ans.	Correct / Skipped
1	C	57.15 % / 30.26 %
2	A	87.78 % / 11.75 %
3	A	87.44 % / 10.38 %
4	C	57.64 % / 37.02 %
5	C	44.35 % / 54.72 %
6	B	23.13 % / 69.85 %
7	C	47.53 % / 34.1 %
8	A	82.36 % / 13.55 %
9	D	45.72 % / 36.84 %
10	D	24.01 % / 73.96 %
11	A	69.42 % / 30.15 %
12	B	26.44 % / 69.38 %
13	C	24.41 % / 73.75 %
14	C	50.41 % / 45.23 %
15	D	19.67 % / 72.32 %
16	A	15.46 % / 76.66 %
17	B	13.38 % / 82.5 %
18	A	62.22 % / 30.98 %
19	C	47.71 % / 42.98 %
20	A	86.97 % / 12.66 %
21	C	24.74 % / 69.58 %
22	C	40.7 % / 42.87 %
23	A	68.66 % / 30.36 %
24	D	63.18 % / 35.37 %
25	C	64.77 % / 31.4 %
26	B	81.55 % / 16.55 %
27	B	76.55 % / 21.73 %
28	C	41.14 % / 46.99 %
29	B	57.84 % / 32.8 %
30	D	83.96 % / 15.02 %
31	D	87.87 % / 10.77 %
32	B	85.29 % / 13.14 %
33	A	67.12 % / 30.0 %
34	A	67.26 % / 30.52 %
35	B	57.26 % / 38.78 %
36	B	44.82 % / 46.18 %
37	C	56.02 % / 34.58 %
38	D	64.17 % / 35.14 %
39	A	62.55 % / 36.34 %
40	A	68.16 % / 31.47 %
41	C	80.29 % / 10.57 %
42	B	56.19 % / 35.79 %
43	A	53.44 % / 39.71 %
44	C	68.12 % / 30.53 %
45	C	42.66 % / 40.85 %
46	C	69.78 % / 30.06 %
47	D	55.18 % / 40.79 %
48	A	78.9 % / 20.12 %
49	A	79.55 % / 18.71 %
50	B	79.61 % / 13.82 %
51	A	58.12 % / 38.83 %
52	D	65.0 % / 34.34 %
53	D	32.5 % / 67.31 %
54	C	83.63 % / 11.87 %
55	C	45.76 % / 46.58 %
56	C	80.08 % / 17.51 %
57	A	44.27 % / 32.09 %
58	C	28.12 % / 70.23 %
59	B	53.43 % / 35.11 %
60	C	68.37 % / 31.4 %
61	C	46.84 % / 50.98 %
62	B	60.07 % / 31.09 %
63	D	52.81 % / 30.61 %
64	A	13.58 % / 72.74 %
65	C	58.97 % / 31.79 %
66	C	42.03 % / 45.44 %
67	A	66.2 % / 31.9 %
68	D	82.36 % / 10.08 %
69	B	62.01 % / 31.05 %
70	D	23.73 % / 72.52 %
71	C	66.43 % / 31.49 %
72	B	78.94 % / 13.45 %
73	C	89.81 % / 10.0 %
74	A	62.28 % / 36.29 %
75	B	52.42 % / 32.67 %
76	B	89.29 % / 10.37 %
77	B	25.97 % / 70.12 %
78	C	40.85 % / 34.23 %
79	B	82.42 % / 17.54 %
80	B	52.07 % / 35.16 %

Q.	Ans.	Correct	Skipped
81	C	76.54 %	21.38 %
82	A	57.46 %	40.45 %
83	C	81.47 %	12.03 %
84	A	50.28 %	47.71 %

Q.	Ans.	Correct	Skipped
85	A	41.63 %	49.37 %
86	A	83.45 %	14.13 %
87	B	62.38 %	31.21 %
88	A	85.16 %	12.85 %

Q.	Ans.	Correct	Skipped
89	D	66.35 %	33.31 %
90	C	86.16 %	11.66 %
91	C	63.59 %	30.47 %
92	C	89.01 %	10.66 %

Q.	Ans.	Correct	Skipped
93	B	43.53 %	53.97 %
94	A	51.17 %	35.73 %
95	D	40.29 %	42.19 %
96	B	47.36 %	43.02 %

Q.	Ans.	Correct	Skipped
97	D	55.42 %	37.13 %
98	C	79.13 %	12.35 %
99	B	41.46 %	43.0 %
100	D	55.74 %	35.84 %

//Hints and Solutions//

1. Total five friends facing south: P, Q, R, S and T

1. Q is sitting in the centre position.

2. P is sitting at the west end.

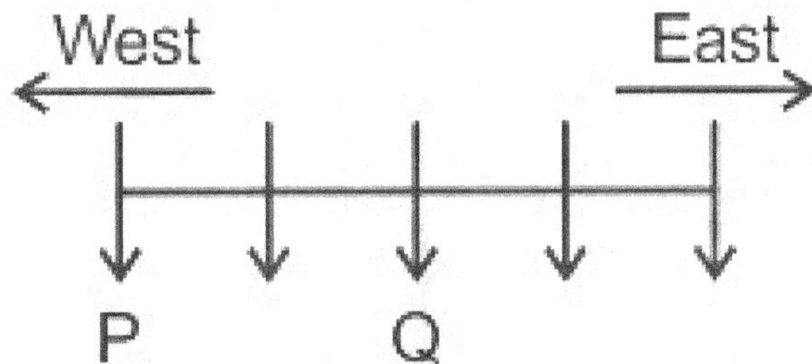

3. Two persons are sitting between P and R.

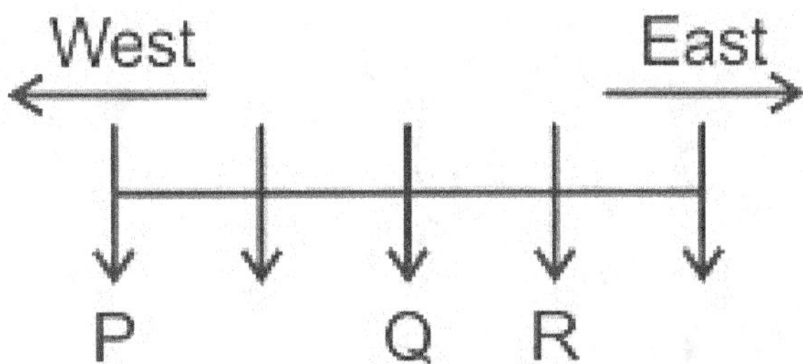

4. T and R are sitting on one side of Q.

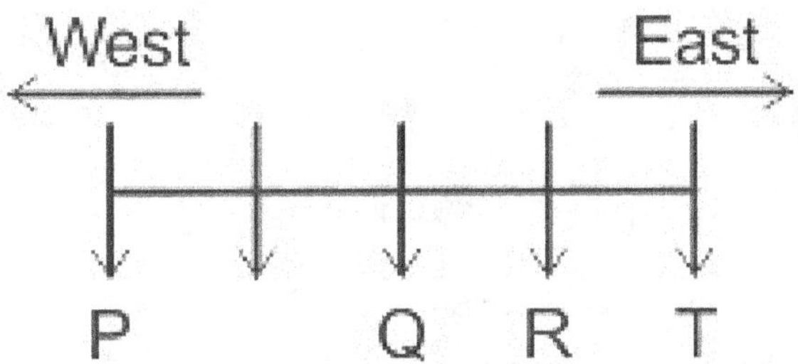

The final sitting arrangement is

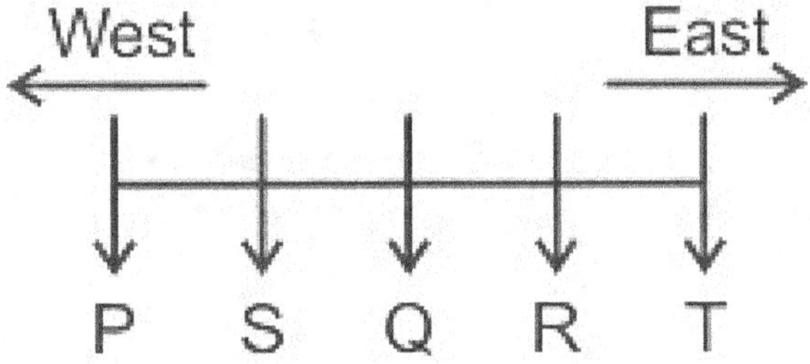

So, 'S' is sitting between Q and P.

Hence, the correct option is (C).

2. The logic follows here is:

Bhubaneswar : Odisha → Bhubaneswar city is the capital of Odisha state of India.

Similarly,

Aizawl : Mizoram → Aizawl city is the capital of Mizoram state of India.

So, 'Mizoram' is the correct answer.

Hence, the correct option is (A).

3. The pattern followed here is:

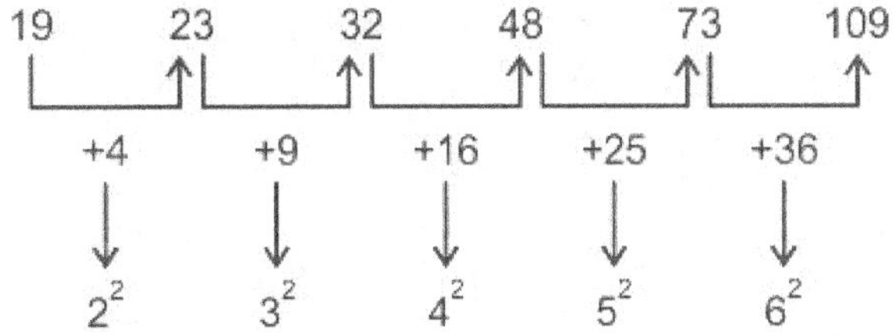

So, 109 is the correct answer.

Hence, the correct option is (A).

4. Given:

13	26	39
30	42	?
17	16	15

Here the pattern followed in each column is:

1st number $+ 3^{rd}$ number $= 2^{nd}$ number

Column 1: $13, 30, 17$

1st number $+ 3^{rd}$ number

$= 13 + 17$

$= 30 \rightarrow 2^{nd}$ number

Column 2: $26, 42, 16$

1st number $+ 3^{rd}$ number

$= 26 + 16$

$= 42 \rightarrow 2^{nd}$ number

Similarly,

Column 3: $39, ?, 15$

1st number $+ 3^{rd}$ number

$= 39 + 15$

$= 54 \rightarrow 2^{nd}$ number

So, 54 is correct answer.

Hence, the correct option is (C).

5. The logic followed here is:

'ARROW' is written as 'FOOSE'

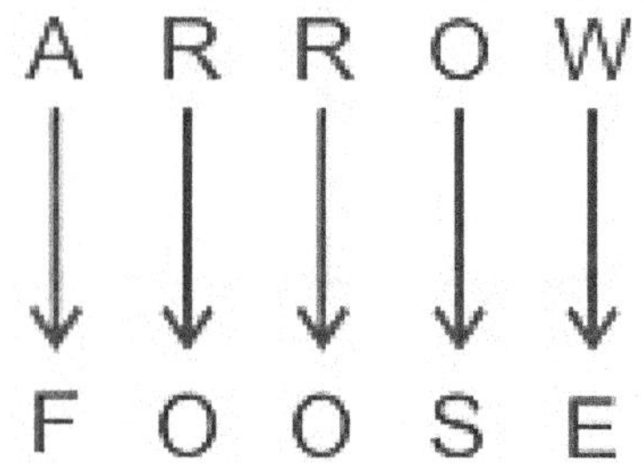

'GERM' is written as 'THOR'

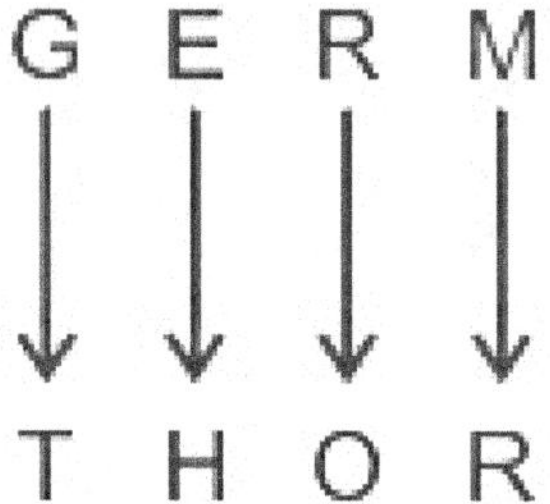

Similarly,

'MOWER' = ?

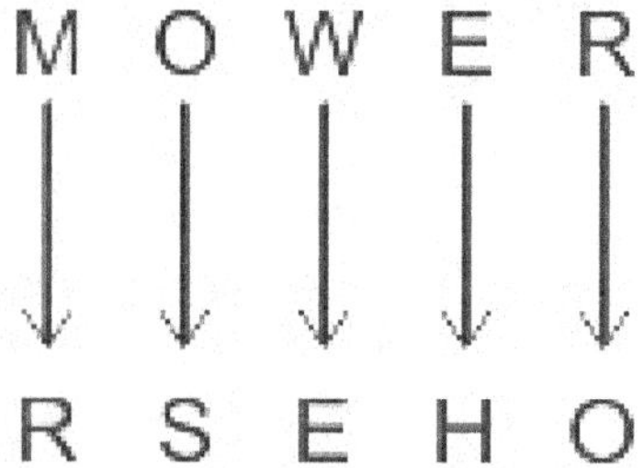

So, MOWER is coded as 'RSEHO'.

Hence, the correct option is (C).

6. Given:

C 2 _ X 2 C C _ X X 2 _ C 2 _ X _ C

By checking options and substituting accordingly.

Options (A) C2X2X → C 2 C X 2 C / C 2 X X 2 X / C 2 2 X X C

Options (B) X2CX2 → C 2 X X 2 C / C 2 X X 2 C / C 2 X X 2 C

Options (C) AXX2C → C 2 A X 2 C / C X X X 2 X / C 2 2 X C C

Options (D) XCX2C → C 2 X X 2 C / C C X X 2 X / C 2 2 X C C

Option (B) gives a cyclic pattern of C 2 X X 2 C / C 2 X X 2 C / C 2 X X 2 C

So, 'X2CX2' is the correct answer.

Hence, the correct option is (B).

7. The image obtained when the paper is unfolded is,

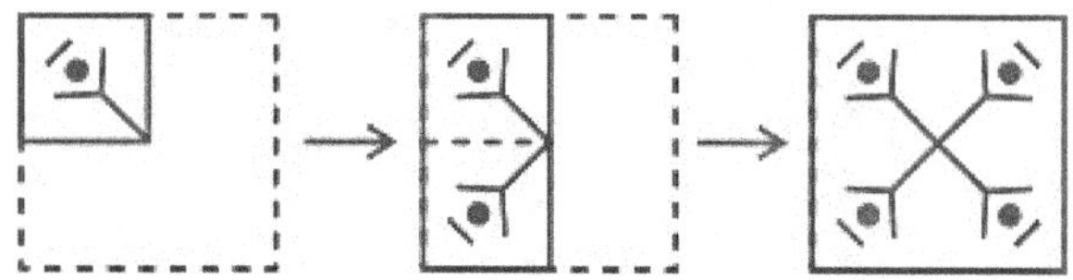

Hence, the correct option is (C).

8. The pattern followed here is:

$$S(19) \xrightarrow{-3} P(16) \xrightarrow{-3} M(13) \xrightarrow{-3} J(10) \xrightarrow{-3} G(7)$$

$$K(11) \xrightarrow{+2} M(13) \xrightarrow{+2} O(15) \xrightarrow{+2} Q(17) \xrightarrow{+2} S(19)$$

$$H(8) \xrightarrow{-1} G(7) \xrightarrow{-1} F(6) \xrightarrow{-1} E(5) \xrightarrow{-1} D(4)$$

So, "GSD" is the complete series.

Hence, the correct option is (A).

9. The pattern followed is,

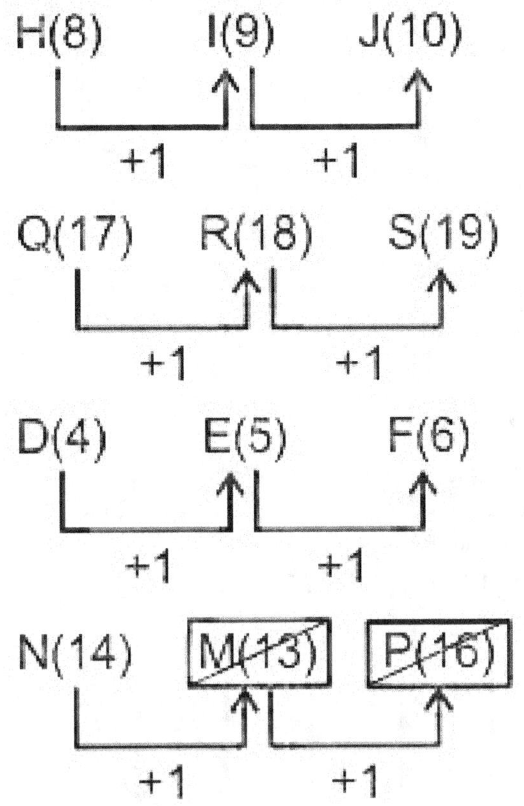

All follow the same pattern, except 'NMP'.

So, "NMP" is the odd one.

Hence, the correct option is (D).

10. Total eight friends facing north: A, B, C, D, E, F, G and H

1. E is third to the left of G. G is sitting at one of the corners.

2. F is sitting between D and G.

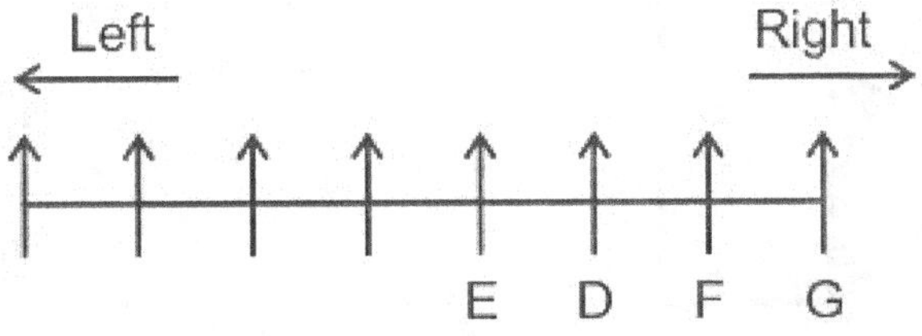

3. H is third to the left of C.

4. B is sitting between H and A.

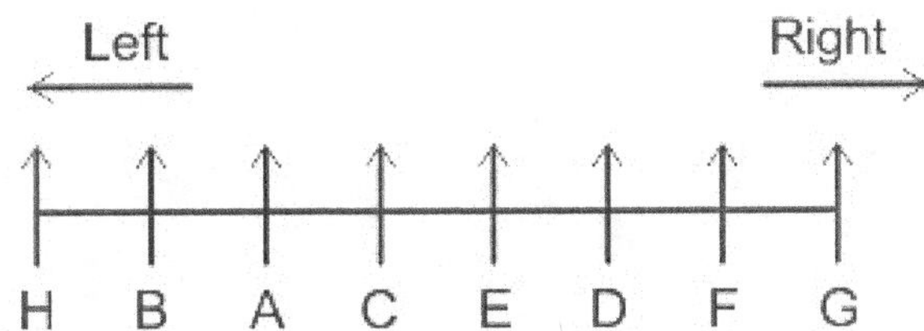

So, 'C' is sitting between A and E.

Hence, the correct option is (D).

11. Give:

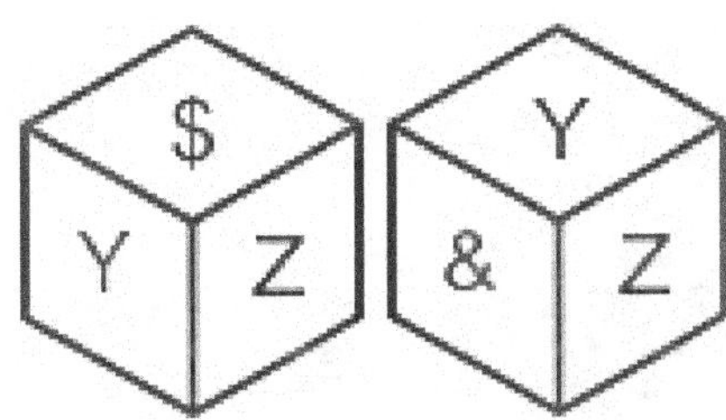

Logic: If two dice have the same two face values in the given image then the third number is opposite to each other.

In first dice and second dice.

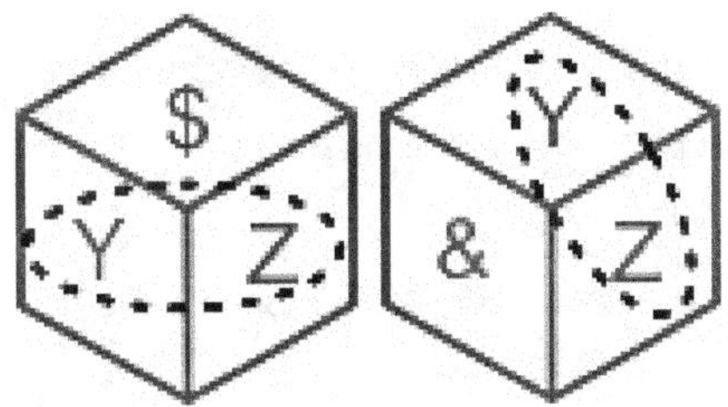

Symbols 'Y' and 'Z' are common.

So, the symbol '&' is the opposite of $.

Therefore, the correct answer is "&"

Hence, the correct option is (A).

12. According to the given information

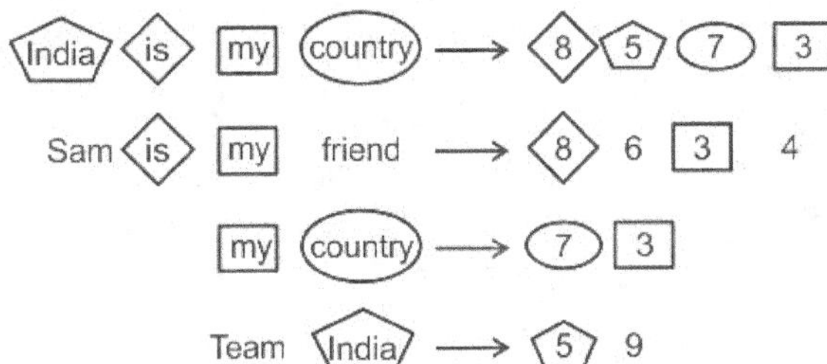

'Country' is coded as 7.

Hence, the correct option is (B).

13. Given:

'R + S' means 'R is the daughter of S'.

'R − S' means 'R is the husband of S'.

'R × S' means 'R is the brother of S'.

Let us first decode the given symbols and then draw a family tree.

R is			
Symbol	+	-	×
Meaning	daughter	husband	brother
to S			

Now break the code 'T × V + Z'

1. T × V

'T × V' means 'T is the brother of V'.

2. V + Z

'V + Z' means 'V is the daughter of Z'.

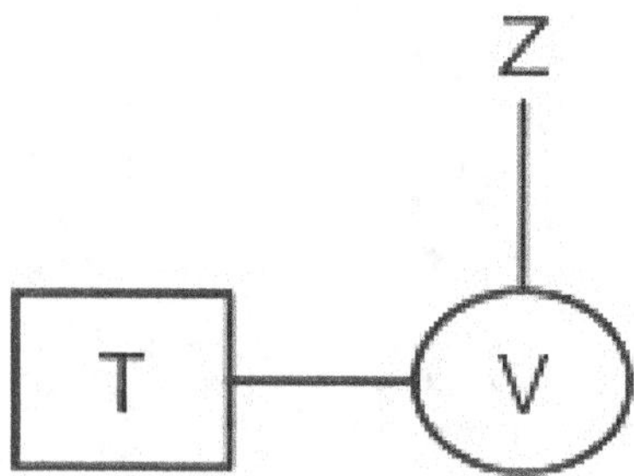

Now, check all the options

Option (A) T is the uncle of Z → False (T is the son of Z)

Option (B) T is the father of Z → False (T is the son of Z)

Option (C) T is the son of Z → True

Option (D) T is the brother of Z → False (T is the son of Z and brother of V)

Hence, the correct option is (C).

14. According to the sequence in the dictionary:

The correct order of the given words is:

Pr is common in all words;

5. Pre<u>mium</u>

4. Pre<u>paid</u>

3. Pre<u>scribe</u>

1. Pre<u>stige</u>

2. Pri<u>stine</u>

So, the correct answer is "5, 4, 3, 1, 2".

Hence, the correct option is (C).

15. The pattern followed here is:

First letters are arranged in reverse order.

And then letters are increased or decreased by +1 or -1 alternatively.

Given:

BLOCK : LBPKC

- BLOCK → Reverse order → KCOLB.
- Now letters are increased or decreased by +1 or -1 alternatively.

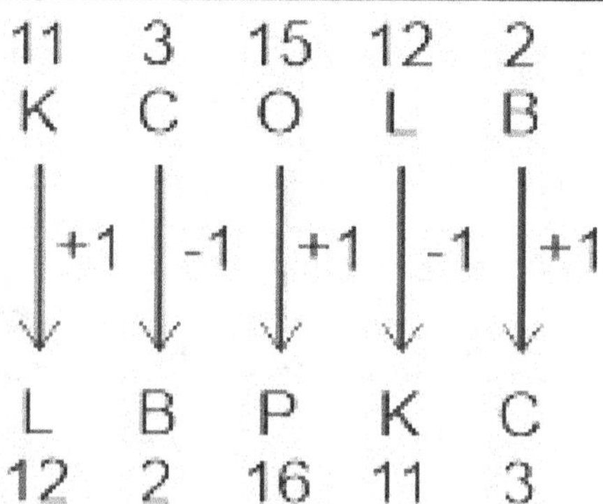

Similarly,

MARGIN = ?

- MARGIN → Reverse order → NIGRAM.
- Now letters are increased or decreased by +1 or -1 alternatively.

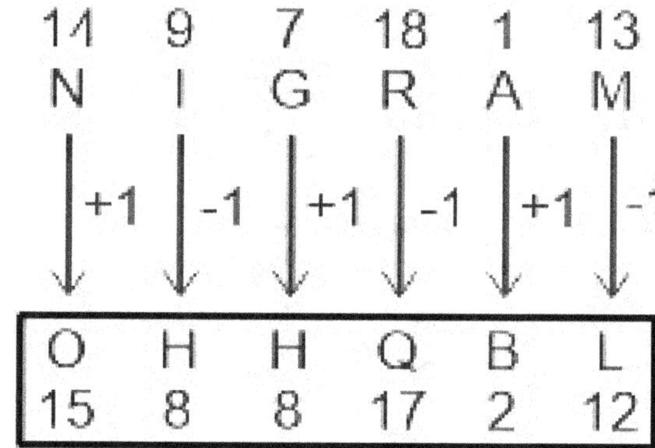

So, 'MARGIN' is coded as "OHHQBL".

Hence, the correct option is (D).

16. The embedded part of this image is:

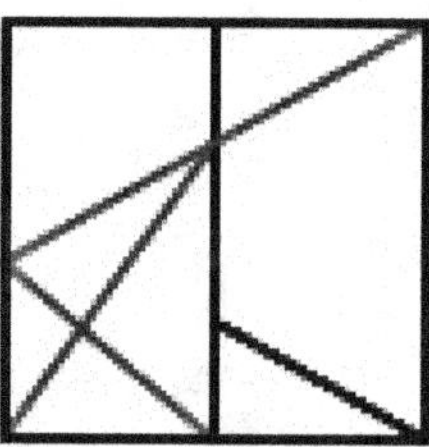

Hence, the correct option is (A).

17. The pattern followed here is:

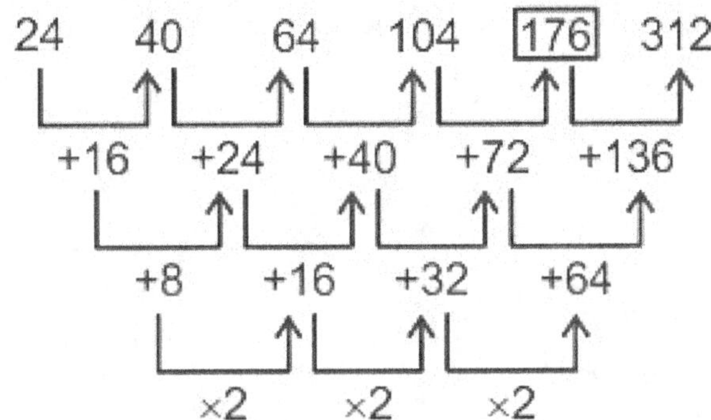

Hence, the correct option is (B).

18. The shaded part represents a set of letters representing root vegetables that grow in summer but NOT in hard soil.

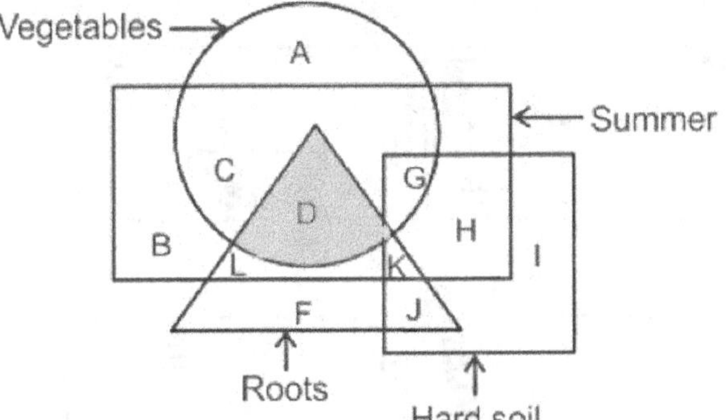

The set of letters representing root vegetables that grow in summer but NOT in hard soil = D

Hence, the correct option is (A).

19. The pattern followed here is,

Let $(1^{st}$ number : 2nd number)

1st number $+59 = 2^{nd}$ number

Now follow the steps:

$31 : 90$

$= 31 + 59$

$= 90 \rightarrow 2^{nd}$ number

Similarly,

$43 : ?$

$= 43 + 59$

$= 102 \rightarrow 2^{nd}$ number

So, 102 is correct answer.

Hence, the correct option is (C).

20. Given Statements:

All blues are whites.

Some whites are greys.

The least possible diagram for the given statements is as follows

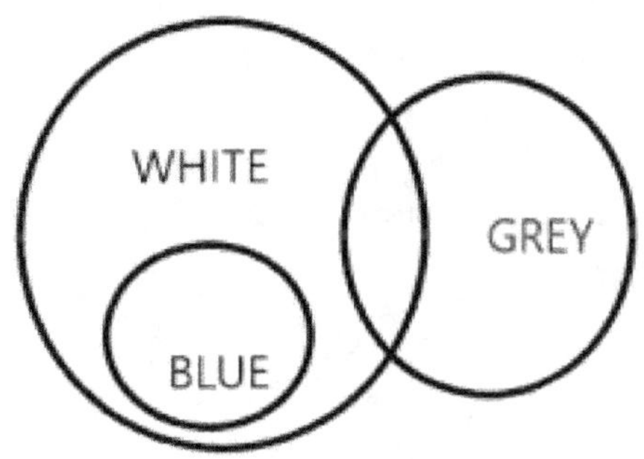

Conclusions:

I. All greys are whites → False (because statement given some whites are greys)

II. All greys are blues → False (because no direct relationship is given between greys and blues)

So, "Neither conclusion I nor conclusion II follows".

Hence, the correct option is (A).

21. We can solve this question by option method,

Option (A):

Let the number be $9,$

According to the question,

$\Rightarrow 9 + 5 \times 9 + 9^2 = 91$

$\Rightarrow 9 + 45 + 81 = 91$

$\Rightarrow 135 = 91,$ not satisfied.

Option (B):

Let the number be $11,$

According to the question,

$\Rightarrow 11 + 5 \times 11 + 11^2 = 91$

$\Rightarrow 11 + 55 + 121 = 91$

$\Rightarrow 187 = 91,$ not satisfied.

Option (C):

Let the number be $7,$

According to the question,

$\Rightarrow 7 + 5 \times 7 + 7^2 = 91$

$\Rightarrow 7 + 35 + 49 = 91$

$\Rightarrow 91 = 91,$ satisfied.

Option (D):

Let the number be $6,$

According to the question,

$$\Rightarrow 6 + 5 \times 6 + 6^2 = 91$$

$$\Rightarrow 6 + 30 + 36 = 91$$

$$\Rightarrow 72 = 91, \text{not satisfied.}$$

Now, we can see only option 3 satisfied.

$\therefore$ The number is 7.

Hence, the correct option is (C).

22. The pattern followed here is:

'CIRCLE' is written as 'DLWAHY'

$$C(3) \quad I(9) \quad R(18) \quad C(3) \quad L(12) \quad E(5)$$
$$+1 \downarrow \quad +3 \downarrow \quad +5 \downarrow \quad -2 \downarrow \quad -4 \downarrow \quad -6 \downarrow$$
$$D(4) \quad L(12) \quad W(23) \quad A(1) \quad H(8) \quad Y(25)$$

Similarly,

SQUARE = ?

$$S(19) \quad Q(17) \quad U(21) \quad A(1) \quad R(18) \quad E(5)$$
$$+1 \downarrow \quad +3 \downarrow \quad +5 \downarrow \quad -2 \downarrow \quad -4 \downarrow \quad -6 \downarrow$$
$$T(20) \quad T(20) \quad Z(26) \quad Y(25) \quad N(14) \quad Y(25)$$

So, 'SQUARE' is coded as "TTZYNY".

Hence, the correct option is (C).

23. Decoding the information,

Symbol	Meaning
$-$	Addition $(+)$
$+$	Division $(\div)$
$\times$	Subtraction $(-)$
$\div$	Multiplication $(\times)$

Given:

$$240 \times 72 + 8 \div 24 - 6$$

After replacing the signs from left to right and using the BODMAS rule,

$$240 - 72 \div 8 \times 24 + 6$$

$$= 240 - 9 \times 24 + 6$$

$$= 240 - 216 + 6$$

$$= 246 - 216$$

$$= 30$$

Hence, the correct option is (A).

24. The correct mirror image of the given figure when the mirror is held at the right side is:

Hence, the correct option is (D).

25. The logic followed here is:

1. Square rotates in a clockwise direction each corner in a box and one by one square part becomes dark in a clockwise direction

2. Line rotate in a clockwise direction and one by one line increase.

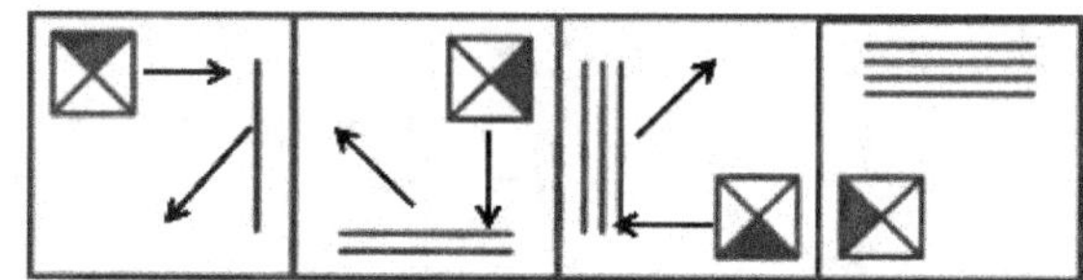

Final series is,

Hence, the correct option is (C).

26. Article 43B of the Constitution of India is related to the promotion of co-operative societies.

- According to Article 43 B of the Constitution of India, the State shall endeavor to promote voluntary formation, autonomous functioning, democratic control and professional management of cooperative societies.

- Article 43 B is included in Part IV of the constitution.

Hence, the correct option is (B).

27. The US nations was India's top trading partner in the financial year 2019-20.

- In 2019-20, the bilateral trade between the USA and India stood at USD 88.75 billion as against USD 87.96 billion in 2018-19.

- In 2018-19, the USA surpassed China to become India's top trading partner.

- The USA is one of the few countries with which India has a trade surplus.

- The bilateral trade between India and China has dipped to $81.87 billion in 2019-20 from $87.08 billion in 2018-19.

- The Government of India is also considering certain steps like framing technical regulations and quality control orders for a host of items with a view to cut import dependence on China and boost domestic manufacturing.

Hence, the correct option is (B).

28. After the death of Guru Gobind Singh in 1708, the Khalsa revolted against the Mughal authority under the leadership of Banda Bahadur.

- Banda Singh Bahadur was a Sikh warrior & a commander of the Khalsa army.
- Since creating his Khalsa rule at Punjab, Banda Singh Bahadur had abolished the zamindari regime & had given "property rights" to the land tiller.
- Banda Singh had rallied together with the lower castes & peasants of Punjab from "Delhi to Lahore" and had undertaken a vigorous "unequal struggle" against the army of Mughal for almost 8 years.
- However, in the year 1715, he was captured and put to death. There many reasons for his failure. One, the Mughal army was very strong, and second the upper castes & classes of Punjab had joined forces against Banda Singh Bahadur because of his campaign for the rural poor & the lower castes.

Hence, the correct option is (C).

29. Raja Ram Mohan Roy founded the newspaper 'Sambad Kaumudi'.

- Raja Ram Mohan Roy was the founder and editor of the following two vernacular weekly newspapers- Sambad Kaumudi in Bengali, Mirat-ul-Akhbar in the Persian language.
- Raja Ram Mohan Roy is known as 'the father of Indian renaissance'.
- He was the founder of 'Brahmo Samaj' and the man who tirelessly fought against the social evils prevailing in the Indian society.

Hence, the correct option is (B).

30. India, Australia, Japan and the US is set of countries participated in the Malabar Naval Exercise 2020.

The 24th edition of the MALABAR maritime exercise, hosted by the Indian Navy (IN) in two phases, concluded in the Arabian Sea on 20 November 2020.

Hence, the correct option is (D).

31. Sarayu river is a tributary of which river Sharda.

The Sarayu is the largest tributary of the Sharda River. It is originated from Surmool and joined Mahakali at Pancheshwar which is at the border of Nepal. It flows through the cities of Kapkot, Bageshwar and Seraghat in the state of Uttarakhand.

Hence, the correct option is (D).

32. On 26 January 2019, the Constitution of India completed 69 years of its existence. In these years, it was amended 103 times (as on 12 January 2019).

It introduces 10% reservation for Economically Weaker Sections (EWS) for admission to government as well as private, unaided educational institutions (except for minority educational institutions).It also provides for similar reservations for employment in government jobs.

Hence, the correct option is (B).

33. 2020-21 marks the beginning of phase 2 of the Swachh Bharat Mission (Grameen).

- The government has launched Swachh Bharat Mission Phase 2 with a focus on plastic waste management, biodegradable solid waste management, grey water management, and faecal sludge management.
- The mission is aimed at progressing towards target 6.2 of the Sustainable Development Goals Number 6 established by the United Nations in 2015.

Hence, the correct option is (A).

34. Deepika Kumari represents India in archery.

- Deepika added more gold medals at the 2018 Salt Lake City World Cup.
- She won the individual event and added another bronze medal in Samsun.
- The year 2021 has been fantastic for the Indian star archer who won individual and gold team medals at the Guatemala City World Cup.
- Deepika Kumari defeated Germany's Michelle Kroppen by 7-3 in the circuit final of Stage III.
- Deepika Kumari has won four silver medals (2011, 2012, 2013, 2015) and one Bronze in the 2018 World Cup.

Hence, the correct option is (A).

35. Pattadakal represents the high point of an eclectic art, which, in the 7th and 8th centuries under the Chalukya dynasty, achieved a harmonious blend of architectural forms from northern and southern India.

- Pattadakal represents the high point of eclectic art as designated by UNESCO.
- In the 7th and 8th centuries under the Chalukya dynasty, achieved a harmonious blend of architectural forms from northern and southern India.
- An impressive series of nine Hindu temples and a Jain sanctuary can be seen there.
- It is located on the west bank of the Mallaprabha River in Bagalkot district in Karnataka.

Hence, the correct option is (B).

36. Cultivation of grapes is known as viticulture.

- Viticulture is the cultivation and harvesting of grapes.
- When the grapes are being used specifically for wine production, the study of grapes can also be called viniculture.
- Both viniculture and viticulture fall under the umbrella of horticulture.

Hence, the correct option is (B).

37. Girish Karnad is best known for his plays 'Yayati' and 'Tughlaq'.

- Girish Karnad was an Indian actor, film director, Kannada writer, playwright, and a Jnanpith awardee, who predominantly worked in South Indian cinema and Bollywood.

- Girish Karnad wrote his first play 'Yayati' in 1961 at the age of 23 when he was still studying at Oxford.

- In the story of King Yayati in Mahabharata, Yayati was cursed to old age for his sexual misconduct and he tries to avert the catastrophe by demanding his son, Pooru's, youth in exchange for the curse on him. 'What makes his version of the tale so resonant, and startlingly original, is that he rejects the traditional glorification of the son's 'self-sacrifice' and, against a backdrop of lust, jealousy, and racial tensions.

Hence, the correct option is (C).

38. Faqir Chand Kohli, who passed away in November 2020, was known as the 'Father of Indian Software (IT) Industry'.

- Faqir Chand Kohli, known as the father of Indian Software Industry, passed away in November 2020.

- Mr Kohli was the founder-CEO of TCS.

- He joined Tata Electric Co. in 1951 where he helped set up the load dispatching system to manage system operations.

- He became director of Tata Electric in 1970.

- He pioneered India's IT revolution and helped the country build the $190-billion IT industry.

Hence, the correct option is (D).

39. In a molecule of water, the ratio of the mass of hydrogen to that of oxygen is $(1 : 8)$.

It is obtained by multiplying the atomic mass of each element by the number of its atoms and adding them together

1 mole of hydrogen $= 1\ gm$

1 mole of oxygen $= 16\ gm$

Water $(H_2O) = 2$ Hydrogen atoms $+1$ Oxygen atom

2 mole of hydrogen $= 2\ gm$

1 mole of oxygen $= 16\ gm$

The ratio of the mass of Hydrogen: Ratio of mass of Oxygen $=$

$$\frac{2}{16} = \frac{1}{8}$$

The ratio of the mass of Hydrogen to the mass of Oxygen is always $1 : 8$.

Hence, the correct option is (A).

40. Union Minister of Education launched a free mobile app called EnglishPro, on 5 September 2020.

- Union Minister of Education RameshPokhriyal Nishank launched EnglishPro, a free mobile app, developed by the English and Foreign Languages University, Hyderabad.

- The App has been developed by University Social Responsibility (USR) is the first-of-its-kind initiative by any university in the country and will help learners develop Indian English Pronunciation in the unique "Indian" way.

- It is an educational resource for teachers, students, and people from varied backgrounds.

Hence, the correct option is (A).

41. α particles are doubly charged ions of helium.

- α-particles consist of two protons and two neutrons.

- They are doubly-charged helium ions. Since they have a mass of 4 u, the fast-moving α-particles have a considerable amount of energy.

- An alpha particle is obtained by removing 2 electrons from a helium atom. So, an alpha particle is a doubly-charged helium ion.

Hence, the correct option is (C).

42. United Nations institutions started the 'Team Halo' initiative in November 2020.

- The United Nations along with "the Vaccine Confidence Project" of the University of London launched an initiative called 'Team Halo' to counter misinformation on the Covid-19 vaccine.

- The initiative aims to tackle misinformation by sharing information on the safety and effectiveness of vaccines via social media.

- Over 100 scientists from different countries have joined hands to tackle the issue of misinformation surrounding Covid-19 vaccines.

Hence, the correct option is (B).

43. With football sports would you associate the team 'Kerala Blasters'.

- Kerala Blasters Football Club is an Indian professional football club based in Kochi, Kerala, that competes in the Indian Super League.

- The club was established in May 2014 during the inaugural season of the Indian Super League.

- The Blasters are the three-time runners-up of the Indian Super League.

- The club is also known for its fan base, including the supporters' group called Manjappada, which has gained a reputational for being one of the most vocal and passionate fan clubs in India.

Hence, the correct option is (A).

44. Cheraw is the traditional bamboo dance of the Mizos.

- Cheraw is the traditional bamboo dance of Mizoram.

- The Cheraw or bamboo dance is a traditional dance of Mizoram.

- It is considered to be one of the oldest dances of Mizoram. The dance is believed to have emerged out of a ritual.

- In this dance form, bamboos are kept in horizontal or cross formations on the ground. Pairs of these bamboo staffs are held by six to eight people.

- The male dancers move these bamboos to a rhythmic beat while the female dancers move gracefully while stepping in and out of the bamboo formations.

- The bamboos are clapped together by the male dancers to a specific beat.

Hence, the correct option is (C).

45. The Third Battle of Panipat between the Marathas and Ahmad Shah Durrani, the ruler of Afghanistan was fought in the 1761.

The Third Battle of Panipat took place on 14 January 1761 at Panipat, between a Maratha Empire and invading forces of the King of Afghanistan, Ahmad Shah Abdali.

Hence, the correct option is (C).

46. In November 2020, the Board of Control for Cricket in India (BCCI) announced MPL Sports as U-19 Team India's kit sponsor till 2023.

- The Board of Control for Cricket in India (BCCI) announced its partnership with MPL Sports, as the new kit sponsor and official merchandise partner for the Indian Cricket Team.

- Under the newly-inked strategic partnership, MPL Sports has entered into a three-year agreement from November 2020 to December 2023.

- MPL Sports association with the BCCI begins with the upcoming India tour of Australia, 2020-21, which will see Team India sporting the new jerseys.

- The senior men and women and the Under-19 teams are also a part of the deal for the new kits.

Hence, the correct option is (C).

47. Raja Todar Mal was the Revenue Minister during the reign of Akbar Mughal emperors.

- Raja Todar Mal was one of the Navaratna in Akbar's Darbar.Raja Todar Mal introduced standard weights and measures, a land survey and settlement system, revenue districts, and officers.

- He introduced a new system of revenue known as zabt and a system of taxation called Dahshala.

- The Kashi Vishwanath Temple was rebuilt in 1585 by Todar Mal.

- The Navratnas of Akbar were as follows: Raja Birbal, Tansen, Abul Fazal, Faizi, Raja Man Singh, Raja Todar Mal, Mullah Do Piaza, Fakir Aziao-Din, Abdul Rahim Khan-I-Khana.

Hence, the correct option is (D).

48. As per calculations done in 2011-2012, the poverty line for a person of rural India got fixed at ₹816 per month.

- In the year 2011 - 12, the poverty line for a person was fixed at Rs 816 for rural areas.

- For urban areas, it is Rs. 1000 under the Suresh Tendulkar methodology.

- The poverty line in urban is quite high due to the high prices of goods and services in urban areas.

- In 2011-12, the number of poor is 26.92 crore.

Hence, the correct option is (A).

49. Five rivers from Punjab (India) enter the river Indus at Mithankot in Pakistan.

- The river Indus rises in Tibet, near Lake Mansarovar.

- Flowing west, it enters India in the Ladakh district of Jammu and Kashmir.

- It forms a picturesque gorge in this part.

- Several tributaries, the Zaskar, the Nubra, the Shyok, and the Hunza, join it in the Kashmir region.

- The Indus flows through Baltistan and Gilgit and emerges from the mountains at Attock.

- The Satluj, the Beas, the Ravi, the Chenab, and the Jhelum join together to enter the Indus near Mithankot in Pakistan.

- The major Himalayan rivers are the Indus, the Ganga, and the Brahmaputra.

- These rivers are long and are joined by many large and important tributaries. A river along with its tributaries is called a river system.

Hence, the correct option is (A).

50. Switch is a simple device that is used to either break the electric circuit, or to complete it.

- A switch is a simple device that is used to either break the electric circuit or to complete it.

- A resistor is a passive electrical component that resists the flow of electric current.

- A transistor is a semiconductor device that acts as both an amplifier and switch.

- A fuse is an electrical device for safety that removes electrical current from the circuit if the current gets too high.

Hence, the correct option is (B).

51. Given:

The perimeter of an equilateral triangle is $36\sqrt{3}\ cm$.

As we know,

Perimeter of an equilateral triangle $= 3 \times$ side

Height of an equilateral triangle $= \left(\frac{\sqrt{3}}{2}\right) \times$ side

According to the question,

$3 \times \text{side} = 36\sqrt{3}$

$\Rightarrow \text{side} = \dfrac{36\sqrt{3}}{3}$

$= 12\sqrt{3}$

So,

Height of the triangle $= \left(\dfrac{\sqrt{3}}{2}\right) \times 12\sqrt{3}$

$= 6\sqrt{3} \times \sqrt{3}$

$= 18$

So, the height of the triangle $= 18 \ cm$

∴ Its height is $18 \ cm$.

Hence, the correct option is (A).

52. Given:

A person crosses a $1600 \ m$ long street in 4 min

As we know,

$\text{Speed} = \dfrac{Distance}{time}$

1 hour $= 60$ minutes

$1 \ km = 1000 \ m$

$1600 \ m = \dfrac{1600}{1000} = 1.6 \ km$

4 min $= \dfrac{4}{60}$

$= \dfrac{1}{15}$ hour

$\text{Speed} = \dfrac{Distance}{time}$

$\Rightarrow \dfrac{1.6}{\left(\frac{1}{15}\right)} = 24 \ km/hr$

∴ His speed (in km/h) is 24.

Hence, the correct option is (D).

53. Given:

Selling price of the chair $= ₹ \ 720$

Discount $\% = 10$

Cost price of the chair $= ₹ \ 640$

As we know,

Selling price $=$ Marked price $-$ Marked price $\times$ discount $\%$

Profit $=$ Selling price $-$ cost price

Profit $\% = \left(\dfrac{\text{profit}}{\text{cost price}}\right) \times 100$

Let the marked price of the article be $10a$.

According to the question,

$10a - 10a \times 10\% = 720$

$\Rightarrow 9a = 720$

$\Rightarrow a = \dfrac{720}{9}$

$= 80$

So, the marked price of the chair $= 10 \times 80$

$= ₹ \ 800$

Now,

Profit on the chair when it is sold at marked price $= 800 - 640$

$= ₹ \ 160$

Profit $\% = \left(\dfrac{160}{640}\right) \times 100$

$= 25$

∴ The profit percentage will be 25%.

Hence, the correct option is (D).

54. Given:

The number $= 2 \times 10^6$

$10^6 = (10^2)^3$

$= 100^3$

According to the question,

Required number $= 2 \times 100^3 \times \dfrac{12}{100} \times \dfrac{4}{100} \times \dfrac{7}{100}$

$= 2 \times 100 \times 100 \times 100 \times \dfrac{12}{100} \times \dfrac{4}{100} \times \dfrac{7}{100}$

$= 2 \times 12 \times 4 \times 7$

$= 672$

∴ Required answer is 672.

Hence, the correct option is (C).

55. Given:

Dimensions of the metallic rectangular block is $112 \ cm \times 44 \ cm \times 25 \ cm$

Radius of the cylinder $= 35 \ cm$

As we know,

Volume of a cuboid $= l \times b \times h$

Volume of a cylinder $= \pi r^2 h$

Curved surface area of the cylinder $= 2\pi rh$

Here,

$l = $ length

$b = $ breadth

$h = $ height

$r = $ radius

Let the height of the cylinder be h.

According to the question,

$$112 \times 44 \times 25 = \left(\frac{22}{7}\right) \times 35^2 \times h$$

$$\Rightarrow \frac{(112 \times 44 \times 25 \times 7)}{(22 \times 35 \times 35)} = h$$

$$\Rightarrow h = 32$$

So, the height of the cylinder $= 32\ cm$

Now,

Curved surface area of the cylinder $= 2 \times \left(\frac{22}{7}\right) \times 35 \times 32$

$= 44 \times 5 \times 32$

$= 7040$

$\therefore$ The curved surface area (in cm^2) of the cylinder is 7040.

Hence, the correct option is (C).

56. Given:

$$45 - 3 \times (4 \text{ of } 6 + 12 \div 3 \times 6 - 4 \times 5) + 6$$

Using the BODMAS rule to solve the above expression, we get

$$45 - 3 \times (24 + 12 \div 3 \times 6 - 4 \times 5) + 6$$

$$= 45 - 3 \times (24 + 4 \times 6 - 4 \times 5) + 6$$

$$= 45 - 3 \times (24 + 24 - 20) + 6$$

$$= 45 - 3 \times 28 + 6$$

$$= 45 - 84 + 6$$

$$= 51 - 84$$

$$= -33$$

$\therefore$ Required answer is -33.

Hence, the correct option is (C).

57. Given:

Profit $=$ SP of $12\ m$ jute

As we know,

Profit $= SP - CP$

Profit $\% = \left(\frac{Profit}{cost\ price}\right) \times 100$

Here,

$CP = $ Cost price

$SP = $ Selling price

According to the question,

SP of $36\ m = CP$ of $36\ m + SP$ of $12\ m$

$\Rightarrow SP$ of $24\ m = CP$ of $36\ m$

So,

$$\frac{SP}{CP} = \frac{36}{24} \text{ or } \frac{3}{2}$$

So, if CP of $1\ m$ jute is Rs. 2 then its SP is Rs. 3

So, profit $=$ Rs. 1

Profit $\% = \left(\frac{1}{2}\right) \times 100$

$= 50\%$

$\therefore$ The gain percentage is 50%.

Hence, the correct option is (A).

58. Given:

Total sum $= ₹\ 2760$

Rate of interest $= 5\%$

As we know,

$$SI = \frac{(P \times T \times R)}{100}$$

Amount $= P + S.I.$

Here,

$P = $ Principal

$T = $ time

$R = $ rate

Let for the 1st part it is $₹\ x$.

So, 2nd part $= ₹\ (2760 - x)$

According to the question,

$$x + \left[\frac{(x \times 2 \times 5)}{100}\right] = (2760 - x) + \left[\frac{\{(2760 - x) \times 4 \times 5\}}{100}\right]$$

$$\Rightarrow \frac{(100x + 10x)}{100} = \frac{(276000 - 100x + 55200 - 20x)}{100}$$

$$\Rightarrow 110x = 331200 - 120x$$

$$\Rightarrow 230x = 331200$$

$$\Rightarrow x = \frac{331200}{230}$$

$\Rightarrow x = 1440$

So, 1st part $= ₹\ 1440$

So, 2nd part $= 2760 - 1440$

$= ₹\ 1320$

$\therefore$ The second part (in ₹) invested is 1320.

Hence, the correct option is (C).

59. Given:

Length of the train $= 725\ m$

Lenght of the tunnel $= 235\ m$

Time taken to cover the tunnel $= 48$ sec

As we know,

$$\text{Speed} = \frac{Distance}{time}$$

$$km/h \times \left(\frac{5}{18}\right) = m/sec$$

When a train passes a bridge/tunnel/platform, then it will cover its own length + length of that bridge/tunnel/platform

According to the concept,

The train had covered $725 + 235 = 960\ m$

Speed of the train in $m/\sec = \frac{960}{48}$

$= 20\ m/sec$

Speed of the train in $km/h = 20 \times \left(\frac{18}{5}\right)$

$= 72\ km/h$

$\therefore$ The speed of the train is $72\ km/h.$

Hence, the correct option is (B).

60. Given:

Total score of the batsman $= 124$ run

He has hitten 6 boundaries and 10 sixes

The batsman scored from boundaries $= 6 \times 4$

$= 24$ runs

The batsman scored from sixes $= 10 \times 6$

$= 60$ runs

Total runs scored by running between the wickets $= 124 - (24 + 60)$

$= 124 - 84$

$= 40$ runs

Required $\% = \left(\frac{40}{124}\right) \times 100$

$= 32\frac{8}{31}$

$\therefore$ He scored $32\frac{8}{31}\%$ of his total score by running between the wickets.

Hence, the correct option is (C).

61. Given:

Ratio of salaries of Ravi and Sumit $= 4:5$

Increased salary $= 6000$ each

New ratio of Ravi and Sumit $= 35:40$

Let the original salaries of Ravi and Sumit be Rs $4x$ and Rs $5x$ respectively.

According to the question,

$$\frac{(4x+6000)}{(5x+6000)} = \frac{35}{40}$$

$\Rightarrow 160x + 240000 = 175x + 210000$

$\Rightarrow 15x = 30000$

$\Rightarrow x = \frac{30000}{15}$

$= 2000$

Current salary of Ravi $= 4 \times 2000 = ₹\ 8000$

Current salary of Sumit $= 5 \times 2000 = ₹\ 10000$

So, increased salary of Sumit $= 10000 + 6000$

$= ₹\ 16000$

$\therefore$ Sumit's increased salary is $₹\ 16000$.

Hence, the correct option is (C).

62. Given:

Anu is four times as good as Binni in completing a task. Together they finish the same task in 7 hours.

As we know,

Total work $=$ Efficiency of the workers $\times$ time taken by them

Let the efficiency of Binni be x

So, the efficiency of Anu $= 4x$

Effective efficiency of the them $= x + 4x$

$= 5x$

Total work $= 7 \times 5x$

$= 35x$ units

Now,

Time taken by Anu to complete the work alone $= \dfrac{35x}{4x}$

$= \dfrac{35}{4}$ hours

$\therefore$ Anu alone will complete the task in $\dfrac{35}{4}$ hours.

Hence, the correct option is (B).

63. Given:

The number of students in class IX and class X is 42 and 45, respectively

The ratio of the number of boys to girls in classes is IX and X is $9:5$ and $8:7$

Number of boys in class IX $= 42 \times \left(\dfrac{9}{14}\right)$

$= 27$

Number of girls in class IX $= 42 \times \left(\dfrac{5}{14}\right)$

$= 15$

Again,

Number of boys in class X $= 45 \times \left(\dfrac{8}{15}\right)$

$= 24$

Number of girls in class X $= 45 \times \left(\dfrac{7}{15}\right)$

$= 21$

Total of boys in two classes $= 27 + 24$

$= 51$

Total of girls in two classes $= 15 + 21$

$= 36$

Difference $= 51 - 36$

$= 15$

$\therefore$ The difference between the total number of boys and the total number of girls in both the classes taken together is 15.

Hence, the correct option is (D).

64. Given:

P, Q, and R can complete a work in 10 days, 20 days, and 30 days

As we know,

Total work $=$ Efficiency of the workers $\times$ time taken by them

LCM of $10, 20, 30 = 60$ i.e total work

So,

Efficiency of P $= \dfrac{60}{10} = 6$ units/day

Efficiency of Q $= \dfrac{60}{20} = 3$ units/day

Efficiency of R $= \dfrac{60}{30} = 2$ units/day

On 1st day P and Q will complete $(6 + 3) = 9$ units

On the next day P and R will complete $(6 + 2) = 8$ units

So, in two days they will complete total $(9 + 8) = 17$ units

So, in $2 \times 3 = 6$ days they will complete $17 \times 3 = 51$ units

Now, remaining portion of $(60 - 51) = 9$ units will be complete by P and Q in $\dfrac{9}{9} = 1$ day [As 6th day P and R will work]

Total time $= 6 + 1$

$= 7$ day

$\therefore$ Required time is 7 day.

Hence, the correct option is (A).

65. Given:

A loss of $10\dfrac{1}{2}\%$ gets converted into a profit of $11\dfrac{3}{5}\%$ when the selling price is increased by ₹ 132.60

As we know,

$SP = CP + CP \times \text{Profit }\%$

$SP = CP - CP \times \text{Loss }\%$

Let CP of the article be $100a$

Now,

SP for 1st case $= 100a - 100a \times 10\dfrac{1}{2}\%$

$= 89.5a$

SP for 2nd case $= 100a + 100a \times 11\dfrac{3}{5}\%$

$= 111.6a$

According to the question,

$111.6a - 89.5a = 132.6$

$\Rightarrow 22.1a = 132.6$

$\Rightarrow a = \dfrac{132.6}{22.1}$

$\Rightarrow a = 6$

So, cost price $= 100 \times 6$

$= ₹ 600$

$\therefore$ The cost price (in ₹) the article is 600.

Hence, the correct option is (C).

66. Given:

The numbers are $398, 437, 5425$

Remainders $= 7, 12, 2$

As we know,

For this type of question, we subtract the remainders from the numbers and then take the HCF of the resulting numbers as the greatest number

Deducting the remainders from numbers we get,

$398 - 7 = 391$

$437 - 12 = 425$

$5425 - 2 = 5423$

Now,

$391 = 17 \times 23$

$425 = 17 \times 25$

$5425 = 17 \times 11 \times 29$

So,

HCF of these numbers $= 17$

$\therefore$ The greatest number is 17.

Hence, the correct option is (C).

67. Given:

The average of the two numbers is 13

The square root of their product is 12

As we know,

$(a + b)^2 = a^2 + b^2 + 2ab$

$(a - b)^2 = a^2 + b^2 - 2ab$

Sum of the numbers $= 13 \times 2 = 26$

Let the two numbers be a and b

So, $(a + b) = 26$....(i)

Now,

$\sqrt{ab} = 12$

$\Rightarrow \left(\sqrt{ab}\right)^2 = 12^2$

$\Rightarrow ab = 144$

Now,

$(a + b)^2 = 26^2$

$\Rightarrow a^2 + b^2 + 2ab = 676$

$\Rightarrow a^2 + b^2 + 2ab - 4ab = 676 - 4 \times ab$

$\Rightarrow a^2 + b^2 + 2ab - 4ab = 676 - 4 \times 144$

$\Rightarrow a^2 + b^2 - 2ab = 676 - 576$

$\Rightarrow (a - b)^2 = 100$

$\Rightarrow (a - b) = 10$

From equation (i) and equation (ii) we can say

$a = 18$ and $b = 8$

Now,

Difference of the two numbers $= 18 - 8$

$= 10$

$\therefore$ The difference between the numbers is 10.

68. Given:

The average of 10 numbers is 46.

As we know,

$\text{Average} = \dfrac{\text{Sum of elements}}{\text{Number of elements}}$

Sum of all numbers $= 46 \times 10$

$= 460$

Correct sum $= 460 - 42 + 142$

$= 602 - 42$

$= 560$

Correct Average $= \dfrac{560}{10}$

$= 56$

$\therefore$ The correct average is 56.

Hence, the correct option is (D).

69. Given:

Ratio of salaries of A and B $= 6:7$

B's salary increased by $5\frac{1}{2}\%$

Total salary of B $=$ ₹ $1,47,700$

Let salary of A and B be ₹ $60x$ and ₹ $70x$

Now,

Increased salary of B $= 70x + 70x \times 5\frac{1}{2}\%$

$=$ ₹ $73.85x$

According to the question,

$73.85x = 147700$

$\Rightarrow x = \dfrac{147700}{73.85}$

$\Rightarrow x = 2000$

So, actual salary of A $= 60 \times 2000$

$= ₹\ 120000$

$\therefore$ The salary (in ₹) of A is 120000.

Hence, the correct option is (B).

70. Given:

Amount $= ₹\ 9982.5$

Rate $= 12\%$

Time $= 2\dfrac{1}{2}$ years

As we know,

$$A = P\left(1 + \dfrac{r}{100}\right)^t$$

Here,

$A =$ amount

$P =$ principal or sum

$r =$ rate

$t =$ time

When interest calculate on certain monthly

Then,

$$r = \left(\dfrac{r}{12}\right) \times \text{month}$$

$$t = \dfrac{\text{total month given in the form of year}}{\text{number of months}}$$

$2\dfrac{1}{2}$ years $= 30$ months $[$ As 1 year $= 12$ months$]$

So, $t = \dfrac{30}{10}$

$= 3$

$r = \left(\dfrac{12}{12}\right) \times 10 = 10\%$

Let the sum be Rs. P

Now,

$$9982.5 = P\left(1 + \dfrac{10}{100}\right)^3$$

$$\Rightarrow 9982.5 = P\left(1 + \dfrac{1}{10}\right)^3$$

$$\Rightarrow 9982.5 = P\left(\dfrac{11}{10}\right)^3$$

$$\Rightarrow 9982.5 = \dfrac{1331P}{1000}$$

$$\Rightarrow P = 9982.5 \times \left(\dfrac{1000}{1331}\right)$$

$$\Rightarrow P = 7500$$

So, sum $= ₹\ 7500$

$\therefore$ The sum (in ₹) is ₹ 7500.

Hence, the correct option is (D).

71. Given:

$89563x87y$ is divisible by 72

As we know,

Divisibility rule of $8 =$ If the last three digits of a number are divisible by 8, then the number is completely divisible by 8.

Divisibility rule of $9 =$ If the sum of digits of the number is divisible by 9, then the number itself is divisible by 9.

$72 = 8 \times 9$

So, the number should be divisible by both 8 and 9

Now,

$87y$ is divisible by 8

The only possible value of y is 2.

Now,

$8 + 9 + 5 + 6 + 3 + x + 8 + 7 + 2 = 48 + x$ is divisible by 9

Clossest value of $(48 + x)$ which is divisible by 9 is 54

So, $x = 6$

Now,

$\sqrt{7x - 3y} = \sqrt{7 \times 6 - 3 \times 2}$

$= \sqrt{42 - 6}$

$= \sqrt{36}$

$= 6$

$\therefore$ Required answer is 6.

Hence, the correct option is (C).

72. Given:

$3 \times 7 + 5 - 6 \div 3 - 9 + 45 \div 5 \times 4 - 45$

Using the BODMAS rule to solve the above expression, we get

$3 \times 7 + 5 - 6 \div 3 - 9 + 45 \div 5 \times 4 - 45$

$= 3 \times 7 + 5 - 2 - 9 + 9 \times 4 - 45$

$= 21 + 5 - 2 - 9 + 36 - 45$

$= 62 - 56$

$= 6$

$\therefore$ Required answer is 6.

Hence, the correct option is (B).

73. Given:

Actual price of the TV $= ₹\ 14{,}500$

On Diwali sale, it is available for ₹ $11{,}890$

As we know,

Discount $\% = \left(\dfrac{Discount}{Actual\ price}\right) \times 100$

Discount $= 14500 - 11890$

$= ₹\ 2610$

Discount $\% = \left(\dfrac{2610}{14500}\right) \times 100$

$= 18\%$

$\therefore$ The percentage discount is 18%.

Hence, the correct option is (C).

74. Given:

A shopkeeper sold an article at a gain of 20%

As we know,

Selling price $=$ cost price $\times (1 + $ profit $\%)$

Let the actual cost price be ₹ $100x$

So, actual selling price $= 100x \times 120\%$

$= ₹\ 120x$

Now,

If he had bought it at 20% less than the actual then its cost price $= 100x \times 80\%$

$= ₹\ 80x$

Now, new selling price $= 80x \times 125\%$

$= 100x$

According to the question,

$120x - 100x = 10$

$\Rightarrow 20x = 10$

$\Rightarrow x = \dfrac{1}{2}$

So, actual cost price $= 100 \times \left(\dfrac{1}{2}\right)$

$= ₹\ 50$

$\therefore$ The Cost Price of the article is ₹ 50.

Hence, the correct option is (A).

75. Given:

A certain sum amounts to ₹ 13200 after 4 years and to ₹ 16400 after 8 years

As we know,

$$SI = (P \times T \times R)100$$

$P =$ Principal or sum

$T =$ time

$R =$ rate

As we know in simple interest the interest is always constant if the rate and sum are same

So, Interest for 4 years $= 16400 - 13200$

$= ₹3200$

So, for the $1^{st}4$ years, the interest will be ₹ 3200 [As mentioned earlier interest will be the same]

So, sum $= 13200 - 3200$

$= ₹\ 10000$

Now,

$$\text{S.I} = \dfrac{(10000 \times 10 \times 16)}{(100 \times 5)}$$

$= 100 \times 2 \times 16$

$= ₹\ 3200$

$\therefore$ The simple interest (in ₹) on the same sum at 10% p.a. for $3\dfrac{1}{5}$ years will be 3200.

Hence, the correct option is (B).

76. Given word:

Visible means something that is capable of being discovered or noticed.

Synonyms: Observable or viewable.

- Example: The house is clearly visible from the beach. Apparent means something clear, obvious or can be easily observed.

Synonyms: Evident or noticeable or recognizable.

- Example: Her happiness was apparent to everyone. Hence, the correct option is (B).

77. In the given sentence, the efficacy of microwave ovens is discussed as compared to conventional ovens.

The qualities of the microwave oven are described before and after the underlined word.

But the underlined word "anxiously" does not exactly describe a quality.

Anxiously means a way that shows you are eager to get or do something in an uneasy or worried manner. Thus, we have to substitute 'anxiously' with a word that describes the quality of the oven.

Efficiently means working or operating in an organized, quick, and effective way.

- From the above-explained meanings, it can be inferred that the correct word to substitute will be "efficiently".

Hence, the correct option is (B).

78. In the given sentence, The quality of the mind is expected to fill the blank.

The mind as described can never be put to rest because inquisitiveness makes it to continue searching for the answers.

Curious means a desire to investigate or learn something.

- Example: I am curious to know about the political shuffle happening in Maharashtra.

Complete sentence: A curious mind rarely meets a dead end; it continues the search for the answers.

Hence, the correct option is (C).

79. The error is in the part "hers umbrella" of the sentence.

- The word "hers" is used incorrectly in the sentence.
- "Hers" is a possessive pronoun that replaces nouns in a sentence. They help us show a noun's possession or ownership.
- They replace a noun or noun phrase already used to avoid repetition. For example: Mine, yours, his, hers, etc.
- The correct word to be used instead of "hers" will be "her".
- "Her" will be used as a possessive adjective that modifies the noun by identifying who has ownership or possession of it.
- In the given sentence, the possessive adjective "her" indicates that the noun "umbrella" belongs to the subject.

Hence, the correct option is (B).

80. A person who knows everything: Omniscient

Omniscient means someone having complete or unlimited knowledge.

Example: They give the impression that the book is omniscient.

Hence, the correct option is (B).

81. The use of preposition "to" after the verb 'told' is incorrect.

The speech of the given sentence is indirect and hence the word 'told' is used correctly.

In direct speech we use the verb 'said' and generally 'to' accompanies it.

- I said to Riya, "Maya wants her book". (direct speech)
- I told Riya that Maya wants her book. (Indirect speech)

Also, "told" is a transitive verb and it is always directly followed by the object.

In the given sentence "Sagar" is the object and the use of "to" is superfluous.

Hence, the correct option is (C).

82. In the given sentence, the possibility of the object to grab the opportunity to earn some money is discussed.

The underlined part "to earn" is correctly used because:

- "to earn" is used as an infinitive verb and the use of 'to' here is not as a preposition instead it is a part of the verb.
- An infinitive verb is essentially the base form of a verb with the word "to" in front of it.

From the above explanation, it can be inferred that the options (B), (C) and (D) is incorrect as the base form of verb is not used.

Hence, the correct option is (A).

83. One who examines a company's financial records - Auditor

Auditor means a person authorized to review and verify the accuracy of financial records.

Example: The accounts were certified by an auditor.

Hence, the correct option is (C).

84. In the given sentence, The manner in which the doctor informed the object is to be filled in the blank.

The doctor in the sentence is giving his counsel to the object regarding her eating habits.

Advised means to tell somebody what you think he/she should do.

- Example: I advised Riya to stop wasting her time on social media.

Complete sentence: The doctor advised her to stop eating fried food.

Hence, the correct option is (A).

85. In the given sentence, the use of the preposition "from" is inaccurate.

- The sentence explains that the subject is required to make the cholesterol get out of her body.
- The double preposition is a proposition that is made by combining two simple prepositions. For example, the phrase "out of" would be a double preposition, since both "out" and "of" are simple prepositions.
- As "out of" is already used as a preposition that talks about movement from within somewhere or something, usually with a verb that expresses movement ("get" in this sentence).

- The use of another preposition i.e. "from" is superfluous.

Hence, the correct option is (A).

86. In the given sentence, what a dialogue is exactly is to be filled in the blank.

The discussion that occurs between two or more people is described in the sentence as a dialogue.

Conversation means a talk between two or more people.

Example: To solve your misunderstandings you both need to have a conversation.

Complete sentence: A dialogue is a conversation between two or more people.

Hence, the correct option is (A).

87. Play for time - To make excuses or do things to gain time

The given idiom "play for time" means to make excuses and delay until you are ready.

Example:
My computer crashed just as the meeting began, so I had to play for time while I waited for it to reboot.

Hence, the correct option is (B).

88. The erroneous spelling is "Aniversary".

"Aniversary" there is no such word in English or we can say that there is some spelling mistake.

The correct spelling is "Anniversary" which means a day that is exactly a year or a number of years after a special or important event.

- Example: The bank will celebrate its 10th anniversary in December.

Thus, the incorrectly spelled word is Aniversary.

Hence, the correct option is (A).

89. Given idiom "to breath one's last" means to die.

Example: This is the room where my grandfather breathed his last.

Hence, the correct option is (D).

90. The erroneous spelling is "Dictionery".

"Dictionery" there is no such word in English or we can say that there is some spelling mistake.

The correct spelling is "Dictionary" which means a book that contains a list of the words in a language in the order of the alphabet and that tells you what they mean, in the same or another language.

- Example: A new dictionary was bought for Riya by her parents.

Thus, the incorrectly spelled word is Dictionary.

Hence, the correct option is (C).

91. The error is in the part "nor the employees was" of the sentence.

In the sentence, the "employees" is a plural noun.

We use "was" when there is a third person singular i.e. he/she, etc. also with first person singular (I).

- He was sleeping on the couch.

Whereas we use "were" with a second person and plural forms in the past tense.

- Dogs were barking on the road.

In the given sentence, with the plural noun "employees", "were" will be used instead of "was".

The correct sentence: Neither the manager nor the employees were aware of the shortage of raw materials.

Hence, the correct option is (C).

92. Anything that leads to death - Fatal

The adjective fatal describes something that is capable of causing death.

Hence, the correct option is (C).

93. "Trivial" is most appropriate antonym of "Vital".

Let us understand the meaning of the given and the marked words:

Vital means something very important or necessary.

Synonyms: Essential, indispensable, or crucial.

- Example: Consistency is vital to success.

Trivial means something of little importance and not worth considering.

Synonyms: Unimportant or insignificant.

- Example: She could remember every trivial incident in great detail.

Hence, the correct option is (B).

94. "Safe" is the most appropriate antonym of "Precarious".

Let us understand the meaning of the given and the marked words.

Precarious means something not safe or certain or dangerous.

Synonyms: Dangerous or hazardous or risky.

- Example: The library is in a financially precarious position.

Safe means something not likely to cause danger, harm or risk.

Synonyms: Secure or guarded.

- Example: This neighborhood is safe from robbers.

Hence, the correct option is (A).

95. "Risk" is the most appropriate synonym of "Threat".

Let us understand the meaning of the given and the marked words.

Threat means an expression of intention to inflict evil, injury, or damage.

Synonyms: Danger or hazard or trouble.

- Example: Global warming is a threat to the environment.

Risk means a possibility of loss or injury.

Synonyms: Menace or peril or hazard.

- Example: All investments have an element of risk.

Hence, the correct option is (D).

96. Given passage, the state of the sunlight is to be filled when the air is clear.

Let us explore the given options to decide which of them fits perfectly in the blank.

- "Is" is a third person singular of the present tense of "be". If we use 'is' in the blank, the sunset will be then declared to be yellow and the existence of other possibilities will be nullified. Hence, use of "is" is incorrect.

- The sentence is in present tense, hence the verb will be used in its base form. Hence, option 3 and option 4 are incorrect.

- We add "s" on the end of a verb in present tense to agree with the singular "he," "she," or "it" subject, in this case "The sun".

Thus, the word which will fill the blank is "appears".

Hence, the correct option is (B).

97. The sentence containing the blank (2) is in present perfect tense.

- It speaks about the event that took place at an unspecified time in the past.

- In present perfect tense, we use verb constructions such as; has been and have been.

- We use 'have been' with third person plural noun and we use 'has been' with third person singular noun.

- In the sentence, "the light" is the singular noun and hence, the use of "has been" is accurate.

- Because of the tense of the sentence, the use of other options will be inaccurate.

Hence, the correct option is (D).

98. In the sentence containing the blank, the appearance of the sunset when the air contains small particles is discussed.

- The correct conjunction to be used in the blank is "or".

- Because "or" is a conjunction that connects two or more possibilities or alternatives.

- In the given sentence, the two alternatives of small particles i.e. natural or artificial are to be connected.

Hence, the correct option is (C).

99. In the sentence containing the blank, the reason behind the orange color of the sunsets is discussed.

Among the given options, the correct alternative to fill the blank is "due to".

"Due to" is used to introduce the reason for something happening.

Synonyms: Because of, owing to.

- Example: The name was omitted from the list due to the employee's oversight.

In the given sentence, due to the salt particles in the air the sunset appears orange.

Hence, the correct option is (B).

100. In the sentence containing the blank, The direction surrounding the sun is said to be reddened.

The area that has been covered by the sunlight is expected to fill the blank.

Around means in a position or direction surrounding something.

- Example: The air around the city has been contaminated.

From the meanings of the words we can infer that "around" is the word that describes the area surrounding the sun.

Hence, the correct option is (D).

// Notes //

// Notes //

www.ingramcontent.com/pod-product-compliance
Lightning Source LLC
Chambersburg PA
CBHW081307130726
47998CB00010B/2965